T0031768

# ONENESS EMBRACED

# ONENESS EMBRACED

## A KINGDOM RACE THEOLOGY FOR RECONCILIATION UNITY AND JUSTICE

TONY EVANS

MOODY PUBLISHERS
CHICAGO

Portions of this book were originally released as *Let's Get to Know Each Other* (© 1995 by Anthony T. Evans) and previously published at tonyevans.org and *Kingdom Race Theology* (© 2022 by Anthony T. Evans).

Excerpt from *Kingdom Men Rising* by Tony Evans, copyright © 2021. Used by permission of Bethany House Publishers, a division of Baker Publishing Group.

Scripture quotations, unless otherwise indicated, are taken from the New American Standard Bible®, Copyright © 1960, 1962, 1963, 1968, 1971, 1972, 1973, 1975, 1977, 1995 by The Lockman Foundation. Used by permission. www.Lockman.org

Scripture quotations marked (NIV) are taken from the Holy Bible, New International Version®, NIV®. Copyright © 1973, 1978, 1984, 2011 by Biblica, Inc. ™ Used by permission of Zondervan. All rights reserved worldwide. www.zondervan.com The "NIV" and "New International Version" are trademarks registered in the United States Patent and Trademark Office by Biblica, Inc. ™

Scripture quotations marked (TLB) are taken from The Living Bible copyright © 1971. Used by permission of Tyndale House Publishers, Carol Stream, Illinois 60188. All rights reserved.

Edited by Kevin Mungons
Interior design: Ragont Design
Cover design: Erik M. Peterson



ISBN: 978-0-8024-2472-3

Originally delivered by fleets of horse-drawn wagons, the affordable paperbacks from D. L. Moody's publishing house resourced the church and served everyday people. Now, after more than 125 years of publishing and ministry, Moody Publishers' mission remains the same—even if our delivery systems have changed a bit. For more information on other books (and resources) created from a biblical perspective, go to www.moodypublishers.com or write to:

Moody Publishers
820 N. LaSalle Boulevard
Chicago, IL 60610

1 3 5 7 9 10 8 6 4 2

*Printed in the United States of America*

*To Rev. John McNeal and Dr. Howard Dial.*
*Thank you for the biblical foundation*
*and model of unity that you gave me.*

# CONTENTS

# ACKNOWLEDGMENTS

A special thanks to my friends at Moody Publishers for their willingness to publish this strategic manuscript, *and*

To my late wife of nearly fifty years, Lois Evans, for her devotion, patience, and support in the original creation of this legacy work, *and*

Rev. Lafayette Holland, Rev. James Womack, Bill Collins, Shari Carroll, and Greg Smith for their interaction with the original material over a decade ago, *and*

Heather Hair for her extensive research, as well as her excellent writing skills and insights in collaborating on both the original and current edition of this manuscript.

# INTRODUCTION

The racial problem in America is the asterisk on an otherwise-respectable reputation. Whether manifesting itself overtly in conflicts between differing racial and cultural groups, or simply lurking below the surface through microaggressions, implicit bias, and other means as a suspicion camouflaging the true depth of the problem, it continues to be the one dominant area of our failure as a nation. In spite of our successes in science, education, medicine, and technology, becoming truly "one nation under God" continues to elude us. Instead, we function as a divided nation apart from God.

Nowhere is this more evident than in the history and contemporary reality of black/white relations in the culture at large and in the church in particular. Whether it is racial tension in Ferguson, Baltimore, Charleston, Minneapolis, Atlanta and elsewhere—the issue has seemed to have only gotten worse in recent years.

While this tension can also be seen in many other ways, through swastikas painted on synagogues, Hispanics marching against the concern of racial profiling, Asians standing up to #StopAsianHate—it is the black/white relationship that has set the bar of racial division the highest. Given the length and volatile history of this divide, if we can ever get this right, we will have developed a template for addressing wherever else this evil shows up in the culture. The church will have established a model on how to biblically address issues such as those found in the current tension arising out of the influx of both legal and illegal immigrants to America, among other things. The church will have put forth biblical and theological answers that have pragmatic manifestations above and beyond mere social and political dialogue about the situation.

It is my contention that the fundamental cause of racial problems in America lies squarely with the church's failure to come to grips with this issue from a biblical perspective. The truth that has been missed is that God does much of what He does predicated on what His church is or is not doing (Eph. 3:10). In the same way that God's purpose, presence, and power in the Old Testament was to flow from His people and through the temple into the world (Ezek. 47:1–12), even so today it should flow from the church into the broader society. When the church fails to act in concert with God's prescribed agenda, then God often chooses to postpone His active involvement until His people are prepared to respond. Our failure to respond to this issue of biblical oneness has allowed what never should have been a problem in the first place to continue for hundreds of years.

This book represents my humble attempt to address the matter of the church, oneness, and social justice from an overtly biblical perspective. It is the contention of this book that what has been lacking in American Christianity is the church's failure to clearly understand and function from a kingdom perspective. Therefore, this work seeks to set forth a *kingdom agenda* approach to oneness and the subsequent issues housed within it. Threaded throughout this book you will encounter the kingdom motif as the underlying basis for embracing racial unity as well as carrying out principles of biblical justice.

I have intentionally chosen the term *embraced* in the title and throughout this book based on the unique nature of the kingdom and its bid for us not to be "color blind" with regard to God's creative diversity, but rather to appreciate, celebrate, and benefit from the divinely created ethnic differences God has embedded in His multicolor creation. This perspective is at the heart of a theological framework I call *Kingdom Race Theology*. A kingdom perspective urges us to open our eyes, hearts, and minds in order to take what we learn about ourselves and from each other with regard to the strengths inherent within each of us, and merge these together to form a more productive union.

Far too often, we have tried to *achieve* oneness through marginalizing racial distinctions rather than to *embrace* it. This is because the church has a limited understanding and execution of reconciliation as its own goal. However, the purpose of reconciliation goes further than merely being able to articulate that we are one. Reconciliation is not an end in itself. It is a means toward the greater end of bringing glory to God through seeking to advance His kingdom in a lost world. This is God's overriding goal in history and thus the central theme of Scripture. Therefore, authentic oneness manifests itself through mutual relationship and service, not in seminars. The degree to which we embrace oneness in the body of Christ is the same degree to which God empowers us to fully carry out His agenda.

The church of Jesus Christ has, on a large scale with some exceptions, missed our calling. How else can we have all of these churches on all of these corners with all of these preachers running all of these programs with all of these members using all of these resources and still have all of this mess? I would like to suggest that the church, while building great ministries and great buildings, has missed the kingdom. The purpose of this collective body of work examining areas of unity, history, culture, the church, and social justice is to promote a biblical understanding of the kingdom foundation of oneness by detailing why we don't have it, what we need to do to get it, and what it will look like when we live it.

If the church can ever merge strength with strength in order to create a more complete whole, there will be no stopping the impact we can have, not only in our nation but in our world. Conversely, the absence of a unifying purpose that is larger than us, a kingdom agenda, will continue to keep us from having a transforming influence. This is because we will remain focused on each other or ourselves as the end result rather than on how we can maximize our uniqueness and gifts together in order to accomplish God's goal in history.

For far too long Christians have wrapped the Christian faith in the American flag, often creating a civil religion and an illegitimate Christian nationalism that falsely equates partisan politics with the kingdom of God. This is foreign to the way God intended His church to function. Our nation's founding fathers are frequently elevated to the level of church fathers in the arguments for the US being founded as a Christian nation. While we should celebrate and affirm the Judeo-Christian worldview that influenced the framework for the founding of our nation, the church must also be careful to judge our nation's founders by their application of that same worldview. Our founding fathers' failure to apply the principles of freedom that they were espousing to the area of race is a prominent reason why many minority individuals today are less than enthusiastic to join in with those in our nation who want to exalt or restore America's history and heritage.

God's kingdom does not allow for human government to either overrule His rule or get so close to influencing His church that it weakens the church's distinctive nature, presence, or biblical worldview operating in the culture. Such a presence of this kind of governmental influence in the church is nothing short of idolatry (Ezek. 43:1–12). This illegitimate union of church and state has led to the breakdown of society by placing the government in a position of influence often higher than spiritual leaders in the body of Christ.

Further, what is often missing in our appeal to return to the heritage and faith of our founding fathers is an acknowledgment and reversal of a major theological contradiction that many held—that of proclaiming justice for all while denying it for many. While much in our national history reflects the call to a biblical worldview on the rights endowed to us by our Creator, we have often appealed to that heritage while simultaneously ignoring the moral inconsistencies that were prevalent in its application.

This has also led to a failure to be fully informed about a major aspect of American history in general, and church history in particular. It is common, for example, for Christian colleges to teach church history with limited or even no meaningful reference to the black church at all, thus keeping students from getting the whole truth about the history of our nation. This is why I have included in this work on oneness a section on black church history.

However, simply recognizing the strengths and struggles of our heritage is not my aim in including this history. God is not concerned with enlarging our egos but transforming our lives. This knowledge should propel us in the black culture to submit to and glory in our God and His sovereign design. I am convinced that many of the social issues plaguing the black community today are due to the vast majority of blacks who have never heard the truth regarding our racial origins and development. When people do not fully know who they are and where they come from, they become more vulnerable to allowing someone else to define these and like issues for them. Also, when members of other ethnic groups do not fully know the value of black culture and black church history, they are left with a limited definition steeped in stereotypical generalizations of who we are as people.

While Anglo Christians have frequently wrapped the Christian faith in the American flag, African American Christians have all too often merged tradition with faith by wrapping the Christian flag in black culture. At times, this has been done to such a degree that it has led to a failure in making the necessary distinctions that should reflect a kingdom-based approach to life. How else can you explain the overwhelming acceptance of musical and comedic artists who have some of the most lewd lyrics and degrading statements in their performances about the opposite sex while concurrently thanking their Lord and Savior Jesus Christ? What's worse is the amount of applause that comes from this overwhelmingly "Christian" audience, both live and at home, at this illegitimate union of faith and culture.

It is this absence of accountability and righteous judgment that keeps many in the African American community from experiencing and fully realizing God's kingdom purpose for us in spite of the mammoth amount of God-given talent and creative genius with which our Creator has endowed us. This bifurcation between what is professed on Sunday and what is lived out from Monday through Saturday limits our individual and collective progress. While passionately and publicly decrying injustice, equal attention must be given to righteousness. Wrong is to be judged and changed, not applauded and excused with no consequences.

While some of the challenges we face in the black community truly emanate from the past and its personal and systemic aftermath, there are also many more challenges that stem from our failure to properly take responsibility for and be held accountable to our actions, morality, families, the quality of services that we provide, as well as the proper management of our human and financial resources. These weaknesses are also exacerbated by an over-reliance on civil government to do for us what God expects us to do for ourselves. This creates a generational cycle of illegitimate dependency that can also lead to a defeatist mindset.

While not seeking to diminish the impact of racism upon a culture, I also want us to recognize that illegitimate or continual cries of racism are self-limiting, self-defeating, and can be an excuse for irresponsibility. They simply foster a victim mentality that reinforces a pathology of dependency. Victimology can be defined as *nurturing an unfocused strain of resentment rooted in a defeatist identity through which all realities are filtered, rather than viewing challenges as opportunities to overcome.* Any form of "wokeness" that keeps black people thinking, acting, or reacting as perpetual victims of racism will certainly undermine black progress. In addition, it reinforces the false notion that black people can only progress, advance, and be delivered by the power of white people who need to prove their racial innocence. Such a posture is doomed to failure since it forever perpetuates the very system of dependency and victimhood that it purports to seek to fix.

I'll speak on this in greater detail in the book, but I'd like to mention it here. While there is some merit to contemporary social issues and the emphasis on teaching a more holistic and accurate history, one of the major challenges of CRT, for example, is that many of its iterations that have gained a popular foothold will forever lock black/white relations in an oppressor/oppressed matrix. To teach or imply to a young child that he or she will always be oppressed is to instill a victim mentality into that child's worldview and, thus, limit that child's ability to pursue his or her full potential. It also reduces personal responsibility or even allowances for righting wrongs or exhibiting mindset changes individually by focusing so heavily on institutional structures and systems. Conversely, to imply that skin color and their concomitant privileges automatically places a person in an oppressor status locks them into a social paradigm from which there is no meaningful exit. Also, social theories that give academic analysis but leave us void of practical solutions create an unsatisfied hunger that leaves us stuck in a never-ending cycle of analysis and critique without resolution.

We must never succumb to the temptation of ascribing to civil government what is our personal, family, and church responsibility to address. It is virtually impossible to be a victor and a victim at the same time. In God's kingdom, victimology (whether promoted by the media, politicians, educators, or social and religious theorists) negates the foundational theological truths of Divine sovereignty and our victory in Christ (Rom. 8:28, 37).

It is my contention that at the core of the problem of racial disunity in America is the failure to understand and execute a kingdom-based theology on both righteousness and justice. A balance between the two is absolutely critical since it is from God's kingdom throne that both righteousness and justice originate (Ps. 89:14).

White Christianity, with all of its strengths, often focuses on personal righteousness at the exclusion of biblical justice. However, there exists within that scope a limited definition of personal righteousness, since the practice of biblical justice is an essential part of living a life of personal righteousness. This limited definition is why a pastor can be fired for immorality, but not for allowing segregation or other forms of injustice either through acts of omission or commission. On the other hand, while there is much within black culture that is to be celebrated, African American Christianity sometimes emphasizes social justice at the expense of personal responsibility.

The balance between righteousness and justice is so crucial that God's commitment to bring His kingdom benefits to bear on one generation is tied to training the next generation in how to function effectively with it (Gen. 18:19). When either side—righteousness or justice—is missed or reduced in significance, then the individual, family, church, and society will be out of balance.

As an biblical kingdomologist, I am unashamedly committed to the authority of Scripture as my final authority. As a black man, I am proud of the unique history and culture God has allowed me to partake of, as well as the unique perspective they give me. As an American, I am committed to this nation of my birth, along with the freedom and opportunities it offers and the oneness it seeks to achieve. It is my goal in this work and in my ministry to provide and promote a kingdom approach to the subject of the church, race, justice, and oneness. I seek to take the issues out of the realm of human speculation and esoteric analysis as well as the limitation of the kingdom of men, and place them squarely in the hands of the kingdom of God, which is where they belong.

Our racial divide is a sinful disease. Over-the-counter human remedies won't fix it; they merely mask the symptoms for a season. What we need is a prescription from the Creator based on the proper understanding and application of His infallible Word (2 Tim. 3:16–17, Heb. 4:12–13, 1 Tim. 3:15) to destroy this cancer before it destroys us. What the church desperately needs is a Kingdom Race Theology (KRT) that gives a biblical framework and practical solutions to our ongoing ethnic divide. I define Kingdom Race Theology as *the reconciled recognition, affirmation, and celebration of the divinely created ethnic differences through which God displays His multifaceted glory and advances His rule in history. God displays His glory through us as His people justly, righteously, and responsibly function personally and corporately in unity under the lordship of Jesus Christ*. This work is my humble attempt to provide such an ecclesiological framework. If the church can ever get this issue of oneness right, then we can help America to finally become the "one nation under God" that we declare ourselves to be. When we get it right in the church house is when we can then spread it to the White House, and beyond.

# Part 1

# A BIBLICAL LOOK AT ONENESS

# Chapter 1

# BROKEN LIBERTY

The racial problem is an unresolved dilemma of America. Racial problems have gone on since America's inception because their root has not been addressed by the people who are most qualified to address it: the church. When we can only bring people together in a limited way, without canceling who they have been created to be, under an umbrella that is bigger than the color that they claim, then how can we expect much more from the world?

The goal of the church should be to glorify God by reflecting the values of God among the people of God through letting the truth of God be the standard by which we measure right and wrong and the way we evaluate and accept skin color, class, and culture. Until we can embrace how we were born and raised, we will never be able to manifest the values of God in history so that people can understand and fully see that God is a God of multicoloredness. God loves the variety in His garden called earth, and each one of us has equal value; after all, He created and died for each one.

## The Contradiction of Liberty

During my college summers, I lived and worked in Philadelphia as an associate evangelist with the Grand Old Gospel Fellowship, regularly setting up tent, church, or outdoor crusades. Frequently, I was able to participate in more than the logistics of the event, but also had the opportunity to do what I am passionate about doing, and that is to posit the truth of God through preaching.

I have always been drawn to the truth. Truth, at its core, is God's view of a matter. It is a powerful entity able to transform lives both in history and for eternity. While truth includes information and facts, it also includes original intent, making it the absolute, objective standard by which reality is measured. The presence of truth brings clarity and understanding. Its absence leads to confusion and the presence of cognitive dissonance—holding contradictory ideas simultaneously.

Located in this same city of Philadelphia where I once preached as a young man is a perfect example of such a contradiction rising out of the abyss of the absence of truth. Hung in the heart of the City of Brotherly Love is the Liberty Bell. Originally cast to commemorate the fifty-year anniversary of William Penn's Charter of Privileges, the quotation, "Proclaim Liberty throughout all the land unto *all* the inhabitants thereof," was especially suited to the circumstances surrounding the intent of the charter and its anniversary. That quotation from Leviticus 25:10 (KJV) came immediately after the command, "Consecrate the fiftieth year." It was followed by the statement, "It shall be a jubilee for you, when each of you shall return to his property and each of you shall return to his clan" (ESV).

At this time in biblical history, according to this passage, all Jews who had been sold into slavery were set free (Lev. 25:40–41). Not only was liberty a possibility in light of the Jubilee, but it was guaranteed. Liberty and the end of slavery were simultaneous realities, mutually dependent upon each other in relationship to the call for jubilee.

Yet at the time in America when the Jubilee was inscribed on the side of the great bell, the liberty it announced had been aborted for many. Slavery continued with no foreseeable end, sanctioned not only by society but also by the church. Fifty years after William Penn's famous charter, our nation's bell proclaimed its own contradictory fifty-year jubilee, ringing out the bittersweet sounds of an emasculated freedom across the hilltops and prairies of our vast land.

## The Breaking of the Bell

My friend Ray McMillan introduced me to the Liberty Bell as a perfect object lesson for America's racial divide. In addressing why "the bell won't ring," Ray describes the crack as a perfect illustration for how our distortion of the Christian history of our nation has helped to maintain the racial divide.

The Liberty Bell rang in celebration of momentous civic achievements or to summon people together for a special announcement. One of these achievements, according to tradition, was the first public reading of the Declaration of Independence on July 8, 1776. It is said that the sound of the Liberty Bell called out to citizens both far and near to join in this heraldic event. Rich and poor, well-dressed and disheveled came together as a community to hear the words,

> We hold these truths to be self-evident, that *all* men are created equal, that they are endowed by their Creator with certain unalienable Rights, that among these are Life, Liberty and the pursuit of Happiness.

The Declaration's truth rang deeply within those who heard it, echoing the resonant tones of the bell. For a moment in time, both the Declaration and the bell proclaimed liberty together. Yet fissures, or cracks, in the bell, a reflection of fissures in the conscience of our land, raised the concern of those most closely working with it. Attempts were made to bore out the cracks before they developed into something more severe.

In 1846, in honor of George Washington's birthday, the bell rang faithfully for hours until ultimately succumbing to the pressure put on the cracks. The *Philadelphia Public Ledger* reported that just after noon, the bell split widely on one side, rendering it unringable:

> The old Independence Bell rang its last clear note on Monday last in honor of the birthday of Washington and now hangs in the great city steeple irreparably cracked and dumb. . . . It gave out clear notes and loud, and appeared to be in excellent condition until noon, when it received a sort of compound fracture in

> a zig-zag direction through one of its sides which put it completely out of tune and left it a mere wreck of what it was.[1]

In a city known for brotherly love, a compound fracture proclaimed otherwise. The jagged divide up the side of the symbol for equality and liberty could not be any more profound in its revelation of dualistic realities. There is a gap in the Liberty Bell, a missing point of connection preventing it from ringing clearly with the smooth tones of a complete union—of oneness and truth.

Something is also missing in our nation today. The election of our first African American president now over a decade ago, and all that led up to it, reignited the discussion in our land on race relations and equality. What many thought would be racial healing in our land only brought to light how deep the racial divide really was. Whether it is reflected in an increase of blame, defensiveness, a large dismissal of glaring inequities, or in heated "language politics" between and within parties, racism has been reintroduced as an issue that hasn't been resolved. Issues of race compete with each other in the news headlines of today in the areas of police reform, racial profiling, hate speech, school curriculum, CRT-influenced training, zoning issues, health issues, as well as economic and educational disparity.

Yet beyond that, and what concerns me personally even more, is that something is missing in the church.

Like the problem with the bell, a compound fracture has zigzagged through the body of Christ, keeping us largely divided along racial and class lines. This division has existed for some time, and while attempts have been made to bore out the fissures through seminars, racial reconciliation events, and well-intentioned efforts at creating experiences of oneness, we have a long way to go toward strengthening the areas that have cracks or filling in the gaps that loom between us.

## Why This? Why Now?

In light of all that has been done and how far we have come, you may be asking, "Tony, why write this book? And why now?"

A battle is going on right now in our nation about the meaning of freedom. This battle concerns the role of the church. Often we are divided over politics. A battle between socialism and capitalism is seeking to divide our nation even further than it already is. The emergence of Black Lives Matter in 2013, along with the later deaths of George Floyd and numerous others, increased awareness of hate speech. Introduction of Critical Race Theory concepts in more schools and businesses along with the radicalism of the political right have heated up the racial debate today to a boiling point.

We, the church, have allowed these battles to divide people of faith even more deeply than before. We cannot afford this. Our nation cannot afford this. Our sons and daughters—whether black, white, or any other color—cannot afford this. We can no longer afford to sit idly by representing the body of Christ as a "mere wreck" of its divine design. The solutions to the issues we face today are found only by applying a biblical and divine standard as answers to the questions before us. The church should be a model at such a time as this to reveal to the world what true oneness, equality, and freedom can produce. Hell advances on the church's doorsteps with fervent speed, and as long as we remain divided, it will continue to do so.

We can resist hell's advances and heal a broken nation if we are willing to come together by first filling in our own gaps—gaps in our understanding, our knowledge of our unique histories, and our relationships—while simultaneously repairing our own fissures that lead to even greater divides.

Our songs ring mournfully flat when the bells on our churches remain cracked. Even so, we continue to belt out our songs with tremendous passion at times, perhaps in hopes that by singing them loudly enough we can somehow cover the silence between us. We sing emotion-filled lyrics designed to draw us together by reminding us that "we all bleed red" until we are blue in the face. But the truth is that when the song is over, we go our separate ways.

We go our separate ways because we have discovered that it takes more than a hug or a friendly "hello" to bridge the gap. While some of us have, many of us have not taken the necessary effort to get to know each other on a level of an authentic exchange. Without a basis of shared knowledge, purposes, and mutual respect, we cannot come together for any meaningful impact. Democracy demands dialogue and yet dialogue is becoming the one thing missing in this mess.

I recently read an interesting quote in a book that highlighted the reality that many of us often don't realize—authentic oneness comes as an outgrowth of shared lives, not simply through a cross-cultural experience here or there, or through reading books like *White Fragility*, *White Awake*, or *Be the Bridge*, and then posting about it online. Edward Gilbreath's words in *Reconciliation Blues* caught my attention as I stumbled across my own name, but then I saw how he summarized a common theme in American Christian culture today. He said,

> I know many of my white friends and colleagues, both past and present, have at times grown irritated by the black community's incessant blabbering about race and racism and racial reconciliation. They don't understand what's left for them to do or say. 'We have African Americans and other people of color on our staff. We listen to Tony Evans's broadcast every day. We even send our youth group into the city to do urban ministry. Can we get on with it already? Haven't we done enough?'[2]

With the racial divide still stretching wide for miles, we obviously haven't done enough. Virtue-signaling actions for the sake of virtue signaling alone, limited authentic engagement cross-culturally, and listening to sermons by someone of another ethnicity aren't nearly enough to heal the wounds that divide us. As former NFL player and son of one of my associate pastors for numbers of years, Emmanuel Acho, states in his book *Uncomfortable Conversations with a Black Man*, "Make sure you aren't engaged in optical allyship—the kind that goes only so far as it takes to get the right post for social media."[3]

*Allyship is a term for a person from an ingroup assisting a person from a marginalized group.*

Much of what has gone on under the designation of racial reconciliation and oneness in Christianity is nothing more than tolerance. To be certain, we have come a long way from slavery, Jim Crow laws of segregation, and other overt expressions of racial hatred. But tolerating each other does not mean we have reconciled. The two are not the same, as demonstrated by the fact that we remain relationally separated most of the time, only coming together for a scheduled event as opposed to living out a desire for ongoing mutual edification and implementation of a shared kingdom vision.

The proof that we still have a long way to go in the church today is that a collective cross-cultural presence is not having a restoring effect in our society. We are more concerned about achieving the American dream than we are about letting the rule of God remake segregated churches and denominations. In so doing, we have limited the degree to which the healing balm of God's grace flows freely down the aisles of our churches into our communities, and ultimately throughout our land. If what we call racial reconciliation is not transforming individuals, families, churches, and communities, then it is merely sociology with a little Jesus sprinkled on top.

Biblical racial reconciliation may be defined as *addressing the sin that caused the divide for the purpose of bonding together across racial lines based on a shared commitment to Jesus Christ with the goal of advancing God's kingdom agenda together.*

In a nation whose middle name is "Me" and where "time is money," being intentional about relationships is required even when connecting with others in our own culture. The very structure of our society impedes many of us in our pursuit of making authentic connections. This is even more true when it comes to developing relationships with others in a different culture than our own. But oneness, as we will see through a careful study of Scripture, is worth the effort. This is because oneness is the preeminent vehicle through which God displays not only His power and His presence, but also His glory. It is also His central tool for advancing His kingdom agenda in history.

This book at this time is set forth not only as a biblical call to oneness, but also as an invitation to an extended handshake. It is my hand reaching out to my white brothers and sisters to say, "Hi, my name is Tony Evans. Let me introduce myself, and the history of my people, in a way that you may not have yet heard." It is also my hand reaching out to my black brothers and sisters to say, "There is a lot more about you, and us, than you may have realized. And it is very good."

More than a discipleship book on reconciliation, the kingdom, and justice, this book serves as a much-needed compilation of the spiritual history and development of the black church and black evangelicalism, stories too long shelved in the attics of our collective minds. This history is shared in order to introduce truth to those in the African American community who may not know the richness of our own heritage in a nation and in churches that have often turned a blind eye. It is also done to introduce this same truth to my white brothers and sisters so that their vision may be clear, and through seeing, they may realize the benefits that can be found when embracing what Dr. Martin Luther King Jr. called our "inescapable network of mutuality . . . [our] single garment of destiny."[4]

While many books have chronicled the history of blacks in America and black spirituality, and many other books have laid the foundation for oneness in the body of Christ, this book presents a holistic story proffering not only a bid for oneness, but also providing the necessary elements to begin to do so by filling in the gaps of black church history. The merging of a biblical foundation for oneness along with a sequential summary of Christianity within the African Diaspora combines to present a broader kingdom perspective of God's view on race.

This perspective flows uniquely out of my personal situation of having been doubly influenced first by black culture through my intimate ties with black individual, family, church, and community life combined with the influence of white evangelicalism, having studied in its institutions and worked alongside its leaders. Weaving these two worlds together and placing them underneath the truth of Scripture has framed a distinctive lens through which to view racial oneness and biblical justice within the body of Christ.

If the truth is supposed to set us free and yet we are still not free from enormously destructive racial and class divisions in the church, then the truth is missing. Only applied truth, as it is revealed in God's inherent Word, is sufficient to bring about the oneness we so desperately need (John 17:17). Read those two sentences again, if you would. They are foundational for all else.

The result of this missing truth in our history and culture has kept large segments of the black community looking to governmental systems for assistance rather than taking personal initiative. This lack of initiative often comes cradled in a victim mentality where racism is blamed for many more things than it should be.

This missing truth has also kept segments of the white community in bondage to a relational style based on stereotypical presumptions as well as a paternalistic expectation birthed in a spirit of entitlement. This prohibits many white Christians from adopting and benefiting from a learning posture underneath the leadership of Christian blacks.

The effect is a stronghold on both groups, keeping pockets of society chained within a prescribed framework, creating pathologies that continue and are reinforced generationally.

This is why I have chosen to broaden the scope of this book beyond a discussion on race relations or oneness in our modern church, and have sought to return, as well, to the realm of what has brought us to where we are now by exploring our historical accounts. When a gap so wide exists in liberty, it is indicative that something is missing. That something, in this case, is the whole truth.

### *Gaps in Our Accounts*

Secular history has often excluded the whole truth from its record of accounts. It has rewritten the annals of our foundation to offer a one-sided and limited view of the founding of our nation. Even though African Americans were involved and present, as freed men and not only as slaves, in the critical junctures of the birthing of our land, our history books, mainstream movies, and often even our artistic renditions show little or no racial diversity. African American heroes of such important battles such as the Battle of Bunker Hill are not only completely absent from mainstream historical accounts, but also, more recently, explained away out of paintings made by those who witnessed the battle firsthand.[5]

What this has done in the American psyche is elevate one group of people, white Americans, above all others. Not only does it disconnect African Americans from any personal heritage to our nation, but it also offers an incomplete and inaccurate view of ourselves. An erroneous view of oneself, or a misguided view of another as is the case when whites are taught an anemic view of black achievement and involvement in our land and churches, leads to actions that perpetuate the illusion, on both sides.

Just over a year before the Liberty Bell rang out calling all to come hear the Declaration of Independence, a young Paul Revere took his well-known Midnight Ride. Few of us who have been raised under the tutelage of our country are unaware of this ride. Yet how many of us know that on the very same night, a black man, Wentworth Cheswell, the freed grandson of a slave, also rode a Midnight Ride?[6] Cheswell was the first black judge elected, in 1768, a devoted husband, church member, father of thirteen children, and for forty-nine years he served our nation in some form of public office such as auditor, assessor, moderator, and "town father."

Cheswell's commission as messenger, given to him by the Committee of Safety, was the same as that given to Revere. Wentworth Cheswell rode north. Paul Revere rode west. Both had a part to play in the fight for the American Revolution. Cheswell's alerting those in the north to make haste and organize themselves to head south for the imminent conflict with the British served our country just as well. Yet Wentworth Cheswell is virtually nowhere to be found in our historical accounts.

Likewise, as the Liberty Bell cracked, creating a gap on the day honoring George Washington, another gap exists in the retelling of the historic accomplishments of the general. This gap belongs to a man named James Armistead. The ending of the American Revolution with the victory at Yorktown and the capture of British general Charles Cornwallis, from a historical perspective, is attributed to General Washington and his troops.

Yet what has been often left out of the retelling of this event is that Washington was able to do what he did with as minimal loss in soldiers' lives that he had—less than a miniscule 1 percent casualty rate—due to information supplied to him that had been acquired by James Armistead, a black man. At great personal risk, Armistead had posed as a runaway slave and pretended to be a British spy, all the while gaining the confidence of General Benedict Arnold and General Charles Cornwallis. The officers spoke freely in front of Armistead concerning their strategies. Armistead's reports documented the movements of the British, giving General Washington all that he needed to bring about a swift end to the war, saving scores of American lives not only in the battle at Yorktown, but in future battles that did not have to be fought.

Similarly, the contributions of the black church have often been neglected or marginalized, thus hindering the oneness of the collective American church. Because much has been ignored, the oneness of the church has missed the opportunity to present a model of highest functionality that the world needs to see.

*Social and Spiritual Realities*

Although some have historical gaps of understanding that need to be filled, others simply have difficulties in reconciling their spiritual beliefs with social realities. My story reflects this difficulty. Yet, what is important to note is that while my story is my own, it is not mine alone. It is not unique to me. My story mirrors countless others still being written on the pages of African American lives. Whether there exist generational, class, educational, denominational, or even theological differences between us, one unifying theme that binds the African American story together is that we all wrestle with reconciling the social and spiritual contradictions prevalent in American Christianity.

Growing up in urban America in a Christian context during a time of racism, segregation, and an incomplete historical education, as referenced briefly just now, not only in the society but also in the church, served to remind me in many ways that I was a second-class citizen. It was frustrating, painful, and confusing. There were places that I couldn't go, opportunities I couldn't pursue, and people with whom I couldn't associate simply because of the color of my skin. In fact, I was even told that I could expect to only go so far in my life because that was the nature of my created being.

These experiences ripped a social and spiritual schism in my understanding that demanded to be resolved. Much like the gaping crack in the Liberty Bell representing a contradiction within realities—that of freedom for *all* in the midst of racism, injustice, and segregation for *some*—I struggled to connect the social reality presented to me as that of being less than someone else with the spiritual reality of hearing that Jesus loved me so much that He died for me. I wrestled in an attempt to come to grips with whether or not I was required to accept this second-class rendering that I was hearing in so many different directions about *who* I was and *why* I was.

What I witnessed in the church only reinforced this conundrum concerning truth. Some of my professors in college and in seminary would either attend or pastor a segregated church while at the same time teach a theology on the oneness of the body of Christ. It forced me, and many others, to seek out an authentic understanding of biblical theology rooted and grounded in absolute truth. It forced me to dig deeply to discover what God had to say about the situation, rather than passively accept the contradiction.

Did God want me to give up my color, culture, background, and history in order to make it in a society that would not embrace me as I was? Or did He want me to see myself as He sees me—a child intentionally designed by His creative abilities whom He has positioned within two culture realities?

Experiencing urban America at the height of the civil rights movement and the formation and implementation of black power and black theology has afforded me a perspective on race distinct to my own culture. However, studying theology for nine years in a white evangelical institution, as well as being the first African American to be graduated with a ThD from there, has afforded me a keen view into the theological thinking of white Christians. Through both realms, I learned how to hone and apply exegetical skills in order to analyze the theology I was being taught.

My perspective for this book, then, and my perspective for all I do with regard to a kingdom agenda philosophy for ministry, flows out of this diverse locus. It is my attempt to tie reality to Scripture in such a way as to emphasize the paradigm for how the Bible reveals that the church and society should address matters of race and social justice. In doing so, I speak not only to others in the church and society, but also to myself and those like me who have had to wrestle with reconciling the schisms between America's social and spiritual actualities.

### *Seeing Clearly*

As an evangelical kingdomologist, I am tightly tethered to Scripture as my final authority on all matters to which it speaks. And it speaks on all matters. I seek to apply this comprehensive view of Scripture to all of life. I am committed to the thesis that there are two answers to every question—God's answer and everyone else's. And when they contradict each other, everyone else is wrong.

As an African American, my vision was formed in the pragmatic reality of racial disparity that caused me to focus on questions about race, oneness, and justice in church history that many of my white counterparts did not have to address. This dualism forced me to read Scripture to shed light on these issues, leading me to the conclusions that are being put forward in this book. I had to look not only to the theology but also the practical application of that theology within the *sitz im leben*—or situation in life—for how that theology fleshes out.

White evangelicalism believed the right things concerning the oneness of the body of Christ, but throughout history it did not consistently apply this belief system in either the church or the culture. In fact, the white church became a primary means, through either or both explicit and complicit manners, of justifying the racism and injustices perpetuated within the broader culture. While there have always been individuals and groups—remnants such as the Quakers, the abolitionists, and the white freedom marchers, among others—in white culture who wanted to apply the right practice of this belief, they did not always have a paradigm through which to express it, nor do they always have that today. There has existed a dichotomy, making it difficult to implement the applicational truth of not only oneness, but also biblical justice. As Dr. Warren Wiersbe, renowned white Bible teacher and father to many in the ministry, acknowledged, this roadblock often led to an ignoring of these and like issues in the white church. He wrote,

> We are handicapped in the white church. If I preached Jesus' first sermon (Luke 4:14–30) and gave to it the social emphasis that he gave, our church has no vehicle for doing anything about the problem. People would respond in one of two ways: (1) "This preacher is off-base, so let's get rid of him," or (2) "I've never seen it quite that way, but what do I do next?" For the most part, our white churches don't have the

> instruments, the organizational structure, to get involved in social action. Our usual solution is to put some inner-city organization into the budget or maybe to collect and distribute used clothing. . . . When it comes to racial issues, many white churches will participate in any number of symbolic activities, but they're hesitant when you ask them to get involved in sacrificial services in the trenches.[7]

Promise Keepers experienced this as a parachurch movement as well. Churches were happy to send their men to listen to a black preacher, or hug a minority person in attendance and verbally commit to racial reconciliation (Promise 6 out of 7). But when it came to diving deeper into the sin of racism, what might be done to address it, the repentance needed for it and the actions that follow repentance, many churches pulled back. "Mark Pollard, a special associate of Promise Keepers in the 1990s, remembers that major donors started to back away, saying they weren't interested if Promise Keepers was going to be a civil rights organization. As he traveled the country with McCartney planning and promoting events, Pollard, who is black, was also asked again and again why race should be an issue at all. Wasn't the gospel colorblind?"[8] Not long after this greater push for reconciliation, the funding for PK began to dry up.

Yet although difficulties and challenges exist, their presence should never be the criteria for whether we give up or keep trying. Views of theology formulated through the lens of any culture will not only produce a myopic view, but also the resultant effects of an inability to carry out the true teaching in Scripture. This inability not only affects those who would be the recipients of the ministry outreaches, but it also affects those doing the ministry because it limits God's involvement in what is being done. Only when biblical truth is the absolute standard by which thoughts and actions are aligned will we experience the full manifestation of God's glory, purposes, and plans in the body of Christ. Maintaining an informational and otherworldly view of theology while neglecting a holistic view of God's kingdom aborts any real opportunity for application.

I will talk more about him later in the book, but my father had an early impact on me in my teenage years to point me to the truth.

I grew up just a few hours away from our nation's Liberty Bell that so proudly proclaimed "Liberty . . . unto *all*." Yet, when I would go to a fast-food restaurant, I was denied the freedom to eat in a public dining room because I was black. The restaurant was pleased to take my money at the takeout window, but eating in was definitely out.

Though I didn't fully understand it at the time, the contradiction between proclaiming liberty while simultaneously denying it sought to shape my mind. Thank God for my father who knew what I was facing and who made a polemic effort to counteract the lie. "Son," he would say, "you're a child of the King. If they don't want royal blood in their restaurant, then don't go in there."

My earthly father pointed me to the truth of my heavenly Father.

As I grew older and looked more closely at the Bible and at Jesus, the Christ, who had come, I discovered something awesome. I discovered that His love for me repositioned me above the class that I had been given by other men. Embracing this truth all of a sudden made what men thought and how men felt about me irrelevant because now I was seated with Christ in a very high place. He gave me recognition, significance, and value, causing me to be fully proud of His creation in me so as not to allow others to denigrate me by how they defined me—or even to make me think more highly of myself than I ought to think—because now I had truth as my reference point.

This book is my attempt to put on paper this reference point, detailing how it applies to both blacks and whites with regard to oneness in the body of Christ. Our unity can then serve as a template for bringing about comprehensive unity for other racial groups in our land. Because until we see ourselves, and each other, as God sees us, and respond with an intentional embracing of His mandate of oneness, we will forever ring flat in a world that longs to hear the liberating cadence of truth.

**Notes**

1. *Philadelphia Public Ledger*, February 26, 1846. Cited in "The Liberty Bell," www.ushistory.org/libertybell.
2. Edward Gilbreath, *Reconciliation Blues: A Black Evangelical's Inside View of White Christianity* (Downers Grove, IL: InterVarsity, 2006), 80.
3. Emmanuel Acho, *Uncomfortable Conversations with a Black Man* (New York: Flatiron Books, 2020), 182.

4. Martin Luther King Jr., "Letter from a Birmingham Jail," April 16, 1963, Martin Luther King Jr. Research and Education Institute, Martin Luther King Jr. Papers Project, 2005.
5. David Barton, *Setting the Record Straight: American History in Black & White* (Aledo, TX: WallBuilders, 2004), 5.
6. "A Black Patriot: Wentworth Cheswell," wallbuilders.com, December 29, 2016, https://wallbuilders.com/black-patriot-wentworth-cheswell.
7. E. K. Bailey and Warren W. Wiersbe, *Preaching in Black and White: What We Can Learn from Each Other* (Grand Rapids, MI: Zondervan, 2003), 105.
8. Daniel Silliman, "Promise Keepers Tried to End Racism 25 Years Ago. It Almost Worked," *Christianity Today*, June 21, 2021, www.christianitytoday.com/ct/2021/july-august/promise-keepers-racial-reconciliation-reconsidered.html.

# Chapter 2

# BRIDGING THE DIVIDE

Every two years nations around the globe send their strongest, most elite athletes to compete against others at what is known as the Olympics. Individual athletes, who are at the top of their game in their particular skill or event, go head-to-head with the world's best. On display for the world to see are their individual prowess, their individual determination, their individual commitment, and their individual abilities.

Yet when the gold medalist stands on the platform, he or she is not asked, "What is your favorite song?" The winning athlete does not get to choose which song will be played as the flag is raised. Instead, the national anthem for whatever nation the individual represents plays loudly. This is done because it is understood that while the individual was the one who sacrificed, practiced, and competed, he or she represents something much larger. The athlete is just one of many who make up a nation that operates underneath the covering of the same song.

Growing up in America, we were regularly reminded to whom we belonged each time we said the Pledge of Allegiance or participated in the singing of our national anthem in school or before sporting or civic events. It was clear that our country did not want us to forget that we are Americans. We recited the pledge day in and day out, allowing it to sink in, enabling each one of us to fully understand that no matter who we were, or what our background was, our history, gender, culture, or color, we belonged to this kingdom called the United States of America.

Even though the pledge had nothing directly to do with what was going on at that particular event or in the classroom, America wanted us to know that it was only going on, and we were only able to participate in it, because we belonged to its kingdom.

## The Kingdom Agenda

The foundational philosophy behind all I do, write, teach, or preach is the kingdom agenda. The kingdom agenda is *the visible manifestation of the comprehensive rule of God over every area of life.*[1] It is a reminder that we, as followers of Jesus Christ, belong to another realm, our allegiance is in another order, and no matter where we live, work, or travel, we are citizens of God's kingdom.

A story is told about a man who needed to get his shoe repaired. He rushed to the shoe repair shop only to arrive there at exactly 5:00 p.m. Scanning the parking lot, he noticed that it was empty, indicating that, apparently, there was no one around. Knowing he wouldn't have another opportunity to go to the shop for some time, he headed to the door to see if, by chance, it was still open.

To his surprise, the shoe repairman was there.

"I didn't think anyone was here," the man said, relieved.

"You came just in time," the shoe repairman replied. "I was almost ready to go home."

Remembering the empty parking lot, the man asked, "How are you going to go home? I didn't see any cars."

"Oh, that's easy," the repairman said. "Do you see those stairs over there?"

He pointed to the corner of the shop. The man looked and noticed the stairs. He nodded.

"I live up there," the shoe repairman said. "I just work down here."

### *We Live Up There*

You and I, as brothers and sisters in Christ, live up there too. "Our citizenship is in heaven" (Phil. 3:20a). That's our home. That's the kingdom to which we belong. We just work down here. Understanding this key spiritual truth is fundamental to all we do on earth.

The kingdoms of this world would have us forget where our home is and lead us to believe that where we work is also where we live. But we, as members of the body of Christ, get our instructions and directions from another realm—from another King who is heading up another kingdom. And as is the case in every kingdom, the King rules.

Briefly, before we dive into our look at oneness, let's touch on the kingdom and its relationship to earth as seen through the Lord's Prayer. I'll go deeper into an examination of the kingdom in the last section of this book, but let's set the table now with Jesus' prayer, a portion of which says:

> Your kingdom come.
> Your will be done,
> On earth as it is in heaven. (Matt. 6:10)

In the words of Jesus, an understanding of God's will as it appears in heaven is the criterion for having God's will done on earth through the establishing of the Messianic kingdom. We know this because the Lord's Prayer has been given to us in Scripture as a pattern for prayer rather than as one designed for recitation. The original Greek term used in the book of Matthew encourages all believers to literally pray "in a similar manner."

Therefore, to pray "in a similar manner" that God's "will be done, on earth as it is in heaven" is to pray that the principles of His heavenly kingdom be reflected in the contemporary rule of God on earth. To reflect God's principles on earth can only be done when we fully understand and apply these principles. Psalm 89:14 offers insight into the core of God's kingdom principles: "Righteousness and justice are the foundation of Your throne; lovingkindness and truth go before You."

Since these, and a number of other principles that we will examine later dealing with God's righteous rule in social spheres, are underscored with oneness rooted in personal dignity, we ought to pray and seek the same end. This is because knowing, understanding, and applying God's comprehensive rule in our lives are essential to experiencing all that God has in store for us while on earth, as well as when we get to heaven.

Submission to God's kingdom rule opens up the flow of heaven's involvement in our lives on earth. Far too many of us are satisfied with the part of Christianity that takes us to heaven, but not the part that brings a bit of heaven down to earth. But in order to bring to earth what "is in heaven," God's will must be done. Jesus' prayer reflects this as well as reflecting His primary purpose while on earth, which was to be solely about His Father's business (see Luke 2:49). Since Christ is our example, we should be about the same.

### *The Business of Oneness*

One of the elements of God's rule and His "business" is His heart for oneness, also known as unity. Unity can be defined in its simplest of terms as oneness of purpose. It is working together in harmony toward a shared vision and goal.

Unity is not uniformity, nor is it sameness. Just as the Godhead is made up of three distinct coequal Persons (i.e., the Trinity)—the Father, the Son, and the Holy Spirit—each unique in personhood and yet at the same time one in essence, unity reflects a oneness that does not negate individuality. Unity does not mean everyone needs to be like everyone else. God's creative variety is replete displaying itself through a humanity crafted in different shapes, colors, and styles. Each of us, in one form or another, is unique. Unity occurs when we combine our unique differences together as we head toward a common goal. It is the sense that the thing that we are gathered for and moving toward is bigger than our own individual preferences.

Through the establishment of the church along with His overarching rulership above it, God has created a reflection of His kingdom in heaven on earth. He has reconciled racially divided groups into one new man (Eph. 2:14–15), uniting them into a new body (Eph. 2:16) so that the church can function in unity (Eph. 4:13). The church is the place where racial, gender, and class distinctions are no longer to be divisive because of our unity and identity in Christ (Gal. 3:28). This does not negate differences that remain intact—oneness simply means that those differences are embraced.

Joining our unique strengths together, we add strength to strength, making a more complete and balanced whole based on our mutual relationship with and commitment to Christ. Biblical unity does not create colorblindness; rather, it gives divine purpose to the diversity of color-uniqueness.

So important is the issue of oneness in the church that we are told to look out for people who seek to undermine it (Rom. 16:17). In fact, God promised to judge those who divide His church (1 Cor. 3:17). This is because the church is to reflect the values of the kingdom of God to a world in desperate need of experiencing Him.

The church is the only authentic cross-racial, cross-cultural, and cross-generational basis for oneness in existence. It is the only institution on earth obligated to live under God's authority while enabled to do so through His Spirit. In 1 Corinthians 12:12–13, Paul wrote:

> For even as the body is *one* and yet has many members, and all the members of the body, though they are many, are *one* body, so also is Christ. For by *one* Spirit we were all baptized into *one* body, whether Jews or Greeks, whether slaves or free, and we were all made to drink of *one* Spirit. (italics added)

The baptism of the Spirit at the moment of salvation, the act whereby God places us into the body of Christ, secures the oneness God wants us to have. This inimitable work of the Spirit positions us under the rule of God. The Greek word for baptism used in the Bible means identification. It was used of a cloth maker dipping cloth into dye so that the cloth would take on the color of the dye. The cloth was then said to be baptized, or identified, with the dye.

When we got saved, we were baptized into the body of Christ. We are now identified with a new family, having been placed into a new spiritual environment while still on earth. No matter our race, gender, or class, when we came to Jesus Christ we entered into God's oneness because we came under His authority.

That is why Ephesians 4:3 says that we are to "preserve the unity of the Spirit." The Scripture uses the term *preserve*, indicating that we don't create unity. Authentic unity, then, cannot be mandated or manufactured. This is so because God desires that His standards alone serve as the basis, criteria, and foundation for oneness. It is also why He thwarts attempts at unity and globalization that ignore or exclude Him (Gen. 11:1–9). The Spirit created unity when we were saved. Our job is to find out what the Spirit has already done so that we can live, walk in, and embrace that reality.

The reason we haven't solved the race problem in America after hundreds of years is that people apart from God are trying to create unity, while people under God who already have unity are not living out the unity we possess. The result of both of these conditions is disastrous for America. Our failure to find cultural unity as a nation is directly related to the church's failure to preserve our spiritual unity. The church has already been given unity because we've been made part of the same family. An interesting point to note about family is that you don't have to get family to *be* family. A family already is a family. But sometimes you do have to get family to *act like* family. In the family of God, this is done through the presence and power of the Holy Spirit.

A perfect example of spiritual unity came on the Day of Pentecost when God's people spoke with other tongues (Acts 2:4). When the Holy Spirit showed up, people spoke in languages they didn't know so that people from a variety of backgrounds could unite under the cross of Jesus Christ. The people who heard the apostles speak on the Day of Pentecost were from all over the world, representing at least sixteen different geographical areas, racial categories, or ethnic groups (Acts 2:8–11). But in spite of the great diversity, they found true oneness in the presence of the Holy Spirit.

Spiritual oneness always and only comes to those who are under God's authority because in that reality He enables them to achieve unity with the power of His Spirit.

### *Broken Oneness*

Our nation has made many strides over the last several decades in attempting to bring people together across racial lines. I was able to witness this firsthand a number of years ago. Joining hundreds of thousands of my closest friends in Washington, DC the week of the forty-fourth presidential inauguration was a surreal experience for me. Even as a child growing up in the racially divided city of

Baltimore in the 1950s and '60s, I thought that one day there would be an African American president of the United States. The anticipation, for me, was always there.

Yet to see the dreams of generations coming true literally and physically before my own eyes was deeply gratifying. No matter what your political views or for whom you voted, the election of President Obama was a symbolic representation of the ultimate prize of progress in a nation that had been historically divided. But like the zigzag crack in the Liberty Bell, this election didn't heal race relations—in fact, the great divide only grew under his presidency. This divide especially grew in the body of Christ, offering the world an anemic reflection of the heart of our Christianity. We have a long way to go toward achieving authentic spiritual unity.

I will talk more about how we can be intentional about our pursuit of oneness at the end of this book as I lay out a vision for transforming our nation's communities and restoring hope to all who need it. But it begins through removing the lens of our own fleshly worldview, our culture's worldview, and even our denomination's worldview, and replacing it with a biblical kingdom-centered worldview. If we want heaven to visit history like what happened in the book of Acts, we have no other choice but to adopt and apply a biblical worldview, God's kingdom perspective, on race. We must view humanity through the lens of Scripture, seeing each other, as well as ourselves, as God sees us.

For some reading this book that will mean a clearer image of who you are as an African American—your exceptional place in both biblical and world history, accomplishments, traditions, and spirituality. For others, this book will open your eyes to see your black brothers and sisters in Christ for who we truly are rather than for how a nation birthed in racial injustice has sought to define us.

As I mentioned earlier, the swearing in of the first African American president of the United States was a historical and meaningful moment. However, as time quickly showed, what was thought to be an answer to a problem only revealed how deep the problem really is. While cultures initially united to bring about the election, a renewed polarization formed afterward as divisions revealed themselves once again.

Rather than bringing our nation together across racial lines, it catapulted the issue of race into the arena of national decision, leading many to either support or oppose initiatives based on racial identification rather than on the policies themselves. Whether you are a Democrat, a Republican, or an Independent, the election of President Obama reintroduced the issue of race, placing it front and center in our nation. The subsequent election of President Trump, coupled with his communication, content, and style, escalated the political and racial divide to an even higher level. It is tearing at the heart of our culture and, unfortunately, it is tearing at the heart of our churches as well.

Admittedly, much has happened to mend the brokenness between the races in our churches over the last several decades, for which we should be grateful. In 1974, my late wife, Lois, and I were informed in no uncertain terms that we were not welcome in a prominent Bible church in Dallas, pastored, by the way, by one of my seminary professors. Now I am routinely invited to Bible churches all over America to preach. In 1985, a number of major Christian radio station managers told me that there was little place for blacks in the general Christian broadcast media because our presence would offend their white listeners. Today, my radio broadcast *The Alternative with Dr. Tony Evans* airs on more than fourteen hundred radio stations daily in our nation and in over 130 countries worldwide.

I can distinctly remember, as I was in my early 20s, when I was told by the leadership of a large Southern Baptist church in Atlanta that I wasn't welcome to worship there. However, in 2021, I addressed—as I have done many times throughout the years—well over ten thousand Southern Baptist pastors at the SBC annual Pastors' Convention as a keynote speaker, being sure to emphasize oneness among the races. Although we have come far, we have not come nearly as far as we often think.

For example, the message at the 2021 SBC Conference came on the heels of a very public disagreement between me and the SBC which took place online only a few months prior. It began when they made a post on Twitter in which they inferred that I opposed CRT. The original tweet stated, "In light of recent statements by Christian leaders regarding Critical Race Theory and Intersectionality, members of the 2019 Resolution Committee of the SBC have drafted the following statement." The statement went on to say, "Recently, we have been encouraged by and agree with statements from Dr. Tony Evans on CRT. In a sermon in which he deals with CRT, Dr. Evans makes a clear affirmation for the sufficiency and authority of Scripture over all ideologies."[2]

Granted, while I do affirm the sufficiency and authority of Scripture over all ideologies, I in no way declared CRT null and void of any merit. My good friend Dwight McKissic noted this publicly as well in his comment on Twitter which stated, "Interesting that the SBC touted a video by Tony Evans (that I fully agree with), making it clear that primacy of biblical authority supersedes CRT. He'd earlier released a video affirming his belief in historic & current systemic injustice. CRT would argue the same & the Bible."[3]

While I may disagree with popular interpretations of CRT's themes or its connections by many of its followers to anti-theistic ideologies, I do not disagree with the totality of its points or purposes as it was originally intended. Having germinated as a hybrid ideology from critical legal studies and traditional civil rights scholarships as far back as the late 1980s,[4] its focus on addressing and dismantling racism within structures, and seeking real solutions to existing racial inequities, is important, and arguably biblical.

Before posting a public rebuttal of the use of my name in opposing CRT by the SBC, I contacted the writer personally through a phone call (Matt. 18:15). We had a healthy dialogue and I felt, in many ways, that the SBC committee members realized what they had done in inferring my statement to mean more than what it did in context. Then I followed up with a public statement online. It read,

> Members of the 2019 Resolution Committee of the SBC, without my awareness or permission, used my name in their recent *Affirmation of Recent Statements from Christian Leaders on Critical Race Theory*. Upon reading this affirmation, I need to state that their use of my name and what I said in a sermon titled *Race & Reconciliation* released on 11/15/20 needs clarification of what I fully said. They have referenced a portion without giving it the context of my sermon. . . .

> As I stated in my sermon, which I encourage everyone reading this to watch, I again affirm that the Bible must be the basis for analyzing any and all social, racial or political theories in order to identify what is legitimate or what is not legitimate. But I did not say, nor imply, that CRT or other ideologies lack beneficial aspects—rather that the Bible sits as the basis for determining that. I have long taught that racism, and its ongoing repercussions, are real and should be addressed intentionally, appropriately and based on the authority of God's inerrant Word.[5]

While we have come far over the years and my message to the SBC Convention in 2021, following this public rebuttal, was received with standing and thunderous applause, I am at times wearied by how far we have not come. The fact that we are still bogged down discussing and debating the semantics of society's structures that we cannot see the obvious disparities and difficulties plaguing certain racial groups, and seek to address them (Mark 12:31, Isa. 58, James 4:17), is mind-blowing.

I regularly get calls from church leaders across the country, both black and white, telling me of the racial tensions in their community and division among their churches. Our national ministry, The Urban Alternative, is frequently called upon to work with individual churches as well as groups of churches on how to help them address the lack of oneness they often experience. As I mentioned earlier, this has led to the casting of a national vision for a Three-Point Plan aimed at reaching our communities in such a way as to ensure a significant and lasting transformation. I will talk more about this in the final section.

Dr. Martin Luther King Jr. was right: "We must all learn to live together as brothers or we will perish together as fools."[6] The Civil War offers us the perfect visual representation of how this truth played out, in that hundreds of thousands of innocent lives were lost due to the absence of the practice of biblical oneness.

God's kingdom includes people from all races and cultures. Spiritual oneness can only be accomplished when we expand our view of God's creation to see each other more intimately and clearly than our often-limited exposure and understanding allows us to.

Due to the unique history of relationship between African Americans and Anglos in our nation, and drawing from my own personal experience, this book focuses on this specific broken arena of racial understanding and oneness. The two most prominent cultures expressing disunity within Christianity in America today are whites and blacks. This being so, I have decided to engage a discussion on oneness in the body of Christ through a bridging of these two groups. However, I want to encourage you to also explore the great variety of family that our Father has created in Native American, Hispanic, Asian, Middle Eastern, and other ethnicities throughout your life and beyond these pages.

Satan spends most of his time trying to divide us in the body of Christ. Why? Because he knows that God's power and glory are both accessed and magnified through unity. He is not spending his time trying to make the world wicked, because he doesn't have to help the world to be wicked. The world is born in wickedness and division. Satan just has to let the world do its natural thing and individuals will divide, fight, and oppress each other. If Satan can keep Christians ineffective due to a lack of cooperation and mutual edification, he will prevent the church from providing a model of the kingdom of God as an alternative to its chaos.

If someone is an alcoholic, it is probably not a good idea for you to listen to that person on how to stop drinking. If the church is divided, Satan hinders our witness on the transforming and unifying power of God.

## The Benefits of Oneness

Oneness brings with it many benefits. One is power. In fact, we see that even God recognizes how powerful oneness is when we read in Genesis 11 about the time when all of the people on the earth used the same language. They gathered together and decided to build a city (i.e., civilization) whose tower (i.e., religious temple) would reach into heaven.

God's response to what they were doing is recorded for us. He says, "Behold, they are one people, and they all have the same language. And this is what they began to do, and now nothing which they purpose to do will be impossible for them" (Gen. 11:6). God then confused their language and scattered them over the whole earth because He knew that oneness is powerful. Nothing expresses the principle of the power of oneness as much as this incident at Babel, because if God recognizes its power and importance in history when embraced among unbelievers operating in rebellion against Him, then how much more important and powerful is it for us?

Another benefit of oneness is that it glorifies God like nothing else because it reflects His image through His triune nature like nothing else. This truth comes through clearly in Jesus' prayer, commonly referred to as Jesus' high priestly prayer, shortly before He was arrested and crucified. He prayed,

> I pray also for those who will believe in me through their message, that all of them may be *one*, Father, just as you are in me and I am in you. May they also be in us so that the world may believe that you have sent me. I have given them the glory that you gave me, that they may be *one* as we are *one*—I in them and you in me—so that they may they be brought to *complete unity*. Then the world will know that you sent me and have loved them even as you have loved me. (John 17:20–23 NIV, italics added)

Jesus Christ placed a tremendous emphasis on His desire for us as His followers to be one just hours before He would lay down His life for us. This isn't something that He is asking us to do only during "Unity Month" or on "Special Oneness Sunday." This is a mandate from our Commander in Chief that we be *one* with Him (vertically) and, as a result, *one* with each other (horizontally).

A benefit of living a life of oneness, as we have just seen in this passage, is letting the world know about the King under whom we serve. Oneness brings glory to God by moving us into the atmosphere where we can experience God's response in such a way that He manifests His glory most fully in history (John 17:24). Thus, illegitimate disunity blocks the manifestation of His glory.

All of the praying, preaching, worship, or Bible studies in the world can never bring about the fullest possible manifestation of God's presence like functioning in a spirit of oneness in the body of

Christ. This is precisely why the subject found its place as the core of Jesus' high priestly prayer. It was the core because it uniquely reveals God's glory unlike anything else. It does this while at the same time revealing an authentic connection between one another in the body of Christ, which serves as a testimony of our connection with Christ. Jesus says, "By this all men will know that you are My disciples, if you have love for one another" (John 13:35).

An additional benefit of oneness is found in the Old Testament passage penned by David,

> Behold, how good and how pleasant it is
> For brothers to dwell together in unity!
> It is like the precious oil upon the head,
> Coming down upon the beard,
> Even Aaron's beard,
> Coming down upon the edge of his robes.
> It is like the dew of Hermon
> Coming down upon the mountains of Zion;
> For there the Lord commanded the blessing—life forever.
> (Ps. 133:1–3)

Unity is where the blessing of God rests, coming down from heaven to flow from the head to the body, and even reaching as far as the mountains of Zion. In other words, it covers everything. The reverse is also true: Where there is disunity, there is limited blessing. We cannot operate in unbiblical disunity and expect the full manifestation and continuation of God's blessing in our lives, ministries, and community impact. We cannot operate in unbiblical disunity and expect to hear from heaven, or expect God to answer our prayers in the way that both we and He long for Him to do. Disunity—or an existence of separatism, from a spiritual perspective—is essentially at its core self-defeating and self-limiting because it reduces the movement of God's favor and blessings.

Jesus made it clear that a house divided against itself cannot stand. Whether it is your house, the church house, or the White House, division leads to destruction (Matt. 12:25). Not only that, but a spirit of dishonor can lead to this same destruction (1 Cor.

12:22–26). Honor promotes unity while dishonor promotes division. Dishonor is not the same thing as disagreeing. A person can disagree with another person but do it in an honorable fashion. However, when dishonor is given to someone of a particular racial, social, or class background that has a history of the same, it negates attempts at unity.

What many conservative Christians fail to realize in a modern-day example is that when our first black president, Barack Obama, was dishonored either through caricatures, name-calling, or disrespectful talk by white Americans, it merely creates a greater chasm between the races. This is because the attack was not merely viewed as an assessment of his policies, but of the race he is publicly identified with and that identifies with him—a race that does not have a heritage established of receiving consistent public honor or respect in our land. To disagree with policy or procedure is a right of every American, but as a believer, any disagreement ought to be framed in a spirit of respect and honor for the position and the person in question. This is also true for how Christian blacks should respond to presidents they don't prefer. Scripture is clear: without equivocation, we are to honor the King (1 Peter 2:17). Otherwise, disunity is bred. However, when we live and work in oneness, God is invited to manifest Himself in ways we could only imagine.

Going deeper into Acts 2, we see the manifestation when the Holy Spirit moved like a "violent rushing wind" and "filled the whole house where they were" (Acts 2:2), in the midst of the oneness of the believers on the Day of Pentecost. At the end of the second chapter, the presence and product of oneness is emphasized as we read, "Everyone kept feeling a sense of awe; and many wonders and signs were taking place through the apostles. And all those who had believed were together and had all things in common" (Acts 2:43–44). Signs and wonders took place when they were "together" and "had all things in common." God manifested Himself when they were one.

What made this place and this period in time so electric was that the Spirit of God had taken over. The miracles that happened did not happen because the individuals had the best program, the best technology, or the biggest buildings in which to meet. They didn't have any of that. In fact, they barely had any income. No one among them had notoriety, a wall full of academic achievements, or charisma. They were simply common people bonded together by a common purpose across racial, class, and gender lines, thus receiving the Spirit's flow among them.

When they were one, God poured His blessing from heaven into history. God chose to do things that He would not otherwise have done if His people had not been one. Conversely, remaining in an environment of intellectual, spiritual, or social separatism limits the involvement of God's blessings in our personal life, family life, churches, and communities.

## The Bridge of Oneness

Achieving God's mandate of oneness is not as simple as reading a book about it. Just as a husband and wife must give up a lot to gain the oneness that marriage offers, so the races must be willing to pay the price of spiritual oneness. Both sides must be willing to experience the potential rejection of friends and relatives, whether Christians or non-Christians, who are not willing to accept that spiritual family relationships transcend physical, cultural, and racial relationships. This is what Jesus meant when He said, "Whoever does the will of My Father who is in heaven, he *is* My brother and sister and mother" (Matt. 12:50, italics added).

Pastors and spiritual leaders must actively remind our congregations of Ephesians 2:14–22:

> For He Himself is our peace, who made both groups into *one* and broke down the barrier of the dividing wall, by abolishing in His flesh the enmity, which is the Law of commandments contained in ordinances, so that in Himself He might make the two into one new man, thus establishing peace, and might reconcile them both in one body to God through the cross, by it having put to death the enmity. And HE CAME AND PREACHED PEACE TO YOU WHO WERE FAR AWAY, AND PEACE TO THOSE WHO WERE NEAR; for through Him we both have our access in one Spirit to the Father. So then you are no longer strangers and aliens, but you are fellow citizens with the saints, and are of God's household, having been built on the foundation of the apostles and

> prophets, Christ Jesus Himself being the corner stone, in whom the whole building, being fitted together, is growing into a holy temple in the Lord, in whom you also are being built together into a dwelling of God in the Spirit.

This passage makes the issue of oneness first and foremost theological, and not simply sociological. Jesus Christ died so that we might be unified as "one new man" in "one body" having access to God in "one Spirit." The absence of the oneness that Jesus died to bring hinders God's involvement and work in the church because the Holy Spirit occupies the church, and His work is directly tied to our unity.

Important as preaching is, it is not enough. Important as teaching and cultural-awareness seminars are, they are not enough. Important as books such as this one can be, they are not enough. The church must follow up with practical opportunities for bridging the cultural divide through mutual acts of service. The time has come to take an active role in inviting not only God's favor but also His blessing into our churches and lives through the intentional pursuit of oneness in the body of Christ. That is why I have purposefully cast a strategy for oneness at the end of this book. Nothing will bond people together more than working toward a common goal.

I go into greater detail about this and other ways of intentionally embracing oneness in the final chapter because while information is a necessary element, it is only the start. Transformation is the revelation that the information has taken root. It is high time for a transformation in the body of Christ. It is high time to rip off the tainted lenses of tradition in order to see each other, and ourselves, for who we truly are: valuable members of one another made in the exquisite image of our God. Only then can the church accurately reflect its spiritual content in this age in such a way that the world can clearly see an alternative to the brokenness of our current state. Having seen this alternative and responded to it, individuals, families, and communities will then be placed in the sphere where they too can experience a bit of heaven on earth until the fullness of heaven comes to earth.

So many individuals today live segmented, compartmentalized lives because they lack implementation of God's kingdom worldview and subsequently lack His blessings. Families disintegrate because they exist for their own satisfaction rather than for the kingdom. Churches are limited in the scope of their impact because they fail to comprehend that the goal of the church is not the church itself, but the kingdom. Communities have nowhere to turn to find real solutions for real people who have real problems because the church has become divided and ingrown, making it unable to significantly transform the cultural landscape. When God, and His rule, is no longer the final and authoritative standard under which all else falls, hope exits with Him.

But the reverse of that is true as well: As long as there is God, there is hope. He's the only one you or I can truly bank on. As long as God is still in the picture, and as long as His agenda is still on the table, it's not over. As long as God, and His rule, is still present in our lives, our families, our churches and communities, there is hope. But in a world where everyone is divided around their own cultural ideas, we end up losing the very thing that can carry us through each day: hope. When truth loses meaning, we cannot be sure about anything. This makes it difficult to find hope since truth, ultimately, is the centerpiece of hope.

I live in Dallas, Texas, and in Dallas there is a loop that I take when I want to get somewhere on the other side of the city but don't necessarily want to head straight through downtown. This loop will take me close enough to the city so that I can see its towering buildings and skyline, but not close enough to actually experience it.

This is precisely what we, as a culture, have done with God regarding oneness in the body of Christ. We have put God on the "loop" of our lives. He is close enough to be at hand should we need His call for oneness in a national emergency, but far enough away that He can't be the centerpiece of who we are each and every day. Therefore, He will not bring hope or deliverance.

It doesn't take much more than a cursory glance around our society today to realize that our world is in desperate need of hope. Our communities need hope. Our churches need hope. Our families need hope. We need hope. Without God's truth as the centerpiece in all that we do and say, we will forever lack hope. We will continue to exist, biding our time rather than experiencing the fullness of a life, family, church, and community pregnant with the sublime.

**Notes**

1. For an in-depth look at the philosophy and theology of the kingdom agenda, see the author's book by the same name, *The Kingdom Agenda* (Chicago: Moody, 2006).
2. 2019 Resolutions Committee of the Southern Baptist Convention, Affirmation of Recent Statements from Christian Leaders on Critical Race Theory.
3. Dwight McKissic, @pastordmack replying to @tombuck @malbritton2016 and @tomascol, December 2, 2020.
4. Angela P. Harris, "Foreword: The Jurisprudence of Reconciliation," *California Law Review* (July 1994), 741.
5. Tony Evans, "Race and Reconciliation," sermon preached at Oak Cliff Bible Fellowship, November 15, 2020. Quoted in Dwight McKissic, "From Boys to Men: My Response to the SBC Seminary Presidents' CRT Statement," SBCvoices.com, December 14, 2020, https://sbcvoices.com/from-boys-to-men-my-response-to-the-sbc-seminary-presidents-crt-statement.
6. Dr. Martin Luther King Jr., speech at Western Michigan University, December 18, 1963, Western Michigan University Speech Archives Collection.

# Chapter 3

# BIBLICAL MODELS OF ONENESS

In the beginning, God created a man. Within the seed of that man rested all of the components, DNA, and characteristic trademarks of all people today. In the beginning, we were one. Scripture tells us in the book of Acts, "He made from *one* man every nation of mankind to live on all the face of the earth" (Acts 17:26). Thus, sharing a common origin in Adam, any form of division or oppression predicated on race is illegitimate, because we all emanate from the same source.

Racial subjugation in our society as well as in the church came about as a result of a divergence from this key biblical truth. It was not only supported by errant theology, but it was also reinforced by pseudoscience, which was called upon to justify slavery by purporting that people in the black race were inferior to those in the white. When theology joined hands with science, this created a double problem in the church by giving both religious and scientific support to the dehumanization and dividing process. Only with a return to biblical truth as our overarching standard by which all else is measured will an accurate view of oneness be seen and actualized.

A major obstacle to overcome in understanding and engaging in oneness, though, is the question of who's in charge: the Bible, science, or one's culture? This leads to a multiplicity of issues, one of which is the hindrance that is caused when authority is given to cultural diversity over biblical truth.

For example, some African American Christians so amalgamate the tenets of black culture with their faith that they frequently fail to make the necessary distinction between the two when it comes to critiquing ourselves. Many times racial hindrances are blamed for blocking forward progress either academically or vocationally. While these hindrances should be acknowledged and addressed, we must also take responsibility for ourselves, in spite of obvious hindrances, to find a way to execute at the level that we should in order to overcome them.

Conversely, Anglos will often leave the Bible when it is culturally convenient to do so in order to protect their traditions and privileges. This has historically been most clearly in the sacred cow of interracial dating and marriage. When the issue comes up, the argument of culture comes up as well. Questions such as: What about the kids? and What will the relatives think? surface much quicker than questions of what the Bible says.

## An Apostle's Bad Example

The problem with both of the previous perspectives is the failure to recognize biblical authority when it clashes with cultural or racial presuppositions. This problem is in no way unique to the contemporary black/white racial landscape as it is equally evident in the world of the New Testament. Galatians 2 records one such incident. This particular illustration is graphic because it involved apostolic leaders, the highest authorities in the first-century church.

Peter was a committed Jew. He loved his people and carried a deep burden for their salvation. God, however, expanded his horizon by giving him the experience of seeing a vision in which God told him to eat the animals on a great sheet, in direct violation of the Hebrew dietary laws. God used this image to tell Peter that he was to repeat the very same work among the Gentiles that was being done among the Jews (Acts 10:11–29). Peter accepted that revelation and seemed to understand it.

The apostle Paul, however, records a confrontation with Peter that revealed old prejudices do not die easily. One day we see Peter had discovered that the Gentiles could cook, among other things. He had joined them for some good old-fashioned chitlins, pork chops, and pig feet. During this time of cross-cultural finger-licking and fraternizing across the railroad tracks, in walked Jewish Christians who had not yet come to grips with their anti-Gentile racism. They put Peter on the spot, telling him to either hand his plate back to the Gentile Christians and walk away or stay over there on his own. Peter didn't want to lose acceptance with his own racial group.

So Peter walked away, leaving the Gentiles to their own. Scripture tells us that Peter's hypocrisy even caused Barnabas, the encourager, to stumble (Gal. 2:13). That's how bad this sin of racial prejudice is. It will make good men—men like Barnabas who was known for encouraging others—bad. A mist in the pulpit is a fog in the pew.

Having caved in to the pressure, Peter failed the test. He had left the Gentiles in order to not offend the Jews. In deference to the cultural pressure of his own race, he discredited the message of the gospel that God had so graphically conveyed to him in the home of Cornelius.

There was only one problem: Paul saw it. Paul was equally committed to his Jewish history, culture, and people, yet he publicly excoriated Peter's non-Christian action, saying that Peter was "not straightforward about the truth of the gospel" (Gal. 2:14). The key point is *truth*. An objective standard transcended Peter's cultural identity and commitment. Paul didn't care what Peter's background was. He didn't care what his racial identity was. All he focused on at that point was that Peter was messing with Jesus Christ. He was messing with the One who came to be our peace, and our point of reference. The One who came to establish one "new man."

The fact that even an apostle could not get away with such an action is very instructional and should not be marginalized in its importance and contemporary application. No one is excused for placing culture above Christ. No one is excused for placing race above righteousness. God's standard reigns supreme, and cultural preferences are to be denounced publicly when a Christian fails to submit to God's standard. Scripture, and only Scripture, is the final authority by which racial interactions and engagement are determined.

Paul did what he needed to do. He didn't hold a meeting. He didn't conduct a sensitivity seminar. He didn't say, "Hey, can't we all just get along?" Nor did he offer Peter a ten-week Bible study. Paul said, "Peter, you are messing with the gospel. Stop it. Don't mess with the gospel."

Racism is a gospel issue, not merely a social one. When people say our Christian leaders should just focus on the gospel and stop talking about this "race issue," I always want to ask them what Bible they are referencing because racism is at the heart of the scope of the gospel. It was this racial issue that led Paul to make one of the most consequential statements on the believer's identity in Christ. He writes in Galatians 2:20, "I have been crucified with Christ; and it is no longer I who live, but Christ lives in me; and the life which I now live in the flesh I live by faith in the Son of God, who loved me and gave Himself up for me."

What is key to note is that this well-known and well-loved verse is within the context of Paul's correction of Peter concerning Peter's racism. Paul was instructing him in this passage, and us, that our identity in Christ—while it does not deny our human uniqueness—does override it. Failure in this regard is spiritual compromise and undermines our confession of faith and our reflection of the gospel power within us.

## A Study on Oneness in Samaria

One of the most informative and poignant teachings from the Scripture regarding culture, truth, and oneness is the story of Jesus' encounter with the woman of Samaria in John chapter 4. This story gives us two overriding principles that are needed to establish true spiritual oneness.

In 722 BC, the Jews living in the Northern Kingdom were taken captive by the Assyrians. An interracial exchange followed. Some Jews were deported to Assyria, and some Assyrians were imported into the Northern Kingdom. The Jews who remained did not entirely relinquish their true worship of God, despite the introduction of Assyrian cults. Intermarriage, however, destroyed the purity of the race, giving birth to a new ethnic group of people called Samaritans.

During the Persian period, the Jews were allowed to return to Jerusalem to rebuild the temple and the walls. This attempt was resisted by the Samaritans, who were now a mixed race of Assyrians and Israelites and did not want to see the city of Jerusalem successfully rebuilt because of their racial hatred of the Jews (Neh. 2:19; 4:1; 6:1–6). The Jews, meanwhile, desired to maintain the purity of the Jewish race and thus would not allow the Samaritans to participate in the rebuilding process (Neh. 2:20; 6:14). A feud developed that continued into Christ's day and served as the historical backdrop to the confrontation between Jesus and the Samaritan woman.

When Jesus traveled with His disciples through Samaria, He was not merely taking a shorter route. He was on a mission to meet needs that He knew existed there. It is important to note that Jesus was intentional about His route through Samaria. The fact that He entered Samaria made it clear that He was willing to go beyond His own culture to meet others' needs. However, overcoming the cultural prejudice of the Samaritans was another issue. Jesus was willing to make the first move, but how could He get the Samaritans to give Him the chance to connect with them? The solution was to recognize common ground, which is the first principle for biblical oneness.

### *Recognize Common Ground*

In Samaria, Jesus rested at Jacob's well (John 4:6). A well offered water and shade, and it was a natural place for a hot, tired man to stop. But Jesus chose this particular well because both the Jews and Samaritans loved Jacob, who was the father of both groups. Jesus was looking for common ground so He stopped at Jacob's well and built a bridge of communication by starting with what He and the Samaritan woman could agree on.

Jesus had rejected the attitudes of His contemporaries in His willingness to go through Samaria from Judea to Galilee, something no good, orthodox Jew would do. This is why in John 4:9 the Samaritan woman asked him, "How is it that You, being a Jew, ask me for a drink since I am a Samaritan woman?" The text tells us, "For Jews have no dealings with Samaritans."

Shocked at Jesus' request, she could not believe that He was asking her, a woman of Samaria, to let Him use her cup. To put His Jewish lips on her Samaritan cup was an intimate act of fellowship and warm acceptance. It was something that wasn't done in this woman's neighborhood. Not only was this an action that signified a willingness for fellowship, but it was also an action that gave the woman value. Jesus was letting her know that He had a need, and that she was in a position to meet that need. He esteemed her with value by placing Himself in a position that acknowledged that she possessed the ability to help Him.

But how did the woman know that Jesus was a Jew? John, the author, does not say that Jesus told her that He was a Jew. So there must have been something about Him that made her know. It could be that He looked like a Jew, or perhaps He had a Jewish accent or some other trait that gave a public indication of His racial and cultural heritage.

Whatever it was, when Jesus Christ went through Samaria, He did not give up His own culture. He did not stop being a Jew to reach a Samaritan, but neither did He allow His culture to prevent Him from connecting with her or meeting a spiritual need in her. While remaining culturally competent, He maintained His unique cultural identity. He just didn't let who He was stop Him from being what He was called to be.

In other words, Jesus didn't let His history, culture, race, and background get in the way of ministering to a woman who had a spiritual need and who would meet him on common ground. Likewise, Jesus allowed the woman to retain her history, culture, and experiences as a Samaritan.

One of our problems today is that we have not allowed the freedom for healthy integration in a context of mutual diversification. We hold so tightly to our preferences either out of protection or pride that we often end up alienating anyone from another cultural background who seeks to join us. Or, conversely, when we seek to enter another cultural group, we shed our own distinctions in an effort to try to become something we were never made to be. This stalls the forward progress of God's kingdom purposes, restraining the kingdom of God from advancing as it is designed to advance.

Jesus didn't do that. Even though none of the other Jews would go through Samaria, He went through Samaria. Even though none of the other Jews would drink from the Samaritan woman's cup, He drank from her cup. This is why Jesus sent His disciples into the city to buy food (v. 8). He would not allow the racism of others to block

Him from doing God's will cross-culturally. The Samaritan woman clearly recognized Jesus as a Jew, but He also entered her world. He did so because He was there representing something much bigger.

God is not calling us to be something we were not created to be when He calls us to oneness. He is not calling you, if you are white, to like soul music, and I'm thankful that He is not calling me to like country and western. What He is doing, however, is calling everybody to take who we are and to work together toward a common goal—a kingdom agenda.

I'm not sure if you realize this, but whatever race you are now is what you are going to be in heaven. If you are white now, you are going to be white in heaven. If you are black now, you are going to be black in heaven. You are who you are intentionally and eternally. God is not colorblind.

But you say, "Tony, I've never seen that in the Bible." Well, it's in there.

In the book of Revelation, John said, "After these things I looked, and behold, a *great multitude* which no one could count, from every nation and all tribes and peoples and tongues, standing before the throne and before the Lamb" (Rev. 7:9, emphasis added).

What I want you to note from that verse is that John *saw* them. The differences were visual. Why? Because God intended there to be differences. God has people from every background, group, and demographic representing His kingdom. Acknowledging and embracing our differences in a context of oneness more accurately reflects the kingdom of heaven than any other thing.

### *Social Leads to Spiritual*

The Samaritan woman saw that while Jesus looked Jewish, talked Jewish, and dressed Jewish, He didn't act entirely Jewish because He was willing to do something no other Jew was willing to do—put His lips to her cup. Please note that this was a tangible, public, and social action on His part. In other words, He wasn't just standing far off saying, "Samaritan woman, you must be born again." Rather, Jesus was willing to engage her socially. Jesus did not ignore her humanity to save her soul. This has been one of the great sins of American Christianity.

One of the greatest hindrances to authentic oneness in the body of Christ today is our unwillingness to engage each other socially. Granted, we have made efforts in the church and society to develop multiracial staff in our ministries, or to link up for special events, but the question is still often posed, or often thought if not stated, "Why do all the black staff members spend their breaktime together?" or "Why do all the whites sit in groups?" Rarely do we witness a natural merging of the races unless it has been forced; however, when it is forced, it cannot be authentic simply due to the nature of oneness. We have misunderstood oneness to mean a denial of racial distinctions. This has left us with the result of forcing oneness rather than actualizing it. This creates polarization and fragmentation since forced oneness can only come as a result of one group imposing its definition of unity on the other rather than an embracing of individuality together toward the pursuance of a common goal.

Jesus understood the value of time, attention, and embracing the other. By engaging the Samaritan woman socially, He brought the opportunity for an even deeper discussion as we read in John 4:10: "Jesus answered and said to her, 'If you knew the gift of God, and who it is who says to you, "Give Me a drink," you would have asked Him, and He would have given you living water.'"

One of the things I love most about Jesus is that He could turn anything into an illustration. What He did is take the simple conversation about a drink and turn it into an evangelistic opportunity. He was able to do this because He was not only willing to spend time with her, but also to drink from her cup. In His willingness to drink from her cup, He gained an opportunity to witness to her soul. Don't miss that. If He had not been willing to engage her socially, He may not have had the opportunity to talk to her spiritually.

A lot of times we want to get people to heaven whom we are not willing to relate to on earth. We want to get people to glory whom we are not willing to even talk to in history. But what Jesus did was use the natural cross-cultural opportunity of common ground—Jacob's well and His need for a drink—to present a message of life to this lady. Through this, Jesus initiated true biblical oneness.

The second principle for biblical oneness is that Jesus refused to allow culture to interfere with His higher priority of representing God's truth.

*Refuse to Allow Culture to Interfere with Truth*

Our second principle is illustrated best through this next passage: "The woman said to Him, 'Sir, I perceive that You are a prophet. Our fathers worshiped in this mountain, and you people say that in Jerusalem is the place where men ought to worship'" (John 4:19-20).

What she is saying, in my Tony Evans translation, is, "Jesus, y'all go to church over there. And we go to church over here. You worship that way. We worship this way. We are different. In fact, not only are we different, we were raised differently. My daddy taught me that this is how you do it because his daddy taught him that this is how you do it. In fact, my great granddaddy taught my granddaddy who taught my daddy who taught me that this is how you do it. This is our history and our background and what we are used to doing."

Jesus responds to her excuses using rather direct language. He says, "You worship what you do not know; we worship what we know, for salvation is from the Jews" (John 4:22).

In other words, "Your daddy was wrong. Your granddaddy was wrong. Your great granddaddy was wrong. And your great-great-granddaddy was wrong. You, and your people, are wrong."

Now, the last time the Samaritan woman brought up cultural differences, Jesus never said a single word about it. But this time Jesus clearly says, "You are wrong." Why does He address the issue now and not before? Because now God has been brought into the equation. Now there is a spiritual truth on the table. Our differences from each other are not wrong except when our differences bring in wrong information about God.

One of the things that you and I have got to understand as brothers and sisters in Christ is that this divide in our culture and in our nation is because people have chosen to pay more attention to their granddaddy than to their heavenly Father. It is because people have held a stronger commitment to the history of their culture than to the person of Jesus Christ. There has been a more faithful allegiance to background than to the Bible.

The problem with race in America is not fundamentally a problem of skin. It is a problem of sin. It is a problem in that people have not been willing to address the sin that has led to a division among skin as we hold tenaciously to our cultures. Our backgrounds, preferences, and unique cultural expressions are legitimate, but when they overrule or conflict with God, that's when Jesus says, "You are wrong."

Whenever there is a conflict between culture and God's truth, culture must always submit to the truth of God as revealed in His Word. When the woman's culture crossed sacred things, Christ invaded her world to condemn it.

This means that to refer to oneself as a black Christian or a white Christian or a Hispanic Christian or an Asian Christian is technically incorrect. In these descriptions, the word *Christian* becomes a noun that is modified by an adjective—black, white, and so on. It's the job of the adjective to modify the noun. So, if you've got Christianity in the noun position, and your color in the adjectival position, you've got to keep adjusting the noun of your faith to the adjective of your humanity. Rather, you've got to put Christianity in the adjectival position, and your color and culture in the noun position so if anything has to change or adapt, it is the noun of your humanity and not the adjective of your faith.

We must see ourselves as Christian blacks, Christian whites, Christian Hispanics, or Christian Asians. We should celebrate the uniqueness of our created humanity while simultaneously submitting that uniqueness to our identity in Christ. This Christocentric identity-focus should serve to enhance the righteous validity of our uniquely created racial distinctives. They should not negate or cancel them.

Our cultures must always be controlled and informed by our commitment to Christ. Whenever we make the adjectives *black, white, brown,* and *other* descriptives of Christians, it may mean we have changed Christianity to make it fit a cultural description. The Bible teaches the opposite—we are Christians who are also black, white, or brown. If anything changes, it is to be our cultural expression, not our Christianity. This is so because cultural history and experience, while important, are not innately inspired. Therefore,

Christianity must always inform, explain, and, if necessary, change our cultures, never the reverse. Similarly, if citizens would take this same approach to our country where we submitted together under our common constitutional bond as Americans, we would have far less confusion in our land. Uniting around a shared identity—without abandoning our racial distinctives—we would work together in a greater unity toward national restoration in that our cultural and racial differences would be subservient to our national identity as Americans.

Black Christians, white Christians, Asian Christians, or Hispanic Christians must decide to live as Christians first, without giving up their cultures, but still submitting it to the authority of Christ when it comes in conflict with Him and His kingdom rule.

*Understand It Goes Both Ways*

Jesus not only critiqued the Samaritan culture by the truth of God's Word, but He critiqued His own culture by that same standard. When His disciples complained that He was talking with a Samaritan woman, He rejected their prejudice by telling them that it was more important for Him to do the will of God than to succumb to their biases.

The disciples hadn't been shocked that Jesus was talking with a woman. They had seen Him talk to women before. He talked to Mary. He talked to Martha. He had healed the woman with the issue of blood. Talking to a woman was not the problem. The problem came in that Jesus had been talking to a Samaritan woman. That's what bothered the disciples. This also explains why Jesus had let them walk a number of miles into town, as is recorded earlier in the passage, and the same number of miles back, just to bring Him some lunch. He knew that He could have never gotten kingdom work done with His prejudiced disciples hanging around.

The principle is that while we can't control what others in our circles do, like Jesus we can control whether or not we let them stop us from doing what the King of kings has called us to do. Obeying the will of God takes priority over satisfying cultural norms and expectations.

While Jesus was explaining this concept to His disciples, the woman was running back into town to tell the men of the city that they should come and see this Man who has told her all of the things that she has done. She had become an immediate evangelist simply because Jesus chose to cross cultural lines to win her to Himself. The disciples, in the meantime, were growing more frustrated with Jesus as they learned that they had just walked nearly all day only to bring food to Him that He refused.

"Jesus said to them, 'My food is to do the will of Him who sent Me and to accomplish His work. Do you not say, "There are yet four months, and then comes the harvest"? Behold, I say to you, lift up your eyes and look on the fields, that they are white for harvest'" (John 4:34–35). The point is that the fields are ready. Jesus is saying that if you will simply lift up your eyes, you will *see* the harvest. Stop talking about how you are going to get around to it next year, or five years from now, or even twenty-five years from now. Stop giving excuses for delaying the harvest when the fields are already ripe. If you will look up, you will *see* that the opportunity to cross over is right in front of you. This is what the disciples saw when they looked at the field and saw the Samaritan men crossing over it to meet them.

We don't need to wait for the next generation to do it. We have opportunities right across the street, around the corner, in a school next door, and in the community near us where we can make a difference for the kingdom of God. The time has come to be rid of our excuses and to start doing kingdom work right here and now.

When we do, we will see things we never even thought could be possible because we will see God show up and let His power flow both to us and through us. This is exactly what happened in Samaria. We read, "So when the Samaritans came to Jesus, they were asking Him to stay with them; and He stayed there two days. Many more believed because of His word" (John 4:40–41).

One of the greatest evangelistic outreaches occurred simply because Jesus took the time to engage and connect with another person from another background than His own. After Jesus had led everyone to Himself, He ended up spending the entire weekend with the Samaritans. Now, keep in mind that He had just met them. Their two cultures don't even talk to each other. They don't share water, nor do they drink from the same cup. But in the same time period that Jesus meets them, He ends up hanging out in their neighborhood all weekend long.

How do we go from "We don't talk" to "Let's hang out together" so quickly? Easy: When Jesus Christ enters the situation and demonstrates the kingdom principle of oneness through kingdom people, He can turn things that are upside down and make them right side up overnight. He doesn't need a generation to do it. It only takes a minute if He's got the right people who are willing to live their lives by His rules.

What Jesus did in Samaria, and what He can do for you and me, is turn distance and doubt—the great divide—into a harmonious fellowship filled with power. When He does, we will see Him do things that we never even dreamed. Lifting our blinders, He will enable us to look across the fields of this life and visualize the art of His creation, His heart, and His unique design. We will see where and how He is working to bring glory to Himself and hope to mankind. Better yet, we will get to experience Him as He pours down His blessings and blows our minds.

Racial harmony and reconciliation do not necessitate that all churches be integrated at all times into one noncultural, robotic format. Don't misunderstand my point. Jesus didn't dispose of His Jewish passport, trim His beard, and adopt Samaritan slang. But He did give us a model of the intentional nature as well as the depth of engagement that we are to follow in cross-cultural relationships. Jesus showed value and esteem to an entire group of people through an authentic respect and intentionality to relate.

God is not asking African Americans to disregard our rich spiritual and cultural heritage and become white in our approach to theology and the full expression of life under the umbrella of a biblical worldview. Nor is God asking white people to adopt other cultural styles of worship and become black in their approach to theology. But He is insisting that, within our differences, we discover a common ground of mutual benefit as we all reflect His truth as revealed in Scripture. When culture does not infringe upon the Word of God, we are free to be what God has created us to be, with all the uniqueness that accompanies our cultural heritage.

However, the objective truth from Scripture places limits on our cultural experiences. As African Americans continue to seek cultural freedom, we must examine every strategy offered to promote social justice and policy under the magnifying glass of Scripture. Every bit of advice given by our leaders and all definitions proposing to tell us what it means to be black must be commensurate with divine revelation. If what we are given as cultural is not biblically acceptable, it cannot be accepted as authoritative or legitimate.

Whites, too, must submit their cultural traditions and privileges to the authority of God's Word if they are going to play their part in dismantling the racial mythology that is a dominant theme in their worldview. Because of this limited and distorted worldview, whites are often unable to see beyond skin to discover the qualitative benefits that would come their way through using and learning from the skills, intellect, and creativity of their African American brothers and sisters.

In the same way that the realm of athletics and entertainment was enhanced by African American participation when it was finally recognized as valuable and included, the kingdom of God would be much more holistically advanced if there were a recognition and use of the gifts, talents, and unique qualities of Christian blacks. But in order for that to take place, there must be a willingness on the part of Christian whites to not only give access to but also intentionally pursue, or respond to an invitation for, ongoing relationships and ministry partnerships with their brothers and sisters in Christ as equals.

I am never more disheartened at the state of our Christian family than when I witness the reality that this access is often much more open, as well as invitational in nature, in our liberal secular society than in our own. In many aspects, our secular society has advanced further in this arena than we have, thus limiting both the influence and impact that we, members of God's kingdom, are able to have on those around us, causing many to even question our relevance.

The great tragedy today is not so much that our society is still divided along racial, cultural, and class lines, but that God's people, the church, are even more deeply divided. This disunity provides Satan with his most powerful tool for crippling the influence of

Christianity. That is why Jesus prayed that believers might be one in order to overcome the world (John 17:21). When we are one, we will overcome. When we are not one, we will be overrun.

Oneness, in a nation structured by the confines of racial autonomy, necessitates that our knowledge of and love for each other must be intentional in nature, just as Jesus' was with the woman at the well. When we come together, unbelievers will see that Christianity is not a secret, and that God alone can jettison centuries of misguided beliefs and traditions. Only then will our unity wash the fabric of our nation's landscape not only on a personal level, but also in our families, churches, and in our communities at large.

Just as it was in Samaria, oneness across racial lines is the greatest evangelistic teaser to the presentation of the gospel that we could ever broadcast, both locally and abroad.

# Chapter 4

# TAKING SIDES OR TAKING OVER

One reason we are not seeing an evangelistic message of oneness permeating our society and world is that the African American community has its own agenda and the Anglo community has its own agenda as well. The problem is that no overarching agenda transcends both. If we were to unite underneath an overriding agenda, a truth-based kingdom philosophy, we would find the common ground with which to reach the world for Jesus Christ. Then we as the church would truly be an impactful and influential missiological entity.

An illustration of this played out when Hurricane Harvey hit Houston. Differences between races took a backseat to the local crisis. Why? Because there was a bigger agenda on the table—namely, the search and rescue of people in need, as well as providing food, clean water, and shelter. A similar thing happened around 9/11 when the equal threat to all of us on the level of heightened terrorism caused people to rally around a common purpose. Individuals from all races gathered together in churches, at city hall, at work, or in homes to comfort and encourage one another as well as to pray. The issue in both of these scenarios, and typically anytime there is a local or national emergency, is not the color, culture, or gender of the persons rushing in to rescue those in need. The only important issue is whether life is protected and preserved.

When faced with a common enemy, a common passion is automatically ignited, resulting in oneness of purpose. The problem emerges, however, when the threat dissipates. The result is all too often a return to the cultural posture that existed prior to the crisis.

We would do well to adopt a joint agenda of purpose that reflects and incorporates the concerns of multiple ethnicities and races, while at the same time reaching broader than our individual concerns. This is because, whether we realize it or not, we do face a common enemy whose agenda it is to wreak havoc in our lives, homes, communities, and world. And by the looks of it, that enemy is doing a very good job at keeping us divided.

A perfect illustration of how we can oppose this enemy together is the abortion debate. The white evangelical church is heavily Republican because of its belief that the Republican party best reflects the concerns of Christians for a moral awakening in our country. Because a large segment of the Republican party is anti-abortion, the watershed issue of the moral agenda, the white evangelical church has made the abortion debate a central component of its concern.

On the other hand, the black church has given its dominant allegiance to the Democratic party because of its belief that the Democratic party is more sensitive to the questions of social justice, racial equality, and the plight of the poor. The black church's heart cry is primarily for the comprehensive well-being of the babies born in the world (specifically in the areas of employment, housing, medical care, equal access, and education), rather than the safety of the fetus in the womb. God's Word makes it crystal clear that His kingdom agenda is whole-life, from womb to tomb, with the full recognition of human dignity in between the two (Ps. 139:13–16; James 3:9). It is the dignity of every human life that serves as the divinely authorized reason for the just use of the death penalty (Gen. 9:6).

What is the solution? It is to establish an agenda that includes both issues because both issues are legitimate and have ample biblical support. In other words, leaders from both sides should establish a purpose that goes from cradle-to-grave and womb-to-tomb—a whole-life agenda. Such an approach would unify the church around a central theme that both sides can agree on while at the same time allowing each side to focus on its primary concern. There would not be sameness, but there would be oneness, and that is what biblical unity is all about.

The bonus to all of this would be that the broader culture would see aspects of the oneness of the church as it works across racial lines, resulting in the fulfillment of Jesus' words, "By this all men will know that you are My disciples, if you have love for one another" (John 13:35). What greater love can we show for one another than by working together to seek the comprehensive welfare of the members of God's family first, and then extending that concern to the culture at large (Gal. 6:10)?

## Another Kingdom

There were critical times in biblical history when God specifically wanted to demonstrate that He alone has an agenda that transcends all methodology, plans, and priorities set forth by man. At these times, when He wanted to remind His people about His kingdom rule, God sometimes let His people get caught in a situation that they could not reason, or resolve, themselves out of. He did this so that they would be forced to submit to His agenda or crumble. I call this getting caught in a catch-22 or between a rock and a hard place. This is when God has intentionally allowed a situation to occur where no human solution is available.

One of these times, for example, was when Israel got caught between Pharaoh's army and the Red Sea. There was no way out. In fact, God's people cried out and complained to Moses that he had brought them there to die. Things had gotten so bad for the Israelites that they could only see death in their future. But that's also when God showed up and told Moses to hold out his rod over the sea so that He would part it, allowing the Israelites to cross over on dry land.

When we look at the social issues rooted in race that are still prominent in our nation today, as well as in the church, it appears that we are in such a time. No one has a solid answer to the plethora of conflicting problems that engulf us. Whether it's immigration reform, police reform, an inordinate number of impoverished black women and children in the midst of one of the most prosperous nations in the world, racial/class distinctions resulting in education disparity, the decline of black voting influence, inequality in health care, or increased crime, everybody knows it's bad. But clear-cut solutions seem nowhere to be found.

We remain in a racial crisis of disunity that continues to cripple our nation in a way that affects us all. We may not live in the midst of these problems ourselves, but their impact reaches into more places than we may even yet be aware, creating cyclical ramifications throughout our land.

I'd like to suggest to you today, though, that a crisis isn't always all that bad even though it may not be comfortable. I say that because when things are in disarray, while they may be difficult and painful, it just might be that our King is up to something great. It might be that God is shaking things up in order to reveal His unshakeable kingdom. The book of Hebrews teaches us that at times God creates discontinuity in history in order to bring the uniqueness of His kingdom to the forefront (Heb. 12:25–29). This is precisely what God did by allowing the multiple pandemics of 2020, which included a worldwide virus, racial conflict, major political divide, and upheaval. While I'm not saying that God brought it about in order to do this, He did allow it to shake up a rebellious, idolatrous world while simultaneously using it to seek to wake up a sleeping and divided church in order to return us to our kingdom identity and responsibility (2 Chron. 15:3–6).

A look into the life of Joshua reveals a time just like that. In the book of Joshua, chapter 1, God told Joshua to "be strong and courageous." Now, when God tells you to be strong and to have courage, He knows that the propensity for fear in the mess that you are facing is pretty high right then. In other words, Joshua was getting ready to face a mess because he was going into some property occupied by Hittites, Amorites, Jebusites, and Canaanites. He was about to march into enemy land.

Joshua served as the military leader over Israel at that time. God had told him one day, "Every place on which the sole of your foot treads, I have given it to you, just as I spoke to Moses" (Josh. 1:3). This promise in the face of his problems came to him as a revelation. One thing we have to understand theologically is that God's promises, while they are legal, must be made literal through our actions. In other words, God will make a promise that most often requires a human action for that promise to be drawn down into a historical reality. It is similar to having a bank account in your name filled with a large amount of money. Unless you access your account either through an ATM card, writing a check, or visiting a teller, that money will no more benefit you than someone else who does not have access to the account. In this case, you must do something to access what is yours.

God said to Joshua, "I have already given you the land, but you need to go and put your foot on it first. Joshua, you need to *do* something." We can see from this condition that while there is a promise to deal with a problem, there is also a process for the promise to take place. A spiritual principle to live by is that God's promises do not extricate us from the process of full participation in receiving them.

### *Whose Side Are You On?*

Skipping forward a few chapters, we see Joshua heading down for reconnaissance near the future battle site of the city of Jericho. He definitely had the thought in his mind that if he could put his foot on it somehow, God would give it to him. But Jericho was a fortified city with a high wall encircling it. In fact, the wall was so thick around Jericho that we are told that Rahab's house was imbedded in it (Josh. 2:15). To have a house imbedded in a wall means it must be a pretty thick wall, even if it's a small house. And yet God had promised victory to Joshua.

Surely, as Joshua studied the wall, he must have wondered how his army was supposed to penetrate such a protected city. He knew he had His promise that every place he put his foot, God had already given it to him, but he certainly couldn't put his foot on Jericho nor the enormous encasement surrounding it.

While Joshua strategized as any good military leader would, we're told that he lifted up his eyes and *saw* someone. He "looked, and behold, a man was standing opposite him with his sword drawn in his hand, and Joshua went to him and said to him, 'Are you for us or for our adversaries?'" (Josh. 5:13).

Joshua saw this military leader come out of nowhere and asked a very relevant question, "Are you friend or are you foe? Before I move ahead, I need to know: Whose side are you on?"

If the military leader is on Jericho's side, then Joshua has a double problem. He not only has the problem of defeating Jericho and Jericho's army, but he's now got the problem of this other captain and his army. So he's fighting on two fronts. That will change his strategy. But conversely, if the military leader is on Israel's side, then that gives him a whole other level of excitement because now he has support for his mission. So he decides to ask him, "Are you for us or for our adversaries?"

To which he is given a strangely odd reply: The military leader said, "No."

Now, I don't know about you but that answer bothers me. Last time I checked, it wasn't a "yes or no" question. Joshua, obviously concerned for his nation's battle strategy, asked a legitimate question to a military leader, and he answered, "No."

I would have thought that the military leader would have said, "Joshua, you are the man! You are God's leading man fulfilling God's promise against the problem that God has already told you about. He has already told you that He will give you this land if you'll just put your foot on it. I'm on your side, Joshua. I'm here on your side."

But, instead, he says, "No; rather I indeed come now as captain of the host of the Lord." In essence, he is saying, "I'm not on anyone's side. I belong to a whole other kingdom. I belong to a different order. I am captain of the Lord's army. Just because you are my people doesn't mean that I'm on your side." What he is communicating is that he has come representing a bigger agenda than Joshua's agenda. In essence, he told Joshua that he didn't come to take sides, he came to take over. Unfortunately, we have unrighteously taken racial sides, political sides, class sides, dignity-of-life sides—rather than God's kingdom agenda side. This fissure has kept God's people weak, ineffective, inept, and ignored.

The failure to recognize, as this biblical example so clearly illustrates, that God is not taking sides with any of our agendas, but rather He has an overarching kingdom agenda under which we must align ourselves, and has been the greatest hindrance to the advancement of the church throughout time. This lack of acknowledgment of and adherence to God's kingdom plan as the comprehensive rule under which all else must fall has kept the church stuck in the Promised Land with the walls of Jericho still standing tall. God never told us to remodel the walls of Jericho; He told us to tear them down.

### *What Do You Want Me to Do?*

One of the reasons that we as the body of Christ have not realized the supernatural presence of God is that we have let our cultures delineate what the church is supposed to be rather than letting God reveal this Himself through the revelation of His Word. We argue, complain, and change the things that we don't like or that don't fit our preferences, unlike Joshua who simply changed his own position. He dropped down to his knees and humbled himself as a servant to receive instruction:

> And Joshua fell on his face to the earth, and bowed down, and said to him, "What has my lord to say to his servant?" The captain of the LORD's host said to Joshua, "Remove your sandals from your feet, for the place where you are standing is holy." And Joshua did so. (Josh. 5:14–15)

Now, Joshua is already on his knees. He's already gone low, but evidently he is still too high because the military leader told him to remove his sandals as well. By removing his sandals, Joshua came in close contact with the very substance that God had used to produce him: dirt. This was a reminder to Joshua that on his very best day, he was still nothing more than sanctified dirt. It was a reminder of his creatureliness before an awesome Creator.

Joshua's posture and question reflected his humility. He asked the only thing he could ask in light of whom he knelt before: What do you want? Joshua's previous question revolved more around what he had gone out there to do—to develop a strategy for taking over Jericho. But when he discovered just who the military leader was whom he was addressing, the issue changed. It was no longer, How am I going to fix this? It became, What do You want me to do? When Joshua asked that question, he got his answer. We read,

> The LORD said to Joshua, "See, I have given Jericho into your hand, with its king and the valiant warriors. You shall march

> around the city, all the men of war circling the city once. You shall do so for six days. Also seven priests shall carry seven trumpets of rams' horns before the ark; then on the seventh day you shall march around the city seven times, and the priests shall blow the trumpets. It shall be that when they make a long blast with the ram's horn, and when you hear the sound of the trumpet, all the people shall shout with a great shout; and the wall of the city will fall down flat, and the people will go up every man straight ahead." (Josh. 6:2–5)

All the reconnaissance in the world would never have given Joshua that idea. Even a professional military man like Joshua wouldn't have thought of that. Joshua had his revelation: I am going to give you the land, God has said. But now, when he bowed in recognition of the supreme authority of another kingdom, Joshua got illumination.

Revelation is what God says, when God unveils or discloses His truth to man. Illumination is when God shows you what to do with what He has revealed. He gives you the details that He hasn't written down. He gives you ideas that were not innate to your thinking, and concepts that you had not preplanned. Illumination is when God blows your mind by giving you answers to problems that were too big for you to solve.

That's what God did for Joshua. That's also what God wants to do for us. But the point I want to emphasize from this biblical event is that Joshua would have never received illumination on how to take over Jericho if he had not bowed beneath another kingdom. By submitting to the plan and program of God, Joshua found the solution to his problem. This means that at our core, we need to first and foremost be kingdom independents. Our political, racial, and class distinctives must submit to our King and His kingdom agenda.

## God Comes to Take Over

We need this same access to God's solutions as we mine through the many issues caused by disunity between the races today, because God does not conduct every battle the same way. We can't execute yesterday's strategy in today's Jericho-wall situation.

A perfect example of this can be found in the inception of black theology. This belief system was formulated in response to the lack of response by white mainline Christian denominations toward the predicament of blacks at the height of the civil rights movement. At the heart of the black experience in America has always been the issue of injustice and oppression. Black theology sought to "plumb the black condition in the light of God's revelation in Jesus Christ, so that the black community can see that the gospel is commensurate with the achievements of black humanity. . . . It is the affirmation of black humanity that emancipates black people from white racism."[1]

Although the mantras of black theology responded to a just need in relation to a sociopolitical cry for liberation, they were far from complete. This was because what black theology neglected to do was posture itself within the principle of the divine authority of Scripture positioned on a literal, historical, and contextual hermeneutic.

My quick reference to black theology at this point is simply a trailer for a subsequent chapter where I address the topic more fully. However, it serves as an illustration that without God's revelation as the focal point for the comprehension of sociopolitical and human understanding, strategies soon dissolve into mere tolerable forms of confrontation, separatist motifs, and an ongoing root of victimology, thus perpetuating the problems for blacks in America rather than resolving them. Thirty years after the creation of this battle plan, the "father" of black theology, James Cone, acknowledged, "Black suffering is getting worse, not better, and we are more confused than ever about the reasons for it."[2] Conversely, however, white evangelicals are far too often tone-deaf to the legitimate biblical priority given to the liberation motif in Scripture. Often blinded by nationalism, implicit bias, and embedded white privilege, they often ignore and neglect a full-throttled verbal and visual response to the plight of the poor and oppressed.

The absence of a kingdom perspective in our personal, family, church, and community life pits us against each other in an unending assertion of divisiveness. This leads to a catastrophic deterioration in our world. Satan doesn't even have to try to defeat us. We, the body of Christ, are defeating ourselves.

However, a kingdom agenda illuminated by ongoing kingdom-based plans garnered through a true humility under God offers us a way to live all of life with a solid hope by optimizing the solutions of heaven. Oneness is not our goal simply for oneness' sake. Oneness ushers in the presence and power of God to such a degree that we can take the offensive against Satan and his tactics in our promised land.

We fail to embrace a oneness perspective rooted in kingdom theology, though, unless we, like Joshua, surrender to the truth that God's kingdom is not here to take sides. God's kingdom is not black. God's kingdom is not white. God's kingdom is not Hispanic. Nor is it Asian, Middle Eastern, or Indian. God did not come to take sides. God came to take over. And until we bow beneath the over-arching rules set forth by the Ruler in His realm, we will continue to live defeated lives in the face of walls too thick to crumble, and an enemy looming too large for us to overcome.

### *One Game, Two Chapels, One God*

Another way to illustrate the kingdom perspective is through my favorite sport: football. I love football. One of the reasons I love football is that many of the attributes of manhood are expressed using gifts, talents, and skills in concert with others for a collective impact without the denial of individual contribution. Football is oneness in action. One of my greatest losses in growing older comes in that I can no longer play football like I used to. Nearly every weekend as a young man in Baltimore, I ran, passed, and blocked. My son Jonathan inherited my passion for the game, and I loved to watch him play.

Some time ago when my son Jonathan played in the NFL, his coach for the Washington Redskins, who was a strong Christian man, gave me a call. He phoned to see if I would come and lead the chapel for the team. So of course I said yes. An unexpected thing happened shortly after his phone call; my phone rang again. This time it was a call from the coach for the Baltimore Ravens, the team that Washington was scheduled to play. This coach also wanted me to lead the chapel for his team, at a different time. So, of course, I said yes again.

I could say yes to both teams because even though my own son was playing for one of them, and I really wanted to see his team win, both coaches were Christian. Both coaches belonged to a higher team, a higher kingdom—the kingdom I belong to as well, the body of Christ. In spite of the fact that the two kingdoms would soon be battling it out against each other, God had called me to stand before them as a representative of His kingdom to declare His truth, His rules, and to seek to manifest His glory.

### *Blow Your Horn*

The great divide in our church today is a schism too wide for us to bridge. The problems are too great. They've been there too long. They are too deep, multigenerational, and multilateral. The walls of our cultures are too thick. Human reason and human reconnaissance cannot fix this. It is time to recognize that there is another team on the field of play in this life, a higher team from a higher kingdom, and the Ruler of that team has already given us the rules by which we need to play.

The first rule is that we need to bow before His sovereign kingdom agenda. Second, we need to take off our shoes, remember our creatureliness, and stop trying to come up with our own solutions. Third, we need to ask God what He wants us to do to experience and use the full manifestation of His revelation of oneness declared by His Son Jesus Christ.

When we do these things, God will give us the solutions to the issues we've been facing in our lives, families, churches, and communities. We will see Him tear down the walls of separation, the walls of elitism, the walls of privilege, the walls of oppression, the walls of judgmentalism, and the walls of victimization. When those walls come down, we will experience not only the relevance of what it means to truly be the body of Christ, but we will also see its power.

Two hundred and fifty years have passed since the founding of our nation and the casting of our now-broken Liberty Bell, and yet we're still working on racial issues in the church that never should have been an issue to begin with. If we will simply bow and become creatures before a Creator, submitting ourselves under His divine rule and authority, there is no telling what God will tell us to do to win this battle. In fact, He may even instruct us, like Joshua, to do something as outrageous as blowing a horn.

One of my favorite passages reveals the all-encompassing power of God that shows up at such a deep level when His people are unified. As a preacher who loves to preach, I find that this passage speaks loudly to me. This is because when the "trumpeters" and "singers" were in "unison" and "with one voice," even the preachers were unable to preach because God's glory was so immense. Now if a preacher cannot preach, then that means there must be a substantive amount of glory!

> When the priests came forth from the holy place (for all the priests who were present had sanctified themselves, *without regard to divisions*), and all the Levitical singers, Asaph, Heman, Jeduthun, and their sons and kinsmen, clothed in fine linen, with cymbals, harps and lyres, standing east of the altar, and with them one hundred and twenty priests blowing trumpets *in unison* when the trumpeters and the singers were to make themselves heard with *one voice* to praise and to glorify the LORD, and when they lifted up their voice accompanied by trumpets and cymbals and instruments of music, and when they praised the LORD saying, "He indeed is good for His lovingkindness is everlasting," then the house, the house of the LORD, was filled with a cloud, so that the priests could not stand to minister because of the cloud, for the glory of the LORD filled the house of God. (2 Chron. 5:11–14, italics added)

When God's glory showed up in response to the oneness of His people coming together "in unison" and in "one voice," the priests were so overcome by His presence that they could not even carry out their duties. God Himself had manifested transformation in His house.

He did it then, and He can do it now.

In His Word, God has given us hundreds of promises that He longs to fulfill while we are still on earth. But He is waiting on us to fulfill the processes that He has set in place so that, based on our submission, He will be ready to invade our history with heaven's glory. One of those processes, as we have learned in the previous chapters, is an intentional embracing of diversity through oneness.

I have purposely used the word *intentional* in this book in a number of places because a great divide cannot be brought together by merely acknowledging the reality of its existence. Standing before the fissured Liberty Bell in full awareness of its massive gap will do nothing to mend its crack. Disunity and separatism have been etched between cultures in our nation over generations. Something so intrinsically imbedded in the social, psychological, and spiritual structures of our land can only be mended through a willful and active compliance on the part of those who have been strategically placed in our culture today to bring about authentic and lasting transformation—the body of Christ.

### *Scoring Together*

Several of my friends play on NFL football teams. They come from different races and different backgrounds. However, when they get on the field, they harmonize their differences toward a common goal. They do this because the goal is larger than their individual distinctions. The moment that your individuality becomes more important than the team, you are of no use to your team. But the moment that your individuality loses its unique skills and attributes, you are also of no use to your team.

God has a team. It's made up of African American, Anglo, Hispanic, Asian, Middle Eastern, and a variety of other people. He never wants you to make your distinction, your history, or your background so precious to you that it messes up His team. Nor does He want you to ignore or diminish your distinction, your history, or your background, thus leaving little with which to contribute to His team.

The reason is that God has a goal. He has an agenda—a kingdom agenda. He has given us the playbook for His kingdom agenda, and it is called the Bible. He has done this so that we, when executing His plays, will "let the world know" that He is God. One way this occurs is when the world looks on and sees brothers and sisters in Christ huddling together across racial, cultural, and generational lines.

But just like in an NFL football game, the huddle is not the play. The huddle accomplishes nothing on its own. In fact, if the huddle lasts much longer than twenty-five seconds, those watching will lose interest and complain, because that's not what they paid over a hundred dollars a ticket to come and see. Instead, they want to see what difference the huddle will make. They want to know, now that you've huddled, can you score? They want to witness what you are going to do as a team with the eleven other men on the other side of the ball daring you to go public with your private conversation.

Our nation doesn't need to see any more huddles by the body of Christ. What people need to see is the church of Jesus Christ, made up of men and women from all backgrounds and cultures, scoring touchdowns for the kingdom of God. This can only be accomplished when embracing oneness enables us to make God's purposes and God's agenda more important than our own individuality and preferences while not negating our own individuality and preferences.

What God wants is for us to live by His rules, execute His kingdom plays against the opposing forces of disunity, resulting in the receiving of His blessing and power. When we as Christians, celebrating our differences, join together as the house of God representing the kingdom of God for the glory of God, we get the response of God to our presence in history.

But all of this starts through a concerted effort to view each other as we have been created to be seen. Just as we saw in the last chapter how Jesus connected with the Samaritan woman, and ultimately her entire town, through intentionally engaging her while simultaneously revealing Himself to her, we are to follow His lead with each other.

The next section of this book is offered to shed light on this process through an overview of black church history. Minority cultures living within the educational and societal systems of a majority culture have the experience of learning much about those in the majority. The history, development, and nuances that make up the Anglo-American culture and church history are widely available to be made known to most everyone living in our land.

However, minority cultures rarely get to acknowledge or explore the inherent self-awareness and satisfaction that comes from a familiarity with one's own culture and background. Likewise, the majority culture loses an opportunity to appreciate, integrate, and learn from both the individual and collective qualities of those comprising the minority cultures among them.

As Martin Luther King Jr. penned in his last book, *Where Do We Go from Here*, "Whites, it must frankly be said, are not putting in a similar mass effort to re-educate themselves out of their racial ignorance. . . . [They] believe they have so little to learn." But I would argue that we all have something to learn about each other and ourselves. Black history and black church history should be taught in our homes, churches, and seminaries by both blacks and whites more than it is done because it is an integral part of our collective history as Americans. The result will be that we experience God manifesting His power, blessing, and presence in our lives to a larger degree as we embrace oneness through the carrying out of His agenda.

The following pages seek to peel away the veneer of modern-day black evangelicalism by revealing the story of the history of the black experience along with the inception, expansion, and system of theology characterizing what many consider to be one of the closest models of the New Testament church in America today.

**Notes**

1. James H. Cone and Gayraud S. Wilmore, eds., *Black Theology: A Documentary History*, vol. 1: 1966–1979 (Maryknoll, NY: Orbis Books, 1979), 101.
2. James H. Cone, "Calling the Oppressors to Account: God and Black Suffering," in *Living Stones in the Household of God: The Legacy and Future of Black Theology,* Linda E. Thomas, ed. (Minneapolis: Fortress Press, 2004), 10.

# Part 2

# A HISTORICAL VIEW OF THE BLACK CHURCH

## Chapter 5

# THE MYTH OF BLACK INFERIORITY

Hundreds of years since the first arrival of slaves to these shores, the myth of black inferiority is still very much with us. It is visibly seen in the rejection and continued disenfranchisement of blacks by many whites and the inability to get beyond the issue of color. Unfortunately, the problem is often as replete in the church as it is in the secular community. Why is this? I would like to posit that it is primarily because of the failure of Christians to approach the issue of race from a theological rather than anthropological perspective.

This theological failure has kept us from appealing to the source of race from whom every family under heaven receives its name (Eph. 3:14–15). God has too often been left out of the debate either by omission when all the data has not been gathered or by commission when the data that is gathered is presented to provide justification and maintenance to existing nonbiblical cultural standards (e.g., the curse of Ham).

Sacralization is the divergence from a comprehensive theology and a biblical worldview into the development of religious beliefs intended to serve the interest of a particular ethnic or racial group. Supported by tradition or generalized prejudices, it is often formulated to carry out a specific end result or to justify a specific behavior.

Sacralization often leads to the creation or furtherance of damaging and devastating myths. One myth that has been perpetuated throughout American history and that serves, for the purposes of this book, as our starting point in understanding the historicity of the black experience and black evangelicalism implicitly and explicitly is the supposed inferiority of black people to white people.

I will never forget the constant word pictures painted for me as a child that were designed to instill the inferiority myth within me. There were the White Tower restaurants that made it unmistakably clear that "colored people" were not good enough to eat there. I remember the "whites only" signs at places of business and the signs that pointed to inferior rear entrances and read "colored people enter here."

Then there were the white churches that praised God on Sunday as we did but would not allow my family to worship there. My father would say, "Son, they believe that God meant for the races to be kept separate, even when it comes to worshiping Him."

I knew the inferiority myth had taken root when as a budding adolescent I thought, as did many of my contemporaries, *Maybe it would be better if I had been born white.* This was the beginning of my love/hate relationship in seeing myself. Loving the personality God had given me, while questioning the package it was wrapped in.

## The Power of a Myth

Myths are traditions passed down over time in story form as a means of explaining or justifying events that are lacking in either scientific evidence or historical basis. The study of myths, mythology, gives great insights into how societies answer questions about the nature of the world and the role of people in it. One very important element of myths is their ability to explain social systems, customs, and ways of life. Myths explain, to some degree, why people act the way they do.

Myths often have strong religious tenets associated with them. Whereas folktales and legends are developed and told for entertainment and amusement, myths are viewed as sacred and, therefore, true. For example, Greek mythology explained good and evil through the creation of stories, such as "Pandora's Box," and through the development of its pantheon of gods.

Myths are powerful because they are believed and therefore become the basis of our actions as individuals, as families, and as a society at large. Myths develop like a pearl inside an oyster's shell. When a grain of sand gets caught in the oyster's shell, it is continuously coated by the secretions of the oyster until a valuable pearl is formed. In the same way, the continuous secretions of societal standards, justified by religious principles, create a mythical pearl that is accepted as both valid and valuable by society.

These myths are accepted by a majority of people and their leaders, and as a result, they become embedded in the culture. Education, politics, religion, economics, science, and every other arena of life are defined by the myth and its traditions. Furthermore, myths tend to authenticate themselves and become self-fulfilled prophecy. Once this happens, nothing short of a catastrophic upheaval can change or reverse them. This is why Jesus had such a difficult time with the Pharisees of His day; their traditions had become so embedded in the fiber of Jewish life that the people wouldn't understand and accept the truth. Fighting myths can often label you as a "revolutionary."

When myths settle in and become traditions, they are then institutionalized, and the culture can hardly define itself without an intrinsic appeal to the myths that help create it and serve to maintain it. Education, politics, religion, economics, science, and every other arena of life are fair game for the myths' influence. Since myths tend to pervade all of society, there is no easy way to get away from them. Furthermore, myths tend to authenticate themselves; after all, everybody believes or accepts them and this false belief system becomes a predictor of future behavior.

The people of the former Soviet Union can give overwhelming testimony to how difficult it is to remove a myth once it has become an ideology. After almost a century of lies, half-truths, myths, and fabrications, the citizens of that once-great country had difficulty believing that any other economic system could work, especially a system that allowed free enterprise. The dictums of Engels, Marx, and Lenin had done much to stifle human ingenuity and aspiration.

## The Rise of the Inferiority Myth

Acceptance of the myth that African Americans are inferior to Anglos has had catastrophic consequences for the psyche of black people, the worldview of white people, and harmony among the races. Worst of all, it has hindered the church from being salt and light in America.

On one hand, this myth has kept the white church from appreciating the black church's great contributions to a true understanding of biblical Christianity and from incorporating those contributions into its own church life and doctrine. You can't appreciate what you do not know. On the other hand, the myth has kept the black community from fully embracing our own heritage and using it as a foundation for addressing the cataclysmic crisis of the African American community.

Spiritual assessments carry great weight in a culture's ability to understand itself as a whole as well as its components. When a culture allows a myth to dominate the way various groups within that culture relate to each other and to themselves, there will be disharmony, injustice, and inequity on every level of that culture. Such has been and still is the case in America. This reality has led to our society's inability to understand itself—and what we do not understand, we cannot fix.

### *The Creation of the Myth*

The American myth of the inferior nature of African people began when the European slave traders subjugated Africans and exported them to the New World without having any understanding of this previously unknown people.

Dr. William Banks, author of *The Black Church in the United States*, describes how traders rationalized their actions through religious purposes:

> The Portuguese and Spanish were the first Europeans to deal in the black slave trade. Rationalizing that it was God's will to bring black heathen into contact with Christianity, even if it meant a lifetime of enforced servitude, their ships carried slaves to labor in the Caribbean colonies as early as 1517. With the approval of their governments and the Roman Catholic Church, the sellers of flesh maintained that "christianized" slaves were better off than free heathen.[1]

Because the slave trade was so extensive and because so many of its promulgators claimed to be Christians, this religious justification had to be promoted with as little resistance as possible. And the myth of inferiority had to be valid in the minds of the slaves as well as in the minds of the white traders so they would accept it as natural.

Thus, early in the exploration and development of the New World, the capture of slaves was done under the pretext of Christianizing the slaves. Because the "savages" needed "true religion" to replace their paganism, it seemed justifiable to bring them to the New World with its strong Puritan heritage. Never mind, of course, that this "noble end" would dismantle African families, orphan African children, often destroy the continuity of African culture, and frequently make African women the victims of rape.

Sociologist Hank Allen describes the plight of these early slaves:

> They came into slavery with varying languages, cultural traditions, rituals, and kinship networks. This, along with an unfamiliarity of American geography, effectively prevented slaves from developing the kind of complex social organization, technology, and mobilization that would be necessary to alleviate their plight. . . . Moreover, to reinforce their brutal social and psychological control, slaveholders often eliminated any bonds of kinship or culture by dividing captured Africans into groups of mixed tribal origins before selling them to plantation owners.[2]

A good friend told me the story of how his great-great-grandfather, Silas Greene, who was a slave, was sold away from his family to another plantation at the age of nine. This must have been a tragic and shocking experience for a nine-year-old, to be taken from his parents for the sake of his master's financial benefit. The economics of slavery were without sensitivity, caring little that a nine-year-old child would be robbed of his mother's love and his father's counsel.

In Alex Haley's famous book *Roots* and the subsequent TV miniseries, Haley's grandfather, "Chicken George Moore," was taken away from his family when George became the medium of exchange for a bet and a cockfight. George Moore lost the opportunity to be a father, whereas Silas Greene lost the opportunity to have a father.

In both cases, the strong familial ties, which have always been a part of the African mentality and ethos, were sacrificed on the altar of a plantation owner's will and whim for the sake of either financial gain or morbid pleasure.

Because many Christians presumed that paganism was inherently part of the African's religion, they looked to the Bible, the sourcebook of the Christian religion, to authenticate the slave industry. Never mind that slavery based on kidnapping was clearly forbidden in Scripture, and punishable by death (Ex. 21:16). This set the stage for the infamous "curse of Ham" doctrine.[3]

### *The Curse of Ham*

Because Ham was the father of black people, and because his descendants were cursed to be slaves because of his sin against Noah, some Christians said, "Africans and their descendants are destined to be servants, and should accept their status as slaves in fulfillment of biblical prophecy."[4]

Due to the curse of Ham theory, there now existed a myth of inferiority with apparent biblical roots. This theological basis provided the raw material necessary to convince the slaves that to resist their assigned inferior status was to resist the will of God. This myth became an authoritative one because it was rooted in a purported theology, and slave owners used this twisted belief system to sustain a perverted sociology.

I knew that something did not sound right about the curse of Ham theory when I first heard it as a teenager. A white minister was giving me the biblical reason that my people and I had to endure the humiliation of American racism. Because I couldn't prove otherwise and because my favorite Bible, the famous Scofield Reference Bible,[5] which had become the official version of American fundamentalism, endorsed the curse of Ham theory, I had little recourse other than to accept it. After all, those promoting it were "trained" in the Bible and theology at the finest fundamentalist institutions in our country—institutions, by the way, that at that time would not allow African Americans to enroll as students.

The endorsement of the Old Scofield Bible, one of the most influential reference works revered by the evangelical fundamentalist community, gave full consent to nourish the notion of a biblically sanctioned black inferiority. This, coupled with the legal status of American segregation, did nothing to ameliorate the already culturally inflicted and discolored perception of black people in the minds of white Bible students, firmly establishing and embedding the myth in the American Christian psyche. This theologically endorsed determinism gave passive sanction to the manifest destiny worldview of the superiority of the white race while simultaneously justifying the use of the Bible to seek to denigrate both the psyche and value of black people.

Never mind, of course, that the Bible says that Canaan, Ham's son, was cursed, not Ham himself. Thus, only one of Ham's four sons, not all four, was cursed. How then could all black people everywhere be cursed?

Never mind that the curse on Canaan and his descendants—"Now therefore, you are cursed, and you shall never cease being slaves"—finds its most obvious fulfillment in the ongoing defeat and subjugation of Canaan by Israel (Josh. 9:23; 1 Kings 9:20–21).

Never mind that the descendants of Ham's other sons—Cush, Mizraim, and Put—have continued to this day as national peoples in Ethiopia (Cush), Egypt (Mizraim), and Libya (Put). In fact, founders of the first two great civilizations, Sumer (Mesopotamia) and Egypt, descended from Ham.

And never mind that God says that curses based on disobedience only extend to three or four generations at most and are reversed when people repent and turn again to obedience (Ex. 20:5–6). This is certainly sufficient to negate the Christian endorsement of the American enslavement of black Christians.

Myths, however, do not need facts; they simply need supporters. Because the myth of inferiority needed as much theological support as possible to make it stick while Christians turned to the New Testament to corroborate the Old Testament verses on masters and slaves, these people quoted biblical passages on slaves submitting to their masters (e.g., Eph. 6:5–8; Col. 3:22) to contemporize the myth to the economic framework of the New World.

The Puritans were attempting to turn America into the "city set on a hill," the manifestation of the prophesied kingdom of God on earth. Slavery provided an economic base for implementing this theology, even among some of the theological and religious heroes of the colonial era. Some of the noted New England leaders who endorsed this perspective of slavery were George Whitefield, John Davenport, Evera Styles, and Jonathan Edwards.[6] They attempted to teach the slaves to docilely accept their inferior status, for to do so was the will of God. To fail to do so was to rebel against God and risk eternal punishment.[7]

With this comprehensive "biblical" strategy, the myth of inferiority took theological wings. These Christians forgot that the apostle Paul told masters to treat converted slaves as equal brothers in Christ (Philem. 15–16). They forgot that the apostle Paul said that slaves had the right to try to change their status (1 Cor. 7:21). And they forgot that the masters' authority over slaves was limited. It was not within the master's rights to treat a slave in an inhumane manner. Masters were to apply the Golden Rule to slaves and were not to treat them as children of a lesser god. The God who rules both heaven and earth will show no partiality to those who commit evil against mankind, whether slave or free, master or servant (Eph. 6:8–9).

The colonial Christians forgot Paul's writing to the Ephesians, which we looked at earlier, that says, "For He Himself is our peace, who made both groups into one and broke down the barrier of the dividing wall, by abolishing in His flesh the enmity" (Eph. 2:14–15). Barriers no longer exist between people's fellowship with God or each other, Paul said.

They forgot the biblical truth that to be members of the body of Christ means that preferences based on class, culture, or race are totally unacceptable to God, and people who make such preferences are candidates for His judgment (James 2:9–13). Such biblical data, however, would not support the inferiority myth. Adding such biblical references would be telling the whole truth, and truth and myth do not mix very well. Therefore, early Americans had to be selective about what Bible verses to use to establish a theological basis to justify slavery and perpetuate the inferiority myth.

The foundational and fundamental failure of white Christianity was its refusal to recognize the *imago Dei* that has been stamped on every human being (Gen. 1:26–28).

## The Impact of the Inferiority Myth

The perpetuation of the inferiority myth is as much psychological as it is theological, because myths affect the way people think.

The myth of inferiority became a part of the psyche of some of the slaves and was often transmitted from one slave to another, developing what some have called a "plantation mentality." Although this mentality was regularly resisted, it nevertheless left its mark, and differs little from a more contemporary labeling of this myth as a perpetual victim or indefinitely oppressed.

Historically, this was seen in the way many blacks held their heads down when talking to whites, perhaps wishing they were white themselves. The law threatened corporal punishment if a black man stared at a white woman. In fact, in 1955 Emmett Till was slain for allegedly whistling at a white woman. In 1989 sixteen-year-old Yusef Hawkins was slain by a mob of close to twenty teenage white boys for allegedly dating a white girl in Brooklyn. When you couple this with almost 4,500 black people being lynched at the hands of white racists with a silent church looking on, or an entire successful business town of African Americans called Rosewood, Florida[8] being literally wiped off the face of the earth, or the Black Wall Street Massacre in Tulsa,[9] it should not surprise us that the myth of black inhumanity was reinforced.

Not only did the myth affect the psyche of adults, but studies have shown that it set in early in children. The infamous 1947 "Racial Identification and Preference in Negro Children Study" done by Kenneth and Mamie Clark showed numbers of children different colors and shades of dolls and then asked them questions such as, "Which doll is the nice doll?" or "Which doll is the bad doll?" The results across the board were unanimously in favor of the light-skin or white dolls.

As recently as April 2010, when Anderson Cooper did a follow-up "doll study" on CNN to see if there had been any significant improvements in our nation over the last sixty years with regard to racial perception, the results, once again, concluded that "white children had an overwhelming bias toward white, and black children also had a bias toward white."[10]

When a person is told either directly or subliminally that the definition of "good," "pretty," or "smart" comes clothed in a certain color, or that he is a "boy," even if he is the senior to the one making the designation, the psychological damage can be overpowering. Or consider what happens when black children are told they are "at risk" simply because of their skin color. Doesn't this decrease their motivation to learn and validate some teachers' belief that black children are unable to learn?[11] The myth of inferiority hits its mark time and time again.

When I was in junior high school, for example, many of my Anglo teachers had limited expectations for my future, and thus they limited their challenges to me. Rarely did they speak to my African American classmates and me about becoming doctors, lawyers, or the president of the United States. This implied that those positions were either reserved for whites or available for only a few blacks who could serve only other blacks, whereas, of course, white professionals could serve both the black and white communities.

From the days of slavery until the present, the inferiority myth has been passed down through the generations, leaving its devastating psychological thumbprint. A contemporary manifestation of the myth's impact is visibly demonstrated in the heavily dependent posture of the black community on government-based social service programs. The independent black church during slavery hewed out a community, culture, religious institution, and antislavery resistant movement with limited support from the government or broader culture. Unfortunately, the heightened infiltration of the inferiority myth into the black psyche, an unforeseen negative byproduct of integration, is seen in the black community's inability to rise above an often self-imposed plethora of destructive characteristics grounded in a victim mentality. In this vein there has developed an illegitimate and unbiblical dependence on government to do what should squarely rest in the scope of the family and the church.

One might argue that the present realities of a large segment of the black community are not a result of the existence of the inferiority myth, but rather a result of systemic racist structures in the broader society or cultural weaknesses within the black community. However, when the actions of those who illegitimately feign superiority dictate the negative actions of others over extended generations, then others must, of necessity, feel inferior to some degree in order to succumb to such dictation.

This illegitimate superiority has been reinforced not only through our legal system, language, and educational system but through our churches as well. The resultant psychological effects of the myth on African Americans have been devastating, culminating by and large in contemporary society through a culture punctuated by definitions of defeatism and victimization.

### *Sociology Reinforced the Myth*

The psychological devastation of the inferiority myth was further reinforced by social structures that served to undergird it. During the era of slavery, landowners granted greater privileges to house slaves who were of lighter skin color than field slaves. Even as late as the 1960s many laws restricted equal access to public accommodations, such as restaurants, restrooms, and methods of transportation, making the myth appear socially acceptable because it was culturally and even legally promoted and enforced.

### *Science Perpetuated the Myth*

If it was not bad enough that religion and theology were called upon to sanction the myth of black inferiority, science also lent its support to the myth when Charles Darwin published his history-altering book *The Origin of Species*, which set forth the theory of evolution. This theory was applied to people in his later book *Descent of Man*. The evolutionary theory fueled racism while providing a basis of justification for both hatred and oppression. His theory that human beings changed from molecules to man over the course of millions of years, with one of our intermediate states being that of an ape, implied that certain races are more apelike than human while others are on a higher level of the evolutionary scale. He concluded that those of darker skin were more apelike than those of lighter skin that had evolved to a much higher plane.

Thus godless science was used to argue for the inferiority of black people, giving whites rationalization for considering themselves as superior. This faulty belief emboldened them to assert the evolutionary theory through the subjugation of those who not only were considered to be grossly inferior, but, in many cases, were not viewed as human at all.

### *Education Perpetuated the Myth*

The first thing blacks were taught about our history in school is that we were descendants of slaves who arrived in America from the west coast of Africa. In contrast, whites were the creators of Western civilization—in Greece, Rome, France, England, and America—thereby producing the first physician of antiquity, Hippocrates; the father of history, Herodotus; great philosophers, Socrates and Plato; and the great scientists, Galileo and Sir Isaac Newton.

Rarely were our children taught about the great nations of north, east, and central Africa, and if they were, they were never taught that all of Africa, including Egypt and Ethiopia, was initially occupied and dominated by blacks. Academia never broadcasted the name Imhotep—a distinguished physician in Egyptian history who practiced medicine before Greece became a nation. Academia never recognized Manatheo—who wrote the history of Egypt before Herodotus was born. Nor was anyone taught about Queen Ti—who once ruled Egypt and whose statues leave no doubt that she was black.

Western education successfully perpetuated the myth of inferiority in our African American children's minds. White children left history classes knowing countries and names of white heroes and heroines. On the other hand, black children left history classes without educators or textbooks acknowledging the accomplishments by those from or in Africa at all, which include producing clocks and calendars, maps, gears, great architecture, engineering, medicine, and mathematics. For example, Africans were the first ones who named and mapped the stars and were the first to teach students from Greece on African soil, and much more. A sampling of the heroes of African descent often neglected from Western education, include:

### *Benjamin Banniker*

Benjamin Banniker was a mathematician, astronomer, compiler of almanacs, inventor, and writer. Banniker was a freeman in the slave state of Maryland and was raised on a farm near Baltimore. He was largely self-educated from books that he would borrow and read.

Around twenty years old, Banniker built a wooden clock that kept precise time. It is noted to be the first clock wholly made in the United States and kept perfect time even until after his death in 1806. Shortly after, he was encouraged to study astronomy, which he also excelled in. By 1788, he began making astronomical calculations, and he accurately predicted a solar eclipse that occurred in 1789. From there, he began making other astronomical observations including predicting other solar eclipses ten years ahead of time.

Banniker's most significant accomplishment was working on the surveying team and designing the layout for Washington, DC and engaging with some of the country's founders in a way no black man had before. Furthermore, as a freeman, he opposed slavery and advocated civil rights—continually sending letters to US leaders, asking for aid in bringing about better conditions for African Americans.

### *Joseph Bologne*

Joseph Bologne was born in Guadeloupe to a prominent French plantation owner and an African slave but moved to France as a teenager.

Because of his elite skill in fencing and horsemanship, he was assigned as an officer of the king's bodyguard and acquired the title Chevalier de Saint-Georges. This was a man of extraordinary talent. He was a champion fencer, master violinist and harpsichordist, classical music composer, and even became a colonel in the French Revolution.

By 1771, he became the concertmaster and music director of a leading symphony in Paris. In 1775, the Paris Opera was considering his nomination to be the next director. However, three of its leading women opposed him because he was a "mulatto." To avoid embarrassing the Queen, Bologne withdrew his name. Nevertheless, he continued to write and direct esteemed operas and classical compositions.

Unfortunately, people called him "The Black Mozart." It may seem like a compliment, but in reality, it was and is demeaning. Bologne doesn't need to be compared to anybody, but celebrated for who he was and what he did. He was the first classical composer of African ancestry, and President John Adams called him "the most accomplished man in Europe."

### *Wentworth Cheswell*

Wentworth Cheswell, the freed grandson of a slave, was the first black judge elected in 1768. He was a devoted husband, church member, father of thirteen children, and for forty-nine years he served our nation in some form of public office.

Many of us are familiar with Paul Revere and his well-known Midnight Ride during the American Revolution. As noted in chapter 1, Cheswell also rode a Midnight Ride. While Revere rode west to deliver urgent news, Cheswell rode north to alert patriots to head south for the imminent conflict with the British. In 1777, he enlisted in a militia unit that joined the Continental Army at the Second Battle of Saratoga.

In 1780, Cheswell was elected as a town administrator of Newmarket and served four terms. He then held various other elected public posts, including assessor, auditor, moderator, and coroner. He helped organize the town's first library in 1801 and helped preserve Newmarket's history by hand-copying important town documents. In 1805, he became justice of the peace for Rockingham County and served there until 1817.

Cheswell should be celebrated on the same level as Paul Revere for being a patriot, for his actions during the American Revolution, and for his public service.

### *James Armistead*

James Armistead, an enslaved African American spy during the American Revolution, was born into slavery in Virginia around 1748. In 1781, he volunteered to join the U. S. Army and enlisted in the Revolutionary War.

He served under Marquis de Lafayette, the commander of allied French forces. Armistead was employed as a spy. At great personal risk, Armistead posed as a runaway slave and pretended to be a British spy, all the while gaining the confidence of General Benedict Arnold and General Charles Cornwallis. The officers spoke freely in front of Armistead concerning their strategies. Armistead's reports documented the movements of the British, giving General Washington all that he needed to bring about a swift end to the war, saving innumerable American lives.

The ending of the American Revolution with the victory at Yorktown and the capture of General Cornwallis, from a historical perspective, is attributed to General Washington and his troops. However, this was only made possible because of the information gained by James Armistead, and we should celebrate him for his patriotic actions.

### *Richard Allen*

Richard Allen, who was born into slavery, originally had no last name—he was simply known as "Negro Richard." At age seventeen, he was converted and began preaching at the local Methodist churches in Delaware and on his plantation. In 1783, he was allowed to purchase his freedom, and he gave himself the last name Allen.

As a free man, Allen settled in Philadelphia and attended St. George's Methodist Church. His preaching and leadership attracted many blacks to the church and caused racial tension. You see, though blacks and whites worshipped together, there was still no equality. Worship was segregated, and blacks were treated poorly. Due to this, Allen left St. George's in 1787 and organized an independent Methodist church. However, Methodist leaders in Philadelphia continued to harass him. Finally, in 1816, Allen formally separated from the Methodist church and established a new denomination, the African Methodist Episcopal Church (AME). He focused on organizing a denomination in which free black people could worship without racial oppression and enslaved people could find a measure of dignity.

Today, AME has over 6,000 churches and over 2 million members.

### *Mary Seacole*

Mary Seacole's mother was Jamaican, and her father was a Scottish lieutenant in the British Army. Being multiracial legally classified her as a "mulatto," and meant that she could not vote, hold public office, or enter the workforce.

However, Mary acquired nursing skills from her mother who ran a boarding house for sick soldiers. To increase her knowledge and medical expertise, she traveled all over the Caribbean, Central America, and England. In 1854, she returned to England during the height of the Crimean War with a heart to serve. However, the British War Office turned her away. Undeterred, she created the "British Hotel" which was nursing quarters positioned behind the battle lines. She nursed wounded soldiers back to good health. She even traveled to the battlefield seeking out injured soldiers to help. Not only did she save numerous lives, but she also became well known among all the soldiers who affectionately called her "Mother Seacole."

In 2004, Mary was voted number one in the 100 Great Black Britons poll. Today, she is celebrated as a pioneering nurse who overcame the tremendous prejudice of being a biracial woman.

### *Henry Ossawa Tanner*

Henry Ossawa Tanner was an African American painter born in Pennsylvania. His father was a minister and tried to discourage Henry's interest in art, but to no avail. However, it did influence him, as most of his paintings carried biblical themes.

At twenty-one, Tanner enrolled in the prestigious Pennsylvania Academy of the Fine Arts as the only African American student. In 1891, he traveled to Paris and enrolled at the Académie Julian. During his time abroad, his paintings brought him notoriety. In 1893, he traveled back to Pennsylvania where he was met and spurned by racial prejudice. Therefore, he left the United States and returned to Paris.

By 1894, his paintings were exhibited at the annual Paris Salon. Over the years, he won awards for Daniel in the Lions' Den and The Raising of Lazarus—a rare accomplishment for an American artist and even more uncommon for an African American. Tanner's paintings continued to win awards in Paris and finally in America as well.

In 1969, long after his death, the Smithsonian honored him through the first major solo exhibition of a black artist in the United States, recognizing Tanner as the first African American painter to gain international acclaim.

### *Charlotta Bass*

Charlotta Bass was a remarkable woman who has, unfortunately, largely been forgotten like so many others. In 1952, she became the first black woman to run for vice president in the United States.

Bass received endorsements from prominent civil rights leaders like Paul Robeson and W. E. B. DuBois. Though her ticket virtually stood no chance of winning, as the Voting Rights Act did not exist and schools were still segregated, it still gave her a platform to raise awareness on racial issues.

Voicing concerns over the treatment of African Americans wasn't new to Bass. She was a longtime editor, publisher, and eventually owner of *The California Eagle*, the West Coast's oldest and most circulated black newspaper. For 40 years, she used the newspaper to shed light on racial issues including police brutality, discriminatory hiring and housing practices, and glorification of the Ku Klux Klan.

She denounced both political parties for neglecting black and women's rights, and she took an uncompromising stance against racial injustices. Both actions resulted in numerous death threats. She was labeled a communist and placed under FBI and CIA surveillance. Though she was viewed as being radical, she accomplished her main goal: placing racial equality in the national spotlight.

### *Bessie Coleman*

Bessie Coleman was raised in Waxahachie, Texas, not far from where I live. She excelled in school and had a proclivity in mathematics. Therefore, Coleman avoided working in the cotton fields.

At twenty-three, she moved to Chicago and made her living as a beautician. She became interested in the field of aviation and dreamed of flying. However, discrimination prevented her from entering aviation school. She did not stop her pursuit. Instead, she learned French and, in 1920, was accepted at the Caudron Brothers School of Aviation in Le Crotoy, France.

On June 15, 1921, she became the first black person to gain an international pilot's license, and the first black woman and Native American to hold a pilot's license. Coleman returned to the United States, where the double stigma of racial and gender biases prevented her becoming a commercial pilot. Therefore, she specialized in stunt flying and parachuting because those were her only career options.

In 2007, the city of Waxahachie unveiled the Bessie Coleman

official Texas historical marker at Freedman Memorial Plaza, and Mayor David Hill declared January 26, 2021, as Bessie Coleman Day in the city of Waxahachie.

### *Sandy Frederick Ray*

Sandy Frederick Ray was a close friend of Martin Luther King Sr. Martin's son, King Jr., viewed Ray as a father figure and called him "Uncle Sandy."

Ray served Baptist churches in Georgia, Illinois, and Ohio, where he became an acclaimed Sunday radio preacher and the first black representative elected to the Ohio State Legislature. In 1944, Ray felt called to Cornerstone Baptist Church in Brooklyn, New York, where he pastored until his death. In ten years, under Ray's leadership, Cornerstone grew from 2,500 to 5,500 members, added multiple buildings and a daycare, and established a credit union.

People travelled to Brooklyn to hear Ray's dynamic preaching, but he also used his voice and platform to advance civil rights. In July 1957, Ray invited Billy Graham to preach on the steps outside his church. More than 3,000 people attended to hear Graham preach against racist segregationist laws, calling for changes to legislation at the national level. Ray remained close to the King family. He fundraised for and assisted King Jr. during his arrests, supported the Montgomery bus boycotts, publicly rebuked southern white supremacists, and condemned segregation before the House Committee. King Jr. said that Ray was one of the strongest orators in the African American church. He should be celebrated for his faithfulness in ministry and involvement in civil rights.

### *Vivien Thomas*

Vivien Thomas, the grandson of a slave, became a heart surgery pioneer. In 1930, Thomas became a laboratory assistant for Dr. Alfred Blalock at Vanderbilt University. However, because of institutional racism, he was classified and paid as a janitor. Nevertheless, Thomas rapidly mastered complex surgical techniques and research methodology.

In 1941, Blalock became Chief of Surgery at Johns Hopkins and Thomas accompanied him. It was there that Thomas and Blalock created a solution for "blue baby syndrome." In the 1940s, operating on the heart was unthinkable. However, Thomas created a blue baby-like condition in a dog, then corrected the condition through heart surgery. Over two years, he successfully performed the procedure on over 200 dogs.

In 1944, the first procedure on a human baby was successful. Thomas coached Blalock throughout the operation from a stepstool. However, Thomas received no credit from Blalock or the medical field.

It took more than 25 years before Thomas received public recognition for his role in creating the blue baby surgery. In 1976, Johns Hopkins University awarded him an honorary doctorate and established the Vivien Thomas Fund to increase diversity at Johns Hopkins University School of Medicine, thus honoring his memory by removing for others the economic and racial barriers that often stood in his way.

### *Mahalia Jackson*

Mahalia Jackson was born on October 26, 1911, in New Orleans, Louisiana. She was known as "the Queen of Gospel" and honored as one of the greatest musical figures in US history.

Jackson began singing when she was four years old at Mount Moriah Baptist Church. She moved to Chicago at sixteen and joined the Greater Salem Baptist Church. She sung with the Johnson Gospel Singers for a few years before working on solo projects with the gospel composer Thomas A. Dorsey.

Jackson was raised in a devout Christian home, but her style was influenced by the blues. In 1947, her song "Move On Up a Little Higher" sold millions of copies and became the highest selling gospel single in history. From there, Jackson successfully toured nationally and internationally, and even had her own gospel program on television.

Jackson was also active in the civil rights movement. She sang at the inauguration of President John F. Kennedy in 1961, the March on Washington, DC in 1963 (right before the "I Have a Dream" speech), and at the funeral of Dr. Martin Luther King Jr. in 1968.

*George Liele*

George Liele, a freed Georgia slave, was one of the most significant figures in the history of Christian missions. He was the first American missionary, and the first Baptist missionary to take the gospel abroad.

Liele became a Christian in 1773 when he was twenty-three. Shortly after, he gained his freedom and began preaching for two years in slave quarters around Georgia and South Carolina. In 1775, Liele became the first ordained African American Baptist preacher in America, and he planted First African Baptist Church in 1777, a church that still gathers today.

However, racial persecution caused Liele to flee to Jamaica in 1782. But once there, Liele used this situation as an opportunity to plant a church, preach the gospel to Jamaican slaves, and begin public baptisms. His evangelism brought more persecution, and he was thrown in prison for "agitating slaves." Eventually, he was acquitted. Nevertheless, he continued to preach, baptize, and build the church.

By 1814, his missionary efforts helped produce 8,000 Jamaican Baptists, and that number grew to over 20,000 by 1832. Liele's ministry had a significant spiritual impact on Jamaica, but it also made a social difference as well. By July 31, 1838, slavery was eradicated in Jamaica. Both these feats are a testimony to his legacy, and we should celebrate Liele for his lifelong missionary work.

There are so many more, such as Frederick Douglass, the runaway slave who subsequently published his autobiography, founded and ran the *North Star* newspaper, and was heralded by President Abraham Lincoln as a statesman, an orator, and a key voice for freedom and equality not only for blacks but also for women's rights. Also, Dr. Percy Lavon Julian, a scientist who synthesized sterol from the oil of a soybean to create synthetic hydrocortisone, reducing the cost of purchase for the general public from hundreds of dollars to mere cents, was the first to mass-produce physostigmine—a treatment for glaucoma—and paved the way for the invention of the birth control pill. And Matthew Alexander Henson, an able seaman from his early teen years, and the first man to place his foot on the North Pole.

Myths breed and grow in an atmosphere of ignorance. When we fail to teach the truth about our history and the many leading contributions those of African descent have made, the myth is left to leave its mark on the collective psyche of mankind. Myths often have a replicating effect when allowed to remain, by all parties involved. They can produce a cycle of a self-fulfilling prophecy if allowed to entrench themselves in the hearts and minds of those whom they are about.

### *The Family Perpetuated the Myth*

One of the most destructive social structures perpetuating the myth, however, was the family structure itself, the most basic of all human institutions. Innocent white children were fed the myth of the innate superiority of their own race and, conversely, the ipso facto inferiority of the black race. Think of the effect this had on children who were unlikely to question the ideas and ideals of those they admired and trusted most—namely, their parents.

This myth has lasted so long because it bears the mark of parental endorsement; after all, "Father knows best." When such parental authority is linked with a fear of the unknown, myths naturally become necessary for one's own survival.

Yet, on the opposite end of the continuum, the inferiority myth was also alive within the black family itself. Martin Luther King Jr. said it best when he declared, "No one can ride your back unless it is bent!" The myth made blacks, at times, wish they were white, and it produced a path of self-destruction and character ridicule within black culture. As a result, African Americans began to view large noses as a sign of ugliness and natural black hair as unkempt. Director and well-known actor Bill Duke reflects the honest feelings of so many young black kids growing up under this myth when he shared how at one point as a kindergartener, he tried to drink bleach in order to be white.[12] Bill shares how his parents' response to his pain of coming to terms with being black in a racist environment in the 1940s was to tell him, "You're no better than anyone else. But, also, no one else is any better than you." He says that this truth in turn helped him go on to succeed as well as he has done over the last 70 years. Bill's parents sought to dig up the seeds of this myth of inferiority early on because they knew how damaging it could be.[13]

Once such mythological representations were made, it was easy to justify laws to enforce the myth. Consider the infamous Dred Scott decision of 1857, which ruled that black people were not US citizens, but instead were property to be bought, sold, or killed at the whims of their masters. It wrongly divided the word of truth, as God's Holy Word was used as a tool to justify slavery, segregation, and racial violence in order for whites to maintain and advance an evil racial, political, and economic superiority.

### *The Church Perpetuated the Myth*

The white church became a dominant major contributor and coconspirator to the expansion of the myth. Hiding behind a biblical interpretation based on cultural expediency rather than exegetical integrity, the white church, following its spiritual leadership, endorsed society's accepted status of Anglos being superior to African Americans. The church endorsed the myth when it was silent to the immorality of parishioners who bred slaves for profit and pleasure. It also endorsed this myth when it allowed its members to buy and sell Africans like cattle which simultaneously resulted in the breaking up of families for financial gain. The church endorsed the myth when it forced blacks to sit in the rear of churches—if they were allowed access at all. The church endorsed the myth when white denominations established schools for biblical learning that excluded African Americans who desired training in God's Word. This practice, which continued well into the second half of the twentieth century in many evangelical Bible colleges, seminaries, and mission societies, accounted for the abysmally low numbers of African Americans that were allowed to be trained for ministry in those institutions.

Such a view taken by the white church at large (even though there were many who rebelled against this hypocritical posture) reinforced an unbiblical separation between the secular and sacred. Not only did the church endorse the myth through segregated theological training institutions, but it also endorsed it through the teaching of only partial, and sometimes errant, beliefs within those institutions while also remaining silent regarding the obvious evils of American slavery. Widely respected Anglo Bible teacher and expositor, the late

J. Vernon McGee, acknowledged these inaccuracies in theological circles when he was teaching on the book of Genesis. He said, "It is so easy today to fall into the old patterns that we were taught in school a few years ago. Now the black man is wanting more study of his race. I don't blame him. He hasn't been given an opportunity in the past several hundred years. The story of the beginning of the black man is that he headed up the first two great civilizations that appeared on this earth."[14]

Even though it is not designated through outward signs, laws, or regulations, the underlying atmosphere of this marginalization and separation still exists today, hindering a bid for oneness within the body of Christ toward the aim of initiating a comprehensive approach to cultural transformation. If Christian whites had devoted the same energy toward protecting the rights of the newborn slave because of his or her value before God that they have devoted toward protecting the unborn baby today, the church would have set a standard that most certainly would have changed and redefined race relations in America.

Probably the greatest visual illustration of this reality in the twentieth century is that of South Africa's apartheid, which cost millions of people their lives because the Dutch Reformed Church maintained a theological stance about the segregation and subjugation of a group of people equally created in the image of God.

### *The Media Perpetuated the Myth*

In 1915, the highest grossing film in the silent film era was *The Birth of a Nation*. This film unashamedly endorsed white supremacy, portraying the members of the Ku Klux Klan as heroes. Quoting then-President Woodrow Wilson, the film opens with the lines, "The white men were roused by a mere instinct of self-preservation . . . until at last there had sprung into existence a great Ku Klux Klan, a veritable empire of the South, to protect the Southern country." The Ku Klux Klan used the film in recruiting men to join them well into the 1970s. As recently as 1992, the US Library of Congress chose to preserve the film in the National Film Registry, declaring it to be both historically and culturally significant.

The rise of media influence in American culture spread the

inferiority myth into every American home as well through the invention of the television. Blacks were good enough to make Americans laugh at all types of buffoonery. (Remember *Amos and Andy?*) This reinforced the general public's conception of the ineptness of black people, even in the minds of blacks. Because such media representations did not spend much time depicting the strengths of black culture (except when black athletes and entertainers impressed us with their skill), society was not able to see the comprehensive contributions people of non-European descent had made to the greatness of America.

Not until the black revolution of the sixties did African Americans corporately reject the inferiority myth, although blacks had attempted to discredit the myth throughout black history. With all of America watching, African Americans categorically rejected the shackles of second-class citizenship and made a progressive push for inclusion. During this period the media became a friend, rather than a foe, as the black case for equality controlled the national debate and demonstrated graphically how debased the superiority myth had become. Laws began to change, opportunities began to come, enhancement programs were established, and massive amounts of funds were allocated and spent. All were designed to appear to address the myth once and for all. Whether they accomplished that, or were simply lip service set to inept policies, is a discussion for another day.

## The Contemporary Status of the Myth

American culture is still reeling from the effects of the inferiority myth. Although the African American church has its own distinctive and valuable appeal, Christian whites presume that the brand of Christianity that comes through the broader evangelical community is the most significant vehicle of Christianity in America. In sociological studies, this is termed "whiteness as normative." It is where life is viewed from the starting point of white culture, and everything else is held up to it as the standard or is to be viewed through that lens. I'll give you a brief contemporary example.

I'll never forget having lunch with a dozen or so Christian leaders from one of the largest Christian organizations in the world on the day the Baltimore Riots broke out. We had convened around the lunch table to discuss ministry partnerships for online theological training. But when the issues in Baltimore got raised for discussion, the dismissive nature in which the conversation was addressed seemed odd. What was said didn't help much. Not only did condemning remarks get made toward the situation at hand, but more sympathy was spoken for the baseball game attendees asked to stay at Oriole Park after the game until the police said it was safe for them to leave (most presumably white fans) than for Freddie Gray, or even his family. Or even for those whose businesses were burning down, or the children who were huddled in their homes in fear as the riots raged in the urban areas.

To view the events of that day through a lens of greater compassion for baseball game attendees shuttered in perfect safety, but having to forfeit quickly leaving after a game, was to view the events through the lens of whiteness as normative. The norm would be to attend a baseball game, watch it, and then go home. And that had been disrupted.

As I mentioned earlier, even in the late 1980s, I was being told by "evangelical" radio stations that blacks in broadcasting might be too offensive to the broader Christian community. The white preacher was normative, and to air anyone different would disrupt this status quo. As in other arenas of life, I was hearing again that blacks could be consumers of the Christian faith from the broader Christian community but could not expect to be producers of Christian ministry for the church at large. This attitude also explains why white Christian groups quickly call upon Christian blacks to join them in their outreach ministries, such as evangelistic crusades, family worship, or anti-abortion rallies, but they are slow to respond when Christian blacks call upon them for their involvement in the justice concerns of the black church and black community. Any invitations of unity usually implied Christian blacks unifying in support of the agenda of the white church, but rarely worked the other way. I was pleased to see this change somewhat during 2020 when many white churches and church members united in peaceful protests with their black brothers and sisters in Christ.

Lincoln and Mamiya, authors of *The Black Church in the African*

*American Experience*, are correct when they state:

> The prevailing American sentiment has traditionally held that the mainline white churches constitute the only relevant spiritual pulse in the nation, and that whatever is outside this narrow ambit is of little if any significance to the American religious profile. This conventional wisdom is widely reflected in seminary curricula and denominational policies to the end that misperception is compounded, and the religious experience of some 30 to 35 million African Americans is clouded in consequence.[15]

Generally, the tendency is to dismiss African American worship and church practices as something that is purely cultural and void of any significant spiritual or theological fiber. The black church member is often viewed as an emotionalist, rather than someone who has a deep, authentic understanding and appreciation of God. Those who peer in from the outside have little or no access to the essence of African American church life and are the worse off because of it. Until there is a willingness on behalf of whites in the evangelical world to sit or serve underneath the leadership and teaching of blacks, and not simply drop in from time to time for a "cultural" experience, true racial progress will not have been achieved.

### *The Myth Remains*

The black community as a whole rejected the inferiority myth and attempted to set the record straight by protesting the superiority myth as well. This process was carried out by using the same authoritative source that was a basis for establishing the inferiority myth in the first place: the Bible. As the black theologian J. Deotis Roberts asserts,

> This explains why the illiterate black slave understood the Bible better than the learned white preacher or missionary who taught him. The Bible has a lot to say about justice, love, and mercy, about liberation from oppression, about deliverance from bondage, and about making life human. The privileged need definitions, rationalizations, logical conviction, and language

> clarity to understand liberation, justice, and mercy. . . . A black man reared in this society does not need a constitutional lawyer or a logic professor to explain "justice" or "injustice" to him. From early childhood the meanings of the words are apparent. Thus, when the Bible speaks of love, justice, and mercy, its message goes right to the soul of the black man.[16]

However, the problem is that the inferiority myth is still with us, and like all myths, it carries with it great power and influence. Just consider the enormous popularity of the book *The Bell Curve*, not only when it was released but even still now, decades later. A nearly 1,000-page book in which authors emphasize a lower IQ average for black Americans than white Americans and how this IQ difference affects life-based outcomes fuels the fumes of inferiority. It does so without allowing for an honest dialogue on environmental and controlled influences on a person's IQ, or even the legitimacy of IQ for determining life aptitudes.

Some African Americans have by their own actions legitimized the inferiority myth through a victim mentality of functioning, which unfortunately may appear to validate the superiority myth that spawned it. The bottom line is that racial victimization, while a real problem, is not African Americans' ultimate problem. In fact, African Americans must take a share of the blame that comes by way of embracing a victimization worldview. This mentality by its very nature keeps a person, or group of people, on the defense and always reacting to what the oppression is doing while also illegitimately allowing us to blame things on racism that are unjustified. It does not encourage a proactive picking up of the ball and running with it. Life becomes a series of reactions rather than the implementation of a transformational plan of action. Cries of racism should never be allowed to define our God-given value, identity or potential.

To admit this, however, would decrease our status as victim and make illegitimate our racial demand upon others to fix what we must take primary responsibility for fixing ourselves. Just as "whites gain superiority by not knowing blacks; blacks gain entitlement by not seeing their own responsibility for bettering themselves."[17] White guilt, coupled with black power, continuously feed off each other, keeping both groups in an illegitimate bondage of negative mutual dependence. Such an unholy alliance can never resolve our continuous racial calamity because it keeps both groups caged in unhealthy worldviews. "For persons who see themselves as victims," writes John Perkins, "it is easy to be ensnared by pride. We can carry our pain as a badge of honor and try to whip others with it. . . . This pride can easily slide into a feeling of entitlement. That I'm owed something."[18]

Once a person realizes his unique position in divine history, however, he begins to realize that no person or racial group has the final say about another person's or group's potential. This realization is by far the greatest need in black America today, and unless it occurs, no amount of "race-hustling" or political protest will reverse the situation a large segment of African Americans now face. A comprehensive understanding of a kingdom agenda view on race and oppression, a Kingdom Race Theology (which I'll talk more about in chapter 16), leaves no room for the embracing of victimology. The Bible clearly teaches that God's children have been given all that we need through the power of the Holy Spirit to overcome, rather than succumb to, opposition and oppression. As former civil rights leader, Robert Woodson, said recently, "It's really white supremacy to assume that blacks have no agency,"[19] which is what the victim-only ideology perpetuates.

Acknowledging how tough the journey to improvement and betterment is remains a valid part of overcoming opposition. But instead of spending too much time seeking to place blame, we must also look for and operate out of the strengths God has given us. Racism is real and evil, making the battle before us a difficult one. However, too much of an unhealthy focus on racism and white guilt will keep us bound to both and keep African Americans in an ongoing state of dependency wherein the "oppressor" defines our existence as the "oppressed." It is like the Dallas Cowboys focusing so much on the eleven men on the other side of the ball that they neglect to implement plays on how to move past them. The idea is to go through, around, and over the opposing forces against you.

To begin this process, both Christian blacks and whites must demythologize the myth of inferiority so the mental fog that clouds the racial atmosphere can be removed. Both of us will then be free to relate to each other on our mutual strengths, derived from the biblically based understanding of our heritage as it is rooted and grounded in the God "from whom every family in heaven and on earth derives its name" (Eph. 3:15).

### *Debunking the Myth*

It has been my desire over the past five decades of professional ministry as a black kingdomologist in America to be one of many evangelical thinkers who help to dispel the inferiority myth which has impacted not only the racial groups of our country, but individuals as well. Each of us is held hostage to the perspectives of our racial group, thus limiting our personal development. Far too many African Americans are hindered from reaching their individual potential because of the black group's demand that they remain in solidarity to the group's definitions and strategies for freedom, even though each individual may not agree with those same definitions or strategies.

Although it is imperative that individuals not be so selfish as to be of little or no benefit to the legitimate aspirations of their racial group, it is equally true that the demands of the group must not impede, destroy, or dismantle individual responsibility, initiative, and goals.

Many blacks who don't vote Democratic are criticized for forsaking the group. Unfortunately this attitude, in effect, negates the very thing we have fought so hard to attain: freedom of political expression. Others are criticized for not supporting black businesses regardless of the quality or cost of service. I have faced criticism from both directions for embracing national politics on both sides of the political spectrum.

Conversely, many Anglos claim individual superiority and/or entitlement because of the myth's doctrine of group superiority. They often question the spirituality of their black brothers and sisters because of a perceived allegiance to the Democratic party. Therefore, whites show a great hesitance to sit at the feet of blacks with the expectation of learning (as opposed to simply being entertained), because the myth has already defined the relationship as that of a superior to an inferior. I personally don't believe in white superiority because I don't believe in black inferiority.

Unless biblical Christians significantly enter the fray and take over the leadership for unifying the racial divide, we will be hopelessly deadlocked in a sea of relativity regarding this issue, resulting in restating more questions rather than providing permanent answers.

It is my uncompromising contention that the only proper perspective is the divine perspective; the only proper agenda is the kingdom agenda, not an American political one. If the Bible is allowed to be the standard by which blacks and whites determine truth, then freedom from this moral and racial malaise will be the outcome; for as Jesus taught, the truth has a unique capacity of making people free.

Only when we define ourselves and see our relationships in light of the absolute authority of Scripture and the overarching rule of God in our lives can we begin to place salve on the open wounds that have kept America in general and Christians in particular in a perpetual state of disunity.

**Notes**

1. William Banks, *The Black Church in the United States: Its Origin, Growth, Contributions, and Outlook* (Chicago: Moody, 1972), 9.
2. Hank Allen, "The Black Family: Its Unique Legacy, Current Challenges and Future Prospects," in *The Black Family: Past, Present and Future*, Lee N. June, ed. (Grand Rapids, MI: Zondervan, 1991), 18.
3. See the "Curse of Ham," *Dictionary of Christianity in America* (Downers Grove, IL: InterVarsity, 1990), 333, for a summary of the argument and how it was used by the Christian church to justify slavery in America.
4. C. F. Keil and F. Delitzsch take this view in "The Pentateuch," *Commentary on the Old Testament*, vol. 1 (Grand Rapids, MI: Eerdmans, 1987), 178: "The Phoenicians, along with the Carthaginians and the Egyptians, who all belonged to the family of Canaan, were subjected by the Japhetic Persians, Macedonians, and Romans; and the remainder of the Hamitic tribes either shared the same fate, or still sigh, like the Negroes, for example, and other African tribes, beneath the yoke of the most crushing slavery."
5. In his note on the descendants of Noah's three sons in Genesis 9, Scofield remarked, "A prophetic declaration is made that from Ham will descend an inferior and servile posterity (Gen. 9:24–25 ix. 24, 25)." C. I. Scofield, *The Scofield Reference Bible* (New York: Oxford Univ. Press, 1909), 16 n5. This note is repeated in the 1917 edition.
6. William W. Sweet, *The Story of Religion in America* (Grand Rapids, MI: Baker, 1973), 170, 285.
7. For a summary of how the slaves responded to this strategy, see Charles V. Hamilton, *The Black Preacher in America* (New York: William Morrow, 1972), 37–46.
8. To learn more about Rosewood, Florida, visit www.history.com/topics/early-20th-century-us/rosewood-massacre or to watch firsthand accounts on YouTube: www.youtube.com/watch?v=cUfhfpuI2i0.
9. To learn more about the Black Wall Street Massacre, see Tom Huddleston Jr., "Black Wall Street," CNBC.com, July 4, 2020, www.cnbc.com/2020/07/04/what-is-black-wall-street-

history-of-the-community-and-its-massacre.html.

10. "Children Learn Attitudes about Race at Home," CNN News, May 25, 2010, www.cnn.com/2010/US/05/19/doll.study.reactions/index.html.
11. Jawanza Kunjufu, *Countering the Conspiracy to Destroy Black Boys*, vols. 1 and 2 (Chicago: African American Images, 1985).
12. Bill Duke, "As A Child I Tried to Drink Bleach after Being Teased for Being Dark" part 3, YouTube, May 12, 2019, www.youtube.com/watch?v=-uICZeiyUmE.
13. Ibid.
14. J. Vernon McGee, *Through the Bible—Genesis* (Nashville: Nelson, 1981), 51.
15. C. Eric Lincoln and Lawrence H. Mamiya, *The Black Church in the African American Experience* (Durham, NC: Duke University Press, 1990), xi.
16. J. Deotis Roberts, *A Black Political Theology* (Louisville, KY: Westminster John Knox, 1974), 38.
17. Shelby Steele, *The Content of Our Character: A New Vision of Race in America* (New York: Harper Perennial, 1991), 17.
18. John M. Perkins, *One Blood: Parting Words to the Church on Race and Love* (Chicago: Moody, 2020), 85.
19. "Civil Rights Activist Bob Woodson Slams New York Times' 'Diabolical' 1619 Project on 'Life, Liberty & Levin,'" FoxNews.com, March 8, 2020, www.foxnews.com/media/civil-rights-leader-slams-diabolical-new-york-times-1619-project-white-supremacy-to-assume-all-African-Americans-are-victims.

## Chapter 6

# THE BLACK PRESENCE IN THE BIBLE

There is a growing satisfaction among African Americans today in witnessing that the broader evangelical community is beginning to recognize the value we have in the kingdom of God. The increased racial calamity and chaos that resulted from the deaths of black men and women brought the issues of racism and injustice to the front page of Christianity. It freshly awakened white Christians to the need for a much more aggressive reevaluation and engagement on the biblical primacy of justice. God's perspective on our value is slowly beginning to filter into the heads, and I hope the hearts, of many of my white Christian brothers and sisters. It seems that every week I get a call from a Christian organization asking me to assist it in identifying and recruiting African Americans for placement in the organization. Sometimes it's a college or seminary. Other times it's a white church looking for an African American staff member to help them minister to their changing multiracial neighborhood, or a parachurch ministry seeking ideas on how to access the black community. A great, fresh awakening and sensitivity is occurring relative to the need to engage more deeply with black Christians. However, we need to be careful to remember that if this fresh awakening leads only to more gentrification, paternalism, and tokenism, it will not make any real strides toward unity.

The rise of this awareness in our collective minds, though, has provided an awakening of black self-consciousness and an appreciation for black culture and achievement. Egyptology and the study of African history and culture are highlighting the unique role black people have played in the development of the human race and world civilizations. Anthropologists of all races are grappling with the increasing plausibility that the roots of human civilization are in Africa with black people.[1] The Rev. Walter McCray, author of *The Black Presence in the Bible*, wrote,

> The preponderance of contemporary evidence being gathered by archaeologists and ancient historians says that Africa (in Egypt's Nile Valley) was the origination of humanity and civilization. It was from here that humanity, an indigenous "Black" humanity, had its beginnings. The preponderance of archaeological and historical facts say that the roots of all people are in Africa! —Egypt, Africa!
>
> Whether one holds to the traditional view of a Mesopotamian origination of humanity, or to the more substantiated view of the origination of humanity in Africa, one point of harmony is certain: indigenous humanity and the originators of the civilizations in each of these areas were Black! They were Black in Egyptian Africa and they were Black in Asia's lower Mesopotamia! Either way one cuts it, the originators of civilization were a Black people.[2]

Such evidence includes the discoveries in the Tanzanian Canyon of the Olduvai Gorge, which reveals that toolmaking began in Africa and then spread to Europe. It includes the discoveries in the Nile Valley that demonstrate that people of Negroid African descent manufactured pottery before pottery was made in the world's oldest known city. Archaeological evidence even suggests African sailors explored the New World prior to Columbus. This evidence includes an extensive number of portraits of Negroes on clay, gold, and stone unearthed in pre-Columbian strata in Central and South America. In fact, paintings by Negro people date prior to 3000 BC.

"Civilization started in the great river valleys of Africa and Asia, in the Fertile Crescent in the Near East and along the narrow ribbon of the Nile in Africa," says historian Lerone Bennett. "In the Nile Valley that beginning was an African as well as an Asian achievement. Blacks, or people who would be considered blacks today, were among the first people to use tools, paint pictures, plant seeds and worship gods."[3] Bennett's conclusion concurs with Moses's assertion that Adam was created from soil in or near the land of Cush, who was Ham's son and originator of the great Ethiopian civilization (Gen. 2:7, 13; 10:6, 8; Isa. 18:1–2).

For African Americans this knowledge is both a great strength and a great weakness. The obvious strength is the very real self-appreciation of the depth of our historical achievements and contributions. Finally scholars, both black and white, are correcting the inaccuracies and deletions that have been taught by many people who have bypassed the truth, by either the sin of omission or commission. We now have the academic tools necessary to refute those who relegate blacks to an inferior status in history and who use erroneous theological, environmental, or cultural arguments to support their perspective that whites are superior to blacks.[4]

On the other hand, black people, particularly Christian blacks, must filter black achievement, history, and culture through the lens of Scripture in order to see it clearly. Greatness must be defined in terms of biblical criteria, not in terms of simple social theory. Black is only beautiful if it is biblical, just as white is only right when it agrees with the Holy Writ.

For whites, this knowledge should cause them to reconsider their culturally laden perspective of blacks, which has hindered their full appreciation, understanding, and acceptance of their brothers and sisters of African descent.

## The Need for a Biblical Perspective of Black Peoples

I prefer to look to the Bible for an understanding of who I am as an African American, and I do so for the following reasons:

### *The Bible Is the Inerrant Word of God*

First of all, because the Bible is the inerrant, infallible, authoritative Word of God, it is the only place we can go to receive a totally accurate and objective understanding of race. Whites and blacks alike have used and misused race for their own advantages. Both races have allowed popular opinion, sociopolitical structures, cultural traditions, and personal preferences to "color" their views about themselves and others.

During the era of slavery whites viewed themselves more highly than others in an attempt to persuade blacks to view ourselves more lowly than others. On the other hand, during the sixties revolution black pride was sometimes taken to violent extremes. The Bible does not suffer from such human lopsidedness because its author is God, and God gives the truth on who we are, Whose we are, and how we ought to think of ourselves (Rom. 12:3).

### *The Bible Is a Multiracial Book*

Second, rooting racial history and culture in the Bible allows me to contradict blacks who write off the Bible as a white man's book and Christianity as a white man's religion. When a person understands the glorious presence of African people in God's drama of redemptive history, Scripture is clearly the primary source for legitimate black pride. Those who reject the Bible stand on shaky racial ground. The Scripture allows blacks to take pride in who we are and what God has made us, without feeling we have to become something other than what God created us to be.

### *The Bible Gives God's Perspective of Racial Prejudice*

Third, because race has played such a major role in the social development and the functioning of American society, it benefits us to discover God's perspective of racial prejudice.

Moses faced racial prejudice when his sister, Miriam, and brother, Aaron, challenged his God-given leadership because he was married to an African woman, a Cushite (Num. 12:1). What apparently bothered them was not simply that Moses's new bride was dark-complexioned, because it has been proven that other Israelites were also dark-skinned. Rather, it was that she was black and foreign. Her

African ethnic origin was unacceptable. It is important to note here that God punished Miriam with the disease of leprosy for her rebellion against Moses "because of the Cushite woman whom he had married." God turned Miriam's skin white, causing her to be "leprous, as white as snow" (Num. 12:10).

Racism, whether based on skin color or ethnicity, has always been a terrible sin in the eyes of God and worthy of His severest judgment. However, such judgment can be reversed when repentance takes place (vv. 11–15). Both white and black people who allow race to determine social and political structures in America need to remember that.

### *The Bible Gives Us an Eternal Perspective*

Fourth, a study of race rooted in the Bible links the pride and understanding of race with an eternal purpose, thereby expanding our understanding of missiology. It is clear from Scripture that black people are objects of God's love and grace. The very lineage of Jesus included blacks, and Africans were among the leaders of the first-century church. Thus, African Americans and white Americans can see that black people are an integral part of God's redemptive agenda and have played a decisive role in disseminating that kingdom agenda to the rest of the world. All Christians need to understand the eternal dimensions of black history.[5]

The Bible is our common ground. It is the guidebook that links black and white Christians to God's eternal truth. Therefore we should look to it for an understanding of race relations, just as we read it to know how to make our everyday decisions.

The Bible is the primary source for legitimate racial pride, self-authentication, self-analysis, intracultural and cross-cultural analysis, and determining God's view of a group's national purpose. The Bible alone fulfills this function with honesty and integrity and should be the starting point for any group to find out its true identity. A biblical perspective is crucial if black people are going to relate properly to their roots and if white people are going to better understand and see us for who we are.

Most black churches celebrate Black History Month, but the focus is usually on black American history because there is very little awareness or appreciation for black biblical history. However, part of the process of discipleship within the black church, as well as the white church, needs to be to equip our congregations by providing biblical, historically accurate, and logical answers to the relevance and value of the ancestral presence of blacks in Scripture. Without it, African Americans are asked to define ourselves with an inaccurate view of our place in history. Anytime people have an incomplete view of themselves, it affects their actions, thus perpetuating many preconceived notions of perception and identification.

In the section that follows we will look to the Bible for a more accurate perspective of blacks in biblical history.

## The Bible and Black People

Voluminous attention is given throughout the Bible to the issues of race, culture, genealogy, and geography as they relate to the identification of groups of people. There is no such thing as cultural or racial neutrality. Every person belongs to some group. Even when groups intermingle, they either lean toward identification with one culture or the other, or they synthesize into a totally new group (such as the Samaritans, who were the offspring of Jewish and Assyrian intermarrying as we saw in chapter 3).

There is really only one race: the human race (Acts 17:26). All humans stem from one root: Adam and Eve. Yet within the human race there are varieties of individuals and ethnicities. One of the ways we distinguish between individuals and groups is by color.

Likewise, the Bible defines individuals and groups of people by color. Yet the biblical definitions are unencumbered by the negative distortions and reactions that have historically been associated with blackness in American society.

When discussing the issue of blacks in the Bible, we must understand that the designation "black" is a term of accommodation. We are using a twenty-first-century mindset to discuss people who, in some cases, lived more than two millennia ago. Thus our distinctions are not necessarily their distinctions. For example, the Romans made a distinction between people who were dark-skinned and people who had Negroid physiognomy. Today both groups would be considered black.

When we say "black" in reference to those peoples of the past, we are, on the one hand, referring to the physical traits African Americans share with those ancient peoples, namely skin color. On the other hand we are referring to the genetic lineage of African Americans and its affinity with peoples of the ancient Near East and Egypt.

There is no question that dark-complexioned people played a prominent role in biblical events. Descendants of African peoples have, beyond a doubt, an ancestral link to certain critical personages in biblical history.

We are sure of this because the color black is used in the Bible to refer to the skin tone of any dark-complexioned people from African or Hamitic descent. Such a descriptive use of color can be found in the actual names of persons, people groups, and places, particularly in the Old Testament world.

### *Descriptive Names Are Common in the Bible*

In biblical times, the names parents gave their children described their hopes for the child or the circumstances surrounding the child. When Rachel was dying in childbirth, she called her son Ben-oni, "son of my sorrow" (Gen. 35:18). Biblical people used descriptive names to relate their experiences at certain locations. Marah, which means "bitter," received its name because of the bitterness of the waters located there (Ex. 15:23).

Names also reflected the character or action of a person. Nabal was like his name; he was a "fool" (1 Sam. 25:25). Names were even changed when there was a need for a new description of a person, place, or relationship. Jacob was renamed Israel (Gen. 32:27; 35:10). Jesus changed Simon's name to Peter, "the stone." Thus, biblical names are akin to our contemporary use of nicknames; they are used to describe some characteristic of a person.

### *Names of Blacks in the Bible*

Names also referred to the actual skin tone of dark-complexioned people. For example, *kedar* means "to be dark,"[6] thus, Kedarites are a dark-skinned people (Gen. 25:13; Ps. 120:5). *Phinehas* means "the

Negro" or "Nubian," who were a dark-skinned people (Ex. 6:25; 1 Chron. 9:20). According to Exodus 6:25, Phinehas was the son of Eleazar and his wife, who was a daughter of Putiel. This is interesting, because when Phinehas was born, Israel was already established as a separate commonwealth, although it was in transit. Therefore, at least some of the citizens within the commonwealth of Israel were giving birth to children whose names characterized them as Nubian or Negroes. Thus the children of Israel must have been heterogeneous.

It is important to remember that the claim to the inheritance of Jacob was not a matter of skin color, but instead a matter of lineage. The critical question was, "Who was your father?" not "What color is your skin?" It is also important to remember that Manasseh and Ephraim were born to Joseph while he was in Egypt. Yet Jacob (Israel) made it very clear in Genesis 48:5 that Manasseh and Ephraim were to be treated as though they were Jacob's sons; therefore they were to receive an inheritance in the Promised Land. Nubian genetics definitely entered the line of Israel at this juncture, if not before.

Perhaps Putiel's name provides us with an understanding of who his people were. The first three letters of Putiel's name appear to have a lexical/etymological link to Put, one of the sons of Ham.[7] Where the name Put is used in the Old Testament, it usually names African peoples (Jer. 46:9; Ezek. 27:10; 30:5; 38:5). This would certainly explain how Phinehas was born a Nubian in the midst of a Semitic congregation.

Furthermore, a total of seventy people from Jacob's family entered Egypt (Gen. 46:27). Yet the Bible says that some six hundred thousand men alone came out of Egypt with Moses (Ex. 12:37). The total number involved in the Exodus, including women and children, is estimated to be more than two million. Marriages to Egyptian women, much like those of Joseph and Eleazar, would have produced dark-skinned offspring such as Phinehas.

Jeremiah 43:7 refers to the place called Tahpanhes, which means "palace of the Negro." The name Ham means "hot" or "heat." The name is an implicit association or reference to burnt or dark skin, especially since he was the progenitor of African peoples,[8] and also because the names of his brothers reflected their skin tone as well; Shem means "dusky," and Japheth means "fair."

Another name associated with color is Simeon, "who was called Niger" (Acts 13:1). A *Greek-English Lexicon of the New Testament* comments on Simeon's nickname in this way: "Niger (dark-complexioned), surname of Simeon the prophet."[9]

As I mentioned earlier, Moses's wife identified in Numbers 12:1 is one of the Cushites, a group of African people coming from the region south of Egypt and characterized with black skin.[10]

The Shulamite bride of King Solomon twice describes her complexion as black (Song 1:5–6). Of special note here is the spirit of legitimate pride associated with her recognition of her color, for she saw herself as black and beautiful.

Jeremiah, likewise, recognized people in terms of color when he raised the question, "Can the Ethiopian change his skin?" (Jer. 13:23). Jeremiah said that black skin color was as basic to the Ethiopian as unrighteous behavior was to the nation Israel. It was a permanent characteristic.

### *A Basis for Black Pride in the Bible*

Because all humanity has its origin in Adam and the three sons of Noah (Gen. 9:18–19; Acts 17:26), this is an appropriate starting point for gaining a proper biblical basis for racial identity. And because we all stem from the same root, it is absurd for any group to claim superiority over another. It was God's intention to reestablish the human race through the three sons of Noah; therefore, God legitimized all races over which each son stands as head and over which Noah presides as father. This is especially true since the Scripture says that God blessed Noah and his sons, and the command to repopulate the earth was comprehensive and equally applied to each of them (Gen. 9:1).

Each son is associated with nations of peoples, as is recorded in the Table of Nations in Genesis 10.[11] Black people, then, as all other races, can take pride in the fact that it was God's intention that we exist, survive, and function as nations of peoples.

One particularly informative verse is 1 Chronicles 4:40, which indicates that Hamitic people living in Canaan positively contributed to community life, productivity, and social well-being: "They found rich and good pasture, and the land was broad and quiet and peaceful; for those who lived there formerly were Hamites." Here, we have a biblical foundation for appropriately placed black pride.

When one examines the biblical data, it becomes distinctively clear that black people have an awesome heritage. To support a basis for black pride in the Bible, all we have to do is look at blacks who made outstanding contributions to biblical history.

## Influential Blacks in the Bible

### *The Sons of Ham*

Noah's son Ham had four sons: Cush, Mizraim, Put, and Canaan. Cush was the progenitor of the Ethiopian people. This is validated by the fact that the names Cush and Ethiopia are used interchangeably in the Scriptures (Gen. 2:13; 10:6). Mizraim was the progenitor of the Egyptian people, who are understood in Scripture to have been a Hamitic people, and thus African (Ps. 78:51; 105:23, 26–27; 106:21–22). Put was the progenitor of Libya, and Canaan was the progenitor of the Canaanites, one of the most problematic foes of God's chosen people, the Israelites.

### *Nimrod*

Of particular importance is the powerful Old Testament figure Nimrod, the descendant of Cush, who ruled in the land of Shinar (Gen. 10:8–10; 11:2). Nimrod eventually became the father of two of the greatest empires in the Bible and in world history, Assyria and Babylonia. He was the first great leader of a world civilization (Gen. 10:10–12). He led all the people on earth and served as earth's protector. Nimrod's presence and accomplishments confirm the unique and early leadership role black people played in world history, albeit not always in a spiritually beneficial way (Gen. 11:1–9).

### *The Tribe of Ephraim*

Hamitic peoples were crucial to the program of God throughout Old Testament biblical history. Joseph's wife, an Egyptian[12] woman (Gen. 41:45, 50–52), was the mother of Manasseh and Ephraim, who later became leaders of Jewish tribes. In fact, the tribe of Ephraim produced one of the greatest leaders Israel ever had—Moses's successor, Joshua (Num. 13:8; 1 Chron. 7:22–27). This Jewish-African link is very strong in Scripture. The prophet Amos said, "'Are you not as the sons of Ethiopia to Me, O sons of Israel?' declares the Lord" (Amos 9:7).

### *Caleb*

Caleb was the son of Jephunneh the Kennizzite; the Kennizzites were a part of the Canaanite tribes (Gen. 15:19) and descendants of Ham. Caleb also came from the tribe of Judah (Josh. 14:6, 14). Judah, the progenitor of the tribe, fathered twin sons by Tamar, a Hamitic woman (Gen. 38). Caleb joined with Joshua as one of the two spies who went to explore Canaan and brought back a positive report to enter the land and take possession of it, as God had declared (Num. 13–14).

### *Jethro*

Jethro, Moses's father-in-law, from whom Moses received the greatest single piece of advice regarding national leadership, ministry organization, political strategy, and personal planning (Ex. 18:13–27) ever recorded, was a Kenite (Judg. 1:16), part of the Canaanite tribes (Gen. 15:19) who descended from Ham. At that time, the Kenites had settled in the land of Midian.

Another interesting observation regarding Jethro is that he is identified as "the priest of Midian" (Ex. 3:1). Since he was a priest, yet he was not a Levite and the Aaronic priesthood had not yet been established, the question is: What kind of priesthood could this have been? The only other priesthood within the framework of Scripture to which Jethro could have belonged was the priesthood of Melchizedek (Gen. 14:18). This is significant because Christ was a priest after the order of Melchizedek (Heb. 7:17). This means that the priest Jethro, who was of African descent, may have been indicative of pre-Aaronic priesthoods, such as that of Melchizedek, which foreshadowed the priestly role of both Christ and the church.

This, then, is another basis for recognizing the strategic role Africans played in the biblical saga that continues today, because all Christians are related to Jethro and his priesthood as part of the royal priesthood.

*Zipporah*

Zipporah was the daughter of Jethro, the African wife of Moses. She bore him two sons and rescued his life from divine judgment when she circumcised her son—a task that belonged to Moses (Ex. 2:21–22; 4:24–26; 18:2–3). If she is the same black wife of Moses spoken of in Numbers, then God intervened on her behalf against the racism regarding their interracial marriage by Moses's brother and sister (Num. 12:1–15).

*Ebed-Melech*

Ebed-Melech was a godly royal black African official in the palace of King Zedekiah of Judah during the time of the siege of Jerusalem. His name means "servant of the King." He was used by God to assist the prophet Jeremiah in his release from prison when Jeremiah had been sentenced to death. Ebed-Melech was rewarded for his heroism with the divine message that he would not fall by the sword during the fall of Jerusalem to the Babylonians because of his trust in God (Jer. 38:1–13; 39:15–18).

*Simon of Cyrene*

Simon of Cyrene, who helped Jesus on the Via Dolorosa, was of African descent. This we know because Cyrene is a country in North Africa (Matt. 27:32). He was compelled by the Romans to carry the cross of Christ to His crucifixion site. This means that the first person to follow behind Jesus, bear His cross, and have Christ's blood run off on him was a black man. This is the spiritual posture of discipleship God calls all believers to have as we identify with Christ and His suffering (Matt. 27:32; Mark 15:21; Luke 23:26).

*David*

King David is known not only as a man after God's own heart (1 Sam. 13:14) but as one of the greatest kings in Israel's history. David's great-grandmother was a Canaanite woman, Rahab, who is also listed in the Hall of Faith (Heb. 11:31). David's grandmother was Ruth, a Moabite, from a people who were Canaanites as well. David, one of the heroes of the faith, hailed from mixed Jewish and Hamitic ancestry and stands as a leader of whom blacks can be proud to call our own.

### *Solomon*

Solomon was David's son with Bathsheba, a Hamitic woman. Bathsheba literally means the daughter of Sheba. The Table of Nations identifies Sheba in the line of Ham, making Sheba a descendant from an African nation (Gen. 10:7). The Song of Solomon describes Solomon's features as "tanned and handsome, better than ten thousand others! His head is purest gold, and he has wavy, raven hair" (Song 5:10–11 TLB). Solomon was not only the wisest man to rule a nation, but he also brought about the greatest extension of Israel's reach as a kingdom (1 Kings 3:3–14). Solomon's great-great-grandmother, great-grandmother, and mother gave him roots within the black race, and place him as an example of black achievement.

### *Zephaniah*

Underscoring the fact that black people are an integral part of God's revelatory process in both the proclamation and recording of divine revelation is the prophet Zephaniah.

The Old Testament states that Zephaniah was of Hamitic origin. He was from the lineage of Cush (Zeph. 1:1), and he prophesied God's judgment on Judah and her enemies for their rebellion against God and their gross idolatry; yet, he proclaimed, the grace of God would save a remnant and restore blessing to the people.

People of African descent can take pride in God's prophet Zephaniah, one of the biblical authors, as their forefather.

### *Simeon and Lucius*

The church at Antioch had two black men as leaders. Their names were Simeon, who was called Niger or black (as I mentioned earlier), and Lucius, who was from Cyrene. These two black men assisted in the ordination and commissioning of the apostle Paul (Acts 13:1–3). This verifies that black people were not only leaders in the culture of the New Testament era, but also leaders in the church itself.

*The Ethiopian Eunuch*

The Ethiopian eunuch, whose impact we'll look at in more detail, is most likely responsible for the establishment or expansion of the Coptic church in a large part of Africa. While, according to tradition, Mark the Evangelist was one of the first to bring the gospel to Alexandria in Egypt where the Coptic branch of Christianity began to develop and spread, the Ethiopian eunuch carried the seed of Christianity into East Africa.

This talented man revealed the high degree of organizational and administrative responsibility that existed within the upper echelons of Ethiopian culture. The Bible describes him as a eunuch of great authority under "Candace, queen of the Ethiopians, who was in charge of all her treasure" (Acts 8:27). According to the standard Greek lexical studies, the word *Ethiopian* is of Greek origin. It literally means "burnt face."[13] The term *eunuch* does not necessarily denote emasculation; it can refer to high military and political officials.[14]

The scriptural account of the Ethiopian official is significant for two reasons. First, it acknowledges the existence of a kingdom of dark-skinned peoples at the time of first-century Christianity. Second, it records the continuation of Christianity in Africa after having been initiated through the first African-Jewish proselytes who were converts at Pentecost (Acts 2:10). This account of Philip's encounter with the Ethiopian official verifies God's promise in Zephaniah 3:9–10: "For then I will give to the peoples purified lips, that all of them may call on the name of the Lord, to serve Him shoulder to shoulder. From beyond the rivers of Ethiopia My worshipers, My dispersed ones, will bring My offerings."

These verses show God's desire: He wishes to call to Himself peoples from the African continent, not into servitude and disdain as some incorrectly surmise, but into brotherhood with all men to serve Him "shoulder to shoulder."

As we see in history, the Ethiopian eunuch's influence has reached generations and transformed an entire culture for Christ. According to tradition, current Ethiopia was once the powerful kingdom of Axum. Its king, Ezaha, became one of the first world rulers to make Christianity the official religion of his kingdom, which became a major center for the faith. When Marco Polo visited Ethiopia, he referred to it as a magnificent Christian land. In 1173, Ethiopians were hosted by a gathering of church leaders in Constantinople. Between 1200–1500 the Zagwe dynasty ruled the land and led an expansion of the church. One of them, Zara Yaqob, worked to purge Ethiopia of traditional African religion. By the 1480s the Church of Santo Stefano degli Abissini was built in Rome specifically for the use of Ethiopian visitors and settlers. Since the Ethiopian church wasn't the product of European influences, it developed its own distinct religious customs and a slightly different canon of Scripture. To this day, the Ethiopian church carries forward these distinctives.

### *Blacks in the Lineage of Christ*

Deserving of our greatest attention is the lineage of Christ, who is the heart and soul of the Christian faith. Over and over again, the prophets prophesied that the Messiah would come from the seed of David. As we have already seen, the Davidic line finds a number of black people within it. Of the five women mentioned in Matthew's genealogy (Matt. 1:1–16), four are of Hamitic descent—Tamar, Rahab, Bathsheba, and Ruth.

The point here is not that Jesus was black. To assert such, as some black theologians and religious leaders do, is to fall into the exclusionist perspective of many whites who would make Jesus an Anglo-European, blue-eyed blond who had very little relevance to people of color. It would also fail to respect the distinct Jewish heritage of Christ. Rather, Jesus was mestizo—a person of mixed ancestry.

It blesses me to know that Jesus had black in His blood, because this destroys any perception of black inferiority once and for all. In Christ we find perfect man and sinless Savior. This knowledge frees blacks from an inferiority complex, and at the same time it frees whites from the superiority myth. In Christ, we all have our heritage.

Black people, as all other people, can find a place of historical, cultural, and racial identity in Him. As Savior of all mankind, He can relate to all people, in every situation. In Him, any person from any background can find comfort, understanding, direction, and affinity, as long as He is revered as the Son of God, a designation that transcends every culture and race and one to which all nations of people must pay homage.

Even when we leave the pages of the New Testament era, we run into African people of the faith who had a profound influence upon the expansion of Christianity.

## The Church Fathers

For centuries church fathers, anointed men of erudition, have sculpted the development of the Christian faith and have postulated ways to articulate the deep and intricate truths of Christian theology. A great disservice has been done to people of African descent in the failure of church historians to identify the African, Hamitic descent of many of the most noted church fathers. By looking at the strategic place black African people have played in the history and development of the Christian faith, both through their piety and intellectual prowess exercised for the glory of God, we authenticate God's continual activity in the black race. We also encourage Christians of African descent to see ourselves as the continuation of a divine legacy. Our opulent heritage should serve to motivate us to continue dispensing God's truth by means of the talents He has deposited in our community, not only for the benefit of the black community in particular but also for the Christian community at large.

Augustine, who was by far the most scholarly and influential of all the church fathers, has influenced our church fathers, anointed men of erudition, who have sculpted the development of the Christian faith and have postulated ways to articulate the deep and intricate truths of Christian theology from his teachings. The greater majority of his doctrinal conclusions have stood the test of time and the scrutiny of many theologians throughout the annals of theological history. Upon observing his life experience through the lens of his *Confessions*, one can easily see his strong view of the grace of God. The thought and contribution of Augustine became the theological foundation for the Protestant Reformation as well as contemporary Reformed Calvinistic theology.

Augustine's words and thoughts are studied in Bible schools and seminaries. He is known as the Father of Theologians and also referred to as the "father of orthodox theology." However, it is often left out that he was not only African, but also most probably was black.[15] We know this because his mother, Monica, was a Berber, and Berbers were a group of dark-skinned people belonging to the vicinity of Carthage.[16]

Athanasius of Alexandria was another prominent church father, theologian, statesman, and Egyptian leader. As a young man he served as secretary to Alexander Bishop of Alexandria. Upon the death of Alexander, it was made known to Athanasius that he had been chosen by Alexander to succeed him as bishop of Alexandria. Athanasius was involved in the theological war against the heresy of Arius and the Arians, who taught that Jesus Christ was not truly God, but a lesser creature. It was because of this heresy that the Council of Nicaea met in the year AD 325, and Athanasius welcomed the definition of the Son that stated He was "consubstantial with the Father."

Like Augustine, Athanasius's words and thoughts are taught in Bible schools and seminaries. He was known as the "black dwarf" because of his dark skin and short stature, a name he was given by his many enemies.[17] Athanasius was exiled five times by four Roman emperors and spent seventeen of the forty-five years he served as bishop of Alexandria in exile. However, he exhibited a cogent understanding of theological issues that was far beyond his own time.[18]

Quintus Septimius Florens Tertullian (c. 160–c. 225), who like Augustine lived in Carthage, was another of the great African church fathers. He is known in church history as the father of Latin theology because he was the first church leader to write his works in Latin. While it is unclear as to his precise skin tone, there is great evidence to support that he was black. He was of Berber and Phoenician origin, and Berbers were a group of dark-skinned people dominating North Africa.

Tertullian received a good education in literature and rhetoric, was trained in Greek and Latin, and became a lawyer. He converted to Christianity some time prior to AD 197, retaining skills in rhetoric and argumentation that impacted the religious environment of his day. Among his greatest contributions to Christian theology were his thoughts toward the foundation of the Trinitarian formula, often receiving credit as the first to use the word "trinity" to describe the Godhead. His notable writings include *Ad Martyras* ("To the Martyrs"), *Ad Nationes* ("To the Nations"), *Apologeticum* ("Defense"), *Adversus*

*Marcionem* ("Against Marcion"), *Adversus Hermogenem* ("Against Hermogenes"), *Adversus Valentinianos* ("Against Valentinus"), and *De Praescriptione Haereticorum* ("Concerning the Prescription of Heretics"). From a historical perspective, Tertullian is known less for what he did than for what he wrote. In his *Prescriptions Against the Heretics* he argued that the heretics of his day had no right to refute the church and that Scriptures were the sole property of the church.[19]

It should be evident from even a limited understanding of the Bible that many people of African descent have had a major role in the development and dissemination of the Christian faith. Yet if these biblical characters and church fathers were living in "Christian" America during the 1940s, they would have had to sit at the back of the bus, use separate restrooms, and be discriminated against in the realms of housing, education, and employment.

Far from being an uninformed people who were afterthoughts in the mind and plan of God, blacks were a well-informed, progressive, productive, and influential people—so much so that we were at the very center of every aspect of God's activity in history. It is only because people have failed to present an accurate reflection of historical truth that this reality is ignored.

I invite Anglos to see African Americans through the lens of Scripture rather than that of culture. In so doing, there can be a basis of equality in relationship building. If we who are black will see ourselves through the same lens of Scripture, we will discover an appropriate basis for racial pride in the God of the Bible. It also means we can give other races the same significance and respect as part of God's creation that we desire to receive from them.

**Notes**

1. See "The Search for Adam and Eve," *Newsweek*, January 11, 1988. A secular anthropologist and a scientist grapple with the data indicating Adam and Eve were African.
2. Walter McCray, *The Black Presence in the Bible: Discovering the Black and African Identity of Biblical Persons and Nations* (Chicago: Black Light Fellowship, 1990), 9.
3. Lerone Bennett, *Before the Mayflower: A History of Black America* (Chicago: Johnson Publishing, 1969), 5.
4. See my book coauthored with Dwight McKissic, *Beyond Roots II: If Anybody Asks You Who I Am* (Woodbury, NJ: Renaissance, 1994), for a comprehensive perspective on the role of black people in history.

5. McCray, *Black Presence in the Bible*, 31: "Black people need to understand all Black history, including that which is revealed in the Bible. If we are ignorant of our history and its heritage we will walk blindly into our future. And without keeping in our minds and hearts the spiritual and eternal dimensions of our history, our future forebodes a hopelessness which many of us would rather not face.

   "From a Christian viewpoint it is important for Black people to understand their Biblical history. Understanding the Black presence within the Bible nurtures among Black people an affection for the Scripture and the things of the Lord. Far too many of our people reject the Bible because they don't understand that it speaks responsibly about them and to their experience. God is concerned about Black people. Furthermore, enough information pertaining to Black people and their experience is written in His Word to convince the honest searcher for truth that God is indeed concerned for the well-being, salvation and liberation of Black peoples throughout the world."
6. Brown, Driver, and Briggs, *A Hebrew-English Lexicon of the Old Testament* (London: Oxford University Press, 1968), 871. The lexicon assigns the meaning to the root *KDR*, as "black-tinted."
7. See Brown, Driver, and Briggs, *Hebrew-English Lexicon*, 806, for the affinity between the names *Put* and *Putiel.*
8. Brown, Driver, and Briggs, *Hebrew-English Lexicon*, 20. See also Professor Charles Copher's discussion on "The Black Presence in the Old Testament" in the work, *Stony the Road We Trod* (Minneapolis: Fortress Press, 1991), 151–52.
9. For other early usages of Niger, see Bauer, Arndt, Gingrich, and Danker, *A Greek-English Lexicon of the New Testament and Other Early Christian Literature* (Chicago: University of Chicago Press, 1979), 539.
10. J. Daniel Hays, "The Cushites: A Black Nation in the Bible," *Bibliotheca Sacra* 153:612 (October–December 1996): 398.
11. For an exhaustive scholarly treatment of the meaning, significance, purpose, and interpretation of the Table of Nations for understanding and validating the black presence in Scripture, see Walter McCray, *The Black Presence in the Bible and the Table of Nations: Genesis 10:1–32* (Chicago: Black Light Fellowship, 1990).
12. Egypt is identified in Scripture as the land of Ham (Ps. 78:51; 105:23, 26–27; 106:21–22), thus giving the ancient Egyptians a black ancestry.
13. Henry George Liddell and Robert Scott, *Greek-English Lexicon* (London: Oxford University Press, 1995), 37. *Aithiops* properly, burnt-face (i.e., Ethiopian, Negro).
14. Gerhard Kittel and Gerhard Friedrich, eds., G. W. Bromiley, trans., *Theological Dictionary of the New Testament*, vol. 2 (Grand Rapids, MI: Eerdmans, 1987), 766.
15. The Original African Heritage Study Bible (Nashville: The James Winston Publishing Company, 1993), 1831.
16. Keith Irvine, *The Rise of the Colored Races* (New York: W. W. Norton, 1970), 19.
17. Justo Gonzalez, *The Story of Christianity*, vol. 1 (San Francisco: Harper, 1984), 173.
18. Walter Elwell, ed., *Evangelical Dictionary of Theology* (Grand Rapids, MI: Baker, 1984), 95.
19. Ibid., 74.

# Chapter 7

# THE BLACK CHURCH'S LINK WITH AFRICA

My ancestors, like those of most black Americans, were brought to this country against their will from the west coast of Africa to serve as slave labor for the economic development of the New World. My great-grandparents worked the land of the South to help America uncover the vast wealth that she had been granted by God. Like virtually all Africans brought to these shores, my ancestors had to endure the agony and shame of American slavery. They were viewed as less than human, savages, thus giving sanction to the abuse and misuse of the legal system of slavery.

The fact that my African ancestors were primarily perceived by whites as savages in need of civilizing gave rise to one of the most inhumane systems of injustice ever to be perpetrated against human beings. It is a system that we are still seeking to recover from today.

My great-grandparents did not come to America from a dark and uncivilized continent. To the contrary, they were forced from their homeland where they lived with personal freedom and dignity and were brought to a country where they could be bought and sold at auction like cattle.

## The Misperception of Africa

Africa! When we hear that word, we may see images of a land untouched by the marvels of modernization. According to the typical Western mindset, Africa is a land rich in raw materials—ivory, gold, oil, and coal. To be sure, at one time the African himself was viewed as a very valuable commodity. Certainly, the African was not valued for his or her intellectual prowess.

Such a mindset spawns men like German scholar Leo Frobenius, who said,

> Before the introduction of a genuine faith and a higher standard of culture by the Arabs, the natives had neither political organization, nor, strictly spoken, any religion. . . . Therefore it is necessary, in examining the pre-Mahommedan conditions of the negro races, to confine ourselves to the description of their crude fetishism, their brutal and often cannibal customs, their vulgar and repulsive idols. . . . None but the most primitive instincts determine the lives and conduct of the negroes, who lack every kind of ethical inspiration.[1]

This point of view was recently reinforced to me when I overheard a white teacher, trying to calm down some overly active black kids in a local elementary school, say, "You kids settle down and stop acting like you are little monkeys just arriving from Africa." Regardless of her intentions, her words emphasize a very popular stereotype—that is, there exists an unbroken continuity between the wild chimps of Africa, the African himself, and the contemporary black American. Many people who would never voice such a philosophy nonetheless hold to its authenticity. Unfortunately, so do some African Americans.

Only by correcting the misconceptions about the African continent can we correct the negative perception that many white people have toward black people in our contemporary society, and the negative way many of us view ourselves.

It is necessary, then, to look at some key facets of African culture and religion without the impairment of Western stereotypes. By

Western stereotypes I mean the cadre of beliefs and images that the Western world embraces regarding Africans and people of African descent as portrayed in the first few minutes of the evening news. In place of an in-depth view of African culture and its strengths, the West adopts a superficial and degrading assessment based on thirty-second clips of starving children, poverty, or people suffering from AIDS.

This propensity on the part of Europe and its satellites to look down on non-European cultures, focusing primarily on their struggles, has caused the Western world to remain in the relational "dark ages." In addition, because European colonialism has often brought with it the advent of Christianity into diverse places of the world, many non-Europeans assess Christianity through the merits of the ones bearing it. Many potential Christian converts link Christianity with a worldview of America formed through a missiological foundation often rooted in colonial sociocultural norms along with the exportation of soap operas, trashy talk shows, and questionable musical artists, and thus form a negative assessment of Jesus Christ and His salvation.

Furthermore, a narrow view of Africa leads to broad generalizations such as the trend toward fetishism (the worship of objects understood to have magical powers, such as idols), which is actually a universal trend and not limited to those in Africa. Scripture verifies this universal trend toward idolatry in Romans 1:22–23: "Professing to be wise, they became fools, and exchanged the glory of the incorruptible God for an image in the form of corruptible man and of birds and four-footed animals and crawling creatures."

Even a cursory walk through the New Testament reveals many horrid practices among the peoples of the northern coast of the Mediterranean and the area of Asia Minor under Greek influence to whom Paul wrote his letters.

In the Greek city of Corinth, people worshiped many deities, including the goddess Aphrodite. Known as Venus to the Romans, this goddess was said to have beauty that made the wise witless.[2] The worship of Aphrodite was centered around the temple erected in her honor. The liturgy involved sexual contact with the temple priestesses, that is, prostitutes. So enraptured were the Corinthians with this vile practice that the Athenian dramatist Aristophanes (ca. 450–388 BC) coined the word *korinthiazomai* (which means "to act like a Corinthian: to commit fornication").[3]

Addressing this aspect of Corinthian life in his commentary, Gordon Fee mentioned the Asclepius room in the present museum in Corinth, which he called "mute evidence of this facet of city life."[4] On a large wall stood a number of clay votives (objects given in fulfillment of a vow or pledge) of human genitals that had been offered to the god for the healing of that part of the body, which was apparently ravaged by venereal disease.

Of course, we have always been taught that venereal disease made it to Europe through Columbus's sailors, who had sex with the native women of the West Indies, which is another great Western myth. In Corinth we have evidence that venereal disease existed in Europe for at least 1,400 years before Columbus was born.

Generally, the Western world fails to acknowledge that the staple of Western society, Christianity, is non-Western. Neither Christianity nor Judaism is indigenous to Europe; rather, they are Middle Eastern in origin. Only via the prompting of the Holy Spirit and the military oppression of the Romans did Europe obtain the prize of Christianity. It was by no craving for virtue and ethical inspiration on Europe's part. However, both Christians and non-Christians often look to Christianity as the white man's religion, and because of this, some Africans have called others to return to their traditional beliefs.[5] Although I cannot in any way endorse a shift away from the Christian faith to any other beliefs, I acknowledge the need to examine black historical and cultural bearings to better equip black kingdomologists.

I agree with Timothy Bankole, who said,

> Putting Christ side by side with Buddha, Muhammad, or Confucius, I find a number of good and admirable attributes in the religions of these leaders, but Christ to me stands out as unique. This is one reason why in spite of the many despicable and un-Christian acts committed by some Europeans in the name of Christianity, I have abandoned neither Christianity nor the Church. In my personal life, I have found Christ to be all-sufficient, and if Christianity is practiced as Christ taught it, I have

> no doubt whatever that God's kingdom will come and his will for mankind be accomplished even in our world and possibly in our time.[6]

As an African American, I was always interested in the truth about Africa and the relation of African religion to my own belief in Christianity. When I was twenty-six, I set out to learn about my heritage.

### *In Search of a Link*

The prospect of discovering my link to African life was quite stimulating to me. I felt much as I had when I watched the last episode of *Roots*. Alex Haley had tracked his family tree all the way back to his clan, his tribe, and his history. It was exhilarating to watch the tears of excitement well up in his eyes. One could not help but share Haley's joy of knowing, "I have roots. I have a history. I have a link!"

When Europeans came to Africa, they did so with the idea that the African understood little, if anything, about God. They also had the idea that Africa had nothing to offer culturally or spiritually to the developing Western civilization. As we will observe shortly, this notion was false in the past and is equally false in the present. This ill-conceived notion is at the core of the contemporary misunderstanding of black people: our perspective, our methods, and our uniqueness. Furthermore, it is at the root of the misunderstanding of the black church.

In order to understand any of these matters, it is necessary to have a rendezvous with African Traditional Religion. This rendezvous provides the cultural antecedent for the development of the black church, black evangelicalism, and the subsequent impact and influence in America.

On a personal level, it helps me both to understand and to appreciate why the view of God held by my ancestors was so inclusive of all of life, resulting in the black church becoming central to black existence.

A major issue of debate among black historians and scholars is whether the slave adapted or lost his African religious heritage when he was brought to the Western hemisphere. The debate historically was waged between black historians W. E. B. DuBois[7] and E. Franklin Frazier.[8]

DuBois argued that the Negro church was the only institution among blacks that started in Africa and survived slavery. Contrary to DuBois, Frazier argued that it was impossible to establish any continuity between African religious practices and the Negro church in America. He argued that the crisis of slavery was too great to sustain African heritage. Moreover, the destruction of the native African languages marked the cessation of certain concepts that were incommunicable in English.

So then, the issue is whether blacks retained aspects of their African heritage. If we did not keep anything from Africa, then the African American experience is a totally new situation with no historical point of reference. However, if we did retain some aspects of our African heritage, we need to know what was salvaged for the sake of determining continuity between the continents.

In recent years, the eminent black religious scholar Henry H. Mitchell convincingly argued, in his book *Black Belief*, that Dubois was right and Frazier was wrong. While not fully understood and appreciated today, much of what you see in contemporary black religion is not only what was seen in slavery, but also, to a large degree, what one saw in Africa and, in fact, still sees in Africa. (I will discuss these similarities later in this chapter.)

Thus, to think of the black Christian church as merely a variant form of white missionary enterprise is fallacious. Rather, many of the fundamental viewpoints were already present; Europeans simply affixed Christian theology to an already existent theological and social structure.

My conviction is that the African heritage of the slave prepared him well for his encounter with the Bible. The tenets and theological structures of Christianity would not have been alien to him. In many cases, his own cultural and religious leanings would have helped him to theologize as efficiently as, and perhaps even more so than, his European counterpart.

The scenario is somewhat similar to that in Acts 17:22–24:

> So Paul stood in the midst of the Areopagus and said, "Men of Athens, I observe that you are very religious in all respects. For while I was passing through and examining the objects of your worship, I also found an altar with this inscription: 'TO AN UNKNOWN GOD.' Therefore what you worship in ignorance, this I proclaim to you. The God who made the world and all things in it, since He is Lord of heaven and earth, does not dwell in temples made with hands."

Paul acknowledges the history of the Greeks' recognition of God by saying, "Some of your own poets have said, 'For we also are His children'" (v. 28). Paul was quoting the Cretan poet Epimenides (c. 600 BC).

As the apostle notes, the fact that we all stem from one seed certainly explains why certain patterns of belief in a supreme deity persist all over the globe. If a Greek could ascend to such grandiose thoughts of deity solely on the basis of general revelation, what would prevent the African from doing the same? The answer is nothing! All peoples grope for God. The difficulty is that our corrupt natures stifle our attempts to find an infinitely holy God. Mankind strains without efficacy through all sorts of ideological concoctions and images made by hand to reproduce the glory above.

Against this tendency to create a menagerie of pocket-sized deities made with hands, Paul is firm in condemning such practices in Acts 17:29. But we would be guilty of exegetical myopia if we did not recognize that Paul insinuates that Greeks may have had a profound understanding of the things above; yet this understanding was aberrant in places and was not effective toward salvation.

When one reads Aristotle's *Metaphysics*, one would think that Aristotle was a Christian. Many of Aristotle's postulations seem as though they were extracted from the Psalms. Perhaps this is why the Catholic theologian Thomas Aquinas found him so intriguing. It is clear in many respects that Aristotle was absolutely correct. But to my knowledge, no one ever confessed his sins and accepted Christ through reading the works of Aristotle.

My point is that if we listen carefully to the rhythmic cadence of African Traditional Religion, we will also find profound reflections of biblical truth that compel us to a greater appreciation for God, the Father of Jesus Christ, as well as for the Africans and their ability to remain committed to that God, even in the most oppressive circumstances.

In order to understand and appreciate the depth of the slaves' spiritual presuppositions, we must first grasp the process by which the African culture was transferred to America.

*The Process of Cultural Transference*

When people transfer or are transferred from one locale to another, they bring their culture with them, in varying degrees: their influences, habits, perspectives, dress, religious inclinations, and a myriad of other aspects of their past.

One has only to visit any major city in America to find a Chinatown, a little Italy, or a Germantown. Located in these specialized enclaves are specific things related to their particular histories and cultures. To dismantle these subcultures is no small feat. Why? In the same way that parents raise children with a view to influencing their future life orientation and decision-making, cultures also raise children so they have a distinct worldview that is hard to shake.

Because slavery was a nonvoluntary enterprise, the only hope the slave had to keep from becoming like his captor and losing his own self-identity in the process was remembering and reinforcing his own cultural heritage. Such was the case as slaves resisted attempts to be deculturalized.

When people take their cultures with them to a new locale, the central elements of the culture are the easiest to salvage, and the centerpiece of the West African culture was God. All of life was interpreted in terms of the Divine. Because God was the African slave's reference point for all of life, He would be the first one to whom the slave would appeal, particularly in a time of crisis.

The worldview of the majority of black Americans is the same as that of the captured African slave: God is central. This explains why the slave and their contemporary ancestors could not separate sacred from secular, personal sins from corporate sins, and religion from politics.

It is important to note here that low religious practices are a part of every religious environment. The Puritans conducted witch hunts to rid the colonies of witchcraft. Also, occultism existed among the peoples of Mesopotamia and in the worship of the mystery religions of the pre-Christian Hellenistic world. Therefore, African religion cannot be singled out as primitive savagery. As a matter of fact, there was no greater expression of low religion than the actions of American slave masters, who practiced inhumanity in the name of God.

But just as the low side of African religion survived in the Americas, so also did the high side. Because the high side was quick to acknowledge the Christian God, it was integrated into Christianity and sustained by it.

This cultural heritage was sustained through the process of reinforcement. This process of reinforcement made me reassess my criticism of the emotionalism of my ancestors in the black church, which evangelicals had taught me to reject as uninformed fanaticism.

### *Reinforcement Sustains Cultural Transference*

This cultural transference was not lost during the trek of the Middle Passage, in which nearly twenty million Africans were made captive over the span of some three hundred years, 1517–1840. The slaves were continuously in touch with their African past because they were continuously in touch with one another. New slaves were constantly brought from Africa to the plantations, and they brought with them the African mindset, which served to reinforce the African disposition, even in the absence of tribal and language similarities. Segregation further fostered cultural continuation.

Another indication of cultural transference was the adoptive system the slave community developed. Coming from a tribal/clan background, the slave was dependent upon his communal environment for security, serenity, and society. The slave recreated that environment in establishing what E. Franklin Frazier, author of *The Negro Church in America,* called "the invisible institution." Christian clan meetings on the plantation became the new tribe. This is further verified in the slaves' migration from the South to the North. The plethora of "storefront" churches that arose in the North resulted from the slaves' demand for a tribal/clan concept to provide them with familiar surroundings in a hostile environment. Religion was the primary point of reference.

Understanding this concept helped me to make sense of the fact that anything significant, or even insignificant for that matter, happening in my community while growing up was either happening at the church, was sponsored by the church, or had to benefit the church. It also explains why the brightest and best black expertise and talent emerged out of the church.

A final method of cultural transference was the rise of the new African priest, the black preacher. The new Christianized leader of African people provided the cohesion and cultural reference point that kept the slaves in touch with the strengths of their past, the needs of their present, and the hopes for their future. Because African religion was handed down from one generation to the next by oral tradition, it would be natural for the African culture to continue to be transferred through that vehicle. The black preacher became the channel for this process. Black preachers were the new African point men in America who maintained the key elements of the African past.

Through an analysis of African Traditional Religion, we see that the African slave's capacity to understand Christian doctrine was not inhibited, but rather assisted, by his own cultural and religious predispositions. Furthermore, the liturgical basis for the slave church lay in these African traditions.

African Traditional Religion, although errant in many of its perspectives and applications—of utmost importance with regard to the understanding of the nature and identity of the one true God—contained a substantial foundation of similar systematic beliefs, thus allowing for the opportunity for a positive response to Christianity. Because it had such a high view of God as well as a holistic view of spirituality, it made conversion to the biblical God and the mediator, Jesus Christ through the Holy Spirit, that much easier.

### *The Similarities Between African Religion and Christianity*

The slave was not a backward, savage person who had no perception of the true God. Yet, as can be said of all cultures, the African recognized God through "His invisible attributes" (Rom. 1:20) but not unto salvation, for salvation is through Jesus Christ. That mankind has a general consciousness toward God is a tenet of the first chapter of Romans. Yet, the gospel is the catalyst that affords all men salvation (vv. 16–17).

Since the slave trade primarily took its captives from West Africa, I begin our assessment of African heritage from that area. We will look at African Traditional Religion through the lens of a prominent group of West African people known as the Yoruba. For centuries the Yoruba have lived in what today is western Nigeria. An examination of the Yoruba will provide us with a thorough and consistent view of the people of West Africa.

The Yoruba did not have a systematic, propositional theology as such; rather, theology was conveyed through the Odu, the vehicle of oral tradition. The Odu is a body of recitals used to convey the Yoruba doctrine and dogma.[9] There are some 256 of these Odu, and within them are 1,680 stories and myths, referred to as pathways, roads, and courses.[10] Some have verses that are almost unintelligible. Such sayings are supposed to be profoundly deep and require special knowledge to interpret. To remember all of this data was a gargantuan chore for the village storyteller, a feat far in excess of memorizing and reciting the entire King James Version of the Bible verbatim!

The question we face is, How did the African perceive his God? Often that perception was closer to Christianity than most Christians realize. There is a great deal of similarity between nine attributes of God as He is revealed in Scripture and that Supreme Being known to the Yoruba as Olodumare.

### *A Supreme Deity*

As we observe the Yoruba form of African Traditional Religion, we see a very high view of the Supreme Deity known as Olodumare. For the Yoruba, the name Olodumare was magisterial and supreme beyond every other name. Does this sound familiar? Olodumare was preeminent overall, whether on the earth or in the heavens. All paid homage to him, including the pantheon of sub-deities (also referred to as the divinities) who owed their existence and allegiance to him. All acquiesced to his will without exception.[11]

This view of the supremacy of God was reiterated to me when I visited my grandmother. If a thunderstorm came through while I was at her home, she had me turn off the radio, the television, and all the lights, and sit quietly. Why? Because God was talking! She saw God as being in charge of all of life and as such, He demands our undivided attention.

For the Yoruba, theology was discourse about God, and it functioned within the matrix of life. Thoughts of Olodumare were always synthesized with the *Sitz im Leben* (situation in life) of the Yoruba. Yoruba theology was never an enterprise reduced to writing, because, like that of other tribes in Africa, it was passed down through oral recitation.

This "grapevine" approach to history and theology was and is a dominant part of black life. When my grandparents wanted to know what was happening in the community, the quickest and surest way to get that information was to go to the barbershop, the beauty shop, or the church house.

### *A God of Goodness and Justice*

One of the fundamental characteristics of the African's God was His goodness and justice. There was no thought of God ever being unfair. One might think that the slave would have rejected his God because he was being enslaved in the name of God. Amazingly, he tenaciously clung to Him. The only rational reason for doing so would be that the slave's own understanding of God told him that his master's interpretation of God was incorrect.

One former missionary to Africa told me about a situation where a curse had been put on the animals in the community where the missionary lived. One after another for several days on end, animals were dying as had been forecast through the curse. Having had no previous exposure to spiritual warfare at this tangible a level, the missionary was disturbed by the reality of the situation to the point of exasperation. Seeing the frustration and hopelessness etched on the missionary's face, an African man with no formal education at all, yet with a faith in God intrinsic to his culture, asked the missionary in disbelief, "Je—hatahujui Mungu?" which translated means, "Do you even know God?"

The question was not intended as an insult, but rather as an honest desire to determine whether this missionary with years of biblical education who had supposedly "left all" to proclaim God in a foreign land even knew the God being proclaimed. The faith of the African man was firmly rooted in God, with or without any classroom education at all, but what he questioned was the faith of the missionary. Similarly, the faith of the African slave transported to America was firmly rooted in God, but what was questioned was the faith of the Christian whites claiming to know Him as well.

The slave's idea of God far exceeded that which was portrayed in the culture in which he lived, or he would never have loved, served, and worshiped the God of those who were enslaving, dehumanizing, and oppressing him. This fact alone demonstrates that African religion was not ignorant religion, but was socially applied religion. It related to the everyday realities of life. It did not rest solely on theological formulas but rather on the ethical realities of human existence. African religion addressed all of life: family life, community life, and business life. This explains why my ancestors looked to the church for direction in resisting the unjust system of American slavery.

This leads me to a major conclusion regarding God's twofold, sovereign purpose for American slavery. On one hand, slavery was allowed by God, not so much to teach the ignorant slave the right way, but rather, as in the case of Cornelius (Acts 10), to acknowledge the slave's faith in the true high God by introducing him to Jesus Christ, the Mediator who would replace all of the sub-deities as the means of access to God. On the other hand, I believe that slavery was allowed as the means by which God would introduce the true meaning of justice and spiritual liberation to American culture, which had neglected these aspects of His character.

The story of Joseph in Genesis 37–50 is an example. Joseph's final position was as second in command of all Egypt. However, his ascension to this lofty post was tortuous. Yet he told his brothers, "As for you, you meant evil against me, but God meant it for good in order to bring about this present result, to preserve many people alive" (Gen. 50:20). As Joseph endured hardship for the sake of an ultimate victory, so did the African slave.

This view affirms what America gained from this dreadful experience—a true vision of justice and spiritual freedom—and what slaves received—Jesus as their Savior and Mediator. If American society would submit to the justice of God the way slaves submitted to Jesus Christ as well as embrace the freedom given through a proper understanding of the cross and grace, then the power, presence, and impact of God in our culture would be beyond our wildest expectations.

### *A Creator God*

Olodumare was the creator. In the genealogy of the gods, all other deities were created by Olodumare. All that existed owed its existence to him. Thus, the heavens and the earth were products of the creativity of Olodumare.

In much the same sense, Genesis 1:1 opens with an all-inclusive statement concerning the creativity of God (Elohim). Moses made use of a rhetorical device known as a *merism* ("the heavens and the earth") to demonstrate that Elohim created everything from the top, which is heaven, to the bottom, which is the earth, and all things in between.

Similar to the Hebrew tendency to use different names for God to emphasize different aspects of His character, Olodumare, in his capacity as creator, was known as Eleda. Also, because Olodumare was the origin and giver of life, he was called Elemi, "the Owner of the spirit" or "the Owner of life."

### *King of the Universe*

Not only was Olodumare considered to be the creator, but he was "the king of the universe" as well. He was over humans and the other deities he created. We've already touched briefly on God's kingdom and His rule on earth, but other passages that delineate this aspect of God include Psalms 47, 93, and 96–99. These chapters are dedicated to the kingship of Yahweh. Psalm 93:1–2 reads, "The Lord [Yahweh] reigns, He is clothed with majesty; the Lord has clothed and girded Himself with strength; indeed, the world is firmly established, it will not be moved. Your throne is established from of old; You are from everlasting."

In much the same way that the Israelites used these "enthronement" psalms to acknowledge the majesty and authority of Yahweh, the Yoruba employed various chants that reflected the same ideas about Olodumare.

### *An Omnipotent God*

To the Yoruba, Olodumare was also omnipotent. He was the most powerful being in the entire universe, able to do all things. The Yoruba would have had no difficulty at all grasping the truths in Genesis 18:14, Jeremiah 32:17, Matthew 19:26, and Luke 1:37, all of which affirm that there is nothing that God cannot do. The Yoruba thought also that things were possible only when and because they were ordered by Olodumare. Isaiah 46:9–10 affirms this same sentiment: that God orders all things after the counsel of His own will (see also Eph. 1:11). To put it simply, the black way of summarizing the great truth about God is to say, God can do anything except fail.

### *An Omniscient Deity*

Olodumare was all-wise, all-knowing, and all-seeing. He and he alone was impeccable and omniscient. The sub-deities might err, but not the Supreme Deity. Olodumare was called Olorun when one referred to his wisdom. A line in one of the songs reads, *Kil'e nse ni bekulu t' oju olorun o to?* —"Whatever do you do in concealment that Olorun's eyes do not reach?"[12]

A similar analogy in Old Testament Scripture is found in Psalm 139. Yahweh is portrayed as the One who sees and knows all. Nothing is hidden from His sight. Or, as my grandmother would say, "Boy, God's a-watchin' you."

### *A Judge of All Things*

E. Bolaji Idowu, author of *Olodumare God in Yoruba Belief*, says, "Olodumare is the final Disposer of all things. He is the Judge. He controls man's destiny, and each will receive from him as he deserves."[13]

This idea that God is the judge of the world is found in several places in Scripture. In Genesis 18:25, Abraham says that God is the "Judge of all the earth." Psalm 7:11 states that God is a "righteous judge." Romans 2:16 reports that one day God will judge men's secrets, while 1 Peter 4:5 says that He will "judge the living and the dead."

So strong was the appreciation for the sovereignty and justice of Olodumare that the Yoruba typically avoided seeking revenge for crimes perpetrated against them. They trusted that Olodumare would render proper recompense for evil. Wickedness would not receive any impunity before Olodumare. "Vengeance is Mine, and retribution" (Deut. 32:35) would be totally in line with the Yoruba concept of justice and sovereignty. In the mindset of the African and of his progeny, the phrase *Fortune Imperatrix Mundi* (Fate, the ruler of the world) never applied, for God was supreme, He ruled, and all would answer to Him, without exception.

In America, we suffer from a "Rambo complex." We feel compelled to pay back evil for evil. If we do not pay back, we feel emasculated and spineless. It is much harder to let our need for revenge go, knowing that God will always deal the last hand. Whereas this concept of allowing God to judge is difficult for Americans, it has always been a way of life for the Yoruba.

Far too often, we in the Western world tend to think that morality and impartiality are Western Christian concepts. Much to the surprise of Western minds, this is not so. God's law is universal. The morality is there because humans are image bearers. We need not try to superimpose our cultural values upon people of diverse places, all the while assuming that our cultural values are uniquely "Christian." God has left a witness of Himself in all places.

### *An Immortal God*

Immortality was foremost in the Yoruba concept of the Supreme Deity. One Yoruba song states, "One never hears of the death of Olodumare." From excerpts of other Odu recitals, we find that Olodumare was known as the "Mighty, Immovable Rock that never dies." As E. Bolaji Idowu comments, "In a sense, this is a comfort and encouragement to the worshipping soul. It is necessary to know that the Deity is alive forevermore, that He is unchanging in the midst of all the changes and decay which have been the constant experience of man, if religion and life are to have any ultimate meaning."[14] As in Christianity, concomitant with the concept of immortality is that of immutability (it follows from the infinite perfection of God that He cannot be changed by anything from without Himself; and that He will not change from any principle within Himself).

### *A Sacrificial God*

Sacrifice was an integral element of the life of the Yoruba. It was through the sacrificial system that one found approval before Olodumare and appeased the divinities. The basic idea was to seek favor from the gods and drive off the evil spirits.

Offerings were never offered directly to Olodumare, but through several mediators, some human (the priests) and some spiritual (the divinities). Only the divinities of the Yoruba bore the supplications of the people before the presence of the Supreme Deity. This was cosmic protocol. No one man could come near to Olodumare.

In Christianity, there is only one mediator between man and God (1 Tim. 2:5). Jesus alone is our advocate before the throne.

The Yoruba did at one time practice human sacrifice. Sometimes human sacrifices were offered so that they might be advocates before the divinities. Thus, the Africans would have had no problem whatsoever comprehending the role of Christ as sacrifice and advocate before the throne of God.[15]

Human sacrifice was often done in circumstances when the livelihood of the community was at stake. Usually, the victim was someone who had been captured in a war. Very seldom was the victim a member of the village; this happened only when a member of the tribe was slated to be an emissary for the community before the gods. Here again we see an advocate motif.

It is clear from the witness of Scripture that human sacrifice is an abominable practice, one that the Bible condemns. This was a detestable practice before God, and He made this known to Israel in Leviticus 20:1–2: "The Lord spoke to Moses, saying, 'You shall also say to the sons of Israel: "Any man from the sons of Israel or from the aliens sojourning in Israel who gives any of his offspring to Molech, shall surely be put to death."'" All sacrifice was to be done after the prescription of God's edicts concerning sacrifice in Leviticus. This meant that there would be a categorical moratorium on human sacrifice of any kind!

Because the Yoruba had such a transcendent view of God, it was difficult for them to accept that the God of Christianity wanted to be near to them. Their concern was how a God so wonderful could come close to ones such as themselves. So then, the difficulty with the closeness of God as seen in the Bible was not born out of ignorance, but out of reverence. But as for the basic concept of mediation itself, the Yoruba had no problem, although certainly their views on the number of mediators required a significant alteration.

As we can clearly see, the Yoruba had an enormously deep appreciation for God and His ways. In fact, the appreciation was so profound that their belief system mirrored that of Christianity in many respects. Therefore, the leap from African Traditional Religion to Christianity would not have been a quantum leap, but rather a simple transition.

The discussion of similarities and disparities could go on *ad infinitum*, but it is sufficient to state that the African Traditional Religion of the Yoruba would have prepared them well for their entrée into Christianity. Also, from the heritage bestowed upon them by African Traditional Religion, three major repercussions entered into the African American church:

- the focus on oral communication;
- the tendency toward orthodoxy and a supreme view of God;
- an essential connection between theology and life.

These three areas are at the heart of a comprehensive kingdom view of Christianity, and while the doctrine of God would not be articulated in terms of formal theological formulas in the African tradition, it would be communicated in the everyday interface of black life. My grandmother would formulate the doctrine simply: "He's so high you can't get over Him, He's so low you can't get under Him, He's so wide you can't get around Him." Somehow she found in this God from her African past all she needed to survive the cruel, harsh world of servitude and injustice.

**Notes**

1. Leo Frobenius, *The Voice of Africa*, vol. 1 (London: Hutchinson and Co., 1913). 2.
2. Edith Hamilton, *Mythology* (New York: Mentor, 1969), 32–33.
3. "Corinth," *The International Standard Bible Encyclopedia*, vol. 1 (Grand Rapids, MI: Eerdmans, 1979), 773.
4. Gordon Fee, *The First Epistle to the Corinthians* (Grand Rapids, MI: Eerdmans, 1987), 2.
5. Cornelius Olowola, "The Concept of Sacrifice in Yoruba Religion," Dallas Theological Seminary Th.M. Thesis, 1976, 3.
6. Timothy Bankole, *Missionary Shepherds and African Sheep* (Ibadan, Nigeria: Daystar Press, 1971), 6. Quoted in Olowola's thesis.
7. W. E. B. DuBois, *The Negro* (New York: Oxford Univ. Press, 1970), 113–14.
8. E. Franklin Frazier, *The Negro Church in America* (New York: Schocken Books, 1963), 9–19.
9. E. Bolaji Idowu, *Olodumare God in Yoruba Belief* (London: Longmans, 1962), 7.
10. Ibid., 38–47.
11. Ibid., 61.
12. Ibid., 41.
13. Ibid., 66.
14. Ibid., 42–43.
15. See Olowola, "The Concept of Sacrifice in Yoruba Religion," 119.

## Chapter 8

# THE UNIQUENESS OF THE BLACK CHURCH

Today, in every major city in America, you can witness a growing number of African American churches that are offering comprehensive ministry to the whole of humanity without compromising the Word of God. These individuals and ministries are committed to biblical preaching, lifestyle accountability, and personal evangelism, but have rejected the social secularism and eschatological escapism of much of the contemporary evangelical church. They are intentionally building communities. As a result, people's lives are being improved by things such as job skill and placement programs, mentors for the fatherless, business development, GED programs, and a myriad of other life-enhancing outreaches.

This contemporary movement is helping with the historical black church's fusion of the best of African culture and the Christian faith. Such a fusion gives rise to what is probably one of the clearest expressions of New Testament Christianity America has ever seen. This is so because of the natural way the slave community accepted Christianity, coupled with the similarities that existed between the experience of the Jews in both the Old and New Testaments. Such a link made untenable any philosophical separation of church and state, for one could not speak of life apart from theology.

When we examine the New Testament definition of the church and juxtapose it with the functioning of the historical black church, it becomes clear that the two institutions were very similar. As such, these two institutions are in a unique position to teach both the black and white churches of today what true biblical Christianity looks like when it operates in a church that truly makes God the center of its existence.

## The Birth of the African American Church

It is unfortunate that many people see the origin of the African American church as little more than a branch that emerged from mainstream white Christianity. When one comes to understand and appreciate fully the circumstances that came together to give rise to this unique institution, it becomes clear that its makeup consisted of men and women of tremendous depth, intellect, wisdom, and pride, who were willing to submit all of these virtues to the work of a sovereign God. There is no understanding or appreciation of the black experience without understanding the importance and centrality of the black church.

The birth of the African American church was the result of a confluence of five strategic factors: the slaves' search for meaning, evangelization, a natural integration of their religious foundations, the Bible, and the black preacher.

### *The Slaves' Search for Meaning*

The reality of slavery forced the slave to look for meaning. Slaves found themselves in a precarious position: They had no freedom, no meaning, no hope, and no help. Where then were they to turn to find these desperately needed facets of life? They looked to the only place available, which was within their history, their culture, and their religious heritage. There they saw the most significant aspect of their past life in Africa: God!

In his book *Black Belief*, Henry Mitchell said, "It is probable that this African, holistic praise of God was also such an important affirmation of Black selfhood that its sense of 'God all in me' was among the most important resources for survival in the unprecedented dehumanization of American slavery."[1] They had to look to that God whom they celebrated in West Africa for His provision of meaning, hope, and freedom, to give them that same definition of existence in their new hostile environment. Immediately, the slaves had the one thing that could keep them keeping on despite the social reality of their plight—they had their God.

Thus, the slaves' minds were already preconditioned for the key role the black church would play in their lives. This intuitive theistic mindset also reveals the depth of the divine consciousness within them.

### *Evangelization*

White organizations, such as the Anglican Society for the Propagation of the Gospel, and movements such as the first Great Awakening, began evangelizing the slaves.[2] What is critical to understand here is that this evangelization process occurred without addressing the slaves' oppressed condition. In 1667, for example, the Virginia legislature agreed that baptism did not alter the state of the slave. Such laws allowed blacks to be evangelized without those evangelizing them ever having to address their sociopolitical plight.

With the influence of the first Great Awakening, Christianity was brought to the level of the common man. This made the African feel comfortable with the appeal of Christianity, especially since the slave was as common a man as you could find. Many of these revivals and crusade meetings were full of emotion, shouting, dancing, and other physical and verbal expressions. This reminded the slaves of their own worship experiences and helped to make the structure of American Christianity palatable to them.

### *A Natural Integration of Their Beliefs*

Slaves began integrating their African beliefs with the new Christian revelations. When they heard the message of the gospel, they heard more than just personal forgiveness of sin. They heard the voice of hope. The Christian message spoke of heaven where earthly trials would be no more and where they would find freedom from all the injustices they were experiencing. They heard about a God who loved them and suffered for them so that they might experience eternal freedom. Given the cry for freedom and the magnitude of

God's suffering love, with which the slave could easily identify, the stage was set for finding that freedom in Christ.

In Christianity the slaves also found a message of liberation from the oppressive historical condition of slavery. They latched onto the Christian message as their means for survival, self-authentication, and historical freedom.

The integration of the eternal and the temporal was evidenced in the worship services of the slaves. They would dress up for their worship services and mimic some of their African rituals in this new Christian environment. They held secret worship meetings if the master did not officially allow them to gather together because he rejected the Christianization of the slave or he feared possible insurrection. At these secret meetings the slaves developed codes to communicate with each other. They communicated these codes in slave songs.[3] This was a major means of communication in the African Traditional Religion. For example, one of the slaves would start singing, "Steal away, steal away to Jesus." Translation: "When the sun goes down there will be a church meeting in the swamp, so steal away to the service."

Songs, then, were not just for personal pleasure. They were also a mechanism for community planning, again revealing the strong intellectual and organizational prowess of the slaves as well as their willingness to risk punishment in order to maintain their worship of the supreme God.

Swamps and forests became the early sanctuaries for slave services. On the morning after a worship service, the slaves in the field would break out with a song, "I couldn't hear nobody praying." Translation: "The master did not hear our worship service going on."

The early African slave church, then, was made up of a brilliant cadre of men and women who had to encode their communication in the natural movement of their lives, with God at the center.

### *The Bible*

The Bible became the first book to which the slaves were exposed. They became acutely aware that the Bible was deeply concerned with the subject of freedom in history as well as in eternity. God had worked in the past with another group of people called the

Israelites, who were, like the Africans, under bondage in a foreign land.

As the story unfolded, it became clear that God was not only concerned about their condition because of His love for them, but He also desired to release them from bondage so that they could worship Him freely. The slaves concluded that if God could save Israel from Egyptian oppression, He could certainly save black people in America. Thus the story of Israel's deliverance was a story that was easy for the slaves to transpose to their own experience. It became clear that God was on the side of the slaves and against the oppression of their masters. Israel's story became the black community's "story."[4]

### *The Black Preacher*

The fifth and final factor that led to the development of the black church was the rise of the black preacher, who would provide the link between Africa and America. We will look at this unique leader in the next chapter.

## The African American Church and Christ

The African American church did not arrive at its Christology through academic study, but rather through the context of slavery. This is not to say that academic information was not available to the black church, but rather that the black church was forced to answer specific questions that reflected the journey from slavery to freedom.

For example, the slaves sang,

*I want Jesus to walk with me,*
*I want Jesus to walk with me,*
*All along my pilgrim's journey*
*I want Jesus to walk with me.*

*In my trials, walk with me,*
*In my trials, walk with me,*
*When the shades of life are falling,*
*Lord, I want Jesus to walk with me.*

*He walked with my mother, He'll walk with me.*
*He walked with my mother; He'll walk with me.*
*All along my pilgrim's journey*
*I know Jesus will walk with me.*

The slaves saw Jesus as a present reality, providing the impetus, support, and direction for their journey. The experience of slavery never allowed the black church to get caught up in the theological and philosophical meaning of Jesus, because the Jesus in black religion was a practical deliverer of the oppressed. Neither, however, did they allow this temporal emphasis to decrease their appreciation of the deity of Christ.

Whereas white preachers and theologians often defined Jesus Christ as a spiritual Savior, the Deliverer of people from personal sin and guilt, African American preachers viewed God as the Liberator in history. The black church saw in Jesus One who suffered as they were suffering; One who had experienced oppression as they were experiencing oppression. Yet, they also saw One who was able, by virtue of His divine power, to overcome the chains of enslavement. The acts and deeds of Jesus' life and ministry were literal acts and deeds, designed to provoke trust and commitment in the midst of present calamity, as the slave songs clearly demonstrated. A similar example can be seen in Thomas A. Dorsey's song "This Man Jesus":

*Jesus walked the water and so raised the dead*
*He made the meats for those saints—He multiplied the bread*
*The blinded eyes He opened and cleansed the lepers too.*
*Then died to save sinners—Now what more could Jesus do?*

*This man never will leave you—This man will not deceive you.*
*This man waits to relieve you—when troubles are bearing you down.*
*Oh, this man when danger is near you—This man is ready to cheer you.*
*This man will always be near you—He is a wonderful Savior I've found.*[5]

This song shows Jesus as actually involved in the liberation process in His earthly life—"blinded eyes He opened"—as well as transcending what occurs now for those who know Him. This illustrates how the "was-ness" and "is-ness" of Jesus are wedded in the black religious experience.

Harold Carter argues, in his book *The Prayer Tradition of Black People*, that the New Testament provided the slave community with a Christ with whom they could identify. He says, "The slave found in the person of Jesus, a savior, a friend, and fellow sufferer at the hands of unjust oppressor, who would do anything but fail."[6] Carter continues, "Doctrines about his theological nature were subordinate to this pragmatic power in life. He was experienced as a savior and a friend. There was no human condition that Jesus could not meet."[7]

At this point, you might again question how the slaves became so amenable to the Savior of those who used Him to enhance black enslavement. The answer is found in the slaves' African past.

In the African religion, God was so high that it took a plethora of mediators to help people reach God. Thus, virtually everything, both inanimate and animate, was called upon to help the African reach the most high God, and he still fell short. When the slaves were confronted with the Mediator, Jesus Christ, however, they found in Him the solution to their greatest religious problem. With Christ, no other mediator was needed to get to God.

Because Christ was the Godman, the slaves not only solved their divine problem—namely, access to the high God—but they also solved a very historical problem. Perfect humanity provided the slaves with someone who could liberate them in history from any and every kind of problem, injustice, and oppression. Sadly enough, this aspect of Christ's work was ignored and misunderstood by the broader Christian society.

Carter agrees that traditional religion from West Africa gave blacks an orientation that allowed them to adapt easily to Jesus:

> It was not hard for Black people to assign to Jesus literal powers. He "came in my sick room." He "cooled scorching fever and calmed troubled minds." He was a "heart fixer and mind regulator." He was a "lawyer in the courtroom, doctor in the sick room,

> friend to the friendless, husband to the widow, mother to the motherless, and father to the fatherless." He saved from sin, had power over the "devil," and guided his children with his eye. All these basic deeds were continually attributed to him in prayer.[8]

The reason that prayer could be made to Jesus in this manner is because His earthly life and ministry demonstrated that He cared and had the power to make a difference. The slaves found a biblical liberation in the Scripture. The African American church saw the liberation motif of the Old Testament and the teaching of the New Testament, combined with the reality of the black religious experience, as validating the existence of Christ as Savior from personal sin as well as Deliverer of the oppressed.

From a biblical perspective, the natural questions here are whether human liberation can be demonstrated to be part and parcel of Jesus' ministry and whether He can be demonstrated to be the very ground of human liberation, as black religion asserts. The answer is an unqualified *yes* on both counts. I will go deeper into this in chapter 10, but for now it is safe to say that the black church was on strong theological footing in seeing Christ as the basis for liberation from oppression. Although such recognition was not understood in exegetical formulas, it was nonetheless biblically sound and the clearest and earliest expression of this Christological theme in America.

The white church needs this Christological understanding if oneness is to be achieved. On the other hand, the contemporary African American church must make sure it does not lose its historically strong spiritual foundation as we seek to expand our social influence and impact. We must not be like Israel, which was an oppressed community in the New Testament because it was in bondage to Rome. Their Christology took them to the point where they recognized Jesus as the One with the message of the kingdom and the power to miraculously relieve their condition of oppression. Yet, when they sought to make Him an earthly king (John 6:15), He refused.

The problem was that a Christology that only leads to political, social, and economic reform is insufficient. Human liberation is part of a comprehensive kingdom agenda theology predicated on spiritual salvation. This is why Jesus said, "Repent, for the kingdom of heaven is at hand" (Matt. 4:17) and why He told Nicodemus, "Unless one is born again he cannot see the kingdom of God" (John 3:3).

Human liberation is also predicated on a willingness to obey Christ as Master. Thus, the process of liberation must be willing to incorporate the principles of Christ if it would present Christ as the leader of the struggle. This is why Jesus said to His followers, "Why do you call Me, 'Lord, Lord,' and do not do what I say?" (Luke 6:46).

Applying this to the black experience means that it is improper Christology to say that Christ is leading the struggle against American racism if He is not first enthroned in the lives of those involved in leading the liberation. The fact that liberation is taking place under the banner of Jesus Christ is not a sufficient statement in and of itself. The leadership must possess both a proper saving relationship to Christ and a proper biblical methodology before the black church can ever return to the strength it has experienced in the past.

### *The Communal Nature of the Black Church*

The historical black church also reminded the slave of who he was in the sight of God, rather than man. One who was considered a "boy" on the plantation became Deacon Jones on Sunday. An elderly woman who was known as a "girl" during the week by her mistress became Mother Smith on Sunday. The church was crucial for maintaining God's view of black dignity and significance under the hand of a good God.

The black church viewed itself as more than just a loose gathering of individuals. It saw itself as a community in which everyone was related. This communal mindset again owed its existence to the African worldview. In Africa, tribal life was family life, and family life was also religious life. E. Bolaji Idowu describes this interrelationship:

> The household grew into the compound—which is usually an oblong or circular enclosure of houses with a common space in the middle and made up in the main of the family which has been extended through procreation, through the living together of blood relations, and the addition to them of "strangers" who came or were brought to dwell among them. In such a compound, there is the central house, a shrine which is

> dedicated to the common ancestor. Worship here is undertaken by the supreme head of the extended family who is "father" or "grandfather" to the whole community. The whole community is the offspring of the ancestor as well as of the central tutelary divinity. This supreme head is entitled to his priestly function because he is the senior of the blood relations in the extended family and therefore succeeds to the priestly function which used to belong to the common ancestor from whom the family descended.[9]

Within the tribal clan, people found support, affirmation, value, protection, meaning, purpose, and guidance. All of these things were experienced in a context of love—with God at the center of tribal life.

When the slaves came to America, the new tribe, of which God was the center, was the black church. Rather than accepting the broader society's definition of church, which oftentimes lacked communal life, they reached back to their African understanding of family. This communal perspective was reflected in the way people related to each other as uncle, aunt, cousin, brother, or sister. This perspective was also responsible for the black church being a successful, beneficial brotherhood that took care of its sick, supported its widows and orphans, educated its children, and developed its independent financial base.

The parallel between the image of the church in Scripture and the communal emphasis of the black church is obvious. The church is to be viewed as a community, that is, a group of individuals inseparably linked together. In the New Testament the church is referred to as the household of the faith (Gal. 6:10), God's household (Eph. 2:19; 1 Peter 4:17), and a spiritual house (1 Peter 2:5). Christians viewed fellow Christians as fellow citizens (Eph. 2:19) and members of one another (Rom. 12:5; Eph. 4:25).

The church is further seen as a tightly knit community by the emphasis on its oneness. Although it is made up of many members, it is one body (1 Cor. 12:20) that suffers together (1 Cor. 12:26) and is fitted and held together (Eph. 4:16). Because all of its spiritual gifts come from one Lord, there is to be no schism in the one body (1 Cor.

12:3–5, 25–31). This mandate for oneness extends beyond the confines of the black church to include the body of Christ at large.

*A Natural Ministry to the Poor*

Internally, the first church began selling "their property and possessions and were sharing them with all, as anyone might have need" (Acts 2:45). This was a voluntary act, not a governmentally imposed social system, of meeting each other's needs so that there would be no unnecessary physical suffering. While the New Testament does not make it imperative that the church use the same exact method of sharing, the church is obligated to meet the physical needs of its members.

The church is commanded to provide money for poor believers' food (Acts 11:28–30; Rom. 15:25–27; 2 Cor. 8:3–4), clothing (James 2:15), and the world's goods in general (1 John 3:17). This can be done by individual members (James 2:15–16) and by the church corporately (2 Cor. 8:18–22). People who are to benefit from the church's internal outreach are those who have suffered misfortune, such as the widows who have no foreseeable means of support (1 Tim. 5:9–10), orphans (James 1:27), and the poor (1 John 3:17).

Because God gives the earthly poor great spiritual riches—namely, faith and future reward—it is an insult to God's value system to treat the poor in an inferior way. The apostle James called the early church to accountability in this area (James 2:5).

James refers to the rich Christians who are dishonoring the poor as "beloved brethren." This does not excuse their acts, but only shows that James saw that their sin of oppression had nothing to do with their salvation, which was a gift from God. They were at the same time brethren and "judges with evil thoughts" (James 2:4 NIV). Here we see that oppression is nothing new to the church, but that such activity is condemned by God and should be vigorously resisted.

The church also has a social responsibility to the broader non-Christian society: "Then, while we have opportunity, let us do good to all people, and especially to those who are of the household of the faith" (Gal. 6:10). It is the responsibility of the church to "speak the truth" about the sin of oppression to the whole culture. I talk more on the issue of the church and the poor in chapter 14.

*Biblical Civil Disobedience*

After Peter and the other apostles were freed from prison, they spoke about Jesus in the temple, a direct violation of the Sanhedrin's command for them not to teach others about Christ. When they were arrested again and brought before the council, Peter justified their violation by saying, "We must obey God rather than men" (Acts 5:29). This shows us that whenever a religious or civil ruling body (the Sanhedrin had both religious power and wide political power)[10] contradicts what God has said or commanded, we are justified to disobey its laws.

God commanded the church to be equitable and honest in its dealings with the unbelievers (1 Peter 2:12), to work honest labor to sustain oneself and family (1 Tim. 5:8), to be hospitable to strangers (Heb. 13:2), to practice justice and fairness (Col. 4:1), and to hold no social distinctions (James 2:1). Therefore, if society (or religion or government) thwarts our efforts to obey these commands, the church has a basis for godly, biblically based rebellion.

In addition, when the government fails to fulfill its divine responsibility of promoting justice (Rom. 13:1–5), then Christians have the right and responsibility to resist, as long as such resistance is within Christian behavior. Paul exhibited an act of civil disobedience; he refused to obey the command of the chief magistrates of Philippi when they asked him to leave jail after he had been illegally beaten.[11] Such an act was justified, however, because the civil authority was unjust. Paul "was trying by legitimate means to compel the Roman authorities to fulfill their God-appointed task. It is to be noted that he did not stage his sit-in because of some selfish personal claim against the authorities."[12]

The black church and the civil rights movement that it spawned, then, stands on solid biblical ground as a liberating community. However, that ground is only as solid as its biblical moorings. A task of black kingdomologists in the contemporary black church is to continue to direct and keep its teachings in tune with biblical methodology. A conspicuous absence of correct theology leads to a number of weaknesses that can plague a society, as is evidenced in the resultant effect of the embracing of a victim mentality. Applying a biblical understanding to struggles within the culture is the only example of authentic solutions that ought to be presented to the broader society on how to address social issues through the private sector.

### *The Contemporary Legacy of the Black Church*

This biblical approach should apply to all of the problems our society faces today, including housing, employment, education, and poverty. The historical black church, with little or no governmental support, was the spiritual hub that connected the community spokes of black-owned and operated businesses, the black press, black colleges, and community-based mutual aid societies. Today we can function in that same role. The black church can be the hub that turns the wheels of black community development and revitalization, as well as the foundation for racial reconciliation and true spiritual oneness in America.

The black church has deposited in its biblical legacy and cultural history the clearest model of biblical Christianity in the history of American religion. This is not because the black church is innately superior to the white church, but because it historically operated more in line with the comprehensive nature of biblical revelation and a kingdom orientation. It did so because the communities' cultural-historical roots and worldview, coupled with the reality of American slavery and racism, forced the black church to grapple with aspects of biblical revelation that were unnecessary for the majority culture to have to deal with in any comprehensive manner.

The contemporary black kingdomologist church stands on a unique pinnacle to be the visual form of the assets of incarnational Christianity: that is, Christianity that visibly displays itself in culture-wide influence, lifestyle, and social ethics. Such assets also include corporate compassion, comprehensive biblical justice, the celebrative nature of worship, holistic ministry, and an integration between the social and the spiritual.

Far from being an uneducated, erratic, and inept folk religion, the historical black church in America was the primary proving ground for biblical Christianity. It uniquely demonstrated the relationship between love and justice. It demonstrated the nature of the church as a family and community of believers rather than simply a gathering of individualized family units. The black church personified the relationship between faith and works and how that relationship transcends the personal matters of life and enters into the spheres of politics, economics, social justice, and law.

The great mosaic of the historical black church shows that there was no distinction between secular and sacred. The church demonstrated clearly that the purpose of the sacred is that it might invade the secular and transform it. It reflected and transmitted God as the epicenter of life, all of life, and it demanded that culture be called to task for any failure to recognize Him as such.

If the lessons of the historical black church are instructional for the culture at large, then they are even more so for the black community itself. If the historic black church, using biblical principles, was able to solidify us, sustain us, protect us, promote us, house us, clothe us, feed us, employ us, and represent us during the worst of times, then how much more should we now appeal to that same biblically based authority today. The black church no longer needs artificial motivators to give us dignity. We already have resident in our biblical God, African heritage, and black church experience all we need to humbly stand tall. In God's definition of us, we operate in a secure identity because who we are is rooted in a sovereign, immutable Being who has the last word about all things.

It is high time for us in the black church to operate and draw from our strengths, and for the white church to draw from and appreciate these strengths as well, rather than both groups being duped into inertia due to illegitimate perceptions that are without substance or authority. It is time for the black church to unite among ourselves again and lead the way in replacing our culture's myopic thinking with long-range, biblically based strategies designed to aggressively reverse the state of affairs in urban America.

### *The Need to Be the Church*

Challenges for uniting today in the black church do exist, and I would be remiss not to mention them. They revolve around the contemporary presence of diversity that has arisen within the black church due to the changes in the economic status of our constituencies, increased mobility, the influence of social media, and our functioning in more integrated communities. We also face the current development of internal class divisions, which present an obstacle concerning how to stay connected as a unified whole and maintain the solidarity that is a necessary component to having any lasting impact on improving the status of urban America. The current increase in the number of megachurches operating with multi-staffed ministries has produced, to some degree as well, a disconnect from the traditional "storefront" churches still in existence. Despite our many differences, though, our singleness of focus must revolve around Jesus Christ and the sensitivity He has shown to social justice and racism, even though our approach may vary greatly as to how to enact solutions.

Not only do we as the black church need to unite together in order to address the many issues plaguing our society, but we also must join hands with our white brothers and sisters, inviting them to work alongside us to impact change within the current dysfunctional trends in our community and in theirs.

The Bible stands as the only sufficient authority and source for providing the appropriate basis for the role of the church in society. Only by allowing the Bible, operating through committed Christians in both the black and white church, to be the standard by which we judge ourselves and others, can we reexperience the power necessary to be the kind of salt and light that can save a decaying society.

The church must operate across racial lines, recognize and use every legitimate avenue to change every expression or repercussion of racism, classism, sexism, and separatism, as well as all other forms of social unrighteousness. Yet, we in the black church must never allow their existence to so cripple us that we are immobilized. A generation of children simply cannot wait until other people change things for us.

In other words, no more excuses! It is time once again for the church to *be* the church.

**Notes**

1. Henry H. Mitchell, *Black Belief* (New York: Harper and Row, 1979), 109.
2. See William Banks, *The Black Church in the United States* (Chicago: Moody, 1972), 17, for a summary of the influence of the Great Awakening on the slaves.
3. See John Lovell Jr., *Black Song: The Forge and the Flame* (New York: MacMillan, 1972), for a comprehensive understanding of the music of the slave community.

4. "Story" in black religious tradition refers to the progressive activity of God within the black community whereby He works in and through them, in keeping with His biblical movement in the deliverance of Israel and development of the church, to bring about their personal and collective salvation and liberation.
5. Thomas A. Dorsey, "This Man Jesus" (Chicago: Thomas A. Dorsey Music, 1949).
6. Harold A. Carter, *The Prayer Tradition of Black People* (Valley Forge, PA: Judson Press, 1976), 47.
7. Ibid., 80.
8. Ibid., 48.
9. E. Bolaji Idowu, *Olodumare God in Yoruba Belief* (London: Longmans, 1962), 131.
10. D. A. Hagner, "Sanhedrin," *Zondervan Pictorial Encyclopedia of the Bible* Vol. 4:271–72. Hagner explains this dual role of the Sanhedrin when he says, "The Sanhedrin certainly had complete control of the religious affairs of the nation as the Mishnah indicates. The high court was the supreme authority in the interpretation of the Mosaic Law, and when it mediated in questions disputed in the lower courts, its verdict was final. Beyond this, the Sanhedrin also governed civil affairs and tried certain criminal cases under the authority of the Roman procurator. The Romans were quite content to let subject nations regulate internal affairs, but there were, of course, always limits. They, for example, would have reserved the right to intervene at will." Thus Hagner says, "The Sanhedrin had every right to prosecute Jesus for alleged crimes whether religious or civil."
11. F. F. Bruce explains why this beating was illegal. "Even if condemned a Roman citizen was exempt from flogging. By the Valerian and Porcian Laws (passed at various times between 509 and 195 B.C.) Roman citizens were exempted from all degrading forms of punishment (e.g., beating with rods, scourging, crucifixion)." *The Acts of the Apostles* (Grand Rapids, MI: Eerdmans, 1968), 322.
12. Charles C. Ryrie, "Perspective on Social Ethics," *Bibliotheca Sacra* (Chicago: Moody, 1959), 316.

## Chapter 9

# THE ROLE OF THE BLACK PREACHER

Without question the black preacher in America has been the most visible, vocal, influential, and strategic leader black America has ever had. On both a personal and corporate level he has been used to bring hope, direction, encouragement, and deliverance to a people needing all of the above and more.

Personally, I have had the unique blessing of having been influenced and encouraged by many godly and effective preachers and pastors. One such person is the Rev. Charles Brisco, the former pastor of the Paseo Baptist Church in Kansas City, Missouri. He epitomizes the historical significance and greatness of the black preacher to the black church and black community. As spiritual leader he faithfully taught his people God's Word. As community leader he served on the Kansas City school board and helped shape the school system into one of excellence and justice.

I have observed with great admiration his loving, tender care for his congregation in the way he greeted them, cared for them when they were sick, and corrected them when they needed it. One of his members summed him up endearingly when she said, "Our pastor loves us." I've also admired Pastor Brisco's commitment to his family. Whatever progress I have made as a pastor I owe in part to his influence in my life. Of profound impact was his statement to me early on in my ministry that encouraged me to remember that our people in the black community needed to be challenged at another level theologically but that delivering that challenge, even if it was critical at times, had to be done out of a heart of love and not merely as a critique or correction.

The late Tom Skinner is another black evangelical preacher who had a significant impact in shaping my preaching both in style and content. Tom entered my life as a mentor, and later became a dear friend. I was captivated early on, like everyone else, by Tom's fiery oratory, his biblical commitment, and his contemporary relevance. His preaching mesmerized black and white listeners alike with his passionately delivered evangelistic message rooted in a kingdom emphasis.

Tom Skinner possessed a courage far exceeding most, and he challenged the white establishment theologically on social issues at a time when it was grossly unpopular to do so. And yet, his commitment to a thoroughly biblical worldview led him to also challenge the black church in areas where it needed improvement as well. Tom was ahead of his time socially and theologically, and because of his presence the road was paved for people like me. He personally encouraged me in my academic pursuits because he recognized the great need for black evangelicals to be able to sit at the academic table of discussion alongside white brothers to offer a perspective on the Bible and theology that reflected the black experience and interpreted social justice through a biblical lens. Tom wanted me, and others like me, to gain access to the tools of theology that white theologians possessed in order to use them in a way, and on subject matters, that they had not previously been applied.

A number of black leaders and preachers influenced me. I could go on extensively, but two more deserve mentioning before continuing our look at the black preacher. Dr. A. L. Patterson, one of the all-time leading black preachers in America, left his mark on me in many ways. In my fiery desire to bring a strong biblically based message to the black community, Dr. Patterson personally exhorted me to never lose sight of my connection to the community I hoped to reach. He challenged me to always stay in touch through authentic relationships in order to best affirm the strengths within the black community by having seen them up close on a daily basis rather than resort to merely critiquing theological aspects that needed to be improved.

Dr. John McNeal, founder and senior pastor of Atlanta Bible Baptist Church as well as a former dean of students and professor at Carver Bible College, invested in my life as well outside of the classroom by pouring into me the conviction to not just preach the Word, but to live up to the Word that is preached.

What is the history of these godly men, and others, to whom the whole black community owes a huge debt of gratitude for their leading us from oppression to freedom? As with the black church, we will find that the roots of the black preacher lie in the African Traditional Religion.

## The Emergence of the Black Preacher

The priest in the African Traditional Religion was characterized by his ability to remember the proverbs and stories (Odu) and communicate them to the members of the tribal communities in an accurate and effective manner. He provided a link between their past and their present. The priest, then, was the embodiment of the history, culture, and heritage of the tribe. H. Beecher Hicks describes this role in his book *Images of the Black Preacher*:

> The vast power of the priest in the African state is well known; his realm alone—the province of religion and medicine—remained largely unaffected by the plantation system. The Negro priest, therefore, early became an important figure on the plantation and found his function as the interpreter of the supernatural, the comforter of the sorrowing, and as the one who expressed, rudely but picturesquely, the longing and disappointment and resentment of a stolen people.[1]

It is little wonder that the black preacher has perpetually served as a father figure to black people, seeing to their welfare in all spheres of life, whether social, political, economic, or spiritual.

### *The Black Preacher as Father Figure*

The New Testament church leaders had little trouble viewing their followers from a paternal perspective. Thus, Paul could call

Timothy his son (2 Tim. 1:2) and Titus his child (Titus 1:4). John could call Christians he was teaching his children (1 John 2:1, 12) and even explain their varying spiritual status within the framework of the different levels of family structure: namely, fathers, young men, and children (1 John 2:13–14). Thus, it is normal to hear black pastors refer to the preachers they ordain as their sons in the ministry.

Here again the African past prepared the preacher well for his posture within the Christian church. While this parental role has at times been abused by some black preachers, it has also served as the driving force behind the development and survival of the black church, in much the same way that the apostle Paul's loving, yet firm, parental role directed the church at Thessalonica (1 Thess. 2:7–12).

### *The Black Preacher as Priest*

The African priestly heritage explains the posture of the preacher as spiritual representative of black people before God. Because God is viewed as a comprehensive part of all of life, the black preacher has traditionally represented God's presence and leadership in every part of black life.

Because God is the center of all of life, Sunday morning involves every aspect of the community. Announcements, for instance, have a dominant place in black services. This announcement period facilitates the wedding between the priest, oral tradition, community life, and the centrality of God. The service gave the preacher a weekly platform with which to guide his people in the comprehensive application of faith to life. The community grapevine would assure that what was announced on Sunday would get disseminated on Monday!

The presence of the priest also provided cohesiveness for the tribe or clan. He served as the point person for their relationship with one another as well as their individual and collective relationship with God. He led them in their ceremonies and festivals, which reflected the essence of tribal life, and he served as the foundation and leader for the totality of the life, activities, and perspectives of the whole community.

Black churches became the new clans, and the black preacher was the new priest. Because access to the formal religious structures of the broader society (white denominations and educational institutions) was virtually nonexistent, black preachers were relatively free to draw intuitively on their African past for many of the elements that would become aspects of black worship. Henry Mitchell says in *Black Preaching*:

> The preaching tradition of the Black ancestors did not spring into existence suddenly. It was developed during a long and often quite disconnected series of contacts between the Christian gospel, variously interpreted, and African men and women caught up in the Black experience of slavery and oppression. To this experience and this gospel they brought their own culture and folkways. In a manner more unusual and powerful than they or we dreamed—until recent decades—they devised a Black preaching tradition. This preaching tradition consisted of the ways Blacks delivered and responded to sermons.[2]

As the African Traditional Religion required the presence of the priest to link the people to each other and to God, the various small gatherings that were part of the black church required the presence of a Christian pastor. Therefore, as these new clan gatherings developed, the roles of the African priest and the Christian pastor merged within the black preacher. The white community allowed the black preacher to have this power, because the position of a pastor who was responsible for providing spiritual leadership to local congregations was within the broader Christian structure.

The African American preacher had significant contact with Anglos and, therefore, was in the unique position to learn, analyze, and interpret their ways. His knowledge had to be communicated to the slave community in such a way as to simultaneously teach the slave about God, protect the slave against oppression, lead the community into a dualistic understanding of freedom (temporal and eternal), and stay within the framework of the social and religious boundaries of the slave master. It should be obvious why the cream of the crop rose to the position of black preacher.

Neither the slave preacher nor the developing black church was hampered in the pursuit of the God of justice because of limited access to academic training. Theology was transmitted orally, from preacher to preacher. This is the only way to explain the perpetual dissemination of the great Christian themes despite the denial of even an elementary level of education.

The Bible became the authoritative sourcebook for the preacher and his congregation's developing understanding of God. However, the Bible was not used as a means of developing an esoteric epistemology. When the black preacher opened his Bible, it was more for the interpretation of recent experience than for detailed exegetical analysis. The different preaching styles between the black and white preacher resulted from their different goals: The black preacher looked to the Bible for an ethical view of life that met the personal needs of the members of his community; the white preacher looked for an epistemological system of thought.

The black preacher, rather than being inferior, had an exceptional ability to lead, communicate, memorize, interpret the times, and link the past with the present. To think that he was able to do this with little or no formal education, opposition from the broader culture, and barely any money is nothing short of miraculous. This fact should dispel any notion of black inferiority and, to the contrary, is an argument for the scholarship of black preachers in the realm of applied theology.

## The Leadership of the African American Preacher

As I mentioned earlier, the African slave saw himself in the saga of the Jewish people, as told from Exodus through the book of Joshua. Moreover, deep in the recesses of his heart he knew that the God who broke the yoke of slavery for Israel could do the same for him. Thus, the slave structured his mental and spiritual framework to complement that of ancient Israel.

Just as the dilemma of Israel required Moses and Joshua to be great spiritual, political, and military leaders, so it was in the African American community. This perspective produced leaders from Richard Allen[3] to Martin Luther King Jr. The holocaust of slavery originally forged this union of priest and presiding officer, and the continued oppression continued the need for the man of God to lead the way.

"The black preacher has been called upon by politicians, parishioners, peacemakers and all others," said black historian Charles V. Hamilton. "He has been a natural leader in the black community. He has a fixed base, the church; he has a perpetual constituency, the congregation, which he sees assembled for at least one to two hours each week. . . . then the preacher's contact far exceeds one or two hours."[4]

The key word that summarizes the leadership role of the black preacher is *link*. He has the perpetual responsibility of tying together the old and the new. This is clearly demonstrated on the four cataclysmic fronts of the cultural transformations black people have experienced:[5]

- the transition from African freedom to American slavery;
- the transition from American slavery to American freedom during Reconstruction;
- the transition from the South to the North during and following World War I;
- the transition from segregation to integration during the civil rights movement.

This leadership role is sometimes perceived as inferior because it focuses on the social and political aspects of life in addition to the theological and spiritual. Such a position, however, results from limited criteria. There were aspects that were inferior, not because they were social or political, but because the method used did not always reflect biblical methodology. Similarly, white preachers who vehemently "contended for the faith" in their legitimate war against the onslaught of liberalism during the early part of the twentieth century did not reflect biblical methodology. Despite their academic knowledge of the Bible, it did not reflect itself in practical social terms. Thus they could argue for the virgin birth while simultaneously maintaining racism, segregation, and classism. Their methodology then operated in a very limited sphere and fell far short of biblical requirements or expectations.

The problem in both cases is a failure to be thoroughly biblical, for God has given a kingdom agenda—clear theological guidelines to govern the social, spiritual, and political issues of life.[6] Anglo Christians did not understand that African American preachers were simply bringing another issue to the theological table which needed to be "contended with," and therefore, their work was written off as social, not spiritual, and by definition inferior.

Yet the issues of slavery and inference were not merely matters of politics and states' rights. They were matters of what was right before God. There was nothing Christian about the dehumanization of one person by another. Where the Bible says, "Love your neighbor as yourself" (James 2:8), it does not mince words. There is nothing neighborly about subjecting a person to something that strips that person of dignity, freedom, and hope since all mankind is created in the image of God (Gen. 1:26–28).

Furthermore, where the Bible is a strong advocate of the family and fidelity in marriage, slave owners used sexual relations (which God had given mankind to make more image-bearers) as a tool for breeding "stock," as though the slave owners were trying to produce the next Derby winner.

The very institution of slavery in America was unbiblical since it was predicated on kidnapping, which was a capital crime (Ex. 21:16). It was imperative that the black preacher voice his concerns as a political activist—but, more important, as a man of God—on this theological issue. For such was the role of a prophet.

Although blacks were no longer wearing iron shackles after the Civil War, other shackles were still there. The new shackles were now set in writing: "Whites Only" or "Colored Restrooms Here." The "master" had also changed. He now wore a suit, and the whip was his ability to deny access to opportunity and equality. Just as the early slave preachers were to lead their people to freedom, even so the task of the preacher remains the same in contemporary America.

Such a consistent posture is not the mark of an inferior people, but rather a tenacious and determined people. We are a people who see a scarlet thread called justice in the character of God, which is so strong that it can keep a people focused and a leadership baton passing from generation to generation without wavering.

## The Uniqueness of Black Preaching

In the black religious experience, preaching is an event. Preaching in the black church thrives on the participation of the congregation. Sermons are not unilateral but bilateral. The term *bilateral* refers to the discourse going on between the preacher and the congregation, known as the "call and response pattern." The preacher initiates the conversation, and the congregation answers back with both voice and gestures. For example, when someone in the congregation raises his hand or says, "Go on!" to a point in the sermon, it serves to let the preacher know that the message or impact of his comment was received. The preacher, the Bible, and the congregation are all intertwined in a rich theological interchange.

In addition to the responses from the congregation, the black preacher engages the listeners during the sermon with questions such as, "Can I get a witness?" and "Are you with me?" With each question comes a collective response of affirmation signifying approval, acceptance, and support for his biblical proclamations.

Toward the end of the sermon, the pace will often slow down or speed up. You can tell that the interpersonal atmosphere is about to take a leap into the ionosphere of even deeper communication. The critical juncture comes when he often changes from third-person delivery to first, introducing statements such as, "When *I* think about the cross." The environment is now ripe for an exchange of personal testimony. The preacher shares that not only is the truth of the cross true because it is in the Bible, but it is true because God has borne witness of its monumental impact in the preacher's own life.

Preaching is not just a sermon. Preaching is not simply a transfer of ideology from one man to a group of people. Preaching is a verbal celebration of God and all of His glory. The preacher seeks out the best, most choice words in order to present the truth of the text in a way that propels the hearer into a new realm of discovery and spiritual growth. The preacher not only engages the mind, but also penetrates the very depth of a person's being. It is in that potent combination of delivery that the seeds of transformation embed themselves and take root.

Unfortunately many black seminarians today reduce preaching

to an academic exercise. That which has always been natural for the black preacher is often programmed for him in evangelical institutions, with the tragic result being that many exit seminary having lost their ability to preach. Black preaching is thirsty for zest. And the black congregation will demand this zest. If there is not lively, earthy appeal in the sermon, it can become difficult to preach to an African American congregation. And you cannot be an African American preacher and not preach. It is not a fair trade to gain exegetical prowess and lose the ability to maintain a vibrant, engaging connection with your congregation.

### *The Black Preacher as Communicator*

The black preacher focuses on retention rather than using notes in the pulpit. This tradition evolved from a couple of factors. The first factor is that his African heritage focused on oral communication and memorization, as I mentioned earlier.

In Africa, storytelling is used to paint pictures of life.[7] The whole culture, its history and its essence, is preserved through oral tradition and celebratory rituals. Stories are also put to melodies and expressed in songs.

Since the Bible is more than two-thirds narrative, the African American preacher is right at home with this type of material. Deuteronomy 6 advocates oral communication as an excellent way to transfer the truth of God to our children. "These words, which I am commanding you today, shall be on your heart. You shall teach them diligently to your sons and shall talk of them when you sit in your house and when you walk by the way and when you lie down and when you rise up" (Deut. 6:6–7). This is similar to African oral tradition, which naturally expressed truth in the normal movement of life. This is why it is still normal to hear black congregations shout back to their pastor during the sermon, "Tell the story," as he powerfully relates Scripture to the black experience.

The second reason the black preacher is tied to oral communication is that for years the black preacher was barred from entering the seminaries, which taught preaching as a technical process. Thus the black preacher simply maintained his heritage, which gave him a great deal of influence in his venue.

The Bible was the first book the slave learned, but in the majority of cases it was not because he could read it. He learned it through what he heard and began interpreting life through it. Even when slavery ended, the Bible remained the black preacher's comprehensive manual on all of life, because he was still denied access to institutions of higher learning. Therefore, African Americans maintained a very orthodox view of Christianity. Our worldview was not tainted by the extraneous and sometimes erroneous thoughts of the American culture.

### *Preaching as a Language Event*

The interpretational grid for the black preacher's preaching was life. Where biblical truth intersected with life (which is how the Bible was written), the black preacher opened the door to a better life both here and in the hereafter. This type of interpretational model is known as a "language event." As Richard Soulen explains, "A language event can be said to have occurred when reality becomes efficaciously present in language. Here the appearance of 'reality' is identified with the simultaneous coming into being of its 'language.' Without language there is no 'reality.'"[8]

Thus, the black preacher used language to paint pictures relevant to life. He got into the text in order to feel it, experience it, taste it, hold it, embrace it, smell it, and tell it. His words interacted with life's realities and experiences. He saw himself as the Holy Spirit's communicative agent who brought relevant application of the scriptural truths to the lives of the hearers.

There comes a time, however, when it is essential to probe the depths of biblical literature for a more precise meaning which may lie upon the pages of Scripture beneath the etymology of a certain word or beneath an ancient cultural innuendo.

The drawback in the African American community is that, traditionally, the clergy has not been trained to employ the tools of exegesis—lexicons, Greek and Hebrew languages, systematic theologies—which serve as reservoirs of knowledge to link us to the ancient culture. The objective is to obtain the meaning of a given passage.

On the other hand, we cannot camouflage bad expository preaching with Greek and Hebrew words. Academics cannot cover up bad preaching. Neither should the presentation of the truth resemble a documentary on some little-known subject on the Public Broadcasting Station. The best scenario is to fuse the uniqueness of black preaching with strong biblical exegesis. Therefore, the preacher should be both interesting and exacting—offering a relevant exposition of the text. Surely it's a crime to bore people with the Word of God.

As we can see, the language event is a very valuable tool for bringing the Scriptures to life, because it uses life as its interpretive key. But what about all those events and doctrines in the Bible that are alien to our life experience? Formal training is needed to bridge these gaps. The white counterpart of the black preacher had a decided advantage in these areas for a number of years.

Historically, black evangelicalism has sought to take advantage of both worlds. In it, the preacher acquires skills in the area of biblical exegesis, yet maintains the vast riches of our African heritage. African American clergymen need exposure to biblical study, not to make us preachers for such we already are, but to make us better preachers.

Furthermore, when an African American walks onto the campus of a predominantly white evangelical seminary, it is not as though he brings nothing to the table. He has a wealth of knowledge about preaching and leadership that should be tapped for the betterment of the body of Christ at large. When black evangelicals and white evangelicals come together, it should be a win-win situation. This is why we must graduate from traditional evangelicalism to kingdomology. Kingdomology is *the theological framework and belief system that asserts that God's purpose in history the manifestation of His glory through the establishment and advancement of His eternal kingdom on earth*. Kingdomology views this purpose as the unifying theme of Scripture that is to be accomplished progressively in history through human instrumentality over and against demonic and human opposition as mankind functions in covenant with Him. This theology finds its ultimate fulfillment in the Person, work, and kingdom rule of Jesus Christ (Gen. 1:26–27; Ps. 8:4–6; Ex. 19:5–6; Matt. 6:10, 13; Ps. 22:28).

I had the privilege of participating in this beneficial connection when I taught "Expository Preaching" at Dallas Theological Seminary while completing my doctorate degree. Most of the graduate students I taught were white. While I included exegetical and structural techniques of effective preaching, I also taught stylistic nuances and methods to help broaden the reach of these future white pastors. The students frequently commented that this taught them how to give life, energy, excitement, and relevance to their preaching.

## Worship: The Context of Black Preaching

Black preaching is set in the context of black church worship, which is formatted from the liturgy of American Christianity. Yet it is African traditionalism that gives the black church and its style of worship the freedom to improvise and innovate. For example, "Amazing Grace" sounds distinctively different when you hear it sung in an African American church compared to the way you hear it sung in a white church. I doubt seriously if the converted slave trader John Newton would have ever envisioned the black church's version of his hymn with its definitive cadence.

Henry Mitchell, author of *Black Belief*, saw three primary sources of black hymns and folk songs:

- The slaves commonly quoted biblical texts.
- They quoted white hymns, which also revealed beliefs they held dear and appropriated.
- They restated doctrines of white origin that were highly significant to them.[9]

Music has always had a significant place in the worship of Africans and their descendants. Remember that much of African Traditional Religion was transferred through hymns and songs, which resembled the Psalms of the Old Testament. The music in the black church takes on the form of the Word of God as it is sung. This notion and appreciation for the genre of song is rooted deep within the core of the African heart. Because the orientation toward the ministry of music is set in this vein, the music of the African American church has had a profound impact on the American culture at large. This is why the Negro spiritual has become such a significant part of

American life. These songs don't just entertain; they tell the story of life and the people who experienced it. They reveal the unique relationship between the person of God, the oppression of blacks, and the power of faith. These songs were to black people what history books were to whites—our link with our past.

In many cases, the music is a way of drawing people into the black church. Thus a partnership is formed between the pulpit and the choir that results in a unique form of evangelism. Few black preachers allow their sermons to conclude without giving a call to discipleship. The choir sings a song about God's grace, power, and mercy, which softens the heart of the sinner and brings him or her up front before all the church to make a confession of trusting Christ for salvation.

I mentioned earlier that the slaves dressed in their best whenever they came to church. This custom was a carryover from Africa, and can still be experienced in African religious ceremonies today. The worship of God was a celebration. It was a festive event celebrating life, which God both supplied and reigned over. For the slave, the worship service was the only time that he was free. The goodness of God could be celebrated without obstruction. Worship was his reaffirmation of hope. This aspect of celebrating God in worship is still visible in the mainline African American church.

Although slavery has ended, the theme of freedom remains. Where there is hope for freedom, there is much joy and exuberance. This joy and exuberance is evident in the music of the black church, which Henry Mitchell calls a "natural application of the principle of black freedom." He goes on to say, "If the Holy Spirit is assumed to take over the specifics of a prayer or a sermon, why not the details of a musical rendition also? Thus black worship frowns on the meticulous adherence to the printed melodic line."[10]

This mode of celebratory worship is quite biblical. Consider the tenor of Psalm 92, titled, "A Song for the Sabbath day."

> It is good to give thanks to the Lord
> And to sing praises to Your name, O Most High;
> To declare Your lovingkindness in the morning
> And Your faithfulness by night,

With the ten-stringed lute and with the harp,
With resounding music upon the lyre.
For You, O Lord, have made me glad by what You have done,
I will sing for joy at the works of Your hands.

Many homiletics departments in evangelical seminaries view the emotionalism involved in black liturgy as superfluous. Yet at the core of biblical worship is the recognition of God for who He is, what He has done, and what we are trusting Him to do. We do not see environments where the people passively sit as spectators while the "professionals" perform when we look at the pictures of worship painted throughout the Old Testament, spoken about in the Psalms, and prophesied in heaven in Revelation. Rather, the whole congregation is called to worship God, using every element of expression from shouting to dancing to praising to crying.

Because the Jews of the Old Testament have much in common with the plight of the African American, it is not unreasonable to find similarities between the two styles of worship. Exuberance and joy should not be anomalies in the worship of God. Sacredness does not necessarily imply that we have to be solemn and silent. We are not the frozen chosen. Of course, silence is appropriate on some occasions (Hab. 2:20), but when the African American considers the care and protection God supplies, especially in light of his socioeconomic plight and history, it is difficult not to be expressive.

Perhaps the same principle is at work in the parable that Christ tells in Luke 7:41–42. In the scene that precedes the parable, the Lord has dined at the house of Simon the Pharisee. At the dinner was a woman whom the Bible refers to as a "sinner" who brought a vial of perfume in order to anoint Jesus' feet. As she knelt at His feet, "she began to wet His feet with her tears, and kept wiping them with the hair of her head, and kissing His feet and anointing them with the perfume" (Luke 7:38).

It seems that Simon the Pharisee found this type of appreciation to be excessive and improper. Furthermore, this woman was a social outcast. Jesus addressed Simon's insensitivity with a parable in Luke 7:41–43:

> "A moneylender had two debtors: one owed five hundred denarii, and the other fifty. When they were unable to repay, he graciously forgave them both. So which of them will love him more?" Simon answered and said, "I suppose the one whom he forgave more." And He said to him, "You have judged correctly."

When most Anglos observe the worship style of black churches, the mode of worship often seems excessive, just as the woman's actions toward Jesus appeared to be much. But the so-called excessiveness is in proportion to the degree of thankfulness due to the God who has granted forgiveness and a promise of a better life. Therefore, it would be abnormal if we did not render our whole selves to God for the sake of worship. It is this tenet that governs the manner of worship in the black church.

This celebratory aspect of worship has even caught on among the middle and upper classes within the white community with the rise of the charismatic movement. What has become new in the white community has been normative for black worship throughout its history.

Certainly, black preaching and black worship that overemphasize emotion and performance can be distracting. If we lose our members amid a storm of confusion, "every wind of doctrine" can blow in. Culture is the vehicle, not the driver. The focus of worship must always be the presentation of truth, whether it is sung, taught, or preached. I pray that we may never glorify the package with its pretty wrapping and ignore the precious treasure inside. This is why the African American preacher must be a relevant and excellent expositor as well as a good storyteller.

## The Contemporary Status of the Black Preacher

Today the black preacher remains at the pinnacle of black community leadership, although it is not as high a peak as in days gone by. Because the black church is still the most dominant institution in black America, and because the black preacher is still its primary leader, he holds the primary role as divine representative and cultural leader.

Unfortunately, this role has diminished for a couple of reasons:

### *The New Diversified Congregation*

The black preacher ministers to a more diversified and stratified congregation. In slavery, all were slaves or severely limited by the social limitations of slavery. Not so since the civil rights movement. Diversity of opportunity has led to diversity of expertise. Thus, blacks do not all automatically look to the black preacher for leadership. In fact, a generation of African Americans do not see the church as relevant to their needs, because many pastors have failed to look to, learn from, and adequately use the variety of skills in the black church to address those needs.

Many of these pastors are limited in perspective and understanding of the needs of their contemporary constituency. They are, therefore, unable to address the complex social, economic, familial, and psychological needs and diversity of modern society. To combat this, pastors must take more seriously the apostle Paul's admonition to prepare the saints to do the work of the ministry (Eph. 4:11–12). Failure to adequately recognize and use the expertise of the congregation for the development of the church and the expansion of its ministry to the members and the community will result in increased disillusionment and a decrease in membership and the church's spiritual and social impact in society.

### *Social Overruling the Spiritual*

Another reason for the diminished role of the black preacher is that the spiritual has often taken a secondary role to the social and political in recent times. Far too many issues are fought without concern for biblical methodology, personal salvation, and theological ethics. This is one of the reasons that the success of the civil rights movement was short-lived. Even though laws were changed, hearts were not. Thus, blacks did not experience the internal spiritual changes necessary to sustain the social and political changes. Throughout black church history, personal conversion was at the root of social conversion. This is a diminished priority today, and the progress of the black church and the influence of the black preacher have suffered greatly because of it.

God is not obligated to bring about social restoration that is not predicated on His standards. Far too many social, political, and economic programs automatically expect black church endorsement and participation simply because of the programs' supposed representation of the black community. These programs want to set the agenda for the church's participation, rather than having the church, based on biblical criteria, establish a kingdom agenda for social change and community empowerment.

Critical Race Theory, for example, must be examined and critiqued based on its conformity to God's Word. Race and racism cannot be the grid for determining theology. Rather, Scripture alone must be the final arbitrator of what is legitimate or illegitimate for this and every other social theory.

In slavery, the black community had to look within itself for meaning, hope, direction, and stability. It drew exclusively from the resources provided by God in order to find the freedom it knew God had granted it. The preacher was the focal point of the community because it could not look outside itself for meaningful leadership. This allowed the black church to rise as a truly independent institution that determined its own direction and destiny under God.

This is tragically not the case today. The African American community has become, to a large degree, a dependent community. In slavery no such dependency existed, because no such dependency was available. The black preacher oversaw a comprehensive institution that clothed the naked, fed the hungry, established businesses, and took care of its orphans. Today many of those responsibilities have been handed over to the state.

Despite the areas of needed improvement, the black preacher still holds the key to the success or failure of the black community's vision of liberation. Just as he provided the comprehensive, qualitative leadership through the most tumultuous times black people have ever faced, he is still poised to accomplish that again as he uses the Bible as his primary manual for hope and freedom.

## We Will Save You a Seat

The fusion of strong biblical exegetical skills with the richly innate prowess of the African American preacher has produced a relevant interpretation of Scripture delivered in a uniquely personal and engaging manner. The shame of the situation is that so few in the body of Christ, outside of African Americans attending African American churches, will experience the full benefit of these insights and discipleship due to the continued separatism that exists within our churches today.

Throughout history, the minority culture(s) integrates into the majority culture in many aspects of life—education, business, and even religion—adopting and adapting to existing cultural norms. However, we should not require legislation in order to recognize and encourage integration among Christian brothers and sisters in the family of God. Especially when there is so much richness and depth of spirituality that can benefit all those who come into contact with it, such as is the case with black kingdomologist preachers today.

I would like to encourage my Anglo brothers and sisters in Christ to, at the least, seek out ways to be discipled and taught by black preachers in the church body—either through books, radio, TV, sermon downloads, or online viewing of sermons. I guarantee that you will be richly fed and go back for more.

But don't stop there. Be intentional in meeting your need for a broader understanding and experience of your faith by looking for ways you can worship and learn under leaders who do not always share your cultural identity or background. Look for African American churches in your area that you cannot only visit, but also attend and even join.

And if you are ever in Dallas, you can find us on Camp Wisdom Road every Sunday morning or Wednesday night. We'll save you a seat.

**Notes**

1. Quoted by H. Beecher Hicks Jr. in *Images of the Black Preacher* (Valley Forge, PA: Judson Press, 1977), from Jackson W. Carroll, "Images of Ministry: Some Correlates and Consequences," paper delivered at Emory University, Atlanta, Georgia.
2. Henry H. Mitchell, *Black Preaching: The Recovery of a Powerful Art* (San Francisco: Harper and Row, 1979), 65.

3. Richard Allen (1760–1831) was founder of the African Methodist Episcopal Church (AME), the first fully independent black denomination in the United States (1816). This came about after he and his ministry companion, Absalom Jones, left the St. George Methodist Episcopal Church in Philadelphia in 1787 over being forced to a segregated galley in the church. He then established the Free African Society (FAS), which was a mutual-aid society that assisted fugitive slaves and new migrants to the city.
4. Charles V. Hamilton, *The Black Preacher in America* (New York: William Morrow and Co., 1972), 102.
5. Ibid., 32–36. Three of the four cultural transformations are identified.
6. Each individual is responsible before God for what he says (Matt. 12:36) and does (Rev. 20:11–15, Matt. 16:27). This means that the fundamental and foundational form of human government is self-government under God. Men, therefore, are accountable to operate with a divinely informed conscience (Rom. 2:14–15). The three institutional governments (family, church, civil) are to operate in such a way that they represent and reinforce God's moral law within their prescribed roles, responsibilities, and limitations.
7. Henry H. Mitchell, "Black Preaching," *The Black Christian Experience*, Emmanuel L. McCall, ed. (Nashville: Broadman, 1972), 54–55. Mitchell summarizes why the Africans' storytelling background adapted them so well to the Bible when he writes: "Blacks took the Bible seriously, and for reasons easily traceable to their African roots. In their African roots, they had known huge quantities of memorized material. Even now, the history, which is still more sung than written, is known by anybody. In one of the festivals, if the performer makes one mistake, at least 200 people will say, "Whoa, go back." I mentioned this because even though many of these men were illiterate, they came out of a culture where people (I Fa priests) memorized thousands of proverbs. In the Yoruba religion, they have sixteen Odus. Each Odu has two hundred proverbs or stories, so that some of those Yoruba priests may know about as much verbatim as we have in the whole Bible. When you go to them for leadership, guidance, or divination, these men can call it right up. This explains to a large extent the way in which blacks adapted themselves to the Bible. The Bible was largely reflecting the kind of culture out of which they came."
8. Richard Soulen, "Black Worship and Hermeneutic," *Christian Century* (February 11, 1970), 169-70.
9. Henry H. Mitchell, *Black Belief: Folk Beliefs of Blacks in America and West Africa* (New York: Harper and Row, 1975), 97.
10. Ibid.

## Chapter 10

# THE BLACK CHURCH, BLACK POWER, BLACK THEOLOGY AND BLACK MOVEMENTS

To refer to myself as a black evangelical means that I am a man who has been doubly influenced. On the one hand I have had the distinct mark of the black experience indelibly etched on my life. That means I, like most black baby boomers, have known the good and bad of being black in America. It means I have experienced the ravages of racism while also having partaken of the great history and culture of African American life.

On the other hand it also means I have been profoundly influenced by white evangelicalism. I have studied in its institutions, interfaced with its church and parachurch organizations, and dialogued with its leadership on its epistemological and theological worldview. I have integrated many of its perspectives and values into my own life and ministry.

It is unfortunate, though, that my appreciation and legitimate pride in my race was not provided me by my study of Christian theology. Instead, it came as a result of the civil rights movement. It was not until the social revolution of this era that I, like many of my contemporaries, developed a new awareness, appreciation, and awakened self-consciousness of blackness. Until that time I lived in a sort of racial twilight zone. On one side, I was being told that I was created in the image of God and therefore had value. On a pragmatic basis, however, it appeared to me that many of the benefits of possessing that divine image were reserved for white people because it seemed that they were the real benefactors of God's kingdom on earth.

The civil rights movement provided me a new sense of being and significance. As I began to grow my Afro, develop my black salutes, and join in the James Brown refrain "Say it loud, I'm black and I'm proud," I began to raise deeper questions about the relationship of theology to the issues of race. As I mentioned earlier in the book, questions competed for answers in my mind. What did God have to say about the fact that many Bible colleges, seminaries, and mission organizations would not allow blacks to enter because of our race? What did God have to say about the Bible-teaching Southern Baptist church in Atlanta that would not allow me to join? Did God have a place for African Americans in His world, or were we an afterthought and second-class spiritual citizens, as appeared to be the case as far as American Christianity was concerned?

This dual reality of race and religion led me and a generation of my contemporaries to examine our theology without simultaneously ignoring or regretting our heritage. The struggle of relating the duplicity in what I was learning theologically from my white professors with what I was experiencing set me on a journey to examine and understand the truth from the Word of God.

## Themes Behind the Rise of Black Evangelicalism

In order to comprehend the hybrid nature of black evangelicalism and its implications for American Christianity and the African American church, it is incumbent upon us to understand the themes that led to this distinctive movement within the black church, and continue to shape it today.

Three themes in particular provide the historical, theological, and social backdrop: the conservative nature of the black church, the theological contradiction of the white church, and the influence of the black revolution, contemporary black movements, and the religious consequences.

### *The Conservative Nature of the Black Church*

The black church was *evangelical* long before evangelical arose as an official term. According to *The Evangelical Theological Dictionary*, evangelicalism is the "movement in modern Christianity, transcending denominational and confessional boundaries, that emphasizes conformity to the basic tenets of the faith and a missionary outreach of compassion and urgency."[1]

Theologically, evangelicalism stresses the sovereignty of God as the transcendent, personal, and infinite Being who created and rules over heaven and earth. Furthermore, evangelicals regard Scripture as the divinely inspired record of God's revelation and the infallible, authoritative guide for faith and practice. In addition, the person and work of Christ as the perfect God-man who came to earth as God's means of providing salvation is at the center of the evangelical Christian message.

Given these generally accepted criteria, we cannot speak of evangelicalism and exclude the African American church, which has always held to historic Protestant Christian doctrine. In fact, the black church was founded and then flourished in a conservative biblical tradition. This has been true without regard to denominational affiliation.

More formally, in 1942, J. Elwin Wright was a leading voice in the charge to join with others in establishing the National Association of Evangelicals (NAE).[2] Harold John Ockenga, the first president of the NAE, would later coin the phrase "new evangelicalism" to refer to progressive fundamentalism with a social message.[3]

The evangelical movement (entirely comprised of white theologians at that time) was born out of a need to purge fundamentalism of its sectarian, combative, anti-intellectual, and anticultural traits. It also sought to have greater influence by unifying the voices of individual Christians. One of the major focuses was gaining greater radio exposure for preachers, as well as influencing public policy on religious liberties.[4] Nestled under its umbrella were Lutherans, Baptists, Methodists, and others such as the Assemblies of God. The NAE made slow but steady gains in growth over the years, representing over 30 different denominations and 1.5 million members by 1960.

The official term "black evangelicalism" emerged not long after the NAE's inception out of a call for a clear, articulate biblical theology for the black experience combined with the necessity for a truly evangelical posture toward social issues within the black church.

Thus, black evangelicalism refers to *a movement among African American Christians that emerged out of the civil rights era and the rise of evangelicalism in the white community, which seeks to wed the strengths of the black church with an emphasis on a systematic approach to theology, ministry, and social impact.*

Yet the white evangelical community did not historically take the African American church seriously. It even encouraged black Christians not to do so either because its theological expression has been an oral tradition, rather than a literary tradition that results in textbooks and formal theological statements.

Given this tendency toward oral expression, we need only to listen to what was preached and prayed and sung.[5] In examining the narratives of Negro history and even the antebellum homilies, it is abundantly clear that the Negro Christian believed the right things about God, the right things about Christ, the right things about the Spirit, and the right things about the Scripture. He did not use the word *omnipotent*; he simply said there's nothing God can't do. The witness of Luke 1:37, "For nothing will be impossible with God," was for the black Christian an all-sufficient statement and was fully credible because Scripture attested to it. The Negro Christian did not talk about the infinity of God, but he knew "God was so high you couldn't get over Him, so low you couldn't get under Him, and so wide you couldn't go around Him," which meant precisely the same thing. He spoke biblical truth in different terminology, but the nature of his theology was evangelical.

Moreover, because blacks were not allowed to attend white schools, they were insulated from the theological controversies of the day, thus limiting the exposure to liberal theology. In the early 1900s, for instance, controversies emerged over the new liberalism, which denied the virgin birth and the inspiration of Scripture.[6] These controversies did not enter into the sphere of black religion because blacks were denied access to the higher educational institutions where such matters were discussed and debated.

For black Christians caught in a web of oppression and injustice, a much more beneficial enterprise was to formulate a theology of existence and liberation. Other issues were moot and thus deserved a mute response, especially since the formal categories of conservative theology were embedded in the African American community's worldview.

The theologian for the black church was the black preacher. Everything that was pertinent to know about God was articulated in Scripture, and that was his lone authority. If he did not believe his Bible, he could never ascend to the pulpit of the African American church. Because the enslaved black church member also had limited access to formal academic training, members were content to listen to the preacher and measure his credibility against what the Bible said.

The preacher had to be conservative in order to be the preacher. Thus, the black church was sheltered from becoming liberal through the 19th century.[7] This began to change, though, as the black church grew in size and scope. The National Baptist Convention, formed in 1895, had over 60% of all African American churchgoers in its membership. By 1916, that number was nearly 3,000,000—making the convention larger than all black religious groups and even larger than the two major white Baptist groups (NBC and SBC).[8] These entities provided a source of stability, strength, and purpose for black people. Excluded from much of the white communities, the black population rose up to provide for our own.

As Henry Louis Gates Jr., writes, "They (African Americans) were left to make their own way in a segregated world. In their darkest hour, they retreated to the safe space that had always helped them survive oppression: the church. 'You have Black churches becoming responsible for so many dimensions of Black life. . . . They are trying to meet a range of needs: educational needs, social needs, economic needs, political needs. The life of Black folks in some very significant ways is being filtered through these organizations. . . . The church has formed a nation within a nation. The church was, then at least, the single most important institution in the Black community.'"[9]

With this growth in size and scope came a variety of beliefs and values-emphases, much of which stemmed from the theological contradictions evident in both the historical and contemporary white church as well as the expansion of basic societal needs to address.

### *The Theological Contradiction of the White Church*

Liberal German rationalism began to infect white churches and their institutions early in the twentieth century. White fundamentalists fought back by establishing alternative religious institutions. These Bible colleges and seminaries sought to train a new generation of youth in conservative theology and prepare them to convert the culture back to God.[10]

As American universities and seminaries became more and more liberal, however, they simultaneously became more and more open racially. Liberal schools led the way in providing religious education to blacks. Conservative schools, on the other hand, were very slow to open their doors.[11] In order to salve their consciences for maintaining the color line, Bible colleges developed separate but equal (most times unequal) evening training programs for blacks, called "Institutes."

Black Christians exposed to these conservative training centers and the ministries that they spawned (such as Youth for Christ, Campus Crusade for Christ, the Navigators, and Young Life) developed a social/theological tension. Although African Americans were being exposed to a systematic approach to understanding the spiritual truths they had always believed, they were also faced with racial segregation, educational disparity, and theological contradictions. As C. Eric Lincoln points out, the existing white theology was a theology singularly lacking in its ability to conceive of humanity beyond the improbable boundaries of the white race—a theology which permitted and sometimes encouraged the sickness of racism and which has on occasion grossly distorted the faith through a calculated attempt to fit the whole of reality into the narrow confines of a doctrine of racial expediency and a deep-seated commitment to a racial manifest destiny.[12]

While white evangelicals nodded their heads toward racial reconciliation through "Race Relations Sundays" and the like, the results were short-lived or superficial at best. In fact, during the season when the black church stood together the most and could have used the support of white evangelical leaders the most, the white evangelical movement kept its distance. "Jerry Falwell gave his 'Ministers and Marches' speech, in which he condemned Martin Luther King Jr. and other ministers engaged in protesting and marching for civil rights, on March 21, 1965, the same day on which King and other black and white ministers were walking across the Edmund Pettus Bridge in Selma, Alabama. Falwell criticized the civil rights movement, declaring that 'preachers are not called to be politicians but soul winners.' He would later apologize for the sermon. . . ."[13]

Black evangelical forerunner Tom Skinner, whom I will speak about more fully in the next chapter, lost considerable influence and support from the white evangelical movement when he addressed the glaring issues in the white Christian movements in a speech titled, "The US Racial Crisis and World Evangelism." Skinner delivered this one-hour talk at the popular InterVarsity Christian Fellowship event called Urbana 70 Student Missions Conference, attended by thousands of white evangelical Christians and roughly 400 African Americans. In his talk, Skinner stated the following:

> Understand that for those of us who live in the black community, it was not the evangelical who came and taught us our worth and dignity as black men. It was not the Bible-believing fundamentalist who stood up and told us that black was beautiful. It was not the evangelical who preached to us that we should stand on our two feet and be men, be proud . . . and that God could work his life out through our redeemed blackness. Rather, it took Malcolm X, Stokely Carmichael, Rap Brown and the Brothers to declare to us our dignity. God will not be without a witness.[14]

Earlier, he had declared,

> To a great extent, the evangelical church in America supported the status quo. It supported slavery; it supported segregation; it preached against any attempt of the black man to stand on his

> own two feet. And where there were those who sought to communicate the gospel to black people, it was always done in a way to make sure that they stayed cool. "We will preach the gospel to those folks so they won't riot; we will preach the gospel to them so that we can keep the lid on the garbage pail."[15]

The same group of people who advocated "the unity of the body" from Ephesians 4:4–6 was also practicing racial disunity. The implicit message was: Let's win their souls, but not value them as people. Unfortunately, this is the exact same sentiment I frequently still hear today. It was expressed as recently as 2021 by the newly elected SBC President, Ed Litton, in a national interview aired by CNN centered on discussing racial issues. In the over six-minute interview, Ed kept returning to the need to "be about the gospel." He summed up his stance by stating the all-too-familiar "save their souls" motif. He said, "It's basically recognizing that people of color in our communities are created in the image of God . . . it's our mission to help get that gospel message to everybody."[16]

While I fully support and stand behind "being about the gospel" message as a believer in Christ, what I do not want us to neglect in our zeal to take the message of the gospel is our call to simultaneously live out the scope of the gospel as we do. Otherwise we are offending the truth of the gospel as the apostle Paul stated. The scope of the gospel includes being intentional about racial unity and equity (Gal. 2). As you recall from where we looked at this more fully in chapter 3, the apostle Paul called Peter on the carpet on his own racial disunity, saying that he had not been straightforward as to the truth of the gospel (Gal. 2:14). To ignore, dismiss, marginalize, or degrade the ongoing plight of "people of color in our communities" through action, word or inaction while trying to "save their souls" is a limited view of the scope of the gospel (Isa. 1:17; Mic. 6:8; Matt. 7:12; Ps. 82:3; Matt. 23:23). Racism is a gospel issue because racism is an affront to the truth that all of us are created in the image of God, and through the salvation of Jesus Christ, become "one new man" in Him. While the content of the gospel gives the believing sinner forgiveness of sins and the free gift of eternal life, the scope of the gospel transforms the personal life and human relationships as it restores human dignity on earth.

Regrettably, not as much has changed over time as we would like to think. As the graduates of these earlier institutions once trekked to the ends of the earth to fulfill the Great Commission of Acts 1:8, they successfully overlooked the Jerusalem, Judea, and Samaria in their own backyard, a focus still prevalent today. In fact, back then even, most mission societies would not even receive black graduates as candidates, whether they were qualified or not, to go "save the souls" of others.

White evangelical theologians understood well the theology of Ephesians 4, but functioned as though these instructions had been given by Immanuel Kant[17] and not the apostle Paul through the agency of the Holy Spirit. It became increasingly apparent that while African Americans could learn systematic formulas for understanding the Bible and theology in these institutions and seminaries, we could only find limited meaningful relationships and empowerment there. Integration came clothed in the isolation of being the lone "black," often viewed as a representation of all black people while at the same time muffled in any real expression of personality or thought. We were allowed in the room, but not given a seat at the table.

It also became evident to most Christian blacks that we were never going to be fully accepted in the broader white evangelical structure throughout the nation. We had been granted a ticket to access another world, but that ticket only opened the door to the stairwell leading to the balcony once again—a balcony ripe with the resultant effects of feeling patronized, marginalized, tokenized, and stereotyped. Essentially, integration meant little more than assimilation.

Unfortunately some black evangelicals thus made the mistake of viewing our own history, culture, and church experience through the lens of white theology. This was a disaster for many as a large number joined whites in assessing Christian blacks as being an "ignorant, uneducated, overemotional group of people." The result of the contradiction within the white church was a contradiction within many Christian blacks as well. This led to an alienation from the very community to whom we had been called to minister and who also had given us birth while supplying us with the rich strengths so greatly needed in the body of Christ at large.

### *The Influence of the Black Revolution*

With the rise of the Negro revolution,[18] which later became known as the black revolution, a community-wide effort developed to change comprehensively the sociopolitical situation in America. Again, the African American church was called upon to provide leadership and cohesiveness to the movement that became a clarion call for identity and empowerment.

An understanding of the black revolution and the subsequent development of a theological and political school of thought is relevant to us not only from an informational standpoint but from an applicational standpoint in how black evangelicalism has been influenced, and at present, why "evangelicalism," and particularly what has come to be known as "white evangelicalism,"[19] has come under fire in a large portion of black Christian culture as nothing more than "Christian nationalism." As Eric Mason explains, "Over the past few years, there's less and less clarity about what it means to be an evangelical. The term has taken on a political agenda that has become disturbing for many."[20]

Mason states elsewhere, "There's so much pain involved with Evangelicalism that the chance to redeem the ideology has lost its fervor. So, now it's kind of like I don't want to redeem the term—I just want to redeem the word 'Christian.' I would rather redeem a word that's in the Bible than a created socio-theological construct which Evangelicalism doesn't realize that it is."[21]

## The Backdrop of the Black Experience

Comprehending the intricacies behind the emergence and existence of the black revolution can be done only by recalling the backdrop of the black experience. This backdrop cannot be denied and should not be underestimated as to its place in the formation and development of not only the black revolution, but also a political agenda, black power, a theological school of thought, black theology, and an expositional approach to theology and ministry.

All have risen out of the post-slavery fumes rife with racist structures held in place by unwritten and written codes of conduct. Police forces armed to uphold unjust laws as well as fire hoses used to intimidate, crush, or even kill placed the backdrop in a frame of oppression. But as Martin Luther King Jr. bellowed on his last night on earth, "There was a certain kind of fire that no water could put out."[22]

This fire enflamed the African American canvas during the black revolution, igniting it with colors of Afrocentric art, literature, music, and ministry. It was during this period that "Negroes," who were previously known as "colored," became "black." That is, the black community no longer viewed itself in terms of the broader white definitions, but sought to define itself. This new self-consciousness gave rise to everything from new hairstyles and dress to a renewed interest and examination of African history and culture. Black people were going to determine for ourselves who we were and where we were going.

*The Birth of Black Power*

On February 1, 1960, four students from the Negro Agricultural and Technical College in Greensboro, North Carolina, were refused coffee at a local variety store because of their color. In an act of rebellion, they sat at the counter until the store closed. This was the beginning of sit-ins that spread across the South. These protests rested on the heels of the Supreme Court decisions on voting and school desegregation as well as the Montgomery bus boycott.

By the summer of 1960, the status of black Americans had become a burning issue on the national conscience. A growing preoccupation with civil rights had infiltrated every aspect of the black community. By the mid-1960s, large demonstrations across the country began taking place to force the issues of justice and equality and to protest the violence done to blacks. The "white backlash" of the Civil Rights Act of 1964 only increased through violent acts of physical, social, and economic oppression.

An example of this occurred in the life of a man named Amzie Moore. Amzie Moore opened the only black-owned petrol station in the Mississippi Delta around that time. Threats against his life and his family ran rampantly like a broken fuel line flirting with the spark of a society enflamed by subjugation. A rifle leaned against the wall near the rear window, ready to fend off any enraged whites. Guarding, not just managing, his business was a twenty-four-hour job similar in risk to an active-duty soldier on the front lines of a war.

A few years later in the same town of Greenwood, a young man named Stokely Carmichael gave birth to a term for what Amzie, and countless others, had spent his sweat and strength attempting to do. Stokely called it "black power." Stokely had joined with Martin Luther King Jr. and Floyd McKissick (leader of the Congress of Racial Equality) in a Freedom March through Mississippi. This March was originally begun by James Meredith, who was sidelined from the March having been shot by a sniper.

Released from jail for the twenty-seventh time for his involvement with the civil rights movement, Stokely poetically reframed the call to freedom in June of 1966 by declaring that he would not go to jail again. His was no longer a fight for freedom on paper; what he wanted was black power.

Black power called for opportunity to rid oneself of the constraints brought on by an internal imperialism. It called for black businesses to begin, a community of black Americans to unite, and a removal of the dependency caused through indirect rule and psychological and physical oppression. I was sixteen years old when blacks around our nation were urged to redefine ourselves based on our own heritage, values, and goals. Structural sins of separate but unequal segregation, educational disparity, and economic limitation offered no real option of forward progress for an entire group of individuals. On one hand, freedom dangled tantalizingly before us, urging us to pursue all that we knew we could become. Yet when tasted, the carrot came laced with the poison of a prejudicial sociopolitical structure.

Stokely communicated that day in Greenwood that deliverance from a societal system of racism through such things as a Civil Rights Act drafted in pen and ink was not the same thing as freedom itself. Just like the proclamation of liberty etched on the steely side of our nation's bell did little to ensure liberty for all, the Civil Rights Act of 1964, while accomplishing much in ending government discrimination, did little to propel society to follow suit. Deliverance is not freedom. Deliverance is the opportunity to pursue freedom. This opportunity would not be maximized, according to the leadership pointing the way for black liberation in America, apart from a call to empowerment through black power.

### *The Emergence of Black Theology*

A year after giving what black people as a whole had been seeking for hundreds of years a public and more official name, "Black Power," riots broke out in Detroit. The Detroit riots of 1967 significantly impacted a young theologian named James Cone. When the riots broke out, Cone was teaching in Adrian, Michigan, at Adrian College after having studied at Garrett Theological Seminary and Northwestern University. Having been called to the ministry at the tender age of sixteen, Cone already wrestled with questions concerning his upbringing in Beardon, Arkansas, and its relationship to biblical truth. Was the God of grace that he had learned about at the Macedonia African Methodist Episcopal Church the same God of the roughly eight hundred white people in Beardon who saw him no higher than a servant, and whose church he dared not visit?

Cone later reflected on these days in Beardon by saying that life in his hometown "meant attending 'separate but equal' schools, going to the balcony when attending a movie, and drinking water from a 'colored' fountain. It meant refusing to retaliate when called a n—— unless you were prepared to leave town at the precise moment of your rebellion. You had no name except for your first name or 'boy.'"[23]

Cone's unwavering faith led him to question these inconsistencies. He later summed up his intellectual and spiritual struggles when he wrote,

> The conflict between faith and suffering was exacerbated by the fact that most of the brutality inflicted upon black people was done by white persons who also called themselves Christians. Whites who humiliated blacks during the week went to church on Sunday and prayed to the God of Moses and of Jesus. Although blacks and whites expressed their faith in their separate worship services in quite different ways, the verbal content of

> their faith seemed similar. That was why many blacks asked: How could whites be Christian and yet do such horrible things to black people? And why does God permit white people to do evil things in the name of Jesus Christ?[24]

These existing contradictions, intensified by the urgency of the Detroit riots, redirected Cone's plans to return to graduate school to pursue another PhD, this time in Literature at the University of Chicago, which he had intended to use in hopes of altering the national landscape through the power of story. Instead, Cone set out to put in writing a system of theology that spoke to the black experience in America. Cone's immediate vision for his future had changed as he confronted the truth that God could not be indifferent to the inequality he experienced as a child. Nor could God be indifferent to the raping of black women, lynching of black men, burning and bombing of black churches, and the ghettoizing of the minds of black children. The problem was, however, that the classical theological disciplines he had studied in seminary did not speak to those realms. It taught him about existentialism, neoorthodoxy, and fundamentalism. It taught him about the council of Nicaea and the Reformation, but no one was talking about the targeted oppression of black people in America.

James Cone concluded that what was needed was a current and more complete way of looking at theology that would emerge out of the dialectic of black history and white culture. The major question he set himself to answer through a study of God's Word was: What has the gospel to do with the black struggle for liberation?

Questions such as this one were raised not only in the spirit of James Cone but in the soul of the black church and community as a whole. They were questions that traditional Christian responses could not answer. Questions included:

> How could Christian whites maintain a clear conscience while using their religion to methodically oppress and strip human dignity from African Americans from the time of slavery through the 1960s?

> How was God involved in what was taking place within the society of the oppressed, and what was He sanctioning the black community to do about it?
>
> What would a life no longer dependent on the agencies, government, and other entities of the white power structure look like?

Questions like these echoed in the collective core of the black mind. While evangelicals would do well to listen to James Cone in the areas where he has argued correctly, we must also recognize the areas of disagreement. Primarily, Cone's black theology greatly overemphasized the black situation of oppression to the point of compromising biblical truth. It also focused heavily on racism to such an extent that no real basis for reconciliation was afforded. Likewise, Cone's interpretation of the relationship of Jesus Christ to liberation failed to integrate it into the whole of God's salvific purpose for mankind.

It became common to hear black people referring to Christianity as a "white man's religion" that failed to address the sum total of experiences, institutions, actions, mentality, and conditions that affected black people in their journey from slavery onward. White religion did not recognize that to grow up black in the structures and definitions of a white-dominated society is distinctly different from growing up white. Without that awareness, there resulted a failure to ascertain the participation of God in the framework of black life.

Black theologians no longer spent time addressing epistemological issues as they had been taught to do for so long, but rather a focus shifted in the black conscience to the ethical outworking of the orthodox epistemological conclusions. Rejecting the concept that Christ was concerned with the black soul while ignoring black oppression, Christian leaders influenced by the black revolution sought to define a biblical, holistic theology of hope. A nascent awareness arose for the need to develop a unified thrust to bring about true liberation and not only a spiritual liberation that will be realized upon reaching heaven.

This component of theological clarification presented the option of a more biblically sound and socially relevant eschatology to that existing in the realm of white theology. Earth, rather than heaven, became the major focus of the church. Having a previous eschatological emphasis on the future had been a common thread throughout African American Christianity, given to it by the teaching of those who sought to subdue any hint of autonomy against them. Wrestling with these and other issues, James Cone wrote,

> White missionaries persuaded most black religious people that life on earth was insignificant because obedient servants of God could expect a reward in heaven after death. As one might expect, obedience meant adherence to the laws of the white masters. Most black people accepted the white interpretation of Christianity, which divested them of the concern they might have had about their freedom in the present.[25]

This perspective changed as a result of the black revolution. Songs such as "We Shall Overcome" replaced heaven-only-focused spirituals such as "I Know the Other World Is Not Like This." A shift was made to no longer wait for a New Jerusalem, but to also strive toward the creation of new cities in the here and now. Eschatology was no longer viewed as an escape hatch that allowed the believer to live without taking seriously the need for helping to shape the earth into what it ought to be. What was not being presented was an idealistic view that this task would be accomplished entirely, for that won't be done until Christ comes back. However, what was being raised at this time in the minds of black theologians was that the church had the responsibility to demonstrate God's justice and righteousness in the world now.

Toward this end, in June of 1969, what came to be known as the "theological arm" of black power was released in a "Statement by the National Committee of Black Churchmen." This statement, largely authored by Cone, set in motion the public intellectual structure already innate in black culture, while giving it the name of black theology. It read,

> Black Theology is a theology of black liberation. It seeks to plumb the black condition in the light of God's revelation in

> Jesus Christ, so that the black community can see that the gospel is commensurate with the achievement of black humanity. . . . The message of liberation is the revelation of God as revealed in the incarnation of Jesus. Freedom IS the gospel. Jesus is the Liberator![26]

Black theology did an essential job in raising and addressing crucial questions that for too long had been overlooked by white American Christianity. It awakened the American theological world to the reality that oppression is an evil affront against God's person and activity in history. It affected the black church profoundly, propelling it forward toward a greater understanding and ability to look after community needs effectively. It reminded all people that theology must find a relevant demonstration in society, that the God of the Bible is not too highly removed that He is not also a God of everyday miry and mucky realities, and that His heart for the suffering and for the poor should be our own.

The black revolution had given rise to a political and theological revolution in black power and black theology that attempted to wrap its systematic arms around the relationship of Scripture to the experience of what it means to be black in America. Concerns were addressed in order to construct an interpretation of Scripture in light of the black experience that spoke to the black soul. Students of the Bible sought to find an integrating point between the oppressed condition of the black community as a whole and the God who is at work freeing the oppressed.

A proper understanding of the black revolution, black power, and black theology is not simply helpful from a historical vantage point, but for contemporary application as well in our church and society at large. Health care reform, immigration reform, bailouts, stimulus packages, climate control, voter suppression, economic disparity, cancel culture, criminal justice reform, and police reform headline the current debate between capitalism and socialism.

This, and other like issues, have been served on the table of contemporary relevance, reemerging to dominate every major news station while becoming the topic of choice around water coolers, on talk shows, and in our church lobbies. In 2008, fueled by the fiery words of an even more fiery preacher named Jeremiah Wright in support of the election of our first African American president, Black Liberation Theology was reawakened as a sleeping giant ready to ask everyone who has ears to hear: How far have we come? The answer to that question varies depending on who steps up to address it but it is a question that has only gained momentum in its asking and need to be addressed, especially over the last few years with the continual rise of a focus on Critical Race Theory, systemic racism, NFL players' national anthem protests, divisions within Christendom and large denominations such as the Southern Baptist Convention, and an exodus from evangelicalism en masse.

## Contemporary Black Movements

On May 25, 2020, the racial conflict in America rose to a whole new level with the very public murder of George Floyd. His death brought about by a white police officer kneeling on his neck was filmed on a cell phone for the world to see. It ignited a racial firestorm throughout America and beyond. Floyd's death was the proverbial straw that broke the camel's back as people black, white, and brown took to the streets in protest, lament, and grief over a past whose effects, both covert and overt, are yet to be addressed or healed.

And while data can demonstrate differing assertions on whether blacks face a higher amount of police brutality than whites or not, the historical root embedded within the systems remains in the DNA of our core. For those who felt that the national outcry of peaceful protests and lamenting displayed online (not the riots) were too much of a display for a man who was a former criminal, let NFL player Benjamin Watson's words help you to understand the collective feeling when we saw what we did. Watson writes,

> White people have no idea of the fear that black people feel toward the police. I cannot say that strongly enough, loudly enough, or forcefully enough. I believe it is a huge point of division between black people and white people. Black people have little expectation of being treated fairly by police in any situation. We have a high expectation of being demeaned, abused,

> and possibly treated violently in any encounter with law enforcement. We have a history that supports this, news headlines that shout this, and personal experiences that confirm this. This is a reality that white people simply don't know.[27]

We need to be careful to keep in mind that while the statistics certainly support that every issue in our nation is not "race-based" nor are the laws any longer overtly enforcing racist structures, the sensitivities are still there because of our shared history. It is this which can make things feel like they are systemic racism or racist, even if intentions may not be. We would do well to be compassionate to these sensitivities in others rather than dismiss them out of hand because we may not agree with their conclusions.

The heartbreaking and stark visual of police brutality that May day in Minnesota catapulted this pain to the public arena on full display. The discourse of social justice dominated our conversations more than it had in a long time, posing questions of: What is it, and Who is responsible to carry it out? One such group that stepped forward to address these questions was Black Lives Matter.

## Black Lives Matter

The focus and support of the mantra *Black Lives Matter* is legitimately born out of tragedy. It originally came to a more formalized structure in 2013 and rose on the national scene after the events of Ferguson, Missouri, and Michael Brown's death.[28] It rose to global prominence after the death of George Floyd. The movement highlights the injustices against black lives in much the same way that white evangelicals emphasize that the lives of unborn babies matter.

The Black Lives Matter movement essentially has two aspects. There is the informal movement by those who stand up for injustice against black lives, using peaceful protests and education to bring about healthy cultural and police reforms. There is also the official organization, trademarked as Black Lives Matter, and founded by Patrisse Cullors (who has since resigned amid controversy), Alicia Garza, and Opal Tometi. The formal entity of Black Lives Matter advocates key elements of an agenda that cannot be supported by serious Christians. It rejects the primacy and protection of the nuclear family while promoting the acceptance of gay and transgender lifestyles.[29] In addition, the founders openly embrace an ideological framework of Marxism, an anti-theistic movement.[30] The Black Lives Matter focus has merit in the overarching mission of social injustice for black lives in particular, an oft-overlooked aspect of social reform. But like all social movements, Black Lives Matter must be examined, analyzed, and critiqued against the backdrop of God's inerrant Word.

## Critical Race Theory

In the wake of the collective upheaval taking place, the Black Lives Matter movement also gave fresh legs to Critical Race Theory, which now stands tall at the core of today's racial debate. I want to explore CRT more fully since it seems to dominate the interviews, talk shows, and dialogue in much of our nation at the time of this writing.

Unfortunately it seems as though there are as many definitions for CRT as there are people discussing it. You might understand a bit better if I were to compare it to fireworks exploding on the 4th of July. Fireworks are shot up into the air and burst into a million separate flames. They start off as solid but once the explosion occurs, it all spreads. You can no longer see what was originally launched because what was originally launched has exploded.

This is what has happened to the issue of race in America, and to Critical Race Theory in particular. An explosion has occurred from an original theory that left everybody asking, "What in the world is CRT, anyhow?" It's become hard to find a definition of it that everyone seems to understand or agree upon because of the explosions that have taken place (the iterations and various nuances). So, I'll define CRT succinctly for our discussion at hand by giving you what many of the originators say it is, or was intended to be, when it was created.

Critical Race Theory may be defined as *a post-civil rights social theory that demonstrates how unjust laws have served as the embedded foundation and filter through which racist attitudes, behavior, policies, and structures have been rooted and continue to influence the fabric of American life, politics, and systems, even after those laws were changed.*

CRT proponents view race as a social construct created to expand or protect power and control. It also holds that the foundation of society's institutions and power structures are based on white privilege. Proponents frequently contend that these institutions and structures are inherently racist in that they are consciously or subconsciously used to maintain and expand the economic and political power of white people at the expense of people of color.[31] Proponents of CRT also contend that storytelling and narrative-based knowledge is a leading element in changing cultures, affecting worldviews, and even addressing systemic issues. One of the leading CRT theorists, Kimberlé Crenshaw, defines it as "a way of looking at law's role platforming, facilitating, producing, and even insulating racial inequality in our country."[32]

Never has there been a more volatile subject separating schools, school boards, churches, denominations, organizations, businesses and even personal relationships through heated emotions and often verbal vitriol. Which is also why I have chosen to examine more fully the historical definition by those who created it to offer context to the conversations at hand. In his own words, one of the founders of CRT, Derrick A. Bell Jr. ,[33] said it is

> a body of legal scholarship . . . a majority of whose members are both existentially people of color and ideologically committed to the struggle against racism, particularly as institutionalized in and by law. Those critical race theorists who are white are usually cognizant of and committed to the overthrow of their own racial privilege.[34]

CRT is said to have germinated as early as the 1960s and 1970s but more formally in the late 1980s, according to Angela P. Harris. She writes that it came about as a mixture of Critical Legal Studies (founded in Wisconsin in 1977) and civil rights scholarship, in hopes of revitalizing "scholarship on race" and correcting the "deconstructive excesses of CLS."[35] Angela writes, "CRT's ultimate vision is redemptive, not deconstructive."[36]

While having ties to Critical Legal Studies, CRT has its own distinctions, particularly regarding approaches to reform as well as caution toward liberal policies. One of the founders, Law Professor

Patricia Williams, emphasizes a key difference "when she acknowledges as example that the paper-promises of enforcement packages like the Civil Rights Act of 1964 have held out as many illusions as gains."[37] Essentially, this difference points out that while laws preventing and prohibiting systemic racism as well as promoting racial equality were passed and enacted by our government (an intended outcome for followers of CLS), due to the underlying nature inherent in culture and collective thought, the positive outcomes of these laws didn't always come to pass.[38]

Critical Race Theory gained its official standing in 1989 in Wisconsin at the first annual workshop on Critical Race Theory. According to historian Ibram X. Kendi, "Several dozen legal scholars met at a convent outside of Madison, Wisconsin, on July 8, 1989, as Public Enemy's 'Fight the Power' topped Billboard charts. They came together to forge an antiracist intellectual approach known as *critical race theory.* Thirty-year-old UCLA legal scholar Kimberlé Williams Crenshaw organized the summer retreat the same year she penned 'Demarginalizing the Intersection of Race and Sex.'"[39]

Kendi continues, "Derrick Bell, Alan Freeman, and Richard Delgado, the early formulators of *critical race theory* in law schools, were also in attendance at the 1989 summer coming-out party for *critical race theory*. One of the greatest offshoots of the theory was critical Whiteness studies, investigating the anatomy of Whiteness, racist ideas, White privileges, and the transition of European immigrants into Whiteness. Critical race theorists, as they came to be called, joined antiracist Black Studies scholars in the forefront of revealing the progression of racism in the 1990s."[40]

Critical Race Theory, much like Critical Legal Studies, focused on how systems served the interests of the wealthy and powerful. But Critical Race Theory differed from Critical Legal Studies in that it did not fully embrace political liberalism, seeing liberalism as unable to truly rectify issues of injustice in society. Professor Derrick Bell stated in his lecture entitled "Who's Afraid of Critical Race Theory?" that CRT's "writing and lecturing is characterized by frequent use of first person, storytelling, narrative . . . and the unapologetic use of creativity. The work is often disruptive because its commitment to antiracism goes well beyond civil rights, integration, affirmative action and other liberal measures." Bell went on to say that CRT's adherents "are highly suspicious of the liberal agenda, distrust its method, and want to retain what they see as a valuable strain of egalitarianism which may exist despite, but not because of, liberalism."[41]

CRT contends that racism has embedded itself in schools, curricula, law enforcement, the legal system, the military, corporations, target marketing, districting, medical industries, infrastructure, and civil government. CRT holds that the virus of racism has comprehensively infected the entirety of American society and must, as a result, be comprehensively addressed.

Three prominent features of CRT involve *interest conversion* (also known as *convergence theory*), *whiteness as normative*, and *intersectionality*. I go into *whiteness as normative* previously in this book but essentially it refers to a mindset that places the "white perspective" as the normative perspective to view all things. It is the grid through which human attributes and behaviors are measured, using whiteness as the "neutral" cornerstone and standard. Also, briefly, interest conversion was brought to public discourse in 1980 when Professor Derrick Bell analyzed why *Brown v. Board of Education* was decided favorably for blacks in 1954 as opposed to any other time period previously in which it had ardently been fought for. His assessment was that this period of time lent itself to desegregation because the white population in power wanted to reduce the threat of internal disruption and rebellion by returning black veterans who had fought alongside white soldiers for the concept of "freedom" in the Korean War. In addition, they wanted to facilitate economic development in the South which was, at that point, being stifled by segregation. In his own words, "the interests of Blacks in achieving racial equality will be accommodated only when it converges with the interests of Whites."[42]

Intersectionality is the view that *an oppressive reality can intersect or connect with other forms and sources of oppression (i.e., class, gender, language, disability) that then places a person at risk of experiencing multiple forms of trauma and oppression*. It argues that an individual's social or personal experience combines to produce different "intersections" of either discrimination or privilege, but that this happens to a greater degree in the lives of the marginalized and poor.

These are not the only features in CRT but they are three of the most-discussed currently, and which you may have heard or be familiar with. CRT proponents often declare that white supremacy, white power, and white privilege are at the root of our nation's historical and contemporary social ills. Writings or lectures frequently claim that this embedded racism is overtly seen in things like police brutality, the effects of redlining, and gerrymandering. They purport that racism is also passive-aggressively manifested in microaggressions. *Microaggressions* involve the sending of racially coded messages, denigrating messages, and actions that insult, stereotype, dismiss, or demean others—minority ethnic groups in particular, but can also apply to other subgroups like the disabled or "English as a Second Language" speakers.

CRT proponents state that even though many of the unjust laws were changed, the systems had already been infiltrated with the previous disparities and prejudices. In this way, the effects of those laws did not automatically, and to varying degrees through today, change with it. So, the fruit (like Adam's sinful fruit manifest in humanity) of unrighteous laws still express themselves in the structures of our contemporary society. One argument of CRT today is that many people still have to struggle with the issue of racism, not because it's a law, but because we live in an environment that was affected by unjust laws, and its ripples still reach our shores.

Take, for example, the law established in the 1930s known as *redlining*.[43] This law was created in order to segment populations by location. It's called *redlining* because zones that were drawn in red indicated a hazardous community environment. A hazardous community meant that mortgages would not be loaned out to home buyers. It meant that businesses would not invest in the development of the area. It meant many things. But what it meant the most was that a certain segment of society found themselves stuck in the Red Line Districts. Generations were born into those districts allowing for the repercussions of the redlining to be transferred from one generation to another. They were, by and large, locked out of segments of society which would have allowed them better opportunities to advance.

At this time, redlining laws do not exist based on race. But that does not mean the influence of those laws do not affect people today. Many people were never able to get out of these zones due to poor education, unstable environmental exposure, economic deprivation, poor education, and an inability to see beyond the red line drawn in the sand.

Lines have been drawn today as well. Different lines. Lines between people of all political, social, racial, and educational differences regarding the legitimacy of these movements and social theories which seek to highlight generational disenfranchisement. Debates rage concerning to what degree they should be taught, funded, resisted, or rejected outright.

While I contend that some of the observations and approaches of CRT are rooted in truthful historical analysis as it seeks to address the insidious racism carried out through overt and covert words and actions, as well as the ineffective policies enacted under the banner of "colorblind" laws of the past and present, its foundation is wrong. I say that its foundation is wrong because the grid on which it exists is based on a sociological perspective rather than a theologically sound kingdom agenda worldview. While racism is an evil sin severely condemned by God, it is neither the first sin, the only sin, nor the defining classification of sin. Idolatry, which is always rooted in pride, is the superintending sin in Scripture. Racism is certainly one major humanistic evil expression of the sin of idolatry since it is an attack on the value of the image of God in which all mankind of every ethnicity is created. On the other hand, the debate on the legitimacy of CRT should not be used for ignoring or shutting down legitimate interaction on the ongoing problem of race and racism in America.

## The 1619 Project

No official curricula of study have been produced by CRT at the time of this writing (it in itself is a theory to be used as an approach to studying subjects and examining constructs in higher education). But a confluence of iterations and interpretations have been introduced into schools and businesses through a variety of other learning tools. One of these is The 1619 Project Curriculum.[44] These have met with harsh resistance. Over 50 political bills in 24 states have been presented to restrict what educators can teach on race and slavery at the time of this writing.

Using the framework of CRT, the 1619 Project was created in August 2019 by Nikole Hannah-Jones with contributors from the *New York Times* and the *New York Times Magazine*. The journalism project argues that the very existence and establishment of America was rooted in the purpose of protecting the institution of slavery that they say began, not in 1776, but in 1619 with the first group of slaves arriving in Jamestown, Virginia. While the year of the first slaves to arrive in America is debatable (some placing it as far back as the early 1500s and some arguing that the individuals in 1619 were indentured servants), the issue of dates isn't the most alarming. The 1619 Project contends, among other historically inaccurate statements, that the American Revolution was fought in order to preserve the institution of slavery, a glaringly wrong conclusion that has brought it a tremendous amount of intellectual criticism.[45] Many historians have criticized its historical validity in other areas as well.

## 1776 Unites

In addition, reactionary movements to CRT and The 1619 Project Curriculum have arisen within the broader white culture, particularly in mainstream Christian culture. But reactionary movements have also arisen among black citizens, parents, scholars, and leaders as well. Many take aim at the attempt to reframe American history with a narrative of victimization and blame, simultaneously planting seeds of the same in the minds of young children. Keisha King, a member of Moms for Liberty, echoes the sentiment of many black parents when she says,

> CRT is not racial sensitivity, or simply teaching unfavorable American history, or teaching Jim Crow history. CRT is deeper and more dangerous than that. CRT and its outworking today is a teaching that there is a hierarchy in society where white male heterosexual able-bodied people are deemed the oppressor and anyone else outside of that status is oppressed. . . . I don't know about you, but telling my child or any child that they are in a permanent oppressed status in America because they are black

> is racist, and saying that white people are automatically above me, my children or any child is racist as well. . . .
>
> This is not something that we can stand for in our country. . . . And don't take it from me, look at the writers of these types of publications, our ancestors, white, black, and others hung, bled, and died right alongside each other to push America towards that more perfect union. If this continues, we will look back and be responsible for the dismantling of the greatest country in the world by reverting to teaching hate and that race is a determining factor on where your destiny lies.[46]

Other black thought leaders target the core of The 1619 Project essays concerning the Revolutionary War as having been proven untrue long before its assertion, in a multiplicity of documented scholarly recordings. For example, Tom Skinner gives what many consider a more accurate recounting of the history of slavery between the years of 1619 and 1660 in his talk referenced earlier, a portion of which can be read in the notes.[47]

In addition, and under the contemporary leadership of Robert L. Woodson Sr., a number of black ministers and civic leaders have joined together to create the black-led movement called "1776 Unites." In the dedication of the book of essays published as a response to The 1619 Project essays, Woodson writes,

> No nation is perfect, but America—more than any other—is a place where people from every imaginable background have been able to pursue their dreams and realize their potential. Americans have never met a problem we are afraid to tackle or a challenge we can't overcome. In fact, those of us who have faced the most formidable challenges in life often become our strongest leaders and our greatest patriots.
>
> This is as true of black Americans as it is anyone else. During the worst of Jim Crow, we built thriving communities full of families, churches, businesses, and countless civic institutions. On the very soil where we once toiled in forced labor, we found the seeds of our liberation.

> At a time when many are trying to pull us apart by stoking grievances and sowing discord, the overwhelming majority of Americans remain devoted to our founding principles and to one another.[48]

In one of the entries of the 1776 Unites movement writings, Rev. Dean Nelson confronts the issues being raised by CRT and The 1619 Project when he writes,

> Learning 'white history' in school did not cause any of us to believe we were inferior to anyone, nor did we somehow naively conclude that the world was free of racism. The racism we did experience did not make us think that America and its ideals didn't belong to us, nor did it deprive us of the ability to love our country and work to make it better. And thankfully, we did not enter adulthood looking for pity or thinking of ourselves as helpless pawns in a white man's world. . . .
>
> My organization, Douglass Leadership Institute, named for Frederick Douglass, works on issues of importance to black churchgoers, which include strengthening the black family, supporting criminal justice reform, and securing economic and educational opportunities for all. In our work on the black family, we have found that there are two opposite dangers that black parents must avoid when teaching their children about race.
>
> We cannot raise our children to think that racism does not exist or not to value and embrace their race as part of their identity. Black Americans will always encounter at least some people who see their race before they see anything else, and we have to prepare our children for those encounters in a way that minimizes the likelihood that they will be traumatized or endangered. However, we also must avoid rearing kids who see every setback they face through the lens of race and look for opportunities to be offended or outraged.[49]

While I agree that teaching a revisionist history of solely oppressed/oppressor constructs should not be the approach, I do believe we need to tell history in its comprehensive truthful context. We are not to marginalize it. We are not to whitewash it. We are to tell and teach the truth; the whole truth. Slavery was horrible. Jim Crow was horrific. Forty-five hundred men were lynched, often on trumped-up charges never proven with due process. We are to teach about towns such as Rosewood, Florida, being completely destroyed until there was no town left at all for illegitimate revenge-killings on charges, once again, not given due process. We are to teach that the town of Rosewood stood as a beacon of black business success where every business was owned and operated by blacks, except for one—until the town was burned down. We are to teach about Black Wall Street and how it was annihilated. We are to teach about Tulsa. We are to teach about how every pocket of progress blacks began to achieve as a group was swiftly met by a new form of oppression or targeted dismantling. I could go on and on. We are not to skip true stories, no matter how ugly or painful they are. We are not to pretend they are not history because they don't fit the popular view of our nation. We are to teach the truth, in large part so we don't repeat it. And also so we can work together to heal from it and undo its lasting legacies of destruction showing up so often today in other ways.

We also, however, are to major on teaching, emphasizing, celebrating, and highlighting the massive number of black achievements that injustice was not able to extinguish. People of all races need to learn from the historical faith-based strength of Black America that in spite of slavery, segregation, and injustice, we not only persevered but also helped to build and promote the social, political, economic, and religious advancement of the entire nation, enabling it to reach the level of greatness that it has obtained.

Much of the criticism of CRT arising within the black community and Christian leaders comes from the need for a greater emphasis on personal responsibility to secure upward mobility, as well as a desire for a greater focus on preserving the black family. Voddie Baucham summarizes these sentiments when he writes what so many of us believe: "This connection between stable families and the rule of law is something most of us know intuitively. It doesn't mean that we have a simplistic understanding of racism or deny it exists. It just means that we understand the importance of the family as it relates to the community at large."[50] As goes the family, so goes the culture.

On these and many issues, black biblicists, having shared the same experience and therefore the same concerns that the black revolution, black power, black theology, and other black movements addressed, offer our answers in line with a commitment to an exegetical and expository approach to Scripture. Historically, black evangelicals were never fully members of the black revolution, although we supported and identified with the call and need for social justice. But neither were we fully members of white evangelicalism, although we benefited from many of its structures of study, ministries, and approaches to theology.

This reality formed a distinction in our approach within both the black church and the broader American evangelical church, providing a unique impetus for the systematizing of a theology on discipleship, oneness, and social justice that is rooted and grounded in biblical truth. This is why I believe that, in time, more and more believers will be identifying as "kingdomologists" instead of "evangelical," no matter what their race is. Kingdomology retains the original emphasis that once proved real in evangelicalism of biblical justice, social focus, and scriptural integrity, but distances itself from the spiritual superiority, political idolatry, and divisiveness which has recently overtaken and, in many ways, consumes contemporary evangelicalism.

**Notes**

1. Walter Elwell, *The Evangelical Theological Dictionary* (Grand Rapids, MI: Baker, 1989), 379.
2. "History," National Association of Evangelicals, www.nae.net/about-nae/history.
3. Harold John Ockenga, Foreword to Harold Lindsell, *The Battle for the Bible* (Grand Rapids, MI: Zondervan Publishing,1976): "Neo-evangelicalism was born in 1948 in connection with a convocation address which I gave in the Civic Auditorium in Pasadena. While reaffirming the theological view of Fundamentalism, this address repudiated its ecclesiology and its social theory. The ringing call for a repudiation of separatism and the summons to social involvement received a hearty response from many evangelicals. It differed from Fundamentalism in its determination to engage itself in the theological dialogue of the day. It had a new emphasis upon the application of the gospel to the sociological, political, and economic areas of life."
4. "History," National Association of Evangelicals, www.nae.net/about-nae/history.
5. For a summary of the relationship of music to the theology of the black church, see James H. Cone, *The Spirituals and the Blues* (Philadelphia: J. B. Lippincott Co., 1970); and Harold Carter, *The Prayer Tradition of Black People* (Valley Forge, PA: Judson Press, 1976).

6. Debate raged because of the propositions of the German scholar Rudolf Bultmann, who contested the validity of miracles in Scripture and thus found it necessary to demythologize the Bible.
7. Also known as modernism, this is the major shift in theological thinking that occurred in the late nineteenth century. It is an extremely explosive concept. The major thrust was to contemporize the archaisms of language and thought of the ancient world into forms and images that were more conducive to the modern world.
8. Henry Louis Gates Jr., *The Black Church: This is Our Story, This is Our Song* (New York: Penguin, 2021), 96.
9. Ibid., 95.
10. The Bible college movement began to call for a reemphasis on the fundamentals of the faith to counteract the growth of liberalism. Out of the Bible college movement came the Bible institute movement, which became an auxiliary means of educating blacks. Schools like Moody Bible Institute and Philadelphia College of the Bible developed night schools for blacks and others who worked fulltime and could not attend during the day.
11. For example, my alma mater, Dallas Theological Seminary, would not admit blacks until about 1968. DTS, which had long been a bastion of conservative Christian education and a school for producing conservative writers, thinkers, and expositors, kept the doors shut to blacks because of the cultural climate of the day. This was true for most evangelical institutions.
12. E. Franklin Frazier, *The Negro Church in America,* and E. Eric Lincoln, *The Black Church Since Frazier*, in one volume (New York: Schochken Books, 1975), 140.
13. Anthea Butler, *White Evangelical Racism: The Politics of Morality in America* (Chapel Hill, NC: University of North Carolina Press, 2021), 53.
14. Tom Skinner, "The US Racial Crisis and World Evangelism," sermon transcript of Urbana Student Missions Conference, 1970, https://urbana.org/message/us-racial-crisis-and-world-evangelism.
15. Ibid.
16. Erin Burnett interview of Ed Litton, "Incoming SBC President Speaks on the Study of Critical Race Theory," OutFront, www.facebook.com/cnn/videos/incoming-sbc-president-speaks-on-the-study-of-critical-race-theory/1904538664148651/.
17. Immanuel Kant was a German philosopher who endorsed the enterprise of human thinking apart from the Scriptures, the church, and the state.
18. For more detailed information, see chapter 31 in John Hope Franklin, *From Slavery to Freedom: A History of Negro Americans* (New York: Alfred A. Knopf, 1968); also see William Brink and Louis Harris, *The Negro Revolution in America* (New York: Simon and Schuster, 1964).
19. For more information on the term "white evangelicalism," see Raymond Chung, "An Open Letter to John Piper on White Evangelicalism and Multi-Ethnic Relations," October 20, 2017, churchleaders.com.
20. Eric Mason, *Woke Church: An Urgent Call for Christians in America to Confront Racism and Injustice* (Chicago: Moody, 2018), 30.
21. Timothy I. Cho, "Interview: Eric Mason Talks Redeeming 'Wokeness' and Abandoning 'Evangelicalism,'" *Faithfully Magazine*, 2019. https://faithfullymagazine.com/eric-mason-wokeness-evangelicalism.
22. "I've Been to the Mountaintop," speech by Martin Luther King Jr., April 3, 1968, Mason Temple, Church of God in Christ Headquarters, Memphis, Tennessee.
23. James H. Cone, *God of the Oppressed* (New York: Seabury Press, 1975), 3.
24. James H. Cone, "The Gospel and the Liberation of the Poor," *Christian Century*, February 18, 1981, 162.
25. James H. Cone, *Black Theology and Black Power* (New York: Seabury Press, 1969), 121.
26. Frazier, *Negro Church in America,* and Lincoln, *Black Church Since Frazier*, 192.

27. Benjamin Watson, *Under Our Skin: Getting Real About Race and Getting Free From the Fears and Frustrations That Divide Us* (Wheaton, IL: Tyndale Momentum, 2016), 91.
28. Most proponents trace its origins to the killing of Trayvon Martin, and its rise in prominence to the death of Michael Brown.
29. Sony Salzman, "From the Start, Black Lives Matter Has Been about LGBTQ Lives," ABCNews.com, June 21, 2020, abcnews.go.com/US/start-black-lives-matter-lgbtq-lives/story?id=71320450.
30. "'We Are Trained Marxists'—Patrisse Cullors, Co-Founder, #BlackLivesMatter," YouTube, June 19, 2020, www.youtube.com/watch?v=HgEUbSzOTZ8.
31. "What Is Critical Race Theory?" UCLA School of Public Affairs, https://spacrs.wordpress.com/what-is-critical-race-theory/: "CRT recognizes that racism is engrained in the fabric and system of the American society. . . . Legal discourse says that the law is neutral and colorblind, however, CRT challenges this legal 'truth' by examining liberalism and meritocracy as a vehicle for self-interest, power, and privilege."
32. Quoted in "What Is Critical Race Theory, and Why Is Everyone Talking about It?" July 1, 2021, https://news.columbia.edu/news/what-critical-race-theory-and-why-everyone-talking-about-it-0. See also the discussion by Ibram X. Kendi, "There Is No Debate over Critical Race Theory," *The Atlantic*, July 9, 2021, www.theatlantic.com/ideas/archive/2021/07/opponents-critical-race-theory-are-arguing-themselves/619391/.
33. Other founders are typically considered to include Richard Delgado, Charles Lawrence, Mari Matsuda, Patricia Williams, and Kimberly Williams.
34. Derrick A. Bell Jr., "Who's Afraid of Critical Race Theory?" *University of Illinois Law Review* (1995), 893–910.
35. Angela P. Harris, "Foreword: The Jurisprudence of Reconstruction," *California Law Review* 82.4 (July 1994), 74.
36. Ibid., 743.
37. Bell, "Who's Afraid of Critical Race Theory?" 900.
38. Note: Much of the opposition to CRT comes through the argument that Critical Legal Studies (CLS) was formed out of Critical Theory (CT), unfortunately without the concomitant research and dialogue to discuss what, if any, of CRT relates to CT itself. The concept of Critical Theory, also known as the "Frankfurt School," was first published in 1937 as "Traditional and Critical Theory" by Max Horkheimer at Columbia University in NYC.
39. Ibram X. Kendi, *Stamped from the Beginning: The Definitive History of Racist Ideas in America* (New York: Bold Type Books, 2017), 443. Some debate exists as to the exact official date of inception.
40. Ibid., 444.
41. Bell, "Who's Afraid of Critical Race Theory?" 899.
42. Derrick A. Bell Jr., "*Brown v. Board of Education* and the Interest-Convergence Dilemma," *Harvard Law Review* 93.3 (1980), 523.
43. See "The 90-Year-Old Financial Policy That Harms Our Health," NYC.gov, https://a816-dohbesp.nyc.gov/IndicatorPublic/Closerlook/redlining/index.html.
44. See "The 1619 Project Curriculum," https://pulitzercenter.org/lesson-plan-grouping/1619-project-curriculum.
45. Leslie M. Harris, "I Helped Fact-Check the 1619 Project. The Times Ignored Me," *Politico.com*, March 6, 2020, www.politico.com/news/magazine/2020/03/06/1619-project-new-york-times-mistake-122248.
46. "Black Mom Torches Critical Race Theory: 'It's Racist,'" DailyWire.com, June 11, 2021, www.dailywire.com/news/black-mom-torches-critical-race-theory-its-racist-its-teaching-hate-will-destroy-america.
47. "On those ships there were approximately forty black people. Notable among them was a couple known as Isabel and Antony, who started the first black family on American soil in 1624. You must keep in mind that one year before the Mayflower, 150 years before the

Constitution or the Declaration of Independence was ever signed, black people had settled this country and were an integral part of this society."

48. Robert L. Woodson Sr., ed., *Red, White, and Black: Rescuing American History from Revisionists and Race Hustlers* (New York: Emancipation Books, 2021), v.
49. Ibid., 73–74.
50. Voddie T. Baucham Jr., *Fault Lines: The Social Justice Movement and Evangelicalism's Looming Catastrophe* (Washington, DC: Salem Books, 2021), 164.

# Chapter 11

# THE RISE OF BLACK EVANGELICALISM

Several influencing factors led to the rise of black evangelicalism as a movement in the mid to late 1900s. First, many "colored" institutes, previously established by fundamentalists in order to maintain both a spiritual and a social segregation at the educational level, began to adopt an evangelical approach to the study of Scripture, which included social issues. Second, white evangelical schools started to open their doors, albeit slowly, to black students, which afforded blacks the opportunity to study in evangelically minded institutions. Third, a number of white parachurch organizations began to intentionally recruit African Americans to join their staff in order to broaden the ministry's perspective on how to reach the black community. And fourth, evangelical Bible teaching spread through the medium of Christian radio, providing broad-based exposure to a number of individuals who would not otherwise have had the opportunity to experience it.

Christian blacks exposed to evangelicalism realized that if they were going to prioritize the evangelization and discipleship of black America successfully while remaining culturally and socially sensitive and relevant, they were going to have to unite for the purpose of ministry. So in 1963 a group of black leaders formed the National Negro Evangelical Association (NNEA), the first distinctively black evangelical organization.

The NNEA became the primary information center for black evangelical outreach, fellowship, theological debate, and ministry exposure. It concerned itself with a commitment to the authority of the Scripture, a burden for the spiritual state of black America, the need for oneness in the body of Christ, and the application of the gospel to the issue of social justice.

Although a distinctive movement, the NNEA did not entirely abandon its denominational affiliations, because black evangelicals needed to be where black people were—in the black church. Maintaining a relationship with the black church was crucial because of the need to maintain black culture from an evangelical perspective. Through organizations such as the NNEA, which later was renamed the National Black Evangelical Association (NBEA), black evangelicalism entered the structures of American society on two fronts: first, through the establishment of independent black evangelical churches, and second, as an expansion into the existing black denominational structures.

Recognizing the strengths and weaknesses in both the black and white churches in America, pastors and theologians in black evangelicalism sought to simultaneously build the strengths of both while addressing the weaknesses of both. This provided the church at large with a greater holistic approach to the topics studied in the Bible and theology, and it provided the black church with a more refined systematic approach to understanding Scripture and its application.

## The Fathers of Black Evangelicalism

Scores of talented men paved the way for the inception and spread of black evangelicalism. The pages of this book are not enough to do justice to them all. However, a few men stand in need of special recognition as fathers to those of us who followed them. These include Dr. John Perkins, Rev. Tom Skinner, Dr. William Bentley, Dr. B. Sam Hart, and Dr. Ruben Conner.

### *Dr. John Perkins*

In 1970, black students leaving a protest in Mendenhall, Mississippi, were rounded up by police, beaten, and taken to prison. This was done as a setup to bait a man named John Perkins who had spent his life as a preacher and social activist, leading protest marches and boycotts against unjust laws, as well as ministering to the poor. When John arrived at the jail to argue for the release of the students, he was immediately surrounded by twelve cops, who searched him and then dragged him into the longest night of his life.

On this night, holed up in a dark room with paintless walls and a concrete floor, John was beaten, bound to a chair, battered with leather blackjacks, and then, after hours of abuse, even forced to wipe up his own blood. Afterward, seeing John drift between a loss of consciousness and a state of physical shock, most of the other prisoners did not think that he would make it through the night. But God spared his life. John remembers a prayer he prayed during the extreme escalation of his pain. He prayed, *Lord, if You will let me survive this, I will devote my life to bringing the races together in love and service to You.*

Not only did John Perkins survive the night, but he went on to lead the way toward unity in America, earning him the affectionate title "the godfather of racial reconciliation." Dr. Perkins personally challenged me on a number of occasions to commit myself to the study of Scripture and the carrying out of its principles toward reconciliation and empowerment among the Christian communities of America.

### *Tom Skinner*

Reverend Tom Skinner, whom I spoke about in a previous chapter as well, initially arose as an evangelist on the national platform. A former Harlem gang member, Tom dedicated his life to God late in his teen years. As early as the age of twenty, he was drawing crowds and conversions through his ability to present the gospel in a compelling yet clear manner. As Skinner grew spiritually, he became a powerful evangelist who shared the gospel for over thirty years and in more than seventy different countries. He was also the chaplain for the Washington Redskins and served as a team motivator for other professional sports teams. He established a high technology learning center that served the inner city and the Skinner Leadership

Institute which provided networking, bridgebuilding, and leadership development.

Tom's success opened doors for him within both the white and black worlds. As these doors opened, Tom addressed the contradiction of the white church and the black experience by bringing a kingdom mindset to the forefront. However, as Tom became more engaged with the white church, he witnessed a level of hypocrisy within it that made him uncomfortable. He saw firsthand an unwillingness to deal with injustices and separatism.

Tom began to speak openly and courageously about these issues in an era when that wasn't done, and as a result he ended up experiencing rejection from many of the Christian whites who had been supporting him. Radio stations found his messages to be too "controversial" and often stopped playing them. These issues propelled Tom even more deeply into challenging the body of Christ to *be* the body of Christ in both truth and in form. Nearly all influential black conservative leaders today will point to Tom Skinner, with his fiery commitment to theology and social justice, as a father to them in their own ministry.

I met Tom Skinner through Dr. B. Sam Hart. He was a true bridge builder, seeking reconciliation and breaking down dividing walls of age, economic status, race, and religion. Skinner emphasized social justice and racial reconciliation, but he did so by presenting the gospel and accentuating the kingdom of God. He had the unique ability to communicate with every age and cultural group—something that he helped teach me. I could not comprehend why the church should just be spiritual while neglecting the social, or why social activism should be done (as it was so often done) absent a sound theology integrated in and through the local church. Skinner helped me to formulate a balanced view of the gospel. His ministry of hope, renewal, and reconciliation changed the lives of thousands of people, and for that, he will forever be remembered in a position of honor among Christian historians.

### *Dr. B. Sam Hart*

Another father in the early inception and spread of black evangelicalism was Dr. B. Sam Hart, who founded the Grand Old Gospel

Fellowship Ministry (GOGF), which sought to plant churches, prepare leaders, and proclaim the gospel through tent crusades, broadcast media, and overseas long- and short-term missions. GOGF also trained pastors in third-world countries and ministered through orphanages.

B. Sam Hart forever changed my life. He is the man who challenged me to go into full-time Christian ministry, and he also encouraged me to attend Bible college, something that I was not considering at the time. Furthermore, when I was seventeen years old, Dr. Hart invited me to travel to Guyana, South America, to help set up a gospel crusade.

In Guyana, I met my wife, Lois, for the first time. I spent one month in Guyana, but I told Lois that I was going to return as soon as I could to marry her. A year and a half later, I kept my promise. In fact, Lois would go on to work for Dr. Hart and the ministry in helping to duplicate ministry tapes shortly after we married. This, along with her later work at the Billy Graham Evangelistic Association, prepared her for her future role of helping me to start our broadcast ministry, The Urban Alternative, and later help to run it as the Executive Vice President. There would be no Evans family, national ministry, or legacy without Dr. Hart's influence.

However, this isn't fully why he should be honored. Dr. Hart was a faithful black evangelist who emphasized biblical literacy and church planting. He not only impacted my life, but he introduced innumerable souls to Jesus Christ and helped them to grow in their faith.

Through his untiring work, Dr. Hart established black evangelical churches outside of traditional black church structures, strongly emphasizing a call to sound biblical theology connected with a strong emphasis on personal evangelism. He emphasized the need for evangelical Bible teaching in these churches. Through his influence, a church-planting movement was spawned on the East Coast. In addition, Dr. Hart was one of the first black evangelicals to gain a platform in the broader media through his weekly radio broadcast.

### *Dr. William Bentley*

Dr. William Bentley was one of the leading architects of the NNEA. He possessed a strong theological desire for the evangelical movement among blacks to reveal how to emphasize the Bible and theology while also addressing racism, segregation, and oppression. Dr. Bentley was a keen black historian as well as an astute black theologian. One of the highlights that I looked forward to in every NNEA convention in the 1970s and '80s was the debates he and I held concerning how to marry the legitimate strengths of black theology's emphasis on the black experience and black liberation with the evangelical emphasis on the authority of Scripture.

### *Dr. Ruben Conner*

Dr. Ruben Conner established Black Evangelist Enterprise (formerly known as Black Evangelistic Enterprises) in Dallas, Texas, which was a church-planting organization designed to bring about a greater emphasis of Bible teaching to black churches in America. Dr. Conner is considered one of the fathers of the contemporary independent urban church-planting movement in America.

In 1931, Dr. Conner was born in a typical African American farming community which suggested he would become nothing more than a third generational farmer. On top of that, his mother died shortly after he was born, and his father remarried seven times. Dr. Conner dropped out of school in the 7th grade.

However, God had a plan for his life. Dr. Conner joined the military when he was 16. After seven years of service, a Bronze Star, and combat injuries, he returned home before moving to Dallas. He converted to Christianity, got married, and opened his barber shop where he began evangelizing and preaching. He then earned his GED, attended Bible school, and made history in 1960 when he planted the first African American Bible Church in the South.

Dr. Conner, who later earned two master's degrees and a doctorate degree, served as the senior pastor at Community Bible Church for 25 years. He also launched Black Evangelistic Enterprises which helped establish over 40 evangelical churches worldwide—including the church I have served as senior pastor for more than forty-five years, Oak Cliff Bible Fellowship.

While at DTS, I began attending Community Bible Church where Dr. Conner pastored. After being accepted as the first African American into the DTS doctrinal program, I was also invited to become an associate professor. However, Dr. Conner, along with some others, challenged me to start a Bible church in Dallas under Black Evangelistic Enterprises as a way of modeling the ideas that I had for connecting the spiritual and social state of my community. There would be no Oak Cliff Bible Fellowship without Dr. Conner.

Dr. Conner was a faithful preacher, pastor, mentor, and church planter who emphasized social change in African American culture. He not only impacted my life, but he impacted innumerable souls for the Kingdom.

## The Fundamentals of Black Evangelicalism

The presence of a black evangelical emphasis provides a number of distinctions that enhance the overall well-being of Christianity both in America and abroad. This is due to the convergence of the existing major theological tenets present in contemporary biblical Christianity with a concern for the oppressed as well as the social realities of the black experience. These distinctions include biblical authority, ministry development, evangelism and discipleship, racial reconciliation, personal responsibility, and biblical justice.

### *Biblical Authority*

There is a vast difference between learning from the past and living in it. While black theology should not be undervalued or ignored as far as it raised and sought to address essential issues within the black experience, the foundational interpretational grid for black theology rested more in experience than in exposition.

Volumes have been written as a critique to black theology as well as the distinction of black evangelicalism. My own ThD dissertation is entitled "A Biblical Critique of Selected Issues in Black Theology." I don't intend, nor do I have the space, to adequately address all of the various systems of thought within black theology and black evangelicalism. And while the term is under attack, for the purposes of explaining its history and impact, I will use it throughout. I want to emphasize a major differentiating factor between Black Theology and Black Evangelicalism, and that is the approach to interpreting

Scripture. I have termed the two varied approaches "black experiential theology" and "black expositional theology."

In an attempt to relate the condition of black people to the teaching of Scripture, black theology elevated the black experience to such a degree so as to impose itself on Scripture, making "blackness" the criteria for true interpretation. This incorrectly elevated the issue of contemporary context above the overall overwhelming issue of revelation. Consumed by the liberation motif, this faulty control given to a culturally conditioned theme gave rise to a school of thought that made the Bible the servant of culture, history, and experience.

This produced a more anthropologically centered theology, since social liberation was made the governing hermeneutical principle through which all of the Scripture is to be interpreted. Biblical subpoints became theological categories, thus giving them a place of preeminence they were never meant to have. Black theology emphasized an experiential revelation to varying degrees from theologian to theologian; however, it is safe to say that a basis of experiential interpretation served as its underpinning.

Black evangelicalism, on the other hand, views Scripture as the standard for judging the black experience. The ultimate goal of revelation, whether general or special, is Godward. It is designed to bring men into harmony with who God is and what He is about. History is crucial to revelation because God is revealing Himself in time and space, and liberation is an important activity of God in history. However, the extraction of the social liberation motif from history as the superintending sufficient revelation of God's activity in history is incorrect because it makes the human situation rather than the divine revelation its ultimate end.

When studying Scripture, the question that any group must ask is whether knowledge of God and the advancement of His kingdom is the goal. To have any other goal is to make Scripture the handmaiden of humanity. No human experience bears divine authority in and of itself. Neither can any human experience capture all of the elements necessary to guarantee an objective approach to the biblical text so as not to impose preconditioned conclusions of experience and culture on the text. Only as experience is validated by the teaching of

Scripture, as in the case of black evangelicalism, can it be considered revelatory.

What must be done when addressing cultural concerns and experience through Scripture is to clearly understand the questions that the culture or experience is raising, take those questions, and place them parallel to a biblical question that was asked or raised in Scripture. Next, find the answer to that question from Scripture, and, finally, apply the answer to the question. Any other approach is subjective and does not align one's thought under the comprehensive rule of God. It forces one to make God and His revelation servants to man rather than having God as the final spokesman. This asks experience to exegete Scripture rather than letting Scripture exegete experience.

The exegesis of culture and experience is indeed a valid enterprise, but only the exegesis of Scripture is an absolute enterprise. Culture and experience may raise the vital and necessary questions and may even illustrate divine answers, but they can never be the starting point for determining the meaning of Scripture. A partial approach to Scripture will never lead to full truth.

We, as African Americans, have been subjected for hundreds of years under the result of an incomplete hermeneutical approach to Scripture. We have been deeply impacted by such an errant methodology. Knowing this, we should be especially careful not to fall prey to doing the same. It can be safely argued that white Christianity did, and even still does, a partial interpretation of Scripture in its maintaining, or failing to seek to reverse, structural sins of dehumanizing separation, disparity, and subjugation brought about by past cultural sins of slavery and legalized racism whose generational effects remain in place at various levels.

James Cone, three decades after first publishing his thoughts on black theology, summarized a common concern still lingering among many:

> What deepens my anger today is the appalling silence of the white theologians on racism in the United States and the modern world. Whereas this silence has been partly broken in several secular disciplines, theology remains virtually mute.

> From Jonathan Edwards to Walter Rauschenbusch and Reinhold Niebuhr to the present, progressive white theologians, with few exceptions, write and teach as if they do not need to address the radical contradiction that racism creates for Christian theology.[1]

Many white theologians are, through a silence on the societal sins brought about by racism and classism, "wittingly or not, accomplices of and contribute to the maintenance of patriarchalism, racism, *apartheid*, and oppression in a variety of its psychological, social, economic, or cultural forms."[2] This may sound harsh, but if it were not a plausible reality, slavery's legacy of a sustaining of the great racial divide—the deepest stain on the soul of our historical American Christianity—would be addressed and amended with the same passion and zeal that other cultural sins and mandates are given in the white church, such as the just defense of the sanctity of life, the teaching against homosexuality, and the spread of the gospel overseas.

A recent example hit me hard when the obviously brutal and inhumane death of George Floyd at the knee of a white police officer went largely ignored by my white brothers who pastor large churches or lead large ministries. I recall commenting on the heinous public act on Twitter the day of his death. While we didn't know all of the surrounding circumstances at that time, I felt we knew enough, and could see enough, to say something against this very publicly inhumane action and ask God for His intervention of grace and mercy for the family, and those impacted by what they saw.

Yet as days, and even weeks, went by I noticed that nearly none of my white brothers serving in spiritual positions of national influence and national platforms would say anything at all. In fact, they appeared to be so callous to the whole experience that seemed to traumatically shake an entire demographic of our nation, that they went on as usual, posting online about their new books or whatever meal they were currently consuming or social engagement they were having. It seemed a bit . . . off.

Yet it was another stark reminder of the undercurrent of a great divide in interests, compassion, and a heart for the plight of those who still face the resultant ripples of a nation historically ransacked by racism. Silence is complicity. It is not enough to merely view racism as wrong, if a person is to live by the Biblical standard of love. Rather, one must intentionally live as an opposing force to racism by actively seeking to change beliefs and behaviors which allow for its continual impact. And, at a minimum, demonstrate some level of empathy or compassion when an entire group of people experiences a very public display of collective pain.

While white theologians should carefully consider their biblical view on oneness, reconciliation, and, where applicable, biblical charity, those who adhere to the principles of black theology should also consider that through its experiential interpretational grid, it has likewise produced a fundamental flaw in that it is rooted in the black experience as that of a victim.[3] Both white theologians' silence and black theology's singular focus on racism promote separatism, thus limiting, through self-imposed means, the ability for the achievement of authentic biblical oneness.

What has been created and perpetuated through both is an enduring platform of separation that allows little opportunity for leadership development, evangelism and discipleship, racial reconciliation, personal responsibility, biblical justice, and cultural impact. Black evangelicalism seeks to place itself under the complete holistic authority of Scripture so as to provide a moral frame of reference under which all of life should align.

### *Ministry Development*

Black evangelicalism seeks to define ministry as any activity in which the needs of people are met by Christians in accordance with the Scripture. Events in themselves do not always help us address the societal crisis that we are facing, while ministry does.

The Bible never describes programs that are not tied to ministry. Unless a program serves the brothers and sisters in Christ or is an outreach to unbelievers in accordance with the commands of God, it is not biblical. For example, Acts 6 records a change in the ministry to widows in the early church. Because the Greek widows were being neglected in the daily giving of food, a complaint arose. When the apostles were told of the problem, they initiated a ministry in the church to work together to meet that social need.

Black evangelicalism recognizes the unique needs often present in urban or predominantly black congregations as reflective of the needs in the black culture. We are no longer a single-tier community; therefore, our churches need to reflect that reality both in the variety of ministries offered as well as their scope. Ministries must be multifaceted in order to deal with the great diversity of needs that are present. They must also relevantly address the unique needs of the next generation who are being governed, guided, and influenced by a whole new world of values and communication vehicles that have increasingly drawn them away from the Christian faith.

Recognizing that the act of service is an integral part of personal spiritual growth, a commitment to serve in one of these ministries is a requirement for every member at our church. These ministries then also offer themselves as a small-group community for those in the church, thereby making a large church of more than ten thousand members have a small-church feel.

Specific ministries relevant to many in the black community include those that minister to single parents by providing godly big brothers or father figures for their sons and daughters. Nuclear families are also formed into a small-group context, thus providing support systems by serving as extended families to the single-parent home. Athletic and summer programs exist for children that not only provide the activities themselves but also teach discipline, determination, and cooperation while fostering an atmosphere of love and acceptance.

In order for these ministries to have their full effect, though, black evangelicalism also recognizes and promotes the need for formal training of its clergy, lay leaders, and volunteers in Bible, theology, and church ministry. A church will only be as strong as its leadership, because God will not bypass the leaders and go directly to the congregation. Church leaders stand as representatives of God before those whom they serve. As such, it is essential that the role of leadership be taken seriously through an intentional pursuit of personal righteousness, spiritual growth, biblical training, and ministry impact.

A formal approach to biblical training includes courses that provide an overview of the Bible, an introduction to each book of the Bible, major doctrines in the Bible, and a systematic approach on how to study the Bible. These elements are necessary because they provide the developmental tools required for effective and sound leadership. A church leader is more than just a person who holds a title or a ministry position; he or she is someone who possesses a heart for service, a thoroughly biblical worldview, an understanding of Scripture, and the essential skills needed to enable him or her to model and teach Jesus Christ and the Word of God to others.

### *Evangelism and Discipleship*

The concern for evangelism within black evangelicalism grew out of the reality that the white church showed less interest in missions across the street in its own black Samaria than in missions around the world. Having been exposed to the quality tools that had been developed to accomplish effective "soul winning," black evangelicals took this mission upon ourselves. This emphasis on evangelism produced a strong distinguishing factor from black theology in its interpretation of the purpose of the gospel. One of the distinctions of black evangelicals, or even currently black kingdomologists, from the black church in general rests in the aggressive nature of personal evangelism rising out of our concern that the social and political movements of the day, while valid and necessary, are at times absent of the eternal aspect of God's kingdom.

The concern regarding evangelism in the black church is born out of the fact that personal evangelism has been downgraded in the emphasis on social justice. This has happened at times to such a degree that the message of the gospel of salvation by grace through faith in the finished work of Christ has become diluted with a culture of religion. Black evangelicalism seeks to stress the need for the clarity of the gospel to be maintained as well as for church members to be directly engaged in personal evangelism.

Intricately woven into the evangelism emphasis of black evangelicalism is the call for sound biblical teaching and discipleship (helping Christians bring every area of their lives under the lordship of Jesus Christ). A great need exists in the contemporary black community for discipleship to address the comprehensive spiritual development of each individual.

Black evangelicalism sought, and continues to seek, to pursue this process of discipleship. Black evangelicalism seeks to instill a different narrative in the black culture by emphasizing personal responsibility and morality, family values and living according to the wisdom of Scripture. It augments biblical discipleship through a variety of ways by first using the strength of personal relationship through one-on-one discipleship, a characteristic already innate in the black church, as the starting point. Added to it are Sunday worship services with church and home Bible studies, Sunday school, fellowship groups, ministry projects that carry a discipleship emphasis, and the use of specially designed study curriculum. Black evangelicalism seeks to emphasize the need for exposure to spiritual growth resources either through books, radio, television, Internet, conferences, or seminars that have personal spiritual development as the goal.

Because black evangelicals have had extensive exposure to the strengths of the established and often affluent white churches that use marketing and growth principles, we gained and implemented new ideas about church structure. These range from multi-staffed ministries to fundraising processes to the development of parachurch ministries that support the local church. Thus, the emphasis of black evangelicals is on the need for a broad-based approach to ministry, with the pastor leading the way, so that the multifaceted needs of the people can be met in a timely and effective manner.

Likewise, while maintaining the celebratory aspects of worship, black evangelicals seek to offer biblical discipleship in the more didactic aspects of Scripture. A particular emphasis on expository preaching is the logical, progressive explanation of a passage of Scripture within its context so that the hearers can understand its meaning and learn how to apply it to their lives. Such exposition, however, must never lose sight of the great biblically based sermonic and worship history and motif of the black church. We must not be guilty of rejecting legitimate aspects of black tradition and worship that should be maintained.

While black evangelicals recognize that many "old-time ways" preserve cultural continuity and spiritual vitality, we also recognize that the contemporary multidimensional generation needs ministry that is relevant to its personal, familial, educational, and developmental needs.

### *Racial Reconciliation*

Biblical racial reconciliation is a further emphasis of black evangelicalism, and kingdomology at large. While reconciliation has always been a desire of the black church, black evangelicals have taken an aggressive posture in order to implement this process with the broader white community.

Black evangelicals, to varying degrees, have historically lived in two worlds and possessed a double-consciousness—partaking of the black heritage, history, and experience while at the same time imbibing the biblical and theological influences coming from the white evangelical world. This has created, much like the black middle class, a hybrid.

Black evangelicals, therefore, are positioned in the distinct location of being able to promote oneness between the black and white church. Because black evangelicals have lived on both sides of the American ecclesiastical divide, we are uniquely placed to mediate the beginning of a new era of mutual benefit and integration among Christians who are culturally different, yet spiritually one.

The bridge of reconciliation has not been easy, on either side, and will continue to require humility on both sides due to the reality that bridges, by their very nature, are walked on from time to time. But the purpose of a bridge is also to take you somewhere that you would not have otherwise been able to go. The bridge of reconciliation takes us, in the body of Christ, to a place where the displaying of God's kingdom agenda is done in such a way that others may "see [our] good works, and glorify [our] Father who is in heaven" (Matt. 5:16).

If the chief end of man is to glorify God,[4] and as we have seen earlier through Jesus Christ's high priestly prayer that "complete unity" (reconciliation) brings glory to God, and that "good works" (biblical justice) also bring glory to God, then we can only reason that a unified effort of good works—reconciliation toward the aim of mutual service—is, and should be, a central objective to our daily Christian life.

Biblical racial reconciliation, as I have said throughout this book, is not an end in itself. It is a means to an end of glorifying God through good works done in a spirit of unity. Reconciliation can never be forced. It comes as the result of an authentic relationship built on mutual respect and understanding. Authenticity necessitates honesty. It also necessitates an acknowledgment of, repentance from, and subsequent forgiveness for the sin that initially caused the relational divide. Whether that repentance and forgiveness be private or public, it is critical that it be genuine and heartfelt.

America is an individualistic society. In many ways this is a positive quality; however, when it comes to addressing corporate sins, it can prove to be a hindrance. Christian whites have historically benefited from the systematic effects of racism, and yet those benefits are often so far removed from direct personal cause that a need for repentance in the area of racial reconciliation often goes unnoticed and unaddressed. But whether or not personal involvement in the sin has taken place, or to what degree it exists, is irrelevant to the biblical model given to us for corporate repentance when national sins have led to national effects. An awareness of this often comes to the surface in backroom discussions or, even at times, public ones. The example of Pastor Louis Giglio in his now infamous exchange with Lecrae, which left Lecrae virtually speechless in the moment, highlighted this.

In a video on "Racism and 'white privilege' in America" between Pastor Giglio, Lecrae and Chick-fil-A chief executive Dan Cathy, Giglio referred to slavery in the context of it having been a "blessing." He said, "We understand the curse that was slavery, white people do . . . And we say that was bad. But we miss the blessing of slavery, that it actually built up the framework for the world that white people live in."[5]

Pastor Giglio later went on to apologize for the statement but the inference remained in the collective conscience of a culture already struggling with centuries of racism, oppression, and pain. To refer to slavery as a "blessing" through what it produced for businesses, systems, and structures of wealth in society for white people is a far cry from repenting for the evils committed both during and after slavery. What our nation needs from our spiritual leaders is a call to repentance and restoration, not a dismissive nod at a past stain.

We see this biblical model in the books of Daniel and Nehemiah where both prophets repented on behalf of their people. While doing so, both prophets included themselves personally in the prayer of repentance even though there is no indication that either prophet participated in the sin itself (Dan. 9:5, 7; Neh. 1:6–7). Thus, personal repentance on behalf of corporate sin that led to any degree of impact, benefit, or privilege for the corporate body ought to be offered in a like manner of sincere humility. When it is not, there runs the risk of cognitively diminishing as well as distancing oneself from the resultant effects of that sin in the lives of those who have been adversely impacted by it.

Likewise, forgiveness is often not acknowledged or granted on behalf of those who have been affected by the sting of historical abuses and institutional racism due to the corporate nature of the sin. Yet we as African Americans must apply the biblical principle of personal forgiveness modeled by Christ (Eph. 4:32), which will then release us from holding our white brothers and sisters hostage to any guilt or obligation toward us on a personal level. While we have every right to seek justice and resist ongoing manifestations of racism, we must also own our responsibility for personal development and progress through not seeking to illegitimately create, amplify or take advantage of any presence of "white guilt."

Superficial racial relationships patterned on paternalism will dissolve before any lasting connection can be made. This is because "white guilt" produces a me-centered struggle for white redemption or white-heroics through liberalism rather than an others-centered focus on authentic connection, learning, empathy, and mutual respect. It keeps blacks stuck in identity politics relegated to inferiority, opportunism, or entitlement. As Shelby Steele writes in his book *Shame*, "the benevolent paternalism of white guilt . . . had injured the self-esteem, if not the souls, of minorities in ways that the malevolent paternalism of white racism never had."[6]

Only through repentance and forgiveness done first and foremost on a personal level, which removes guilt and shame, will we be free to forge relationships that allow us to embrace dignity and diversity. We must be mindful that it takes time together in order to learn how to build trust, relate across cultural differences, and learn from each other. Unless our personal motivation is pure during the initial ups and downs of that time, we will become easily offended or wearied and fail to last in the ongoing effort that is required to learn how to embrace true oneness.

It is important to note that throughout the history of the church in America, there has always been a remnant of the white culture who, based on their capacity, intentionally sought out reconciliation, partnership, and a mutually respectful relationship with blacks in support of the black effort toward freedom and equality. This remnant has done so under their conviction of biblical justice and oneness, even when doing so meant great personal risk and sacrifice. These Christian whites have stood in the gap for their culture as a testimony of reconciliation and good works.

While that is true, a common challenge that has arisen in attempts toward reconciliation among the broader white population, particularly in evangelicalism, as a whole is that the terms of oneness have often been set and established by the white community void of any substantive input on the front end by the black community. Reconciliation cannot be achieved by one group imposing its ideas, preferences, context, and programs on another. Nor can it be achieved by simply inviting the other group to participate in a program, an idea, or a ministry after the agenda and procedures have been established. This limits the contribution and intermingling of unique qualities needed in order to produce a stronger, more complete whole. It also reinforces the paternalistic practice of whites toward minorities. This was recently reflected in the Southern Baptist Convention when white seminary presidents rejected out of hand "Critical Race Theory" without first seriously including and interfacing with godly black leadership on what aspects of CRT, if any, might be valuable.[7] While they did meet with African American ministers roughly a month after the fact, a conversation ahead of time would have been appropriate.[8]

Both groups must be brought to the table on the front end of the discussion and planning so that there is full participation, recognition, appreciation, and use of the strengths of both groups. True reconciliation occurs through a merging of strengths toward the pursuit of a shared purpose under the lordship of Christ, not a begging to participate by a marginalized group to the ingroup. Bryan Loritts addresses this rift in contemporary evangelicalism when he summarizes the thoughts of many black spiritual leaders seeking to be heard at the table:

> I'm tired of begging white evangelical academics to include people of color on their required reading lists. I'm tired of begging white homiletics professors to lengthen their references of good preachers to preachers of color. I'm tired of urban hipster church planters, planting churches in gentrifying neighborhoods never once considering existing minority churches in those neighborhoods as ones to learn from and partner with.
>
> I'm tired of recommending young minority leaders to serve on white church staffs, and watching them get used as tokens to show how "serious" the church is about diversity, only to see it end very badly. I'm tired of the silence of other minority leaders who, in their pursuit of climbing Mount Significance, are scared to speak the truth for fear of not being invited to some conference, missing out on a book deal, and not having their brand established or extended. I'm tired of the insensitive comments I'll get to articles like this from our white friends, not because it's pushback, but because they have grown up in all white churches that refuse to educate them on biblical, gospel issues like diversity and racial reconciliation.[9]

Both groups need to sit at the table but also both groups need to be heard. Both will also have to give up something, to yield in some areas, in order to fully implement the strengths of the other group; however, neither side should be asked to give up everything.

### *Personal Responsibility*

Black evangelicalism also emphasizes personal, family, church, and community responsibilities, similar to kingdomology. Rights belong to God. Responsibilities belong to the people. These should not be lessened in light of systemic issues that make the implementation of wise life choices more difficult for many more blacks than whites in America. What the African American community needs to understand is that while racism is a problem and a challenge that must be ultimately addressed, it is not our chief adversary. While racism is real, it should no longer be viewed as determinative. It should not be seen as the primary impediment to our progress individually or as a people. How a person chooses to view something will have a large impact on his or her mindset, beliefs and—ultimately—actions. If we would seriously take responsibilities for the things we *do* control, then racism's negative impact can be greatly limited, and we would flourish more freely as a community.

These responsibilities include getting a good education and not dropping out of school; taking care of our families and not abandoning our marriages and children; getting regular health checkups, adopting overall healthy eating habits, and not abusing substances like alcohol, cigarettes, and drugs that are debilitating to our physical and mental well-being; as well as being honest and equitable in our dealings with those inside and outside of our own community.

Of particular concern is the growing and disproportionate number of abortions taking place in the black community, thus participating in what many feel is, and has been, a targeted genocide. The number-one killer among African Americans is not heart disease or cancer—it is abortion.[10] Since the legalization of *Roe v. Wade,* more than 20 million African Americans have lost their lives at our own hands due to abortion. To put this into context, in 1960 there were approximately 18 million African Americans according to the census. Since 1973, abortion has killed more than the entire population in existence in 1960.[11] We must garner enough personal responsibility to analyze the data and ask ourselves why this is happening and why we, as a race, have been targeted in this way.

Other minority groups are increasing in size in America at a much quicker rate than the African American community, which is somewhat due to the increase in abortions among African American women.[12] African American women are five times more likely to have an abortion than white women.[13] According to the CDC, African American women (who account for approximately 7% of the national population) had the highest percentage of abortions performed between racial groups at close to 40% of all abortions. The abortion rate among African Americans was over three times higher than that of white Americans, and even higher than that of Hispanic women.[14]

Alveda King, the niece of the late Martin Luther King Jr. , recently campaigned against Planned Parenthood when a light was shown on the founder, Margret Sanger's, obvious eugenic aims as a member of the American Eugenics Society and a frequent speaker at events held by the Ku Klux Klan.[15] Alveda called the removal of a connection with Margret Sanger at a New York abortion clinic, similar to the removal of confederate statues throughout the country, was simply "window dressing." She went on to say, "Margret Sanger sought what was an Aryan race, thinking that was more perfect. . . . "[16] This statement is reflected in her own writings, her own programs such as the "Negro Project" established in 1939[17] and the legacy of targeting African American communities where nearly 70% of all clinics are within walking distance of urban, poor minority-dominant neighborhoods.[18]

The church is complicit in our role in failing to own the responsibility for preserving our own lives. In fact, Margret Sanger knew how powerful the African American church and our leaders were so she specifically chose to use them to quiet any uprising against her attack on the Negro population. In a letter to Dr. C. J. Gamble dated December 10, 1939, she wrote, "The ministers work is also important, and also he should be trained by the Federation . . . We do not want word to get out that we want to exterminate the Negro population and the minister is the man who can straighten out that idea if it ever occurs to their more rebellious leaders."[19]

The question on the table is how can a community that has fought for the full expression of life as well as fighting against systems that would deprive us of that life join in on the destruction of life in our own community? We have turned a blind eye to what was clearly set up as our own participation in our own ethnic cleansing.

In addition, we must focus on where we can improve as a culture and strengthen our families and personal lives. We must stop excusing errant behavior in the name of racism. Even though racism was and is a major contributing factor to the decline of the black community structures, it is still our responsibility to take ownership for the things that are within our power to control. We cannot expect others to take us any more seriously than we are taking ourselves in addressing our needs. We must not illegitimately use racism as a convenient scapegoat for irresponsibility, mediocrity, or criminal and immoral behavior.

If a Super Bowl champion team complained when they took the field that there were eleven men on the other side of the ball trying to stop them, or if Michael Jordan had whined each time he took to the court that there was always someone in his face trying to block his shot, neither would have reached the goal they had set before them. While God is a God of liberation, God is also a God who divinely uses opposition as a tool that, when responded to correctly, develops perseverance, strength, determination, compassion, faith, and even, at times, greater and more personally satisfying opportunities than what would have been granted without it.

Jesus Christ does not guarantee freedom from racism, classism, sexism, or oppression while we still live in a sinful world. What He does promise is freedom from personal sin and strongholds coupled with the provision of the power to overcome. Although this freedom may not change the world, it will change each of us by giving us a divine perspective through which to deal with the problems that we face. What good is it to be at peace with your neighbor and not be at peace with God or yourself? What good is it to gain freedom from others and still be a slave to yourself?

Without a biblical view toward the principle and practice of overcoming adversity, a victim mentality takes root. This victim mentality bears the fruit of foreshadowing a wrong conclusion, thereby casting a self-fulfilling vision of limitation brought about in the context of having been, or being, at the mercy of someone else's intentions. Victimology exists far more than it should within black culture today and serves as a constant reminder of the obstacles blocking the movement toward forward progress. Unfortunately, it has become our own internally based form of oppression.

Black evangelicalism emphasizes the *truth* in the statement that it is in knowing the *truth* that one is set free. This truth includes the good, the bad, and the ugly. It includes principles on personal responsibility, sin, accountability, spiritual power, and authority along with a need for pursuing a right relationship with God based on the foundation of His work in Christ, and our identity with Him.

We cannot afford to be like the children of Israel who let the influence of more than four hundred years of servitude in Egypt keep them from moving forward to experience the Promised Land that God had for them (Num. 13–14).

### *Biblical Justice*

Increasingly, concerted efforts are being made to address the ethical issues of our day; however, a lack of properly applied biblical justice is the underpinning for the continuation of societal and familial breakdowns as well as class and racial disparities. Biblical justice, when carried out correctly, naturally leads to the improvement of race, gender, and class divisions.

Due to the relevant significance of biblical justice with regard to the church's practice of oneness, I have dedicated an entire chapter to this topic in the next section. Yet, for the purpose of introducing it now as a fundamental of black evangelicalism and kingdomology, we will look at a foundational principle through a cursory glance at Isaiah 58.

We read in this chapter that the Israelites sought God's help and assistance—what we could call His "blessings." In fact, it says, "Yet they seek Me day by day and delight to know My ways" (Isa. 58:2). Not only did the Israelites seek God, but they also fasted (v. 3) in a desire to experience the "nearness" of God (v. 2). Basically, they went to church, read their Bibles, prayed, sang, humbled themselves, and attended their small-group studies. Yet, despite all of that, God did not respond to their pleas to bless them, nor did He respond to their requests for Him to execute "just decisions" (Isa. 58:2) on their behalf. Starting in verse 5, we read His reason why. It says,

> Is it a fast like this which I choose, a day for a man to humble himself? . . . Will you call this a fast, even an acceptable day to the Lord? Is this not the fast which I choose, to loosen the bonds of wickedness, to undo the bands of the yoke, and to let the oppressed go free and break every yoke? Is it not to divide your bread with the hungry and bring the homeless poor into

> the house; when you see the naked, to cover him; and not to hide yourself from your own flesh? (vv. 5–7)

Essentially, what God told the Israelites, in my Tony Evans translation, is that seeking Him, going to church, having regular prayer meetings and the like was not enough. Because in spite of all of that, and more, their relational actions revealed a contradictory reality, which showed that they were fasting as a means of argument while pursuing their own desire (Isa. 58:4).

The problem occurred in that their theology never affected their sociology. The thing they offered an "amen" to on Sunday never got carried out on Monday. They would come to church and sing about love, but return to the world and withhold that love. They would proclaim unity, charity, and equality in the house of God, but fail to practice that unity in the global body of Christ. Thus, the missing component of their ethical relational outworking within their theology nullified their religious activity.

The interesting thing about this passage is that the thing the Israelites sought from God ("just decisions") was the very thing that He says they withheld from others. Simply stated, the principle is: Whatever you want God to do for you personally, you must be willing for Him to do through you to others. God is not looking for cul-de-sac Christians. He is looking for Christians who are willing to be a conduit of His blessing and justice to those in need (Luke 6:38).

It is not right to say, "Lord, help me," but then not help someone else whom you can. We cannot say, "Lord, deliver me," but refuse to be the deliverance for another person in need. That is contradictory Christianity. What we have often done in the area of biblical justice is relegate it to others while at the same time complaining to God that He is not responding to our needs. We have neglected to see that the two are often interlinked.

Also, while many of us do not directly carry out overtly unjust actions against others on a regular basis, the importance of biblical justice has become diminished in our minds. But the critical aspect to note concerning biblical justice is the biblical definition of sin. Because a sin is not only a wrong action that is done, but a sin is also a right action that remains undone (James 4:17). The question of biblical justice is not simply, Have I done anything wrong? The question is, Have I done anything right? It is good that you do not hate your brother or sister in need, but what are you doing to show that you love him or her? Isaiah 58 reminds us that the foundation for biblical justice exists in the principle that our horizontal relationships must accurately reflect our vertical beliefs about God, or we will limit God's response to our needs as well.

James clearly tells us that "pure" religion is to "visit orphans and widows in their distress" (James 1:27). Orphans and widows represent the helpless and marginalized in society, those who cannot defend or empower themselves. This prescription isn't about what we do *against* the needy and the poor, it concerns what we do *for* them.

God says that He will do for us in response to what we do for others. Biblical justice is not a passive awareness of human needs, but rather an action taken to execute God's justice in the midst of an unjust society. Only when our biblical theology leads to a just and righteous sociology does God promise to make our lights shine, answer our prayers, and make us successful agents of reconciliation (Isa. 58:1–12; 2 Cor. 5:18–19).

## The Present State of the Black Evangelical Movement

While none of us are completely removed from a connection to our own personal experience, black evangelicalism adheres to the conviction that we are not to allow our experiences to have an authoritative hold when it comes to interpreting and applying Scripture, whether that be a black experience, white experience, or any color. The Scripture assumes itself to possess a basis of authority and priority that transcends cultural distinctives and needs regardless of how tightly woven that experience is in the lives of the audience involved. When a theology based on experience rather than a biblical exposition of revelation is applied, interpretational and applicational methods of study are concomitantly transposed, leading to incomplete conclusions and diverting us from living out a kingdom-based model for life, especially in the areas of racial relationships and social justice.

The black experience is real, but not revelatory. It is important, but not automatically inspired. Recognizing this to be true during the social and theological revolution of the 1960s and 1970s placed theologians like me at the critical juncture of the emergence and development of black evangelicalism, in a position of being caught between two worlds. Holding tenaciously to a conservative hermeneutic of theology gave us, black evangelicals, a link to the white evangelical world. However, we also had to respond, both personally and on behalf of our calling given by God of faithfully and accurately shepherding those under our care, to the valid questions raised by the black revolution, black power, and black theology along with the inconsistencies taught by many of our white mentors.

As a result, black evangelicals serve in a long line of strategic links to help strengthen the ministry of the black church while simultaneously educating the white church to the far-reaching cultural impact of the gospel. The enslaved black church married the best of African religion and culture with the Christian faith to forge a unique imprint on the American religious scene. In the same way, black evangelicalism facilitated the fusion of the best of the black church with the best of the white church to hew out what could very well have been the strongest contemporary expression of biblical Christianity in America. The current divisions which plague us as Christians in our nation have sought to redefine many of the terms we have looked at in this chapter and in this book. And, often, rightfully so. Yet we still face a culture and a world in decline with a seemingly inept approach at addressing the real issues of the day. It is my belief that we will only experience the full expression of biblical Christianity in our nation, and in our world, if and when we are willing to come together underneath the overarching rule of God in every area of life—respectfully, as one.

While hugely important in shaping the history and even current structures of the conservative Christian black experience in our nation, the organized black evangelical movement has waned in its influence over the years. This applies both to the overall group as well as organizations such as the NBEA. For example, in the 1970s and early 1980s, the NBEA conferences and teachings were highly regarded. Yet following its peak in the early '80s, it began to decline as many of its younger members began to grow and develop our own ministries and focuses, which eventually proved to be larger than the NBEA itself. This specific organization was crucial during the embryonic days of evangelical integration and once stood alone in addressing the social issues at large, but these concepts then filtered into larger ministries, schools, and even cross-cultural institutions as the overall cultural climate matured on social issues.

In addition, personally, it was hard to stand with organizations such as the NBEA when they began to experience what many of us felt was a theological drift. That is why Ruben Conner, Eddie Lane, and I submitted our official resignation from the NBEA Board of Directors in 1980 due to what we saw as too much of a non-biblical framework influencing the conferences and dialogues.[20] Going too far to satisfy the black experience at the expense of biblical clarity had birthed what I and others believed to be an unclear gospel message which many of us could no longer align with. Thus, our commitment, and many others like us, to biblical inerrancy had placed us between two distinctly divided worlds once again. Had the concept of "kingdomology" existed at that time as a movement, I'm sure I—and many others—would have embraced it. But it didn't. It was still germinating in the seeds of the minds of those of us seeking to know God's heart for both the social and spiritual in the context of His overarching rule and role in our lives as His followers.

The author of Hebrews tells us that when God is ready to do something new, He creates a disturbance. The reason He creates the disturbance, according to Hebrews, is to shake earthbound and physical things up in order to reveal that which cannot be shaken. In other words, God shakes our physical, human reality in an effort to get us spiritually back on point.

I don't think anyone would disagree with me when I say that the black evangelical movement has been shaky over the recent years. In fact, I don't think anyone would disagree with me to suggest that evangelicalism has been shaken too. I would like to suggest that one reason for these disturbances is that evangelicalism (black and white) has gotten off-point. Evangelicalism has lost its way. We are being written off, dismissed, critiqued, and criticized—often with just cause. The very Word we proclaim has fallen into disrepute. Not because the Bible isn't true or we don't believe the Bible as white or black evangelicals, but because the presence that we ought to be having due to the truth of the Bible has not been manifested in the culture as our Creator designed it to be.

We have become the outcasts. And not because we are being persecuted for our faith but rather because we are being persecuted for our foolishness. This problem of race should never have been allowed to seat itself in the Church of Jesus Christ for generation after generation after generation. When Paul dealt with it in Peter and the others, he dealt with it both swiftly and soundly. What's more, Paul didn't confront Peter with sociology, an essay, or theory. He confronted him with the very truth of the nature of the gospel we all claim to love and cherish so much. Paul let Peter know the position on racial segregation and prejudice he had taken that day was intolerable and misaligned with the gospel.

Far too many evangelicals have not understood that while the gospel is narrow in content, it is broad in scope. The unity of the church is a gospel issue, and it is a gospel issue saints need to know about. We cannot dismiss it by calling on the content of the gospel that gets us, or someone else, to heaven—while we skip the scope of the gospel which ought to change how we relate to one another on earth.

So, to help the church out today, God is calling us out too. God is confronting us. He is shaking up the culture to reveal what's going on. Since the church has become content to continue to use illegitimate diagnostic methodologies for determining relationships, fellowship, and unity, then He is messing up the culture enough so that we can no longer get away with skipping the issues we need to address.

We've got too many Bible-believing churches, Bible-believing Christians, Bible-believing books, Bible-believing programs that all give God a lot of respect—on paper. We're just not getting anything done. We're not making much progress. We're not demonstrating a King who is ruling a kingdom. Because if we were, the culture wouldn't skip us or marginalize us. No, they would come to us for guidance and direction. They wouldn't ignore us. Unfortunately today, we have become too evangelical and not kingdom enough. The Bible is all about the glory of God through the advancement of His kingdom. It is about the rule of God to which we are to be subordinate. And since we sit under divine rule, we need to act like it.

We serve a God who is demonstrating to us through the tumultuous times in our land and in our world that He is the builder of the only unshakeable kingdom. He rules over all. And until we align ourselves underneath His overarching command and obey His commandments, it doesn't matter what we call ourselves or how many programs we fund or conferences we hold. It is only when we intentionally live our lives underneath God's rule that we will advance His kingdom agenda together.

**Notes**

1. James H. Cone, *Risks of Faith: The Emergence of Black Theology of Liberation, 1968–1998* (Boston: Beacon Press, 1999), 130.
2. Daniel Patte and Gary Phillips, "A Fundamental Condition for Ethical Accountability in the Teaching of the Bible by White Male Exegetes: Recovering and Claiming the Specificity of Our Perspective," *Scriptura* 9 (1991), 8.
3. Anthony B. Bradley, *Liberating Black Theology: The Bible and the Black Experience in America* (Wheaton, IL: Crossway, 2010), Introduction.
4. Westminster Shorter Catechism, answer to question 1.
5. Sarah Pulliam Bailey, "Atlanta Megachurch Pastor Louie Giglio Sets off Firestorm by Calling Slavery a 'Blessing' to Whites," *Washington Post*, June 16, 2020, www.washingtonpost.com/religion/2020/06/16/atlanta-megachurch-pastor-louie-giglio-sets-off-firestorm-after-calling-slavery-white-blessing (a video of the event is embeded in the article).
6. Shelby Steele, *Shame: How America's Past Sins Have Polarized Our Country* (New York: Basic Books, 2015), 2.
7. "Prominent Black Pastor Pondering Exit," ABCNews.com, abcnews.go.com/Politics/wireStory/prominent-black-pastor-pondering-exit-southern-baptists-75456007.
8. "Seminary Presidents Meet with Black Pastors But Don't Change Position on Critical Race Theory," BaptistNews.com, baptistnews.com/article/sbc-seminary-presidents-meet-with-black-pastors-but-dont-change-position-on-critical-race-theory/.
9. Bryan Loritts, "More on Leaving White Evangelicalism: A Response from Bryan Loritts," *Christianity Today*, October 20, 2017, www.christianitytoday.com/edstetzer/2017/october/response-to-ray-changs-open-letter-to-john-piper.html.
10. Charlene Aaron, "The Number One Killer of All African Americans," CBN.com, July 8, 2019, www1. cbn.com/cbnnews/us/2019/june/the-number-1-killer-of-all-African-Americans-black-denomination-battles-the-racism-of-abortion.
11. Catherine Davis and Bradley Mattes, "Since *Roe* Abortion Has Killed More Black Babies Than the Entire Black Population of the US," *Washington Examiner*, www.washingtonexaminer.com/opinion/op-eds/since-roe-abortion-has-killed-more-black-babies-than-the-entire-black-population-of-the-u-s-in-1960.
12. "Resident Population of the United States by Race from 2000 to 2020," www.statista.com/statistics/183489/population-of-the-us-by-ethnicity-since-2000/.
13. Zoe Dutton, "Abortion's Racial Gap," *The Atlantic*, September 22, 2014, www.theatlantic.com/health/archive/2014/09/abortions-racial-gap/380251.
14. Katherin Kortsmit et al., "Abortion Surveillance—United States, 2018," Centers for Disease Control and Prevention, November 27, 2020, www.cdc.gov/mmwr/volumes/69/ss/ss6907a1.htm.

15. Mary Anne Dion, "Hitler, the Ku Klux Klan, and Margaret Sanger," *Courier Herald*, April 10, 2019, www.courierherald.com/letters/hitler-the-ku-klux-klan-and-margaret-sanger.
16. "Window Dressing: Alveda King Says NY Planned Parenthood Removing Aryan Racist Sanger from Clinic Not Enough," CBSNews.com, https://www1.cbn.com/cbnnews/us/2020/july/window-dressing-alveda-king-says-ny-planned-parenthood-removing-aryan-racist-sanger-from-clinic-not-enough.
17. Tanya L. Green, "The Negro Project: Margaret Sanger's Eugenic Plan for Black America," http://www.blackgenocide.org/negro.html.
18. "Is Planned Parenthood Targeting Certain Neighborhoods?" FoxNews.com, August 14, 2015, www.foxnews.com/transcript/is-planned-parenthood-targeting-certain-neighborhoods.
19. Margaret Sanger to C. J. Gamble, December 10, 1939, Margaret Sanger Papers, Smith College Library Archive, https://libex.smith.edu/omeka/files/original/d6358bc-3053c93183295bf2df1c0c931.pdf.
20. Jimmy Lockyear, "Theology Culture Rift Surfaces Among Evangelical Blacks," *Christianity Today*, May 23, 1980, www.christianitytoday.com/ct/1980/may-23/theology-culture-rift-surfaces-among-evangelical-blacks.html.

# Part 3

# A KINGDOM VISION FOR CULTURAL IMPACT

## Chapter 12

# THE REALITY OF RACISM

As we enter into this final section, I want to examine what racism is, how it works, and what the resolutions should be to our current racial crisis. I've chosen to focus the majority of my time in these pages on the biblical case for oneness. This book differs from many of the books written recently which delve into the inner workings of structural and personal racism, or the denial thereof, in that I've aimed to look at the importance of unity, why and how we've lost it, and what we can do to regain it. Much of the debate and dialogue has devolved into nothing more than language politics, offering us no real dialogue or solutions for the real problems at hand. We must learn to discuss hard issues with an open heart. We must be willing to read or listen to people we don't agree with. We must search for the kernels of truth, wherever they may lie, so that we can learn, improve, grow, and impact our culture for Christ. This has always been my aim when talking about the reality of racial concerns.

At the time of writing the first edition of this book in 2010, finding readers interested in the topics of race, unity, or even racism was about as common as finding the abominable snowman in Texas. Even the publisher didn't feel it would circulate well. And, at first, it didn't. But I wrote the book more out of obedience to God and His call to tell the truth whether there are ears to hear or not. Racial unity was a topic that needed to be discussed even though few seemed interested. Racism was a sin that needed to be uncovered and addressed, with a solution to overcoming it and healing from it offered. Yet the focus in our nation, at least in that season, contented itself on other things, much to my personal disappointment and concern.

However, in the more than ten years since I first released this book, I am thankful to see that the interest and discussion on racial issues has exploded, to put it mildly. Where there used to be only a handful of books on the subject by Christian and secular thought leaders, volumes now line bookstore shelves. Where there used to be only a mention on a daytime talk show here or there, and that typically in February (Black History Month), the news hours and investigative programs, as well as many of our podcasts, films, and certainly our social media influencers, speak on the subject ongoingly. While there used to only be what appeared to be tokenism by the white church or even by the white secular entities and shows/films, there now seems to be an attempt at real inclusion. With the rise in awareness of real issues concerning race and unity—issues like economic disparity, the wealth gap, ongoing repercussions of systemic racism, police reform, educational inequities, hate speech, implicit biases, microaggressions, environmental and healthcare imbalances—our collective conscience has reawakened the slumbering giant within.

Gone are the days of sweeping this subject to the side. No longer can ignorance nor apathy serve as a cover for ill-used words, actions, inactions, or failed systems, policies, and their consequences which can linger even generationally after they have been disbanded. The topic of racism, and antiracism, is finally getting the attention and conversation it needs in order to have the opportunity to deal with its ugly stain on both the history and present nature of our nation and, most importantly, the church.

Surprisingly, to me at least, there has not been widespread embrace, though, of this increase of focus on racial issues. Certain terms such as *systemic racism, white privilege, implicit bias, microaggression, victimization*, and others trigger emotional responses which often kick opportunities for authentic conversations to the curb. A mixed bag of personal definitions of these terms combined with a variety of personal experiences have turned the dialogue on diversity into a heated battle of hearts oftentimes leading only to confusion. This has caused many, on both sides, to throw the proverbial "baby out with the bath water" through rejecting concepts, ideologies, or viewpoints holistically rather than pursuing an honest intellectual exchange on what may be valuable or what may not.

The redefinition of terms and multiple meanings of words, often dependent on who is using them, has made it almost impossible to discuss relevant issues reasonably. As Thomas Sowell puts it, "One of the many signs of verbal virtuosity among intellectuals is the repackaging of words to mean things that are not only different from, but sometimes the direct opposite of, their original meanings."[1] Thus, before we start any discussion on racism and reconciliation, I want to start by giving you my definitions for what I'm about to address.

## Racism and Systemic Racism

Many people define racism in many different ways. This is due to the tremendous variety in both the practical and emotive experiences that form the perspectives through which life is viewed. I define racism as *the conscious or unconscious belief in the superiority of one race over another race or ethnicities, which manifests itself in a variety of dismissive, oppressive, or exploitive ways.* Racism shows up in the use of power, influence, resources, or communication, which is employed to discriminate against, marginalize, exploit, and/or subjugate people of another race or ethnicity. When unaddressed prejudice gets married to power, there is going to be an unintended pregnancy that will give birth to the evil of racism.

I have heard the assertion, as I'm sure you have, that "systemic racism" no longer exists. I often hear that from people who with their next breath say they are not racist, and some might even add that they never owned slaves. These two statements are often tied so closely that they appear to be a defensive posture. By negating the existence of systemic racism or its consequences, they attempt to absolve any personal feelings of attachment to it. The white author Ken Wytsma connects this defensiveness to a need for personal comfort. After being told to not use the term *white privilege* in a talk at a Christian university, he observed that "our desire for comfort leads us to defensiveness when we are confronted with questions of race." He continues with a good question: "But when did our comfort become the driving value?"[2]

Yet I have also heard the same denial of systemic racism by many well-known black scholars and conservative black theologians, who do so with a focus on personal responsibility and moral values. They seem hesitant to acknowledge the existence of lingering corporate, social, political, and economic effects of racism, as if this somehow eliminates the possibility and primacy of promoting personal responsibilities.

And while I agree that our laws and legal systems on paper have been addressed and corrected over the years, I would assert that certain cultural repercussions remain. Just as a football team may win or lose on paper but perform very differently in the actual game, paper laws intended to help don't always produce equitable outcomes. This is because the carrying out of those laws, as well as the residual effects of the earlier laws, applies to people, not paper. Whenever you insert humanity into the equation, you've inserted sin, and sin invariably messes things up.

Systemic racism, or the resultant lingering effects of it, continues to show up in pockets and places across our land. You see it in unequal access to quality health care and lack of affordable nutritious meal options in urban centers. This leads to increased obesity and negative health outcomes (physical and mental), as well as lower access to quality job opportunities. It also leads to the disparate amount of transferable generational wealth largely due to the equally disparate numbers of home ownership over the last century.

It can also be argued that systemic racism exists through less overt but cyclically produced ramifications of decades of racist-based legislation (again, whether or not the legislation still exists). Urban crowding and its lasting legacy of poor education, dismantled families, and high crime is one example. There is no "law" keeping black Americans living in highly populated urban centers, but there is also not much of a way out since many of the individuals there face so many hardships at such a young age, coupled with inadequate training, which often prevents upward mobility.

In addition, the targeted rampant funding and promotion of unhealthy lifestyle norms which have annihilated the framework of the black family in many areas in our land, not just in urban centers (such as values-damaging movies, music, abortions, drugs), have sealed in much of the systemic limitations and resultant self-sabotaging behaviors which show up in the inordinately high prison rate among black males, the frequency of teenage pregnancy and abortion, single-parent homes, and a lack of initiative in career training and the seeking of advancement. Many people do not recognize this but another insidious form of racism was the illegitimate use of welfare which targeted and encouraged the destabilization of the black family. Welfare entered the scene just as legally based racism was beginning to be eradicated through the Civil Rights Act and other reforms. And while many claimed that welfare was implemented in order to help lift the plight of the poor, it took aim at that which would have helped the poor to lift themselves: personal responsibility, the promotion of two-parent homes, and self-respect. Rather than seek to train, or in the Christian terminology "disciple," individuals to make every use of opportunities for personal growth, welfare and other policies like it undermined the upward mobility of certain segments of our society.

Discipleship, by its nature, intends to deepen and expand its impact by speaking to life's challenges through the establishment of a stronger spiritual foundation as the starting point, as opposed to a sociological foundation.

Sociology, in and of itself, does not make good biblical theology. Nor does sociology, in and of itself, offer a strong framework for discipleship. In fact, many of the sociological systems which have been enacted in an effort to help lift black Americans (i.e., war on poverty, Head Start, affirmative action) have actually—from a statistical standpoint—only compounded the issues within the black communities through the dismantling of core building blocks such as the nuclear family, personal responsibility, and self-worth.

The data prior to the 1960s, before the Civil Rights Movement ushered in many of these policy changes, cannot be argued in that the nuclear black family was stronger, the wealth gap tighter, and even the overall educational attainments were higher.[3] The difference in median household income between black Americans and white Americans in 1970, shortly after many of these new initiatives took place, was roughly $23,800. That amount was measured to have increased to $33,000 by 2018.[4] Not only that, the median net worth of African Americans in 2020 was $24,100 as compared to $188,000 by white households.[5]

Anyone who runs a business or an educational institute knows that you must examine outcomes to determine whether or not an approach is effective. The outcomes for the black status in America since the Civil Rights Era should be taken into consideration when examining policies for impact, both those in the past and how they have performed (or caused harm, despite any well intentions) and policies for the present. In addition, any policy that strips a person of his or her innate personal responsibility, ownership, and ambition—particularly those which promote a victim or oppressed mindset—can undoubtedly lead to a self-fulfilling cycle of personal and collective sabotage.

In essence, the antipoverty initiatives (while arguably well-intentioned by many) subsidized the destruction of the strength of the black man by seeking to replace the virtues of work with welfare. This then led to the dissolution of the black family. The number of black children born to two-parent households before these policies were enacted was roughly 75%. But over five decades later, that number is now representative of the over 70% of black children born to single-parent homes. It has flipped. As former President Obama said in his talk on fatherhood as a then-Senator at the Apostolic Church of God in Chicago,

> We know the statistics—that children who grow up without a father are five times more likely to live in poverty and commit crime; nine times more likely to drop out of schools and 20 times more likely to end up in prison. They are more likely to have behavioral problems, or run away from home or become teenage parents themselves. And the foundations of our community are weaker because of it.[6]

History has shown this trend of negative outcomes to be true, no matter the racial demographic, when policies which remove or undermine personal responsibility and value are applied to any racial demographic through any set of systems, legal or not.[7]

It is my belief that racism has embedded itself not only in many individual hearts throughout our history but also, to varying degrees, in the many structures of our society. Whether those structures are political, economic, legal, or many others, they impact how entire groups of people think and live.

Systemic racism is said to exist whenever racism has become part of the policies, procedures, and mindset by which a particular entity or societal structure operates. And while law-based existences of systemic racism may have been overturned or done away with through nationwide reforms, the lasting implications of many of these systems can still be felt by many. Some people get stuck in semantics over whether or not officially sanctioned "systemic racism" exists in our nation through governmental laws, or whether it exists through cyclical and cultural effects. Instead, believers ought to be open to examining real-life struggles and how to solve them.

Systemic racism recognizes that the sin of racism is, or was, not only a personal issue, but a corporate one as well. In fact, systemic racism even recognizes that while individuals themselves might not be racist, the structures and entities in which these individuals live or function can be established and still run on racist policies, practices, ideals, and intentions. I have heard many people argue against systemic racism through arguing that not all people of a certain race are racist. But that is not what systemic racism is. To acknowledge that systemic racism exists is not the same thing as declaring all white people to be racist. Systemic racism speaks to the structures, policies, and institutions of a society and not to the entirety of the individuals who inhabit it.

Thus, I define systemic racism as *the presence, or cyclical resultant effects, of racist practices and processes embedded in and shaping the social, political, economic, legal, educational, religious, infrastructural, and medical systems and policies of a society—initially established and perpetuated by the government*. These then overlap and interconnect in such a way as to give an unjust advantage of resources, rights, mindsets, and privilege for a majority number of one race while denying or limiting it to a majority number of other races or ethnicities.

Systemic racism's impact over the decades when it loomed large still impacts a myriad of things such as employment, education, housing, incarceration, health care, family dynamics, wealth gaps, and much more. Whatever the system or structure of racist realities (known or unknown), these contribute overall to inequitable opportunities for personal advancement or personal wholeness. These same principles can apply to class divisions or caste systems and have existed in other nations divided by ethnic or racial constructs. It is not only a white/black matrix, depending on the nation and the group in power.

### *Theological Comparison*

Perhaps a theological comparison can help illustrate the point. Men are born under the evil law of sin and death. This sentences all mankind to the slavery and oppression of sin (Rom. 8:2; Eph. 2:1–3). Upon conversion, that law is canceled and replaced with a new law, the law of the spirit (Rom. 6:6). This new law legally frees believers from the law of sin and death. However, just because the law changed, the abiding struggle with sin did not automatically disappear (Rom. 7:14–25). Only consistent growth in the application of the law of the spirit can overcome the flesh's attempt to keep us functioning as spiritual slaves (Gal. 5:16–18). Failure to apply the new law means that the abiding effects of the evil system of the old law continues due to the historical power of the old laws' influence on our flesh, even though it has been replaced. This reality serves to deny believers the full experience of freedom the new law promises (Rom. 8:3–13; Gal. 5:13). Likewise, the abiding effects of racism continue at various levels depending on the willingness of people to submit to the new laws of justice that have been established.

### *Historical Comparison*

Our shared history begins with the system of whites enslaving blacks, which arguably began as far back as the 1500s. Of course we are all aware of the evil system of slavery, a legal system enacted to oppress black people based on the color of our skin. But what many people do not realize is that when slavery was dissolved, the ideologies within it merely got embedded into other structures in society. So while the practice of slavery was outlawed, the principles that undergirded it remained present through other legalized systems from the Black Codes to Jim Crow. Thus, when people point to slavery as a contributing factor to present-day issues, they are pointing to slavery and the resultant practices and policies that flowed out of it up until now.

For example, after slavery there immediately developed a practice called debt servitude (peonage), where an employer would compel an individual to work in order to pay off a debt. This was primarily used by landowners or merchant suppliers as a way of keeping blacks in a state of perpetual servanthood. On the surface, debt servitude does not necessarily seem evil. It is only when you uncover the ways in which it was enacted upon minority ethnicities after slavery that you see the evil for what it was. Price gouging on life-sustaining items such as flour, eggs, or milk in order to create lifelong dependence and debt was commonplace. And while this form of peonage was outlawed by Congress in 1867 due to its imbedded evils, many people found a way to continue the principles of the practice through other means.

In addition to debt servitude, the criminal justice system sought to exploit a clause in the Thirteenth Amendment that stated a person was free unless they were a criminal. This resulted in an extension of peonage well into the 1900s, through the profitable practice of convict leasing.

What this clause unleashed was an avalanche of criminal charges against black boys and men for even the most minor of infractions. Often no crime was committed at all, or it was invented, such as an accusation of littering with no proof, or planted proof. For example, certain vagrancy laws even made it a crime to be unemployed at a very young age.

Once put in prison, these young boys and men would frequently be held way beyond what they were arrested for, and forced to live and work in conditions that in many cases were worse than the conditions in slavery. From a purely business standpoint, the wellbeing and the health condition of the slave mattered more to the master than to the prison owner. If prisoners were lost to death or disease, they could be replaced with another criminal without much effort. The prison owner also had no long-term view of the life and long-term contribution of the convict to seek to preserve. Thus, conditions deteriorated rapidly as people learned how to work, and fill, the system. For example, "In the first two years that Alabama leased its prisoners, nearly 20 percent of them died. In the following year, mortality rose to 35 percent. In the fourth, nearly 45 percent were killed."[8]

The *New York Times* gives insight into why so many died when it described the condition of these prisons in December 1882. It "told of black prisoners packed into a single cramped cabin like slaves on the Atlantic passage. The building had no windows. Vermin-ridden bunks stacked three high were covered with straw and 'ravaged blankets.' 'Revoltingly filthy' food was served cold from unwashed coal buckets, and all 150 black convicts shared three half-barrel tubs for washing."[9]

As you can imagine, many black families had their strongest male contributors plucked from their homes at a young age during the decades of convict leasing. Convict leasing was a lucrative practice to produce goods at a low cost. The price of using criminals for work assignments was less than a fraction of a penny. For instance, in 1866, Texas leased 250 men to two railroads for $12.50 a month.[10] A dollar could buy the labor of twenty black prisoners for a full month.

Not only did these systemically racist policies increase the wealth and opportunities for powerful whites in America (a generational wealth handed down through inheritances, which still contributes to the wealth gap today), but the policies also dismantled the nucleus of the black family by removing a large percentage of black males from homes. This strategy by those in power (i.e., that of dismantling the nucleus of the black family) has continued over the centuries through a variety of approaches. As believers in the Word of God, we know that Satan's primary way to keep a people group subjugated or in a perpetual state of cyclical self-sabotage is to attack, and destroy, the family unit. Satan is not above using sinful people and broken systems to carry out his agenda.

Many point to the war on drugs and the war on crime and other policies created in the late 1960s and early 1970s as an intentional response to thwart the gains achieved through the Civil Rights movement and a strategic extension of this targeted attack to dismantle the nuclear black family. In fact, although less easy to see, the outcomes of the policies left many calling it the "new Jim Crow." As Stanford

Law School graduate Michelle Alexander writes, "No other country in the world imprisons so many of its racial or ethnic minorities. The United States imprisons a larger percentage of its black population than South Africa did at the height of apartheid. . . . These stark racial disparities cannot be explained by rates of drug crime."[11]

But in addition to its root, peonage, and before the new Jim Crow, systemic racism showed up as our nation grew in numbers through the way people were denied employment or educational opportunities during the actual era of the Jim Crow segregation. Jim Crow laws of the South were the official standards that inculcated and established that one group would be allowed to benefit while another group would be disenfranchised. It also showed up in churches that were unwilling to accept people of a different race, or theological institutions that were unwilling to train people of a different race.

### *My Experiences With Racism*

Systemic racism impacted me personally in a number of ways. When I tried to enter the media ministry in my mid-30s, I was turned down by every station I sought to get on, except for one in Houston. Some would even go so far as to tell me that a black speaker would offend too many of their white listeners. While there was no law stating a black preacher couldn't air his sermons on white-owned radio stations, there was an embedded cultural system in place denying black preachers equal opportunity and equal access for upward mobility.

Now does that mean every radio station listener was racist and would have been offended at that time? No. Did I think every white person was racist at that time because I couldn't get on radio stations to broadcast my sermons? No again. That's because the existence of systemic racism, or its cyclical outworkings, does not mean that every white person in America is racist. But it did mean that the system of Christian radio in the early 1980s and before functioned, to some degree, with unwritten yet very clearly racist processes, standards, and assumptions.

I have plenty of personal illustrations where I have faced systemic racism. One took place when I was asked to go speak to a group of Christian golfers at a golf club. Those who invited me wanted me to teach the Bible in order to make a spiritual impact on the members.

I went, but after I got there, I discovered that I was visiting a place that I could not join. I was welcome as a preacher but not as a person.

Not too long ago, the church where I pastor purchased the golf course adjacent to our church, 155 acres of prime acres in the southwest section of Oak Cliff. I did not propose buying the course because I like golf—in fact, I don't even play. I wanted us to purchase it in order to have a say in what happens in our community. We own several hundred acres of land in this area for that very purpose—to invest in the well-being and maintenance of our urban community.

The interesting history about the golf course was that black people could not play on it until the 1990s. This is because blacks were not allowed to be members when it was built in the 1950s.

Now when the golf course turned into a member-owned course some years later, there was no longer a law that kept black people from joining. The law got removed because our culture was changing and that kind of law was no longer viewed as acceptable. But even though the unjust law had been removed, the system was still plagued with racism. For example, before a person could become a member, an existing member had to recommend you. That shouldn't be much of a problem until you find out that after you are recommended, two-thirds of the membership had to also vote for you.

So let's say a white man recommends a black man to join the golf club. They are going up against a system that states that two-thirds of his peers have to agree with the way he is thinking, which is why no black man was voted in until 1994. Not because there was a law against it. There wasn't. But there was a system in place that operated on racist principles.

But taking this further—let's say as a white man you are part of the one-third who voted to have the black man admitted to join. Or you are the white man who proposed he join. Well, you still lost because of the two-thirds who were the majority in the system. Now, you could argue that you are not part of the two-thirds and are not like those people. You could also argue that you are not a racist, and you could be absolutely right. But the point is that the system you were a part of was racist. Acknowledging the existence of systemic racism is not the same as saying that all white people are racist. But denying its existence out of a spirit of defensiveness or an honest lack of personal involvement is insensitive to the plight of the many impacted by it either in the past or present.

While there are varying views on the degrees to which systemic racism is reflected in our lives today, one thing is clear: wherever systemic racism (or its repercussions) exists, or whatever you choose to label it, there are real issues plaguing millions of Americans today. And much of this shows up in affecting primarily lower-class black Americans (and certainly other subgroups and class groups). Rather than spend all of our time arguing semantics or trying to pin blame (or deflect it), we as Christ followers ought to acknowledge the issues at hand and righteously address them.

A person merely needs to walk through the urban center of Baltimore, where I grew up, to witness the inadequate facilities for equal educational opportunities for Baltimore's minorities, as compared with the educational systems in the suburbs. And while admittedly there have been opportunities to address these issues by electing minority leadership, there has been an obvious failure to take advantage of those positions to bring about a greater good for the community at large. Historic systemic corruption can become so deeply imbedded that it can show up even in those who you would think would want to change it.

As recently as 2020, graduation rates in the urban areas of Maryland were only 69.9 percent while the average rate for the entire state is much higher at 86.7 percent.[12] Not only that, graduation requirements have been so grossly lowered in the urban schools that the Baltimore City Community College reported that 93 percent of all incoming students (70 percent of whom come from Baltimore's city-schools) required remedial classes.[13] Lowering standards does not prepare an individual for success. In fact, it often sets them up for induced failure. This contributes to a lowering of their own personal esteem through the concept of mismatched placement, which can then be handed down generationally, according to famed black economist Thomas Sowell.[14]

### *Systemic Racism and Political Ideology*

Systemic racism isn't a politically-neutral-perpetuated issue either, as both sides often like to believe. Both sides of the aisle have contributed to its generational mess. In fact, much of it has been produced most recently through what people have labeled liberal progressive legislation and policies, beginning in the mid-1960s with the war on poverty. Any policy that seeks to strip individual responsibility, ambition, and values from people or dismantles the primacy of the nuclear family does more harm than good. Systemic racism camouflaged as charity is another insidious form of injustice.

In fact, compare the statistics of racial income gaps prior to the war on poverty and other civil rights legislation and after it. The income gap has remained the same, if not worsened in some areas.[15] Liberal policies, along with an errant view of the legitimate divinely created scope of civil government, fall short in producing the outcomes that the liberals claim they will. Rather, the policies produce an unhealthy and illegitimate dependency on government.

Shelby Steele describes this conundrum between liberal ideology and outcome as the "great internal contradiction of white liberalism: that its paternalism, its focus on whites rather than on blacks as the agents of change, allows white supremacy to slip in the back door and once again define the fundamental relationship between whites and blacks . . . Whites are agents; blacks are agented."[16]

Elsewhere in his book, Steele describes neither side's true solutions (liberal or conservative) in the context of his father's life. He was gainfully employed as a truck driver yet unable to join the Teamsters Union, thus receiving less wages. He also had to hide his home ownership from his employer in fear of being fired for "getting above himself." Steele said his father thus lived in "an insecure nether land with no harbor among either capitalists or socialists."[17] In summary, "his society quite literally labored to defeat his ambition even as it left him entirely responsible for his life and family."[18]

Systemic racism, or its ensuing effects, often comes stacked over a lifetime, but it can also be viewed like dominos standing on a table. If you knock one domino over, the rest will likely fall. Children and youth need opportunities to excel in education, starting with a strong nuclear family, strong church, limited exposure to damaging influences, strong role models, healthy food and life balances, character development and behavioral accountability, and an accurate view of personal potential. Without this foundation, their opportunities for social and vocational successes diminish later in life as well. One thing leads to another. And this then is passed down generationally as poor life choices lead to generational consequences stacked on each other in what can appear to outsiders as communal self-sabotage. The net result is that hopelessness rules.

### *Systemic Racism and Education*

In addition to the personal and cultural contributing factors, the education system itself continues to add to the problems. This includes the refusal to offer parents school choice (where the funding follows the kids and not vice versa). This greatly disadvantages the opportunity and progress for the disenfranchised, locking them into an inefficient educational monopoly that underserves them. From a kingdom perspective, education starts with the family, not with the state. Such competition in the marketplace will inevitably lead to improved educational opportunity for those who need it most.

Education is merely one domino on the table that enacts separate standards based on color and class. When a person is faced with several realities of systemic racism in his or her life (this is referred to as *intersectionality*), along with an often-generalized and dismissive stance by the culture at large on whether or not he or she faces any inequitable hardships at all, he or she confronts an emotional, psychological, and practical barrier toward personal growth and development. Sometimes, and far too often, paralyzingly so. This creates a self-imposed prophecy of living up to the lowered expectations offered through permissive policies.

## Our Responsibility

While an individual today may not be personally racist, they can contribute to the racist structures by supporting the inequitable systems still in place, or by denying that they exist. If you are nonracist yourself but do not actively oppose racism (willing to speak or work against racism and racist systems where they show up), you are failing to fulfill the whole letter of the law of love (Rom. 13:8). As we saw earlier, sin is not just a bad behavior you do but rather sin is also knowing something good to do and choosing not to do it (James 4:17; Isa. 58).

Yes, sin is personal. Far too many people argue that racism is not something to be addressed by the church because the church should focus on personal sins only. But Nehemiah 1:6–7 coupled with Daniel 9:4–6 links our personal sins to the collective group and to the systems upon which culture is founded and runs.

Think of a sprint where some racers are allowed to start earlier or are allowed to start at a point much ahead of another group. The other group spends their whole time just trying to catch up—the sprint is intrinsically not equitable. This illustration may help you develop more empathy for this historical reality of systemic racism. When you can grasp this reality, how frequently it appears in our culture, and its resultant cyclical effects, you can gain sensitivity to the conversations at hand or legitimate protests taking place. Again, the existence of racism cannot and must not be used as a reason for rejecting personal and corporate responsibility, even as injustice is being properly addressed. It should also be noted that while righteous protesting is biblically based (Acts 16:35–40), rioting is not (Rom. 3:14–18). Rioting must never be accepted as a righteous way of redress.

Despite all of our forward progress, there still remains within our society certain critical elements that need to be corrected, adjusted, or even entirely revamped so that equal opportunity toward emotional, physical, and psychological health as well as personal development in education and skills training is granted to all people, irrespective of race. I have seen a tremendous increase in virtue signaling and social media posting about racial unity over the last few years but what I have not seen much at all is any real changes in the true racial integration of relationships, Christian organizations' staff or church makeup, or even personal investment in addressing the broken systems that continue to plague pockets of our land. Reading a book is great. Posting about it online gets the word out. Also, good. But when you close this book, seek to do something to make a difference for good in the world in which we live. This difference should be led by the church publicly operating with a Kingdom Race Theology, not a culturally determined sociology.

*Simultaneous Pandemics*

As I write this chapter, our nation finds itself in the middle of multiple, simultaneous pandemics. Not only are we contending with the aftermath of a global medical pandemic brought on by COVID-19 but we are also living in the midst of a cultural and societal pandemic. Yet deeper still and at the root of these is a spiritual pandemic.

We have wandered far from the value system established by God for how human beings are to live, act, and relate to one another. Across racial and class lines, we have come up with our own standards for how we treat each other, and it has not done us any good.

The solution starts in understanding how the world works. We gain one of our greatest insights into this through reading 2 Chronicles 15, which we will look at more closely in the next chapter. But in this passage, we see that when the spiritual principles are placed aside, there is no peace in the culture. In fact, it clearly states in 2 Chronicles 15:6,

> Nation was crushed by nation, and city by city, for God troubled them with every kind of distress.

The Israelites had so hardened their hearts toward God, and rebelled against His righteous rule, that God initiated an ongoing state of distress. Now, if God is your problem, it doesn't matter what programs you come up with, because only God is your solution.

The root of the racial problems we face in our nation today are clearly spiritual. It's only when we identify and understand the spiritual components that we are then able to translate them to the pragmatic realities of the cultural crisis at hand. Sometimes it takes a mess to make a miracle.

God has been known to allow chaos for the purposes of creating a heartfelt calling by His people to Him for help. When we appeal to Him according to His kingdom rule, He is then able to reintroduce Himself into the scenario and usher in the healing we so desperately need.

Everyone knows what it's like to suffer for a long time from stomach pains only to later throw up and feel better relatively quickly. The throwing up is a messy situation, but the reason you feel better afterwards is because you have purged the toxins.

There are a lot of toxins swirling around us today. We have toxins of injustice, toxins of racism, and toxins of hate. We have a multiplicity of toxins coagulating in the same space at the same time. But if we miss the reality that God has allowed this in order to bring about a correction and a cleaning, then we will just move from one symptom to another symptom. We will miss the opportunity to address the root that has produced the fruit which has led to the confusion of hopelessness on display.

God has spoken on the issues at hand, and He has not stuttered. He has spoken about racism. He has spoken about systemic and individual injustices. He has spoken about classism. He has spoken about culturalism. He has spoken about politics. He has spoken about freedom. He has spoken about division. He has spoken about equity, elitism, indulgences, empathy, and more. God has spoken about all of these subjects, but until we align our hearts, thoughts, words, and actions underneath His overarching rule based on what He has said, we are living in rebellion and will continue to suffer the consequences for it.

What many people do today, unfortunately, is pick and choose what they will obey. As a result, we are experiencing a dearth of kingdom disciples who observe all that God has commanded, not just the parts they like. From God's throne comes both righteousness and justice. These are not seesaws to go up and down on. Rather, these are twins who are joined at the hip. You don't skip injustice and call for righteousness. Likewise, you don't skip righteousness in the name of injustice. We are created for a higher calling, that of following the whole counsel of God.

If we are to ever fix this madness and solve this mess—on these issues of injustice, racism, the pain of our shared history, and the systems which perpetuate inequity generationally in areas of our land—it will only be due to a right response, collectively as the body of Christ, based on God's Word. Until the spiritual issues are prioritized and addressed, the social, cultural, and racial ones won't be solved. This is why we need a Kingdom Race Theology.

## Notes

1. Thomas Sowell, *Intellectuals and Society* (New York: Basic Books, 2012), 78.
2. Ken Wytsma, *The Myth of Equality: Uncovering the Roots of Injustice and Privilege* (Downers Grove, IL: IVP Books, 2019), 23.
3. Georgina Tzanetos, "The Money Gap Between Black and White Americans is Wider Than Ever—Can Businesses Fix It?" MSN.com, April 9, 2021, www.msn.com/en-us/money/savingandinvesting/the-money-gap-between-black-and-white-americans-is-wider-than-ever--can-businesses-fix-it/ar-BB1fuc8W.
4. Katherine Schaeffer, "6 Facts About Economic Inequality in the U.S.," PewResearch.org, February 7, 2020, www.pewresearch.org/fact-tank/2020/02/07/6-facts-about-economic-inequality-in-the-u-s/.
5. "Black and White U. S. Inequality," CNN.com, July 3, 2020, www.cnn.com/2020/06/03/politics/black-white-us-financial-inequality/index.html.
6. "Obama's Fatherhood Speech," Politico.com, June 2008, www.politico.com/story/2008/06/text-of-obamas-fatherhood-speech-011094.
7. Thomas Sowell, "Affirmative Action: A Worldwide Disaster," *Commentary*, December 1989, www.commentarymagazine.com/articles/thomas-sowell-2/affirmative-action-a-worldwide-disaster/.
8. Douglas A. Blackmon, *Slavery by Another Name: The Re-Enslavement of Black Americans from the Civil War to World War II* (New York: Doubleday Anchor, 2008), 57.
9. Ibid., 72.
10. Ibid., 54.
11. Michelle Alexander, *The New Jim Crow: Mass Incarceration in the Age of Colorblindness* (New York: New Press, 2010), 6–7.
12. Chris Pabst, "Baltimore City Schools Graduation Rate Drops to Six-Year Low," FoxBaltimore.com, March 31, 2021, foxbaltimore.com/news/project-baltimore/baltimore-city-schools-graduation-rate-drops-to-six-year-low.
13. Ibid.
14. Thomas Sowell, *Intellectuals and Race* (New York: Basic Books, 2013), 66–67. Sowell cites a Massachusetts Institute of Technology study showing nearly one-fourth of its black students failed to graduate, though they would have thrived at other institutions, due to a system that "turns minority students with all the qualifications for success into artificially induced failures, by mismatching them with the institutions that admit them under lower standards."
15. Heather Long and Andrew Van Dam, "The Black-White Economic Divide Remains as Wide as It Was in 1968," *Washington Post,* June 4, 2020, www.washingtonpost.com/business/2020/06/04/economic-divide-black-households/.
16. Shelby Steele, *White Guilt: How Blacks and Whites Together Destroyed the Promise of the Civil Rights Era* (New York: Harper Perennial, 2006), 147–48.
17. Ibid., 48.
18. Ibid., 49.
19. Jeff Raikes, "We Can Challenge Systemic Racism One School District at a Time," *Forbes*, September 9, 2019, www.forbes.com/sites/jeffraikes/2019/09/19/we-can-challenge-systemic-racism-one-school-district-at-a-time/? sh=4ea209cc7e42.

## Chapter 13

# MY EVANGELICAL JOURNEY TO THE KINGDOM AGENDA

My personal path toward black evangelicalism, and later kingdomology, began at a very young age and eventually took me on a journey toward the formation of a biblical and theological philosophy called the kingdom agenda. The initial impetus for this worldview came through witnessing firsthand the impact the Word of God had in transforming my own family.

For as long as I can remember, my father worked as a longshoreman on the harbor in Baltimore. My father had to drop out of high school in order to help his father make ends meet in their home. He later went to night school as an adult to get a high school equivalency degree. Yet as a black man without a diploma raising a family in the 1950s and '60s in urban America, his work options were limited. Basically, he had to get work wherever he could find it.

Sometimes the work at the docks was unpredictable. Longshoremen often had extended periods of time without any work at all due to layoffs, strikes, or a lack of ships coming in. But during those times, I never saw my father sitting idle. He was a jack-of-all-trades, repairing anything that anyone needed fixed in a makeshift shop in our basement. In fact, he even made homemade brandy in our basement to sell before he was saved. I never saw my mother sitting around idle either. She was either cleaning, cooking, getting groceries, ironing, or doing whatever needed to be done to make sure that we had what we needed as a family. Both of my parents worked extremely hard at whatever they did.

However, prior to the transforming impact of God's Word in our home—which came when I was around ten years old—our home was very volatile. There were arguments and resistance to such a degree that I frequently wondered whether we would even make it as a family much longer. As the oldest of four children, I experienced both sides of this transformation—the unstable home life and the stable home life—more than my siblings.

## My Parents Transformed

The transformation began when my mother had been invited by a friend to attend a small, predominantly black Plymouth Brethren Assembly called the Glad Tidings Chapel. Somehow, she got my father to go with her. This turned out to be the Sunday that changed not only my father's life, but ultimately changed mine as well.

Two men approached my father after the service that day asking him if he knew whether or not he was going to heaven. My dad was uncertain of his answer, and so they shared with him the gospel of salvation by grace through faith in the finished work of Jesus Christ. My dad trusted Christ for salvation when he returned home that day at the age of twenty-nine. The resultant life change was not only immediate, but also graphic.

Frustrated that he had grown up in a Baptist church and was even serving as the choir director there at the time, where he had never heard a clear presentation of the gospel, my father left his church and joined the Brethren Assembly. He dove headfirst into his newfound faith, spending hours studying the Scripture, starting a Bible study in our home, leading devotionals with our family, listening to evangelical teaching on the radio, preaching in jails, and passing out gospel tracts on street corners.

My mother, however, was slower to embrace change. If she was not excited about my father when he was a sinner, she was even less excited about him when he became a saint. For months, she challenged and rejected his conversion and distanced herself from experiencing it with him. She even threatened to leave him after his conversion, saying that his change was too much for her to deal with. But late one night she came downstairs while he was working in the basement. Tears flowed down her face that evening as she told my dad that whatever he had must be real because, although she had doubted it and fought it, his life had clearly been changed. She told him that she wanted this change as well. So that night my father got on his knees with my mother as she trusted Christ for her salvation. Our home was never again the same.

I'm not going to tell you that I was a perfect child growing up in our home, either. I had my moments too. But in them my parents did everything that they could to not only instill the fear of God in me, but also the fear of them. They refused to tolerate, nor did they model, inexcusable or lazy behavior.

## Early Life Lessons

One of the greatest lessons I ever learned came as a result of a poor choice that I made. It happened when I was in the eighth grade. I remember going through the lunch line to get my food and seeing the sticky buns for sale on the counter. The sticky buns looked extra good that day, but I knew that I didn't have enough money to buy one. So instead, I glanced around me to see if anyone was watching. When I didn't see anyone watching, I snuck a sticky bun onto my plate. Later, as I was seated at my table getting ready to take my first bite, one of the ladies from the cafeteria line walked over to me.

"I saw what you did," she said. Terror instantly seized every ounce of my body, quickly spilling over onto my face. "I saw what you did," she said again. I'm pretty sure I stopped breathing at that point. "But do you know what?" she asked. "I'm going to show you mercy. I'm not going to turn you in." Relief flooded me everywhere.

"On one condition," she threw in. I nodded my head—anything, I was thinking—just name it. "You have to promise me that you will never steal again." I promised, and I kept my promise.

Another time while at Garrison Junior High I got into a fight with a fellow student. One of the teachers caught us battling it out together and dragged us to the principal's office. The principal had my father called in to the office in order to let him know what had happened. For my father to come in, though, meant that he had to take off work. Translation: He was going to lose some pay. I remember sitting in the office completely horrified at the thought of this.

When my dad arrived, he made two statements. First, he told me, "Tony, I'll see you when you get home." Next, he told the principal, "You will never have to worry about seeing him here again."

At home, my father sent me downstairs for what he called a "session." Essentially, a "session" meant you would get to "feel" my father's disappointment. Sessions weren't frequent in our home, but when they happened, they were difficult to forget. When my father walked downstairs, he told me to assume the position. That meant placing my head between his knees. So I did. With each strike, he asked, "Are you ever going to get suspended again?"

Everyone in the next county could hear my reply, "No!" And I never did.

## Community Backup

Many people in the neighborhood I grew up in had a similar approach to behavior as my parents. Bad behavior wasn't tolerated. If I did something wrong and an adult saw me, I was in trouble. It didn't matter if I was ten blocks away from my home. It didn't matter whether the adult even knew me. It was perfectly acceptable that whatever adult saw me could grab me by the collar, spank me, and then walk me home to my mother. My mother would then kindly reply to the stranger standing before her, "Thank you for caring enough to discipline my son," and invite her in. After my mother's newfound friend left, my mother would spank me again because someone else had to correct me. I had shamed God's name and the family name as well.

That was the community that I knew early on. It was a functioning, relationally oriented, and stable community. People shared food and struggles with each other. You could tell that there was a genuine care for each other. We didn't have much by way of material goods or opportunity, but we had a community governed by a moral code of mutual respect and personal responsibility in spite of segregation and poverty.

As time went on, due to several influencing factors, fractures began to appear in the urban community I lived in. Families began to break up more frequently. Joblessness and poor academic achievement, juvenile delinquencies, and the growth of alcoholism and drug use slowly began turning a blue-collar working community into our contemporary understanding of an inner-city neighborhood. A sense of hopelessness crept in as the community wrestled with the realities of a socially imposed oppressive psychology playing out within the tantalizingly close image of a democracy, in spite of the achievement of desegregation. These two mutually exclusive realities became difficult to synchronize for many of us.

As a result, one of the tensions that I experienced as a Christian was what it meant to be separated from the world's way of viewing life, yet still be an active participant in the world. I wanted to enjoy the things that I saw others enjoying and stand up for the things that I saw others standing up for, but I questioned how to go about either while remaining true to my growing biblical worldview.

Racial issues also heightened this tension when they became even more overtly hostile in the 1960s. I remember the week of April 4, 1968, in particular. As a seventeen-year-old boy, I sat staring out our house window upon row after row of National Guardsmen. The assassination of Martin Luther King Jr. led to explosive riots in our area. I stood there staring out my window at all the National Guard members, fully armed, who lined the streets. It looked like a war zone. I remember seeing them and fully feeling the anger present in many of us during that time of curfews and heightened security. I felt conflicted inside because I was dealing with a reality that could only be summarized as painful. These men in the National Guard had been called on and positioned there to do their job. But their job was to keep people like me, black teenagers, in our homes. It was confusing and shaming in many ways, especially in light of the reality that "people like me" had just lost one of our greatest peaceful voices for civil rights, through the violence of an assassination.

But at the same time, I was also wrestling through the teaching and training I had received from my father. My father never wasted his words. "Love your enemy, Tony," he would say. He explained that you didn't have to love what they did, but you had to love them. You could hate the sin but love the sinner.

Growing up, I had to balance all of this within me emotionally. Struggling through this season led me to a life principle I've applied ever since: Faith must overrule everything, even my feelings. I learned that I had to operate on what I believed, not what I felt. I had to make my decisions based on the truth of God's Word, causing me to do what was right rather than allow my emotions to encourage me to do something wrong.

So, on that day as I stared out the window as a black teenager in a city with streets lined by soldiers, I asked my dad if I could take them something to drink. I asked if I could take them some water. It was my way of putting feet to my faith. It was my way of demonstrating grace and kindness in the midst of confusion and chaos. It was my step in seeking not to succumb to the vitriol that the cultural environment called for, even though it was based on legitimate pain, but to rise above it.

Yes, my pain was real. The injustices were real. The killing of a peaceful leader who was helping us move forward as a nation cut deep. But I chose to respond in truth rather than react on emotion, based on the Word of God.

I've tried to carry that principle with me throughout my life since then. This does not mean endorsing the wrong. We are to condemn what is wrong. Yet, at the same time, we are to rise above it so we do not become trapped in it as a personal stronghold of bitterness or pain. Let me give you an example of how this played out in everyday life later on.

I'll never forget the time a man came in to do some work on our house. Everything was going fine until the man, who was white, called me "boy." At that very moment, all of my history rose up to the point of threatening to boil over. I just turned toward him with a glare. I'm black. He's white. He's using a term of denigration based on the past. What's even worse is that I was older than he. And a pastor.

All of that was hitting my emotions at the same time. I wanted to respond out of my feelings, but I decided to pause instead, based on this principle I learned as a teenager. I decided to whisper a quick prayer asking God to give me wisdom because I wanted to address the situation appropriately. It's always a good thing to pause and pray when you don't know what to do. It could be that your emotions are responding without all the information to be had. Ask God for wisdom.

I'm glad I did because a few moments went by when a white man came in who was also around my age. The gentleman also called him "boy." Apparently, this was a term that was a habit to him, and he was unaware of the cultural context on how it might be offensive to me. Seeing him call the white man boy changed the whole atmosphere because, at first, I had taken it personally. But when I got more information, I understood his intent more clearly.

Waiting to learn intent, especially in today's contemporary culture, can deescalate situations that might otherwise turn hostile. My concern is if we all remain so sensitive about anything that can cause an offense, driving us more deeply toward "cancel culture" before examining the heart, we'll never move forward. We've got to learn to push pause and discern, question, and speak truth in love. Let the person know that what he or she did or said offended you and then ask them if they meant it, or if it just came out wrong. Minister through grace. We all need grace at some time or another.

I learned these difficult lessons through the cultural environment I grew up in. Inequality among the races was always a fact of life for me early on. I remember often being called the "n-word" by white kids and adults whom I came across in life. At times it made me fearful, yet at other times it made me determined to work harder in order to outdo my white contemporaries. In spite of the strength of biblical discipleship and evangelism that the Brethren Assembly was known for, they were segregated based on race like other denominations. These and other disparities among the races raised questions in my mind about what was true and what was purely human concoction.

Like my father, I turned to God for answers. I had seen how my father merged his belief in God into all areas of his life. He frequently took me with him on ministry outings including street evangelism, and he modeled responsibility throughout our family's life, such as being the one to take me for weekly allergy shots or to rush me to the hospital for epinephrine when I suffered from asthma attacks. He also discipled me through normal, everyday activities by pointing out spiritual connections to physical realities. My father made learning and living the Word the priority of our home.

Because of his desire to learn and apply the Word of God, my father kept Christian radio on in our house most of the time. This exposed me to the white evangelical teachers of the day who, while they didn't often address social issues, used exposition as the proper means of approaching Scripture. This, coupled with growing up in the Brethren Assembly, deepened my desire to understand, explain, and apply scriptural principles to life.

As a high school student, I couldn't get enough of the Bible. My love for the Word of God caused me to be very public about my profession of Christ. I witnessed to other students at school personally as well as through passing out tracts. This sometimes led to ridicule, but it also led to respect. When people needed advice in a crisis, they often came to me. This response propelled me to witness all the more.

I was very active in my school and community through sports, playing both organized and sandlot football every moment that I could. I also swam the backstroke on the high school swim team and started as a catcher on our baseball team. These activities provided natural relationships within which to express my faith and public witness.

## People Who Changed My Life

My life forever changed in 1968 when our church joined the other black Brethren Assemblies to host Dr. B. Sam Hart and his ministry, The Grand Old Gospel Fellowship, for a tent evangelistic crusade in Baltimore. As I mentioned in an earlier chapter, on the first night of the crusade, Dr. Hart challenged Christians in the audience to fully commit themselves to God in order to reach more people for Christ. Having already sensed a strong call on my life by God since the age of fifteen, I chose to go forward and make a public commitment to full-time Christian ministry.

I spent a great deal of time with Dr. Hart throughout the remainder of the crusade. He challenged me in two directions: First, he encouraged me to consider going to college in order to get a strong, biblical foundation. With my father being a high school dropout and my mother working in the home, college was not in my immediate plans at that time. While my parents believed in my abilities and potential, college wasn't something we discussed often.

Second, Dr. Hart encouraged me to work with him in evangelism since that was what I felt God was calling me to do. A month after the crusade, he asked me if I would go to Guyana, South America, to help set up a crusade that was being planned there. I agreed. Having never flown on an airplane before, I left America as a seventeen-year-old and headed to South America to set up the crusade.

I noticed several things when I first got to Guyana. It was an independent, black-run nation that had recently secured freedom from British colonialism, and it was both impressive and exciting to witness this reality. I instantly saw how faith played a strong part in the culture as it was visibly woven throughout business, government, and society. Faith not only dominated but also threaded itself through the fabric of the land.

I also noticed that Guyana wasn't as advanced as American culture. Having only received its independence from British rule in the previous three years, it had not yet organized itself to be recognized on the international trading scene as a viable entity. Despite this reality, I sensed a strong determination in the heart of the people with whom I interacted.

The head of the crusade committee hosting me in Guyana was a man named James Basil Cannings. James Cannings was an elder in the main Brethren Assembly. He took me to his home for dinner that was being prepared by his daughter Lois. During my one-month stay, I became enchanted not only by Lois's cooking but also by her beauty, spiritual commitment, ministry involvement, musical talent, and administrative skills. As you can tell, I could go on and on about Lois. Lois's gifts and spirit won me over immediately, and after my month in Guyana, I told her that I was going to come back as soon as I could to marry her. She agreed, and a year and a half later Lois Cannings became Lois Evans—my life partner, ministry partner, and best friend for almost 50 years until she passed away.

During my involvement with Dr. Hart both domestically and abroad, I also became exposed to Tom Skinner. While both Sam Hart and Tom Skinner were evangelists, Sam Hart emphasized biblical literacy and church planting. Tom Skinner, on the other hand, emphasized evangelism, social justice, racial reconciliation, and the kingdom of God. I was profoundly influenced by both men as I sought to discover how both emphases could merge together to create a greater, stronger whole. I could not comprehend why the church should just be spiritual while neglecting the social, or why social activism should be done as it was so often done absent a sound theology integrated in and through the local church.

Another man who influenced my journey at that time was a Jewish man named Martin Resnick. I met Martin when I went to work for him while in high school. Needing a job to help out at home, I followed up on the lead given to me by a friend about a job opening for a dishwasher at Martin Resnick's catering service.

I had thrown newspapers before and bagged groceries at the supermarket, but this was my first real job. After some time, Martin called me into his office and told me that he had been watching me work and was impressed with what he saw. He asked me if I would consider chauffeuring his kids as part of my job. Of course I agreed, and began driving his two children to and from school, practices, or wherever else they needed to go on the weekends.

The Resnicks lived on what was considered the white side of town, making it necessary for me to drive over there frequently. One day as I was driving to pick up Martin's children, a policeman stopped me. Pulling me over for no apparent reason, he retained me for an inordinate amount of time wondering why I was in that neighborhood. I tried to explain to him that I needed to leave to pick up some children who needed to go to school, but he wouldn't let me go. Finally, after some time, I was released, only to arrive at the Resnick home to an impatient and frustrated Mrs. Resnick. She asked me why I was late, so I told her what had happened. Mrs. Resnick told Martin, who then told authorities connected to the police department, which then immediately transferred the policeman to night duty.

Not only did Martin stand up for me in that situation, but he also always encouraged me. He saw the *me* in me—the potential. At one point, after I graduated from high school, he asked me if I wanted to go to work full-time for his business on a professional level. I told him that I would be interested in pursuing it, so, like Dr. Hart, he encouraged me to go to college to get the training that I needed to pursue a career in social catering as a manager. In fact, he even offered to pay for a significant portion of my college expenses. I took him up on the offer until I was able to get scholarships and other funds to pay for the rest.

After high school, I never worked for Martin Resnick again because God had a different plan that involved theology, pastoring, and running a national ministry, but we have remained great friends over the years. Whenever I go home to Baltimore, we always get together. In fact, the Resnicks routinely hosted and participated in our family reunions or birthday parties, held at one of their local banquet facilities. His business has boomed, and he is—and will always be—incredibly important to me.

Until I had become exposed to what I could do through mentors like Dr. Hart and Martin Resnick who believed in me and encouraged me to see that I had a future beyond what I could see, I had never really thought much about college. However, these men, along with my parents' approval, propelled and motivated me to go beyond what I had envisioned for myself.

## Education and More Exposure to Racial Issues

So in 1968, I boarded a train and headed from Baltimore to Atlanta to attend Carver Bible College. Carver was a small black college that had been started by white fundamentalist missionaries to train "Negroes" in the Scriptures. While at Carver, I was mentored by Dr. John McNeal, the Dean of Students. Dr. McNeal took me under his wings, assuming the role of a father figure in my life. Recognizing my insatiable passion for learning and preaching the Word of God, he challenged me to always balance biblical study with personal spiritual depth.

Because Carver was located just minutes from the Atlanta University system that included Morris Brown, Morehouse, Clark, and Spelman Colleges—the centerpieces of black educational and cultural life—there was never any lack of sociological discussion. Carver was also located just minutes from the Interdenominational

Theological Center, which was a predominantly black seminary that emphasized black history, black culture, and black theology.

Here I was at a Bible college that stressed biblical theology, evangelism, and discipleship in the midst of a city of great diversity of thought of civil rights and black culture. You can imagine the confluence of perspectives with which I had to deal in an area so inundated with differing views. Students from ITC often challenged us from Carver about our relevance to the social realities that blacks were facing. Carver students challenged the students at ITC about their liberal orientation to Scripture. These debates, along with living in Atlanta in 1968 at the height of the civil rights movement, provoked questions in me that traditional theology had not clearly addressed. I began formulating answers to these questions out of a kingdom theology that continued to develop as I went deeper in my study of Scripture.

Living in Atlanta brought the issue of race even more to the forefront of my mind because racism in Atlanta was more overt than it was in Baltimore. For example, one of my white "evangelical" professors asked me to do some work on his house for him one afternoon. When it came time for lunch, he put me in another room to eat by myself. He told me that his mother lived with him and that she would never eat with a black man. That was an eye-opening moment, one of many to come.

I also remember being very nervous when I had to drive through small Georgia towns because of the horror stories I had heard about the South. A white medical doctor had been told about my passion for theology and proclaiming God's Word at Carver, and had hired me to conduct an outreach Bible study to Christian blacks in his area. He paid my way and provided me with a place where I could sleep at night. As best as I can remember, though, he never once came to the Bible study he initiated.

The Bible study was located several hours away from Atlanta, making driving there an experience. The "n-word" got thrown at me if I was in an area where I needed to slow down. I saw black men and women walking with their heads held down. If I stopped for gas (I tried not to stop at all), I saw black men and women who wouldn't even make eye contact with the whites around them. These realities along with two major events affected me greatly toward devoting myself to theologically grappling with the contradiction between the white "evangelical" church and what it taught in comparison with the segregation that it was practicing.

One of these events was the time Lois and I visited Bob Jones University. Bob Jones University was a leading evangelical school that taught that the Bible was the inerrant Word of God, yet it also publicly practiced racial segregation. Not only did BJU publicly promote racial segregation, but it actively taught that it was biblical. In *Is Segregation Scriptural?* published just a few years before Lois and I visited the university, Bob Jones III said,

> A Negro is best when he serves at the table. . . . When he does that, he's doing what he knows how to do best. . . . And the Negroes who have ascended to positions in government, in education, this sort of thing, I think you'll find, by and large, have a strong strain of white blood in them.[1]

I will never forget driving onto the campus of this "Bible-based" university and being followed and stopped by the campus police not only to inquire what we were doing there, but to ask us to leave.

The second impacting event was when I attended Colonial Hills Baptist Church in East Point, Georgia, with my mentor and professor, Howard Dial. Dr. Dial was white. He was a committed Christian man who had a heart for racial reconciliation. He was the academic dean at Carver, but he was also close to me in age. Over my time there we became very good friends. We were contemporaries in athletics, shared theological discussions, and Lois and I even babysat his children when needed.

The Sunday I attended church as a guest of Dr. Dial just so happened to be the Sunday that the leading candidate for the vacant pastorate was preaching. He preached a powerful message while giving a call to come forward in a commitment to discipleship at the end. I responded to the call, not realizing that the focus would turn to me when I did.

First, the man who received me at the altar to pray with me made it clear, not only to me but to everyone in the church, that there was a monumental difference between making a spiritual commitment to discipleship and making a commitment to come to church. Those were two very separate deals.

Next, the leadership made it explicitly clear that they did not want blacks coming to the church on a regular basis. In fact, the church ended up splitting over this one event and the prospective pastor declined the invitation to become senior pastor, saying that he could not pastor a church steeped in racial segregation.

These and other less dramatic events brought the major disconnection between evangelical belief and practice to light for me on a highly personal level. I understood afresh the anger and frustration of the black church in America at the hypocrisy of white Christianity in general and white evangelicalism in particular.

Experiencing firsthand the reality of what black theology and black power sought to correct propelled me to wrestle with theological issues at a deep level. I already had a passion that had been birthed in Baltimore and Philadelphia to address these issues, but studying in Atlanta at the height of the civil rights movement fired my passion to a supersonic level. In fact, it thrust me into a desire to study further at seminary so that I could address the issue not only from a popular level (such as a pulpit), but also from an academic level. I set my mind to bridge the divide both on theological and practical terms in a way that would be consistent with the kingdom concepts that I had been introduced to and had become extremely inquisitive about.

In August of 1972, Lois and I arrived at the campus of Dallas Theological Seminary. I had originally planned to go to Grace Theological Seminary, a school located in a predominantly white city. However, a man named Doug McIntosh challenged me to consider going to DTS instead since it was located in a more urban environment, which would provide me with the practical experience of applying the theology I was learning within an urban environment. Doug was so convinced that I should attend DTS that he paid my application fee in order to encourage me to choose that path on my journey. I was the fourth African American student accepted into the master's degree program at a school that had begun nearly fifty years earlier. The first three were Eddie Lane, Ruben Conner, and Ron Roberts.

Not wanting to distance myself from my own culture while learning in a nearly entirely white evangelical culture, I began attending a black church called Community Bible Church pastored by Dr. Ruben Conner. This provided me the contextual reality to keep before my theological queries.

The environment on the DTS campus was welcoming to me by most of the professors, but it also became clear that many of the students had not been around African Americans up until then. Therefore, either they didn't necessarily want to relate to us or just weren't quite sure how to do so. Some were reacting to the social climate and felt like the actions of the African American community were not keeping in line with how Christians should act. But what that meant to me was that, while not all of the actions they were witnessing on the news could be justified, the white students likewise did not understand the social, political, and economic realities that prompted much of what they were seeing and hearing about.

Yet, given that my personality is very outgoing and I genuinely like to meet people and make them feel comfortable, a lot of these barriers did come down over time. But I did have to assume a lot of the initiative just to meet people and show myself warm, friendly, and receptive to them for starters.

I would categorize the professors into three distinct groups at that time. The first group was very open and welcoming to me. They wanted to interact and initiated mutual engagement and discussions, inviting my perspective. Four who stand out to me the most were Howard Hendricks, Haddon Robinson, Charles Ryrie, and Steve Slocum. All four, plus others, were very welcoming. I would often spend hours in their respective offices talking one on one. Or we would go to lunch together, or they would invite Lois and me to their homes for dinner.

The second group were clearly not comfortable. There would never be an outright rejection but you could tell that they either didn't know how to interact with you or with the concerns of the culture, or simply resented having to do so. The third group were somewhat in the middle. They had chosen to go with the flow, as it were.

I'll never forget one of my earliest conversations with Dr. Walvoord. We were talking about the fact that Dallas Theological

Seminary had been segregated for so long. And while I realize he had addressed this issue as far back as the mid-1950s by saying the openness was there but that there were not any qualified African Americans to accept into the program, I felt that was an insufficient, and convenient, answer to the problem, especially when no real effort had appeared to have taken place to locate qualified applicants. I wondered why, so I asked. His statement to me was, "Tony, I'm not a fighter. I kind of go with the law—the protocol." Another professor pastored a church in Dallas and informed me that the deacons at his church would not allow me to even visit. That seemed to be the atmosphere of the Bible churches at that time. It was a culture of self-segregation without the overt rejection. It was subtle, but real.

Yet in the midst of these disparities, I was given the freedom to pursue the question of race as well as to offer a biblical response without the fear of unwarranted opposition. In fact, it was DTS who first sent me and Eddie Lane, as representatives of the school, to the National Black Evangelical Association (NBEA) conferences. They encouraged us to become involved not only as an attendee but as a voice to speak into this community that highlighted the black experience as it related to Biblical theology. DTS gave me the exegetical, expositional, and theological tools to evaluate for myself the ethical, social, economic, racial, and political implications of the theology I was learning. My doctoral advisor, Dr. Charles Ryrie, continuously challenged me to systematize my theological conclusions effectively and efficiently.

My natural temperament has always been very relaxed. In fact, my children often say that they have only seen me get upset once. This being so, when racial tensions arose due to the topic in class, I often made a joke to lighten the mood. For example, I would tell Dr. Pentecost that I was going to come to the other side of the tracks and visit him on the north side of the new Jerusalem when we both got to heaven. Comments such as these often lightened the atmosphere when heartfelt issues had made it tense. I was so passionate about what I was doing that any racial problems that did arise were often muted quickly.

In DTS's effort to reach out to black students, Steve Slocum realized that black students would often come from a more limited economic base so he went out to find scholarships. He actively encouraged us to attend NBEA conferences and other forums, while also investing in us personally by inviting us to his home oftentimes to just hang out or share a meal. He had a real heart to make things happen for the African American community both financially and personally. In fact, when he eventually left to go to the American Tract Society, he put Eddie Lane in the position to recruit more black students and function more in terms of inclusion. Both Steve Slocum and Hadden Robinson led the way for the opening of doors into DTS for minority students as students and in future leadership roles there ourselves. Hadden would often speak definitively on racism, segregation, and inequities. Of everyone there, he became my closest friend.

The school also made efforts to include and encourage us in the area of spiritual growth. Over the years, the momentum of black students applying to and enrolling at DTS increased. Between Eddie Lane's active recruitment of potential black students in urban contexts, my appointment as an adjunct professor in the area of Expository Preaching, as well as the expansion of my national footprint through traveling and speaking, along with Ruben Conner's organization (Black Evangelistic Enterprise), coalesced to give a broader picture of DTS as a school ready and able to receive minority students well. Ron Roberts was simultaneously influential as the Associate Pastor of St. John Missionary Baptist Church while attending seminary. This being a highly respected traditional black church in the black community began to link DTS to the more traditional parts of black culture and raise awareness of the school there too.

Even so, early on, it was disconcerting to know that some of my professors still went to and pastored churches that practiced segregation. Perhaps the most influential church that was attended by many professors was First Baptist Church of Dallas, pastored by the late Dr. W. A. Criswell, who publicly proclaimed segregation based on the "curse of Ham," a position he recanted shortly before he died.

When I finished my ThM in 1976, having graduated with honors, I decided to look for another school to pursue my doctoral degree. That was when I called James Cone, the founder of black theology. I wanted to find out more about the program where he taught because I had been challenged from reading his material even though I used a different hermeneutic in addressing the issues he addressed. Dr. Cone had captivated me with his insistence that God's perspective on this issue of racial disparity and oppression was not a minor biblical theme.

I enjoyed my phone conversation with Dr. Cone. He was a very warm and friendly man, but due to other reasons, I eventually decided to pursue my doctorate at DTS. However, I chose to make Dr. Cone's theology the topic for my doctoral research and dissertation.

## Beginning Ministry

After being accepted as the first African American into the DTS doctoral program, I was also invited to become an associate professor. Simultaneously, Dr. Ruben Conner and Dr. Gene Getz challenged me to start a Bible church in Dallas under Black Evangelistic Enterprises as a way of modeling the ideas that I had percolating within me resulting from my theological training and burden for connecting the spiritual and social state of my community. These ideas had become foundational concepts for what would become a kingdom perspective on ministry.

Lois and I prayed about whether I should be a full-time professor at the seminary or whether I should start a church. Being a professor would have been a lot easier for me at that time with a wife and small children and a doctoral program to complete. However, Dr. Getz encouraged me instead to live out my beliefs. He and his church also committed to financially support this effort over the initial years of starting up a church. So, after being confirmed by God that this is what He wanted us to do, interestingly enough over a dinner at Dr. Ryrie's home, Lois and I agreed to begin a church in the southern section of Dallas. That is when I also became an adjunct professor at DTS.

Oak Cliff Bible Fellowship was organized on June 6, 1976, in our home with about ten people who joined us for a weekly Bible study. We set forth a vision of building a church that would not only be about making disciples, but that would also have a social impact in the community. As the church began to grow, these concepts of connecting the spiritual and the social began to be implemented through ministries designed to affect our community.

The primary vehicle of making this influence came through the formation of The TurnAround Agenda (TTA) which uses resources, volunteers, and paid staff in the church to deliver social services to the community. These include public school mentoring, family support services, a crisis pregnancy center, food bank, thrift store, job fair, free community health screenings, and many other social outreaches. These ministries, which I will talk about more in the following chapters, have expanded to such a degree that we now directly reach into more than forty schools in the Dallas/Fort Worth region and service the southern section of Dallas with many ministries designed to meet social needs.

Because I was a man of two worlds, I strove to integrate what I felt was the best of the black church with what I thought was the best of the white church. I sought to embrace the biblical strengths in each culture through the forming of a new culture under the umbrella of black evangelicalism through the implementation of a kingdom worldview. I also set about to create an environment of intentionality concerning racial diversity in the church by adding non-African American staff and leadership to our existing governing body.

The one uniting feature was the positive response to the emphasis on a kingdom perspective revealed through expository preaching. This perspective became solidified at this point in my life, having grown out of my personal involvement as the senior pastor of the church, my own personal background, as well as my biblical training. All of these arenas emerged into a theological and biblical philosophy called the kingdom agenda that serves as the basis for this work, the basis for the way our church operates, and the basis for the upcoming strategic approaches to biblical justice and community transformation that you will read in the following chapters.

I began teaching from this kingdom worldview from that point forward, addressing issues in the church and community from the perspective of having discovered that the reason the breach between the spiritual and the social existed in our nation to such a degree was that we had not been focused on God's unifying kingdom goal in history. Therefore, we had let the secular world divide us along racial, class, gender, and denominational lines. To overcome the many issues plaguing not only our communities but also our churches and families, we needed to apply a kingdom strategy and solution to every area of life. In my view, traditional evangelicalism has failed to achieve this goal.

As the church began to grow, people outside of our congregation began requesting my tapes. Yet, even so, when I first attempted to broadcast my sermons on radio in the late 1970s, the radio stations would not even carry me. And they weren't shy to say why. The only station that did was a small station in Houston, KHCB. I mention Bruce Munsterman because I want to highlight the reality that there have been all along, and still are, good people fighting systemic racism. The other stations all turned me down because they said a black man would offend their white listeners. It wasn't until a highly influential white Christian leader intervened by making phone calls and sending a letter to each of the stations, imploring them to change their ways, that a few stations began to open their doors. Opportunities then began to open up for increased radio exposure. Lois, using her excellent administration skills as well as her experience previously with B. Sam Hart's ministry and Billy Graham's ministry, set up shop in our garage to begin fulfilling orders from those who wanted to keep up with my teaching. This developed The Urban Alternative, founded in 1981, into a national ministry. As national exposure expanded, increasing numbers of opportunities came to address both black and white audiences on a kingdom theology as well as its implication on the subject of race.

At that time, in the mid-1980s following my graduation from DTS with a ThD, I was invited to speak to the National Religious Broadcasters Convention (NRB). After my address, new radio stations began to inquire about my broadcast. It was then that The Urban Alternative took off. Since that time, God has expanded our reach to air our broadcast on over 1,400 stations in America and in more than 130 countries internationally. We also broadcast the Word of God over multiple television and Internet channels around the world. In July of 2017, the Tony Evans Training Center was launched to provide an online training program designed to develop kingdom disciples in the comprehensive biblical worldview of the kingdom agenda. At the time of this writing, we have roughly 2,000 active enrolled students and we offer over 40 comprehensive courses on subjects ranging from bibliology to preaching to spiritual growth to cultural engagement. Our church and national ministry have also grown in ways I didn't even know how to imagine. I'll talk more about our local outreach in the very last chapter, which is on a kingdom strategy, but I will say now that God has done great things. I am constantly amazed at what He has brought about. Included in all He has done is giving me one of my greatest joys over the years which was to have had the opportunity to serve as chaplain to the Dallas Cowboys during the Coach Tom Landry years and as chaplain for the Dallas Mavericks for more than forty years, getting to experience many ups and downs with them. God has also privileged me to be the first African American to write a complete Study Bible and Commentary. The joy of seeing this Study Bible and Commentary on display at the Museum of the Bible in Washington, DC pales in comparison to seeing the posts from people who use these study tools regularly and share the thoughts they are learning from it online, practically every day.

My passion today is even stronger than it was when I first began. I desire that God will use the confluence of my background, history, training, experiences, and work to hew out a distinct biblical community of evangelical Christians. In fact, I desire that God will use my unique footprint to clarify and codify a fresh new subgroup of His followers in contemporary culture. It is my hope that this specific community will embrace the uniqueness within our racial and cultural identities while submitting together under our common commitment to the lordship of Jesus Christ, the authority of Scripture, and the righteous and just advancement of the kingdom of God in history. Connecting the social with the spiritual underneath the overarching rule of God is my mission to live out as well as to proclaim the kingdom agenda.

## From Evangelicalism to Kingdomology

As mentioned earlier, and as I'm sure you are aware, the term "evangelical" has become somewhat toxic in the broader culture, and even in many Christian circles. It has become an inadequate unifying designation of true biblical Christianity for those who understand and are committed to the comprehensive nature of biblical faith. One of the primary reasons for this is the marriage of evangelicalism with cultural and political movements and personalities that compromise, to varying degrees, the comprehensive application of God's Word.

While the term evangelical is a biblical one, many of its adherents have distorted its contemporary effectiveness along with muting its ability to bring unity to the body of Christ. Unfortunately, it has often become synonymous with what is seen as a "white Republican racially insensitive Christianity." It has, in short, become known as a form of Christian nationalism. While this is certainly not true for many of my white brothers and sisters, it unfortunately has become the normative perception today.

Conversely, many Christian blacks, who by and large reject the term "evangelical" because of its perceived racial, social, and political overtones, stay committed en masse to one political party primarily due to its purported emphasis, whether actualized or not, on the issues of race and social injustice. This also contributes to the lack of oneness and unity among believers.

It is my contention that we need a new, more clarifying designation that has not become tainted by its identification with American politics, politicians, and cultural movements. We need an identity whose biblical framework promotes the unity of the body of Christ rather than the idolatry of race—an idolatry which only continues to divide the church of Christ.

Since the central theme of Scripture is the glory of God through the advancement of His Kingdom, and since the overarching mission of the church is the making of disciples (Matt. 28:19–20), then, for me, an appropriate new designation for a collective approach to biblical perspectives is kingdomology. To review, kingdomology is *the theological framework and belief system that asserts that God's purpose in history the manifestation of His glory through the establishment and advancement of His eternal kingdom on earth*. Kingdomology views this purpose as the unifying theme of Scripture that is to be accomplished progressively in history through human instrumentality over and against demonic and human opposition as mankind functions in covenant with Him.

Christians who adhere to this approach are known as kingdomologists. These kingdomologists understand that their primary God-given task in history is that of modeling and making kingdom disciples who function as kingdom agenda disciples of Christ. Kingdomologists apply the whole Word to all of life and as they do so, they become the visible and verbal representatives of Jesus Christ. Such a fresh designation can move us one step closer to the biblical oneness that we need to have and that the world needs to see, regardless of our racial and political uniqueness and differences.

When it comes to the matter of politics, I believe that we would do well if every Christian viewed themselves as a kingdomologist at their core. Thus they would function as a kingdom independent regardless of the political party with whom they identify. A kingdom independent is a disciple of Jesus Christ who partners with God in expanding His kingdom rule, as kingdom citizens, through their engagement with civil government. Their commitment to the values of the kingdom of God must overrule their allegiance to any political party. This is an area where a large segment of "evangelical" Christianity has failed. Spiritual leaders would do well to serve as kingdomologists whose primary task is to develop kingdom disciples to function in a way that equips and empowers God's people to make a lasting individual and collective kingdom impact in our churches and on our culture and world.

**Note**

1. Bob Jones III, quoted by Robert Sherrill, "Bob Jones University: New Curricula for Bigotry," *The Nation* (March 29, 1965), 326–33. The article was later reprinted in Robert Sherrill, *Gothic Politics in the Deep South: Stars of the New Confederacy* (New York: Ballantine Books, 1969), 248–49. For background, see also Bob Jones Sr., *Is Segregation Scriptural* (Greenville, SC: Bob Jones University Press, n.d.), a booklet transcribed from an April 17, 1960, radio address.

# Chapter 14

# THE KINGDOM-MINDED CHURCH

In every recognized country in the world there is an American embassy. An embassy is fundamentally a little bit of America a long way from home. Embassies are sovereign territories, meaning that they do not belong to the countries they are in. They belong to the countries from which they came.

If you get into trouble in a foreign land, make your way to the American embassy. Because once you cross the gate and enter the realm of its dominion, you are in America again. You are where the laws of America rule.

The church is supposed to be a little bit of heaven a long way from home. It is to be that place where the values of eternity operate in history. The church is a place where weary people can go to find truth, acceptance, equality, freedom, forgiveness, safety, joy, justice, and hope. It is heaven's embassy on earth.

Yet how is it possible for the number of churches in our nation to be ever increasing while the impact of the church only wanes? How can we have so much preaching, praising, and programs and yet so little demonstrated power? Why does the church merely react to society's agenda rather than offering a kingdom agenda for society to embrace?

The answers to these questions lie in the reality that the church today bears little resemblance to the kingdom from which we came.

This is because we have failed to function from a kingdom perspective. The church has stopped *being* the biblical church that it was designed to be, and as a result, we have limited our impact on contemporary society, both inside our walls and without.

## The Kingdom Agenda

Throughout Scripture, God's agenda is His kingdom. The Greek word used for kingdom is *basileia,* which essentially means "rule" or "authority." A kingdom always includes four crucial components: First, a ruler empowered with sufficient authority; second, a realm of subjects who fall underneath this authority; third, the rules of governance; and fourth, a realm over which the ruler rules. God's kingdom is the authoritative execution of His comprehensive governance in all creation.

Therefore, the universe we live in is a theocracy. *Theos* refers to God, and *-ocracy* refers to rule. A kingdom perspective means that the rule of God (theocracy) trumps the rule of man (homocracy). Psalm 103:19 (NIV) expresses it this way, "The LORD has established his throne in heaven, and his kingdom rules over all." Therefore, the kingdom agenda is *the visible manifestation of the comprehensive rule of God over every area of life.*

God's kingdom is larger than the temporal, political, and social realms in which we live. It is not confined to the walls of the church in which we worship Him. The kingdom is both now (Mark 1:15) and not yet (Matt. 16:28). It is among us (Luke 17:21) but also in heaven (Matt. 7:21; 2 Tim. 4:18), since it originates from above, from another realm. Jesus revealed that truth shortly before His crucifixion, when He said in response to Pilate, "My kingdom is not of this world. If My kingdom were of this world, then My servants would be fighting so that I would not be handed over to the Jews; but as it is, My kingdom is not of this realm" (John 18:36).

Since it originates from another realm, God established covenants within the world we live through which to implement it. A covenant is a divinely created relational bond through which God administers His kingdom agenda in history. These covenants are governmental systems or institutions designated as family, church, and civil government (state). God rules them all and each one is to be accountable to Him and His standards as their sovereign. Whether or not mankind functions in alignment with His rule is another story. Regardless, God has given the guidelines by which all three are to operate because He is the originator of all three. Failure to operate under His authority within those guidelines results in negative consequences. The three, while distinct in their responsibilities and jurisdiction, are to cooperate with each other with the common goal of producing personal responsibility and individuals who govern themselves under God. None of these governing spheres is to be viewed or is to operate as an all-powerful, centralized, and controlling authority over the others.

The foundation on which all three operate is that of an absolute standard of truth. This standard of truth is nonnegotiable, nonadjustable, and transcends cultural, racial, and situational lines. Truth is fundamentally God-based knowledge on all subjects since God is both the originator and the author of truth.

Not only does the kingdom agenda operate on this foundation of truth, but it also operates under the only all-inclusive principle presented to us for understanding the work of God and His kingdom. This principle is His glory. Romans 11:36 says, "For from Him and through Him and to Him are all things. To Him be the glory forever. Amen."

Glory simply means "to be heavy" or "to have weight." It denotes significance. Since all things come from God, are through God, and go to God, God's glory exists intrinsically in Himself. Whether we ascribe glory to God or not is irrelevant to the amount of glory God has; His glory is already fully present in Him. However, we experience and access that glory when we place ourselves under His comprehensive rule. This is because it is then that God radiates and magnifies His glory to, in, and through us.

A primary position for bringing glory to God is that of surrender to His sovereignty. To surrender to God's sovereignty is to acknowledge His jurisdiction, along with the validity of His supremacy, over every area of life. God is accountable to no one. He either causes all things to happen, or He permits them to happen. Sovereignty means that God never says, "Oops, I missed that one." When we live by the principles of the kingdom agenda, we experience God's hand in every area of life and thereby witness His promise to work all things together for good (Rom. 8:28).

However, what we often do is limit our opportunity to experience God working all things together for good by defining God according to our purpose rather than His. Humanism and socialism—whether it be in the form of modern-day church-ism, materialism, me-ism, statism, liberation theology, or Marxism—offer an insufficient understanding of the purpose, work, and revelation of God. They attempt to box God into a "kingdom" confined within the perspective of man. Yet, when the human condition is used as the starting point for seeing the whole of God's revelation, rather than a surrender to His sovereignty over the whole of the human condition, faulty theology and sociology emerges. What we wind up with is a God fashioned in the image of man.

A kingdom perspective does not view man's condition first and then assign to God what we feel would best reflect Him. Rather, a kingdom perspective ascertains how God has determined to glorify Himself and then aligns itself with that despite our inability to always understand God's processes. God *is* good, all the time. All the time, God is good. However, God's definition of good isn't always ours. In fact, God often uses the very thing that we call "not good" as a tool to bring about an ultimate purpose, as well as the resultant manifestation of His greater glory.

For example, according to the covenant with Abraham in Genesis 15, slavery in Egypt was an intricate part of God's program for the nation. We read, "God said to Abram, 'Know for certain that your descendants will be strangers in a land that is not theirs, where they will be enslaved and oppressed four hundred years. But I will also judge the nation whom they will serve, and afterward they will come out with many possessions'" (Gen. 15:13–14).

The point here is that God, in accomplishing His kingdom agenda, allowed a negative reality that could have been avoided if He had chosen for it to be. Yet, the reality of the Israelites' slavery in Egypt accomplished a higher purpose of establishing God's theocratic relationship with them based on an exodus that would serve as a constant reminder of who had brought them out (Ex. 12:41).

This truth served as a foundational relational principle in the future movements of God with the Israelite community.

God's sovereignty in the midst of what we do not understand is echoed elsewhere throughout the Bible. Another example is found in the life of Joseph who had been sold into slavery by his brothers. Joseph later said to his brothers, "As for you, you meant evil against me, but God meant it for good in order to bring about this present result, to preserve many people alive" (Gen. 50:20).

The freedom that is actualized through a kingdom perspective—that of embracing God's sovereignty while simultaneously cultivating an intimate relationship with Him—generates a faith more powerful than any human weapon or system of philosophy could ever produce. It accesses God's grace in such a way as to grant a freedom that is not incumbent upon externals. This is the only true authentic freedom as it manifests God's ability to bring about good in any and every situation surrendered to Him.

While God is a God of liberation and justice—and while we should be about the same—a kingdom perspective recognizes that in His sovereignty, His timing is not always the same as our own. However, a kingdom theology also recognizes that while oppression and injustice remain in the world's systems, they should never be tolerated within the church of God or among members within the body of Christ.

In fact, whenever Jesus proclaimed the "kingdom of God" during His earthly presence, He did so while simultaneously healing, helping, feeding, and freeing the hurting and the lost. Therefore, any ministry that minimizes legitimate social needs has failed to model itself after the One whom we have been given to follow, thereby reducing the glory it gives to God (Matt. 5:16).

While we may not always understand God's processes or His timing, a kingdom theology recognizes that God's purpose does not change, and that purpose is to glorify Himself. The ultimate goal of the kingdom is always Godward. Therefore, living the kingdom agenda means that the comprehensive rule of God is the final, authoritative, and governing principle in our personal lives, family lives, churches, and communities in order that God may manifest His glory in all of society through advancing His kingdom.

*The Sociopolitical Distinction of the Kingdom*

The problem we face in the church today is that we have misunderstood the kingdom, thereby marginalizing its authority and influence not only in our lives but also in our land. Many in the church have so spiritualized the kingdom that its sociopolitical rules have become little more than an ethereal ideology to be displayed at a later date. This has led to a reduction of the vast socioethical implications in and through the church, creating an organism whose function offers little power toward the transformation of society. However, the sociopolitical nature of the kingdom of God is very real, biblically substantiated, and relevant to the embracing of spiritual oneness.

We first witness the sociopolitical distinction of the kingdom in Satan's challenge to God's rule. This challenge, while spiritual, was also political in nature in that it involved an attempt to secure a throne only God held the right to possess (Ezek. 28:11–19, Isa.14:13–17). Satan said, "I will ascend to heaven; I will raise my throne above the stars of God, and I will sit on the mount of assembly" (Isa. 14:13). Satan's desire to "sit on the mount of assembly" was his attempt to hold the seat of divine government in the spiritual realm while getting Adam to surrender it in the physical realm. From the beginning, politics was an issue in the rule of God.

Other demonstrations of the sociopolitical nature of God's kingdom include the command God gave to Adam that he was to subdue the earth under him, revealing the combination of the spiritual and physical aspects of a theocratic kingdom (Gen. 1:26).

Next, the specific institution and creation of national government directly relates God's kingdom program to the social and political aspects of man as well, especially since capital punishment is instituted in this period (Gen. 9:1–7). That capital punishment was predicated on the fact that man is made in the image of God (v. 6) underscores the truth that God's kingdom rule in the area of human justice has a spiritual basis.

Further, under the patriarchs, Abraham was a participant in a covenant that included both land and seed. This covenant became the basis for Israel's spiritual as well as sociopolitical existence (Gen. 12:1–3). Likewise, whether in the conflict of Moses with Pharaoh or in the judges, a theocratic role in governing the nation involved social, political, and economic forces as the means of expressing God's rule on earth.

Looking toward the millennial kingdom, Messiah's righteous rule, we also see a reflection of the social structure of the kingdom demonstrating the inseparability of the sociopolitical aspects from the spiritual. Christ's future rule will bring about changes within the structures of society. It will mean that military warfare will cease (Ps. 46:8–9; Mic. 4:3; Isa. 9:6–7), slums will be removed (Ps. 72:16), political wrongs will be righted (Isa. 2:4; Ps. 72:4), and physical disease will disappear (Isa. 35:5–6; 33:24).

### *An Alternative Model for the World*

The contemporary purpose of the church, in light of the nature of the kingdom, is to reflect the sociopolitical and socioethical aspects of the kingdom. It is to be a model for the world operating in the world while providing an alternative to the world. When the church functions as a community, not as a reaction to the world's oppressive system but rather as a divine structure operating in a liberating manner according to the way God has ordained it to be, the church sets itself apart as a haven, much like an embassy. This then shows those who are in the kingdom of darkness a preview of what the kingdom of God is all about.

In the movies, previews advertise coming attractions. Designed to entice, the preview focuses on the hot clips of the movie such as the chase scenes, love scenes, and fight scenes. The point of the preview is to whet our appetites for the upcoming attraction.

Someday a big show is coming to town, and it's called the kingdom of God. Jesus Christ is the star, and it will be a worldwide production. But until then, God has left previews in the world. We are His hot clips. God has left His church here to provide clips of the major production that is to come.

Unfortunately, most of our clips have been so weak in demonstrating the power and wonder of the feature film that few people show interest in picking up a ticket. Instead of previewing an epic, we often merely reflect the sitcoms and soap operas around us. Until we, as God's people, intentionally embrace, apply, and reflect the kingdom, the church has little to offer the world.

While there is war in the world, there ought to be the existence of peace in the church (Eph. 4:3; Col. 3:14–15), and prayer for peace by the church (1 Tim. 2:1–2). While there is oppression in society, there ought to be liberation and justice in the church (James 2:1–9). While there is poverty in the world, there ought to be voluntary sharing with the goal of meeting existing needs in the church (Acts 2:44–45; 2 Cor. 12:12–24). While there is racism, classism, and sexism in the world, there ought to be authentic oneness in the church (Col. 3:10–11; Gal. 3:26–29). Thus the world is presented with the option of Christ by being what the church is supposed to be in the world—an alternative model for the world, a community functioning in relationship with and under the rule of God in the mediatory kingdom on earth.

Members of the biblical church model this alternative on the basis that we are citizens of the kingdom (Col. 1:13), having been designated as workers for the kingdom (Col. 4:11), promised victory because of the unshakeable nature of the kingdom (Heb. 12:28), as well as heirs of the kingdom (James 2:5). Further, the fruit of the church reveals itself to others as the "good seed" sown during the period of the mysteries of the kingdom (Matt. 13:38). The church is therefore uniquely positioned and authorized to carry out the mandates of the kingdom under the authority of Christ (Eph. 1:22–23) when we seek the kingdom above all else (Matt. 6:33), empowered by the spiritual priorities of the kingdom (Rom. 14:17).

Since the church is to serve as a model partaking of this universal and eternal kingdom, and since this eternal kingdom is sociopolitical as well as spiritual in nature, the church, as a spiritual body, also partakes of the sociopolitical realm. The question is, then, what is the picture of the biblical church and its role with regard to justice? The remainder of this chapter will look at the nature of the biblical church, laying the foundation for our discussion on justice and social action in the following chapter.

## The Biblical Church

Let me begin by saying what the biblical church is not. First, the church in the New Testament—which serves as our picture for the church age—is not a social club. It is not a place to come and be entertained. Neither is it an outpost for an official political party. While functionally it has sociopolitical structures and intents, it is never commanded to impose itself governmentally on the world. The church, rather, functions as a model revealing and influencing the principles of the kingdom. The biblical church is *a community of individuals spiritually linked together with the purpose of reflecting and legislating the values of the kingdom of God.* A kingdom church prioritizes building kingdom disciples who function as kingdom servants in order to make a kingdom impact for the advancing of God's kingdom agenda.

The church is to function as an internally legislative and familial community with an emphasis on oneness. By the biblical church, I am referring to the church that Jesus Christ established that is to be reflected or modeled through the local gathering of believers, a local assembly, as defined shortly before the end of His earthly ministry (Matt. 16:18–19).

Several key verses in this chapter are very important for us to look at in order to understand who we are as a church and what we do. We begin by reading that Jesus had just asked His disciples an important question. He asked them to tell Him who people were saying that He was. Everyone offered flattering answers in reply. Some said that He was Elijah while others said Jeremiah or a prophet. While all were compliments, all were wrong. Then Jesus turned to His disciples and asked, "But who do you say that I am?" (Matt. 16:15).

It isn't evident in the English translation, but in the Greek text we discover that when Jesus asks, "Who do *you* say that I am," the "you" is plural. In Texas, we'd say, "Who do y'all say that I am?" The plural form of the word "you" reveals to us that Jesus is not just asking this question to Peter, who subsequently offered an answer. Rather, this is a question to the group as a whole.

When Peter answered, he answered representatively as a leader of the disciples. One way we know that Peter is a leader is that whenever we see a list of the names of the disciples in the gospels, Peter is always listed first. He is a natural spokesperson. While he may be one to slip up due to suffering from foot-in-mouth disease at times, he is also one who steps up when needed. Peter doesn't have the paralysis of analysis. He speaks his mind and offers Jesus the collective answer, "You are the Christ, the Son of the living God" (Matt. 16:16).

Jesus responds by affirming him and changing his name, which had been Simon Barjona, to Peter—which means "a stone." He continues by saying, "And upon this rock I will build My church; and the gates of Hades will not overpower it" (Matt. 16:18).

### *Many Makes One*

Several important principles are given to us in this passage. First, the biblical church is made up of many interlinking pieces.

Once the disciples individually recognized and agreed upon who Jesus was, they were ready to come together and *be* the church. This is critical because Christ is both the foundation and the cornerstone. Once He saw that they understood who He was, Jesus esteemed their commitment to His identity by empowering them to carry out His work. He did this because their reply showed Him that they were a group of individuals who could jointly make an impact on society, which is exactly what they have done. Their impact has left a legacy that is still alive today.

What we sometimes do when looking at this passage, though, is make the mistake of interpreting Christ's statement as meaning that He is building His church on one man: Peter. However, the word Jesus used for Peter was the Greek word *petros*. It indicated a single stone that can be easily thrown. That is not the word Jesus used for "rock."

Jesus used the Greek word *petra* indicative of a mass, or cliff, of rocks that consists of something much larger than any individual rock. This mass of rocks interlinks individual rocks together to create a stronger whole. While there are a multitude of rocks in *petra*, they do not function as individual rocks, but are intimately joined together. The best exegete of the passage would have to be Peter himself. We see his interpretation in 1 Peter 2 where he says, "You also, as living stones, are being built up as a spiritual house" (1 Peter 2:5).

It is not insignificant that Christ described the church in this way. Oneness, as we saw in the first several chapters of this book, is an essential element used by God through which He manifests His power and reveals His glory. Therefore, if we, as the church, are going to *be* the church that Jesus is building, we have no other choice but to embrace our call to oneness.

Jesus did not place option B or option C on the table. He did not say that He will build a black church over here, and a white church over there, and a Hispanic church over here, and a National Baptist church over there, and a Southern Baptist church over here, and a denominational church over there, and a nondenominational church over here. Jesus did not give us that option. When we limit ourselves to those options, we have perverted His definition of His church.

Rather, we are all individual stones coming together to form a larger, more complete whole upon which Christ, serving as the foundation and cornerstone, will build His church (Eph. 2:20–22).

### *The Purpose of One*

Second, not only are we all interlinking parts to one church, but the biblical church also has a legislative capacity. We learn this in Ephesians 2 when we look at the definition of the term *church*.

*Ecclesia* essentially refers to a group of people who had been called out from the general population to serve in the parliament, congress, or counsel of the community in order to establish the governance, guidelines, rules, and regulations for the broader citizenry. In other words, if you were a part of the ecclesia in Greek societies, you were part of the governing council who legislated on behalf of the Greek population. Ecclesia wasn't a place where you came to sing a song or hear a sermon. Ecclesia was the place where you came to legislate on behalf of the nation. The term is negatively used this way in Acts 19:39–41 to identify the assembly of those who sought to illegally pass legislation against the church and the expansion of Christianity.

Most of the time when we use the term *church* today, we simply mean a place where people can go to worship, find encouragement, teaching, and fellowship. However, while those things are important, when we limit ourselves to them, we have reduced the word from its intended meaning. To be a part of the church of Jesus Christ, as Jesus defined it, is to be a part of a spiritual legislative body tasked to enact heaven's viewpoint in hell's society. In the midst of a place of war and conflict, God has deposited an ecclesia: *a group of people who have been called out to bring the governance of God into the relevant application and practice of mankind.*

This legislative role of the church is clearly evident in this passage, since what is resisting it are the "gates of hell," and "gates" are used in Scripture to refer to a place where legislative activities occur (Zech. 8:16; Deut. 16:18). This is reinforced by the fact that "keys" are given that gain access to heaven's authority to be executed by the church on earth (Matt. 16:19). Jesus sits at the right hand of the Father to legislate from heaven, and we sit with Him (Eph. 2:5–6). This explains why God decides what He's going to do from heaven tied to what the church is doing in history (Eph. 3:10).

When the church settles for spiritual inspiration and information only, as important and foundational as those things are, we wind up with temporal encouragement with little lasting transformation. The church is supposed to be where the values of eternity operate in history so that history sees what God looks like when heaven is operating on earth. The job of the church is not to adopt the culture, or to merely assess and analyze the culture, but to set heaven within the context of culture so that culture can see God at work in the midst of the conflicts of men.

### *The Progression of One*

Third, the biblical church exists to advance the kingdom, not simply to defend it. Please notice the progressive nature of the language Jesus used. Jesus said that He is going to "build" His church. He did not say that He was going to stop hell. Rather, hell has come to stop Him. It happens this way: As Christ builds His church, hell sees Him doing it. Hell does not like what Christ is doing, so hell tries to stop it. Jesus and His church are on the offensive. Hell is on the defensive.

However, for far too long the church has operated on the defensive side of this battle. We've been reacting to the movements of hell rather than setting the pace of heaven. Jesus clearly says that the way you will know that the church is His church is that hell will be trying to stop it, and hell will be failing. The reverse of that is true as well. The way you will know that the church is not operating as

Jesus' church is that it will be reacting to hell's advances, and it will be failing to stop them.

Jesus said, rather, that His church, *as one*, will be hewed together around a common vision and purpose, making it not only capable of withstanding the strongest oppositional forces on the planet—the gates of hell will not prevail—but also able to make a progressive impact. However, if the church is not joined together as one, a rock, the reverse of that will occur as well, because that is the way Christ has designed the church to function. Without oneness, the gates of Hades—Satan and his minions—will overpower and engulf us.

This reminds me of when Hurricane Katrina made her appearance in New Orleans. Hurricane Katrina was bad, but she wasn't the ultimate problem. Katrina had come into town, done her thing, and she was on her way. The trouble didn't just come from Katrina. The trouble also came when the levee broke. That's when the city flooded.

The job of the levee had been to hold the water back. Had the levee held, Katrina would have been remembered as just another strong storm in a long line of others like her, rather than as the disaster that she became.

God has placed a levee in history. He has called it the church. The church is designed to hold back Satan's forces being unleashed against mankind. The church isn't solely about choir fests, programs, and luncheons, while those things are good. The church isn't just about feeling something, praying, clapping, singing, or saying "amen," although those things are good. The church was intentionally designed to *be* the church, because when it *is* the church, even the strongest forces cannot break it down. The gates of hell will not overpower it. In fact, when the church is *being* the true biblical church, the church will storm in and overpower the gates of hell.

But if hell is on the doorstep, in the lobby, or in the pews and pulpits of the American church—which many would argue that it is—it can only be the result of the body of Christ failing to join together across racial, class, and gender lines as a unified whole in pursuit of a kingdom agenda. We know this is true because Jesus made it clear that He would build His church in such a way, when done His way, that the gates of hell would not overpower it.

That doesn't mean we become "one race," ignoring our different preferences in worship, music, preaching, fellowship, or even how long we want to meet together on a Sunday morning in what we call "church." The kingdom of heaven where we will one day go as the bride of Christ will be made up of racial and ethnic diversity (Rev. 5:9; 7:9); therefore, we ought not to try to strip ourselves of our unique differences now. Rather, we need to welcome God's creative distinctions in such a way so as to make a stronger, more unified body in our land by joining church congregations together—rock and rock together—embracing an intentional strategy of edification through mutual service, thereby impacting not only our families and churches but also our nation with the transforming power of Christ. The realms of athletics, entertainment, and technology have grasped and implemented this idea to their advantage far more than we have as the body of Christ.

If we could ever see the kingdom as God sees it, and if we could ever see each other as God sees us, designed to come together in a unified goal underneath His overarching agenda, then the world would have to deal with the strength of the church of Jesus Christ. Now the world merely needs to deal with this segment over here and that segment over there as we divide ourselves over preferences.

Reconciliation through mutual service rather than in seminars, songs, or events makes us the church Jesus designed us to be. When we do this, we serve notice that the kingdom of God is here, real, and advancing.

### *The Power of One*

Fourth, the biblical church operates with full access to supreme authority and power. The next verse in this passage in Matthew 16 tells us, "I will give you the keys of the kingdom of heaven; and whatever you bind on earth shall have been bound in heaven, and whatever you loose on earth shall have been loosed in heaven" (Matt. 16:19).

Jesus says He will give the church the "keys of the kingdom of heaven." What do you do with keys? You gain access (Isa. 22:22). Have you ever been in a hurry and you can't find your keys? That means that you're not going anywhere anytime soon. Or perhaps you are like me and you have a number of keys on your keychain, but you have forgotten what some of them unlock. Those keys are no longer of any benefit to you.

Jesus says that the church He is building will have the keys to the kingdom of God, giving it the authority to bind and loose from heaven to earth. Binding and loosing refers to the divinely given authority to forbid and permit. It authorizes exercising heaven's authority on earth. The implications of this truth are staggering. If we could only grasp the potential of this reality, there is no end to the impact we, as the church, could have on our land and in the world.

Yet why are we not experiencing this power and authority in the church today? Because we are not operating in the way Jesus designed His church to function. We are operating according to churchdom while not operating according to the kingdom. Therefore, we are trying to use our own church keys to unlock kingdom doors and finding that they don't open much of anything at all.

This reminds me of a time I flew from New York to Chicago. In New York, I had stayed at the Marriott Hotel. But when I got to Chicago, I went to another hotel. I checked into the hotel and they gave me my keys. I made my way up to the twentieth floor and stuck my key card into the lock. A red light came on, so I tried my key again. A red light blinked again. At this point, tired from a long trip and not wanting to drag my bags all the way back down to the lobby again to tell them that they had given me the wrong key, I'll admit that I got evangelically ticked off.

But down I went, making my way to the front desk. When I handed the lady at the front desk my key, she apologized and let me know that she would exchange it for me. Then she paused. Looking at my key card, she handed it back to me and said, "I'm sorry, sir, but this key is your problem. It doesn't go to this hotel." I had put my New York key card in my pocket, and once I arrived in Chicago, I mistakenly took that key out to try to open my hotel door. Understandably, it didn't work.

In other words, the keys Jesus is giving the church are the only keys that will work. These are not program keys, ministry keys, sermon keys, or song keys. These are the keys that belong to the kingdom. So if our churches are not kingdom-minded—if we have failed to comprehend, let alone adopt, a kingdom theology, ideology, and methodology—we will not be able to open heaven's doors. We will have prayer meetings, preaching, choir songs, and seminars, but no authority. We will have no authority on earth because the authority is directly tied to the kingdom. The keys don't belong to Church A or Church B, or even Church AB & The Redeemed C; the keys belong to the kingdom alone and only the church has been given the authorization to possess and use them.

I referenced this "other kingdom" earlier in chapter 4 when we looked at Joshua and the military leader outside of the city of Jericho. God's kingdom isn't here to take sides; it is here to take over. This principle can be further illustrated through a look at my favorite sport, football. Most people think that when a football game begins, there are only two teams on the field. That is a common misunderstanding. Each time a football game is played, there are three teams on the field. There are the two opposing teams battling it out for victory, and then there is the third team—the team of officials.

The team of officials, while in the game, answer to a higher authority—the NFL League office. They represent another kingdom. They rule within the established purview of their own rulebook. You don't see officials on a football field asking the home team what it thinks about a certain play or penalty. You don't see them requisitioning a poll to determine whether or not the ball was trapped or caught. I've never gone to a game and seen an official ask the visiting coach if he thought his running back fumbled the ball, or if his knee was actually down.

If the officials did that, there would be mass confusion. Some people would say it was a fumble. Others would not. Some people would say the play in question should draw a penalty. Others would not.

In football, the officials rule. They make the decisions. Bottom line: What the referees say goes. When they give their decision, they do so without hesitation. Because it doesn't matter to them who likes them. It doesn't matter to them who claps for them. It doesn't matter to them who boos them. The referees are not there to win a popularity competition. They are there to ensure order so that a victor can be ultimately declared.

Likewise, the church does not exist for the church. The moment the church exists for the church, it is no longer being the church. God created the church for the benefit of the kingdom. The church exists for the league office that sets the rules, governance, and guidelines that determine who the church is, what the church does, and how the church is to function on the game field of life.

God established the church to give us the keys to a whole other realm. He didn't place us here to be popular or to merely mimic the views of the secular society. Sometimes the crowd is going to boo us, but that's okay. We don't work for them. We serve a King from another kingdom who rules with supreme authority. Whatever we bind, the kingdom backs up just like the NFL League office backs up the officials when they make a decision on the field. Whatever we lose, the kingdom backs up. This is because the keys of the kingdom access the authority of the King.

## The Kingdom and the Church

Our society is not changing today because the church has settled for buildings, programs, personalities, and cultural acceptance instead of accessing the authority of the kingdom. We've had church, but we haven't had transformation. Unless the church becomes kingdom-minded, we are not being the church Christ came to build. In fact, Jesus only mentioned "church" three times in His earthly ministry, and all three times are recorded in the kingdom-focused book of Matthew. The word *kingdom,* however, is found fifty-four times in the book of Matthew alone,[1] and 162 times in the New Testament (*basileia*).

Yet, surprisingly, we often hear more about the church than the kingdom. We "plant churches" rather than promote the kingdom. Our seminaries teach our future leaders how to *do* church rather than how to *be* about the kingdom. We ought to focus on both the kingdom and the church because both are interconnected. We can't have church without the kingdom. Yet the kingdom carries out its agenda through the church.

It is high time we become kingdom people as a church representing something bigger than our own individualized groups and preferences. It is high time we made God's kingdom our rule and His glory our goal. God didn't establish the church to make us feel good. Rather, we are a people with a purpose made up of many members brought together in one body (1 Cor. 12:20), who suffer together (1 Cor. 12:26), and are fitly joined together (Eph. 4:16) in order to allow the full expression of the diverse spiritual gifts that have been given to each of us for the building up of the church for the impact on society, the opposing of Satan's forces, and the manifestation of the glory of God (Eph. 3:21).

As we saw briefly in chapter 2, Paul describes this when he compares us to a body. We read,

> But to each one is given the manifestation of the Spirit for the common good. . . . For even as the body is one and yet has many members, and all the members of the body, though they are many, are one body, so also is Christ. For by one Spirit we were all baptized into one body, whether Jews or Greeks, whether slaves or free, and we were all made to drink of one Spirit. (1 Cor. 12:7, 12–13)

A danger in our culture today is that in our well-intentioned songs, events, and Sunday cross-cultural exchanges, we have emotionalized our call to oneness rather than embraced it. While campfire lyrics evoke sentiments of spiritual unity and connection, and that is important, it is never to be an end in itself. Oneness is a means toward achieving a greater purpose of carrying out the will of God on earth "as it is in heaven." It is the environment created through the merging of diverse strengths through which the glory of God manifests itself within the power of God working in and through the people of God carrying out the purpose of God.

Unless we view oneness in this regard—as a kingdom strategy ordained by God against the schemes of the devil—we will continue to falter in our personal lives, family lives, churches, and communities simply because we fail to realize that the call to become one goes deeper than emotion. We *need* each other (1 Cor. 12:21–22). We are remiss not to embrace each other as God has ordained us to do, "whereas our more presentable members have no need of it.

But God has so composed the body, giving more abundant honor to that member which lacked, so that there may be no division in the body, but that the members may have the same care for one another" (vv. 24–25).

If the church is ever going to make an impact on society, we must realize that we are a part of an established kingdom where God makes the rules. He has given us authority in the earth, but we are only able to exercise that authority according to His rules. Escaping those rules is as impossible as escaping the effects of gravity. Just like there are natural laws that govern nature, there are spiritual laws that govern the spiritual world. If you jump out of a window, you're going to crash to the ground. There's no way around it. Likewise, if we try to *do* church individually rather than *be* the church collectively, we're going to remain powerless and ineffective. This is because a preeminent rule for being the church is that we are one. That is foundational: "There is neither Jew nor Greek, there is neither slave nor free man, there is neither male nor female; for you are all one in Christ Jesus" (Gal. 3:28). Only when the church embraces righteous diversity across racial (Jew nor Greek), class (slave nor free man), and gender (male nor female) lines will we be the haven God designed us to be in a world of lost people in search of a kingdom embassy.

## The Priority of Discipleship

To accomplish this kingdom-minded goal, the church must make a radical return to our primary mission of developing kingdom disciples. Traditional evangelicalism and cultural church life have lost their way. Spiritual leaders are to serve and train the members to serve as kingdomologists who are developing kingdom disciples who become kingdom servants that make a kingdom impact.

Again, a kingdom disciple is *a believer who is progressively learning to live all of life under the lordship of Jesus Christ and who is transferring a comprehensive biblically centered kingdom worldview to those within their sphere of influence.* Jesus makes it clear in His great commission to the church (Matt. 28:16–19) that He only shares His kingdom authority with disciples, not with all Christians in general (John 2:23–25).

When discipleship is not the primary goal of the church, its members become useless to the kingdom (Luke 14:34–35; Matt. 5:13) and therefore fail in impacting the culture. Discipleship is where believers learn to imitate Christ's character and conduct, attitude and actions (Matt. 10:24–25). True kingdom disciples publicly confess (identify) their allegiance to Christ at home, work, and in their recreation and entertainment choices. They are not part-time Christians but rather are full-time saints representing and reflecting Him and His kingdom values in everything they do.

With the development of disciples there is the transfer of kingdom authority through the church into the culture. A powerful church will have an impact and influence not only on individuals but also on the environment and structures of society. This is why Jesus commands us to disciple the nations. Nations are not only made up of the individual people who live there, but also the structures and systems in society that govern them. So, discipleship should also affect the institutions of a society and bring both righteousness and justice to bear on how they should function.

An effective church can only be measured by the amount of kingdom disciples being made of the converts, not merely the amount of people who attend worship services. Only disciple-making churches are kingdom-useful churches and only unified kingdom churches are useful to God in reversing the downward spiral our culture continues to experience.

**Note**

1. Matthew Allen, "The Kingdom in Matthew," bible.org, May 1, 2004, https://bible.org/article/kingdom-matthew.

# Chapter 15

# A KINGDOM APPROACH TO BIBLICAL JUSTICE

Before the pandemic of 2020, my favorite place to go was New York City. If I could have picked anywhere in America to go for a week, I would have chosen New York City. The streets were alive with activity and vitality at any time of night or day. One of the things I have always loved most about New York City is its diversity. Walking down the crowded streets, riding in a cab, or stopping in a store or restaurant takes one across the path of people from a variety of cultural backgrounds.

It shouldn't be a surprise that the Big Apple is full of so many different groups of people. After all, there is a lady standing in her harbor whose crown has seven spikes representing the seven seas and seven continents whose inhabitants have been invited to come. Inscribed near a broken chain at the base of Lady Liberty read these words,

*Give me your tired, your poor,*
*Your huddled masses yearning to breathe free,*
*The wretched refuse of your teeming shore,*
*Send these, the homeless, tossed to me,*
*I lift my lamp beside the golden door!*

Lady Liberty proclaims freedom every day to anyone with a heart to hear her. Freedom can be defined as *the unimpeded opportunity and responsibility to choose to pursue one's divinely created destiny righteously, justly, and legally.* Biblical freedom is God's gift to the human race which cannot be truly experienced without functioning within His divinely authorized boundaries (Gen. 2:16–17). Although the opportunity to experience the benefits of legal freedom exists in our nation today, many people still live in bondage to a number of injustices in America, as well as around the world. These can include economic, relational, societal, educational, health, vocational, or familial injustices. Like the Liberty Bell, Lady Liberty proclaims freedom at a time when many are still seeking to find it.

An often overlooked and yet critical aspect of the kingdom and the church with regard to oneness is this area of freedom. The kingdom agenda involves promoting this freedom in Christ through the vehicle of what is often called, in our contemporary society, *social justice.*

However, *social justice* has become a convoluted term meaning different things to different people. It is often used as a catchphrase for illegitimate forms of government that promote the redistribution of wealth as well as the collectivistic illegitimate expansion of civil government, which wrongly infringes on the jurisdictions of God's other covenantal institutions (family and church). Such a view of social justice is a contradiction and denial of biblical justice since biblical justice seeks to protect individual liberty while promoting personal responsibility. For example, the biblical injunction of "Thou shalt not steal" includes areas such as government-sanctioned theft through state-enforced redistribution of wealth and illegitimate taxation. When God's guidelines for freedom are compromised, then the state seeks to become god resulting in a corresponding loss of freedom. You then become a slave of the state (1 Sam. 8:9–18).

For our purposes in this chapter, the term I have chosen to use is *biblical justice* rather than social justice, because biblical justice provides society with a divine frame of reference from which to operate. The word *justice* in Scripture means to prescribe the right way. Since God is just (Deut. 32:4) and is the ultimate lawgiver (James 4:12), His laws and judgments are just and righteous (Ps. 19:7–9; 111:7–8).

They are to be applied without partiality (Deut. 1:17; Lev. 19:15; Num. 15:16) seeing as justice identifies the moral standard by which God measures human conduct (Isa. 26:7–8). It is the government's role, then, to be His instrument of divine justice by impartially establishing, reflecting, and applying His divine standards of justice in society (Ps. 72:1–2, 4; 2 Sam. 8:15; Deut. 4:7–8).

Biblical justice, therefore, is *the equitable and impartial application of the rule of God's moral law in society.* Whether exercising itself through economic, political, social, or criminal justice, the one constant within all four realms is the understanding and application of God's moral law within the social realm.

## The Spiritual and the Social

It is the division of the sacred and the secular that has led to the cultural disintegration we are now experiencing. It was never the Creator's desire to have such a separation exist in His world. From Genesis to Revelation, it is inextricably clear that the spiritual and the social are always to be integrated if life is to be lived the way God intended.

In fact, the Bible expressly states that the reason there is social disintegration in the form of all kinds of personal, domestic, urban, and international chaos is that man wrongfully segregates the spiritual from the social (2 Chron. 15:3–6). When God created man, he was given the responsibility to rule the earth under divine authority while simultaneously spreading God's image throughout the world (Gen. 1:26–28). Social justice should simply be the application of biblical justice to the issues and institutions that affect society and its citizens.

However, it was man's refusal to submit to divine authority that led to the first social disintegration. When man disobeyed God, the result was family breakdown, economic struggle, emotional instability, and physical death (Gen. 3:1–19).

When God established Israel, He wrote their constitution in the form of the Ten Commandments. These commandments were divided between man's vertical responsibility to God and his horizontal responsibility to his neighbor. Consequently, God deemed the spiritual and social relationship necessary for the proper functioning of society (Ex. 20:1–17). God also wanted His people to reflect His character through charitable works and acts of kindness to people outside of Israel as a reflection of their gratitude for His goodness to them (Deut. 10:17–19).

Biblical justice is not a man-made, socially imposed, top-down system ultimately leading to the negation of freedom. Biblical justice promotes freedom through emphasizing accountability, equality, and responsibility in providing a spiritual underpinning in the social realms.

Each of the four jurisdictions in God's kingdom—personal, family, church, and state—is called upon to promote justice and responsibility under God in its own distinct way. Through these jurisdictions, God has given man the task of impartially protecting the "unalienable rights" He has granted to each of us. One way this is done is through the just removal of illegitimate boundaries that prohibit people from pursuing and fully experiencing all that God has created them to be.

Biblical justice is not the removal of all boundaries since boundaries are an essential component of experiencing freedom. For example, a tennis player isn't free to play tennis if there is no base line. A baseball player isn't free to play baseball if there is no foul line. A fish is not free to roam the jungle, nor is a lion free to live in the ocean. The reason that God allows boundaries is to create the opportunity to take full advantage of freedom. However, biblical justice seeks to remove illegitimate boundaries so that the full expression of freedom can be made manifest. Biblical freedom can be defined as t*he unimpeded opportunity and responsibility to choose to righteously, justly, and legally pursue one's divinely created destiny*.

Only God can declare what is a legitimate or illegitimate boundary because only God determines what is right or wrong. His Word is the standard by which the aspects of His law, reflected in truth and righteousness, govern what we do. God's justice is therefore predictable because His standard does not change. He does not show partiality in His judgments (Rom. 2:11), nor is He a respecter of persons (Acts 10:34; Eph. 6:9). He is the righteous judge who renders judgment in equity without regard to status (Rom. 12:19;

Num. 15:16), and He expects civil rulers to do likewise (Ps. 72:1–2). So important is the principle of justice that God rejects worship where injustice prevails (Amos 5:21–24; Mic. 6:6–8; Isa. 1:10–17). His instruction given to Moses indicates that humanity is to do the same: "You shall not show partiality in judgment; you shall hear the small and the great alike. You shall not fear man, for the judgment is God's" (Deut. 1:17). Jesus makes it plain that to miss the primacy of justice is to ignore one of the weightier matters of God's revelation to man. In spite of any other religious activity one does, the failure to understand and apply biblical justice keeps us from understanding and applying one of the major themes of Scripture (Matt. 23:23).

### *God the Deliverer*

Repeatedly throughout the Scripture, God has revealed Himself as a defender and deliverer. The exodus out of Egypt dramatically portrays God's execution of biblical justice on behalf of a group of people who were oppressed. Later, when God gave His laws to Israel, He reminded them of His deliverance. He said, "You shall not wrong a stranger or oppress him, for you were strangers in the land of Egypt" (Ex. 22:21).

God regularly tied either a presence, or an absence, of biblical justice to a presence, or absence, of His blessing. For example, Israel's worship was rejected because of an absence of justice in society (Amos 5:21–24). The Israelites were taken into captivity and held in bondage because of their rebellion against God. God had repeatedly told them to turn from their sin and practice "justice and righteousness," pay back what was stolen, and secure every pledge (Ezek. 33:10–20).

The destruction of Sodom and Gomorrah, as another example, is often attributed to the blatant practice of homosexuality; however, God clearly links His wrath toward them to their lack of concern for and oppression of the poor (Ezek. 16:49).

The prophets of the Old Testament regularly condemned the people for their social injustices as well. These social condemnations were not merely viewed as secular affronts to communities, but also a spiritual affront to God (Zech. 7:9–12). God's people were specifically instructed to seek the welfare of the secular city in which they were living and to pray for its well-being so that it would become a better place to live, work, and raise their families (Jer. 29:4–7).

Therefore, the role of the church, as a participant in God's sociopolitical kingdom and as His bride, is to execute divine justice on behalf of the defenseless, poor, and oppressed. Scripture relates biblical justice distinctly to these groups as a primary concern because it is these groups that most represent the helpless in society and bear the brunt of injustices.

The church is not to mistreat or marginalize the poor (James 2:15–16), or to have class and racial prejudice (Gal. 2:11–14). Rather, the church is commissioned to meet the physical needs of the "have-nots" within it. Note, this is not to be confused with subsidizing irresponsibility, which the Bible strictly prohibits (2 Thess. 3:10; Prov. 6:9–11; 10:4; 13:18; 24:30–34). Even in the biblical practice of gleaning (Deut. 24:19–21)—which was leaving behind portions of a harvest for the benefit of the poor who collect it—the poor needed to exercise responsibility in accessing what had been left behind. The amount of work that was put forth resulted in the amount of food that was obtained.

The Bible is clear on spiritual ministry and social responsibility working hand in hand. When the two are properly connected and integrated, people become productive citizens of society while also becoming prepared for life in eternity.

### *Loving God, Loving Others*

A strong biblical connection exists between our knowledge and relationship with God and our concern for the poor and the oppressed (Jer. 22:16; Matt. 25:34–40). Micah 6:8 reveals this: "He has told you, O man, what is good; and what does the Lord require of you but to do justice, to love kindness, and to walk humbly with your God?" We "do justice" in a humble response to a just God as a natural reflection of His presence in our lives. We are not just to talk about it and believe it; biblical justice demands action. Religion becomes authentic when it manifests itself in ministry to others in need.

The second-most-talked-about subject in Scripture, after money, is the poor. More than three hundred verses directly relate to the treatment of the poor, strategies to aid the poor, God's intentions for the poor, and what our perspective should be toward the poor. Space doesn't allow us to go through all of them, but the point is clear that God cares about the poor particularly because they are the most vulnerable to suffering from oppression and injustice.

Ultimately, *doing justice* fulfills the two greatest commandments given to us by Jesus—that of loving God and loving others (Matt. 22:37–40). Christ says, "On these two commandments depend the whole Law and the Prophets." Both the content and meaning of the Law and Prophets were centered not only on one's relationship to God, but also on whether one was rightly related to his neighbor. The implication is that understanding of and love for God that does not also express itself in love for one's neighbor does not satisfy the biblical definition of love.

Thus, Jesus linked our attitude toward God (spiritual) with our attitude toward others (social). When asked who is my neighbor that I am to love, Jesus responded by telling the story of the Good Samaritan, pointing out that your neighbor is the person whose need you see and whose need you are able to meet regardless of racial differences (Luke 10:26–37). Jesus concludes the story by exhorting us to love in like manner.

It is important to note the meaning of love because we often confuse love with an emotion. While love can, and does, contain emotions, the Greek word used in this command to love God and love others is the word *agape*. It is not referring to "liking" someone or preferring a certain personality or race. Love is *the decision to compassionately, righteously, and responsibly pursue the well-being of another.* Jesus used the condition of injustice as an intrinsic aspect to a proper perception of defining the meaning of loving one's neighbor. Therefore, since loving one's neighbor includes seeking his best interest by relieving him from injustice or oppression when it is necessary and we are able, love for God is validated through a liberating love for others. To love is a command, whether or not it is accompanied by any emotion (John 13:34–35; Matt. 5:43–44).

Jesus' earthly ministry to people consistently modeled the integration of the spiritual and the social that He taught about in that He dwelt among the oppressed (John 4:39–40), ate with them (Luke 5:27–30), comforted them (Luke 12:22–34), fed them (Luke

9:10–17), restored them (Luke 5:12–16), and healed them (Luke 7:18–23) in fulfillment of His Father's will. All of Jesus' good works were clearly connected to the spiritual purposes of God (Matt. 4:23–24).

When Jesus gave His great Sermon on the Mount, He instructed His disciples to be the salt of the earth and light to the world (Matt. 5:13–16). Salt was used as a preservative to stop decay, and light was used to dispel darkness. Christ's followers were to influence society for God, accomplished by the good works they did for others in the name of God. Therefore, good works done for the benefit of helping people must include, not exclude, God. Good works originate from God, are done through God, and align under the truth of God in order to bring glory to God. In other words, God gets the credit for everything. Good works are not good words, nor are they simply good things. You don't have to be a Christian to do good things. The unsaved can build orphanages and houses, give money, visit the sick, and do a lot of other good things. But what the unsaved cannot do is glorify God through good works. Good works must always be tied to God's glory.

The apostle John also stressed the connection between love for God and love for others when he said, "If someone says, 'I love God,' and hates his brother, he is a liar; for the one who does not love his brother whom he has seen, cannot love God whom he has not seen" (1 John 4:20). John reminded us that this love is to be expressed through actions and not just words as it is carried out in "deed and truth" (1 John 3:18).

Further emphasis that this love should be given to the poor and oppressed as special objects of God's concern comes when James writes, "Did not God choose the poor of this world to be rich in faith and heirs of the kingdom which He promised to those who love Him?" (James 2:5). He also defines true religion by how one treats the widow and the orphan (James 1:27). While Jesus does not reject the rich who have legitimately acquired their wealth, He does condemn them when they are insensitive to or use their resources, influence, and power to oppress others (James 5:1–6).

This same emphasis continued within the operation of the early church. As a result, the influence of the first-century church was so powerful in society that it brought great joy to the entire city (Acts 8:8) and was said to have turned the world upside down (Acts 17:6). The church became known for its good works (Acts 4:32–35; 5:11–16). Members of the church were taught to do good not only to other church members but also to all people (Gal. 6:10).

Biblical justice isn't simply a ministry to be relegated to a special event. Biblical justice is a foundational part of fulfilling the purpose of the church as intimated by the heart of God. It is a result of God's people becoming one through being what God has called us to be and participating in what He has called us to do—*justice.*

## The Scope of the Gospel

There is some confusion today about the implications of the gospel, and to what degree the gospel includes this mandate of justice. Some Christians believe that to include social liberation and justice in the gospel is to preach a "different gospel." Others believe that to exclude social liberation and justice as part of the gospel is to deny the gospel. Black liberation theology was formed on this latter thesis.

To resolve this dilemma, KRT makes a distinction between the gospel's content and its scope. This distinction is important because through it is determined the extent that we are to "do justice" as the church as part of our comprehensive responsibility of proclaiming the gospel.

The content of the gospel message is limited, narrow, and contained. Paul made this unmistakably clear when he said,

> Now I make known to you, brethren, the gospel which I preached to you, which also you received, in which also you stand, by which also you are saved, if you hold fast the word which I preached to you, unless you believed in vain.
>
> For I delivered to you as of first importance what I also received, that Christ died for our sins according to the Scriptures, and that He was buried, and that He was raised on the third day according to the Scriptures. (1 Cor. 15:1–4)

Clearly, the content of the gospel message is the death, burial, and resurrection of Jesus Christ. Scripture is plain that it is personal faith in the finished work of Christ that brings people the forgiveness of sin, a personal relationship with God, and eternal life (John 5:24; 6:47).

The gospel's scope, however, reaches further into sanctification, within which is located the concepts of justice and social action. We see this scope in Paul's use of the word *gospel* when he informs the Christians in Rome that by the "gospel" they are established (Rom. 16:25). Likewise, in the book of Romans the gospel is called "the power of God for salvation" (1:16) and is said to include "the righteousness of God . . . revealed from faith to faith" (v. 17). This righteousness includes sanctification, since "the righteous man shall live by faith" (Hab. 2:4; Rom. 1:17).

In addition, the gospel is viewed as the criterion of Christian conduct (Phil. 1:27), and believers are viewed as being obedient to the gospel when they are active in the ministry of love to poorer believers (2 Cor. 9:12–13). Paul further explained that the gospel involves more than the initial reception of salvation, but also a life of liberty, freedom, and multiracial relationships when he rebuked Peter for drawing evil racial distinctions between Gentiles and Jews on the basis of circumcision. Paul said that in doing so Peter had not been "straightforward about the truth of the gospel" (Gal. 2:14).

The gospel that sanctifies also encompasses the whole man as directly stated by Paul: "Now may the God of peace Himself sanctify you entirely; and may your spirit and soul and body be preserved complete" (1 Thess. 5:23). A view of mankind that divides the invisible world (soul) from the visible world (body) narrows the understanding of the scope of the gospel. This is reflected in a desire to save people's souls, thus compartmentalizing a section of man; that is, to save an aspect of man as opposed to the man himself.

This division between the immaterial and material parts of man leads to a lack of application by way of biblical justice through emphasizing the spiritual over the social. However, the relationship of the soul to the body is to be seen as a unified whole. Biblical terms referring to the spiritual aspects of man support this reference to man's whole person, including the body. The Hebrew word for soul (*nephesh*) refers to the whole person, which includes the body (Gen.

2:7; Lam. 3:24). In the New Testament, the Greek word for soul (*psuche*) is used to refer to Christ's body, seeing as souls do not die and go to the grave (Acts 2:27).

Therefore, KRT argues that the church is commissioned to deliver the content of the gospel (evangelism) so that people can come into a personal relationship with God through faith in Christ. Yet the church is also commissioned to live out the scope of the gospel (sanctification) so that people can realize the full manifestation of it and glorify God. The content of the gospel produces oneness in the church as we evangelize the world together. The scope also produces oneness through good works that are based on the principles of biblical justice and the eradication of racism. When the two are illegitimately separated, you wind up with Christians doing evangelism while simultaneously supporting racist and unjust laws, actions, and perspectives.

Many years ago I had the opportunity to sit down with one of the great evangelists of our time, the late Billy Graham, at his home in North Carolina. While we spent the afternoon together, he expressed the concern weighing heavy on his heart. He told me how ministers and churches would work together across racial lines to both plan and implement his crusades; however, after the event was over, these same ministers and churches had little or no relationship with each other at all.

Billy Graham asked me why I thought this was so.

In response, I told him that this happened because the event was only tied to evangelism and not to community transformation as well. When invited, black pastors joined with white pastors to put together an evangelistic outreach. But the heart of African American Christianity hinged on a broader perspective of the scope of the gospel rather than solely on the gospel's content. When asked to participate in community impact and legitimate justice initiatives by their fellow African American pastors, the white church has, as a general rule, often not shown the same enthusiasm of partnership that they receive in their outreach requests.

KRT says that while we must never convolute, conflate, or contaminate the content of the gospel with the scope of the gospel, neither are we to allow the content of the gospel to obscure the necessity for a broader understanding, need, and application of the scope of the gospel. Without a comprehensive understanding of the scope of the gospel, we lack the common goal necessary to bring us together, in oneness, to evoke real and lasting change in our churches so that it can be expanded to our nation.

## Jesus and the Gospel

The greatest illustration of both the content and scope of the gospel is found in Luke chapter 4. This passage took place at a time when the Jews were living in social, political, and economic oppression under Rome. The Jews hated the domination of the Romans, were looking for a messiah to deliver them, and desperately wanted their freedom.

Roaming the hillsides at that time was a man named Barabbas. Barabbas was a leader of a group of counterrevolutionaries known as the zealots. These zealots wreaked havoc along the Judean hills in order to protest and resist Roman imperialism and oppression. Caught in the middle of one of these pillaging raids, Barabbas was eventually arrested and sentenced to death on a cross.

A contemporary of Barabbas was Jesus. Jesus was known at that time as a man of no reputation who had been born in a tiny country town called Bethlehem. While news had begun to spread about Him around the other parts of the country, His greatest claim to fame in His hometown of Nazareth was that He was the son of a carpenter.

One day, Jesus had returned to Nazareth. As was the custom when there was a visitor, He was given the opportunity to read the Scripture and offer the morning's commentary. Having been handed the book of Isaiah, Jesus turned to the place in Isaiah that He wanted to read. We know that He purposefully turned there because Scripture records that He "found the place where it was written . . . " (Luke 4:17). Jesus looked for a particular passage that would deliver a particular truth at a particular time to a particular audience with a particular need. He did so because He had a particular point that He wanted to make. When He found the passage He was looking for, He read,

> The Spirit of the Lord is upon Me,
> because He anointed Me to preach the gospel to the poor.
> He has sent Me to proclaim release to the captives,
> and recovery of sight to the blind,
> to set free those who are oppressed,
> to proclaim the favorable year of the Lord. (vv. 18–19)

Then "He closed the book, gave it back to the attendant and sat down; and the eyes of all in the synagogue were fixed on Him. And He began to say to them, 'Today this Scripture has been fulfilled in your hearing'" (vv. 20–21).

Don't overlook that Jesus said, "*Today* this . . . has been fulfilled." The timing of the reading of this passage is crucial. Jesus intentionally chose this passage at a time when the Jews were in the middle of an economic, political, and social crisis. He came on the scene in the midst of a society experiencing the devastating effects of injustice and said that the Spirit of the Lord was upon Him to proclaim good news: the gospel.

What is essential to note from this passage is that Jesus Himself said that He had good news (the gospel) for those in the economic crisis—*the poor*. He had good news (the gospel) for those in the political crisis—*the captives*. He had good news (the gospel) for those in the social crisis—*the oppressed*. This good news that He had was the gospel of the favorable year of the Lord.

### *The Day of Atonement*

This "favorable year" is called the Jubilee in the Old Testament. To understand it more fully, we need to look at the contextual framework in which it first appeared. We read in Leviticus,

> You shall then sound a ram's horn abroad on the tenth day of the seventh month; on the day of atonement you shall sound a horn all through your land. You shall thus consecrate the fiftieth year and proclaim a release through the land to all its inhabitants. It shall be a jubilee for you. (Lev. 25:9–10)

The year of Jubilee, as noted in this passage, was inaugurated with the Day of Atonement. This was the day set aside to atone for the sins of the nation of Israel both individually and corporately. The Day of Atonement was when Israel got right with God through the shedding of blood—the slaying of a sacrifice. In other words, they didn't get the Jubilee (i.e., God's involvement economically, socially, and politically—an aspect of the scope of the gospel) without first getting their sins addressed by God (a type reflecting the future content of the gospel). They didn't get the social—which included reversing the evils of injustice, slavery, family instability, generational poverty, and oppression (Lev. 25:11–55)—until they had the spiritual. If they skipped the Day of Atonement in order to get the social benefits of the Jubilee, they lost out on the Jubilee altogether because there was a prescribed method for how God instituted His agenda.

A common problem we find in the church today is that we want God to do things for us without the Day of Atonement. A lot of people cry for justice, or for God to pay this, fix that, redeem this, or vindicate that while skipping the very thing that inaugurates God's Jubilee—the addressing of personal and corporate sin. God's wrath against sin must always be addressed, which in the dispensation of the church comes through our relationship with Jesus Christ, before He is free to give the social freedom we are looking for. If the spiritual is not foundational, there isn't going to be a Jubilee. KRT seeks to bring the spiritual to the forefront without abandoning or marginalizing the social. This is why the concept of justice is intentionally and intimately connected to righteousness throughout Scripture. They are twin towers that are to never be separated. From God's throne: righteousness and justice (Ps. 89:14). Fathers are to train their children in righteousness and justice (Gen. 18:19). Righteousness is the foundation of justice (Deut. 32:3–4). Thus, the spiritual must never be separated from the social. Biblical justice, then, means doing the right thing in the right way to obtain the right result in the right proportion as God defines it in His Word.

The reason that the Jews didn't receive the freedom that Jesus proclaimed to them was that they rejected Him and His atonement. They wanted the social action without the spiritual interaction. However, Jubilee came as the result of the atonement.

It is important to note that Jesus "proclaimed" the good news of the gospel, just as Lady Liberty proclaims her offer of freedom to anyone who has ears to hear. Lady Liberty does not give freedom to someone coming from Tibet or Burma any more than she does for someone from Kenya. Nor does she force her freedom on anyone who doesn't want it. A person needs to make his way to America and go through the process of applying for and accepting what she has to offer in order to bring her proclamation of freedom out of theory and into reality.

Likewise, Jesus proclaimed good news. He proclaimed the gospel. He proclaimed release for the captives and sight for the blind. He didn't force it by eradicating capitalism and developing a spiritualized socialism. He simply offered it under the condition that it must be accepted through a prescribed atonement before it can be experienced. This is why the biblical church operating on a kingdom agenda worldview through KRT is the only longterm solution to our racial malaise.

Jesus couldn't give Jubilee to the Jews because they refused to deal with their sin and receive Him as their Messiah. Jesus could have provided them with the deliverance from Rome they so greatly desired if they had recognized Him as their future atonement and their Lord. However, the Jews wanted the benefits of the Messiah without the relationship with the Messiah. But that's not how God's justice works. No guarantee of deliverance exists without first addressing the spiritual through the atonement. This is why the church stands poised to be the most effective and most strategic entity in the culture because it is composed of people who are already living and interacting with the spiritual. Not only that, but since Jesus is the fulfillment of the Jubilee in the church age, and since it is the responsibility of His body to reflect and extend what He has accomplished (Eph. 1:22–23), then it is the responsibility of the church to manifest Jubilee's liberating principle in history. The effectiveness of the church is the key to the wellbeing of the culture.

### *Christ as King*

Many of the Jews witnessed Jesus feeding thousands and healing the sick, but they demanded that He be crucified in exchange for the release of the rebel leader Barabbas. They chose the revolutionary who was attempting to free them from Roman bondage via a revolution, not the One who would do it via the cross. This is because they only wanted a welfare program rather than to be made well through spiritual transformation. They wanted deliverance, but not the King who delivers. And ever since then, mankind has been trying, and failing, to solve the problems of our societies in like manner, not via the favorable year of the Lord through the Day of Atonement, which is the supremacy of the gospel of Jesus Christ.

There is a direct correlation between the preeminence given to Christ as King and the freedom one experiences. To the degree that Jesus is exalted in personal lives, family lives, churches, and communities is the degree to which the rivers of justice and racial harmony run freely (John 4:1–42).

Jesus' ministry gave the proper order for how to approach all issues of justice and social action. He could have snapped His fingers and delivered all of the poor, the widows, and the oppressed. Instead, He was very particular about His involvement. He became involved in connection with the proclamation of His kingdom message. His purpose was to provide not only physical freedom and relief, but spiritual as well, because He knew that the spiritual and the physical are connected with each other.

KRT insists that Jesus' gospel, as recorded in Luke 4, is the good news that includes the spiritual, physical, and social. To make His proclamation merely social is not good news. If a person has the best food to eat, the nicest clothes to wear, and the greatest job at which to work and yet still dies without a relationship with Christ through His atonement, he ends up not having anything at all.

But to make His proclamation merely spiritual is not the full experience of "good news" either. To tell a person that Jesus can give him a home in heaven, but that He can't do anything about where he lives on earth—or to tell him that he's got shoes, I've got shoes, and all of God's children have shoes in heaven, but that we all have to go barefoot on earth isn't all that good of news either.

Jesus' gospel includes both the spiritual and the social. It is designed to build God's kingdom rather than try to save the world's systems. It is designed to provide a model of a different system, one created by God, which provides a divine alternative so that the world can see what God can do in broken humanity. All of the social activity in the world cannot solve the world's problems. In the long term, social action is limited; lasting solutions can only come from the kingdom of God because that's where the atonement guarantees lasting freedom.

Unless social action is based on spiritual discipleship, it will lack the power for longterm transformation. This is because there is a spiritual reality behind every physical and relational problem. By addressing the underlying theological or spiritual issues along with the physical, we can achieve longterm solutions because we have addressed the entire problem, not just its physical manifestation. Secular society does not understand the spiritual reality that causes physical, racial, social, political, and economic problems. Therefore, secular society is limited in its ability to impact and transform society.

## Implementing Biblical Justice

God has a vision. His vision is His kingdom agenda. The kingdom agenda is God's methodology for impacting and transforming the world in which we live. What the body of Christ needs today is to combine our individualized congregations and unite around a fresh view of God's vision carried out in a way that does not negate our own unique distinctiveness. This is why KRT is so critical.

God's vision promises hope both for time and eternity to all who will receive it by connecting the social with the spiritual in a biblically based frame of reference. The social without the spiritual may help people in time but leave them impoverished for eternity. The spiritual without the social may have people looking forward to a great eternity but missing what God wants to do to, through, and for people in history. As we have seen, both are essential for the transformation of not only individuals, families, and churches, but also our nation.

The church operating on a Kingdom Race Theology is in the unique position of implementing biblical justice in a country in desperate need of an alternative. John Perkins declares this boldly: "There is no institution on earth more equipped and capable of bringing transformation to the cause of the reconciliation than the Church."[1] But in order to do so, we must pursue reconciliation through a shared pursuit of biblical justice. We must similarly rally around three key principles for implementing this biblical justice: restitution, reconciliation, and responsibility. Much can be accomplished when like-minded kingdom disciples embrace one another's strengths to work together toward a shared Kingdom Race Theology vision.

*Biblical Justice and Restitution*

If the principles of biblical justice were implemented in our society today, we wouldn't have prisons full to overflowing. This is because the aim of biblical justice is always a cessation of the crime coupled, when possible, with restitution to the victim.

In biblical times, this was carried out in one of three ways: capital, corporal, or economic punishment. Capital punishment addressed heinous offenders by applying a severe penalty to severe crimes. Corporal punishment regulated a controlled form of physical punishment, along with the potential for restitution (Ex. 21:22–25, 28–30). Economic punishment put economic justice into effect through the repayment with interest of what had been lost through the crime (Ex. 22:1–15; Luke 19:1–10).

Regardless of the arena of application, biblical restitution was always specific to the offended victim. It included a designated amount that had a predetermined end for when full restitution would be realized and forgiveness granted (Lev. 6:1–7; Num. 5:7). If these guidelines had been used for our modern-day approaches to seeking equity-based opportunities for all, we would not have gotten burdened down in endless debates regarding their effectiveness and conclusion. We would have looked for a predetermined outcome which would affirm this. Not only that, we would have analyzed, measured, and even adjusted the initiatives and policies when they failed to produce the intended results they had been established to target.

In addition to restoring to victims what was unjustly taken, there must also be repairs made to the ongoing damage created by the sin. This means investing in the familial, educational, and economic development of those who bear the negative consequences of injustice. While governments have a strategic part to play in delivering justice, what we as the body of Christ need to remember is that God did not create governments to take care of the things He has called the church to do. The specific biblical role of civil government is to maintain a safe, just, righteous, and compassionately responsible environment for freedom to flourish. Civil government is created to protect the rights given to us by God. The solution to our problems won't land on Air Force One, nor does God ride the backs of either donkeys or elephants. To put it another way, Christians should be representing God's kingdom by caring for people across racial, gender, political, and class lines so well that government experts come to us to find out how we do it. Jesus could feed, heal, lead, and minister to people in a way that was a witness to the world. Because He was able to minister to their needs, Jesus turned the people's eyes toward Him and not toward the Roman government.

In our legitimate, biblical call on government to promote justice, we in the African American church have often become overly dependent on its programs, grants, and assistance to the degree that we have failed to adequately develop the means of addressing our own needs through the church. Conversely, the white church—while complaining about waste in government programs and redistribution of wealth—has done little to equip itself to place justice back in the church. Slavery, racism, criminal leasing, and Jim Crow could never have flourished in our nation if the white church had not remained silent, thus serving as religious and theological coconspirators to the evil of American injustice. Both sides have often missed the mark of what it means to be a biblical kingdom-centered church.

In the church I pastor in Dallas, we have a justice process that renders decisions on everything from restitution to marital disputes, divorces, business lawsuits, juvenile delinquency, and so on. Of course, capital crimes fall solely under the jurisdiction of the state (Rom. 13:1–4). However, this ministry—run by fully qualified legal representatives—serves the church and community in a myriad of ways.

An example of how this functions is illustrated in the life of a man whom I'll call Chris. Chris had stolen $1,500 from his employer and had been caught by the police. The judge was going to lock him up for three years at a cost to the taxpayers of about $18,000 per year. Besides the cost, Chris would be going to prison where he would only learn how to become a better criminal. Along with that, his employer would never be repaid for the loss.

I sent a group of men from our church to the judge and one said, "Your Honor, if you will give Chris back to us, we will assign a man to be responsible for him, get him a job, and garnish his wages to pay back his former employer."

The judge was happy to do that. So we placed some men in Chris's life to influence him in the right way, got him a job, garnished his wages, paid back the money he stole, saved the taxpayers money, and held him responsible. Six months later we took him back to the judge, who was astonished. Later, we got a call from the judge: "Will you take twenty more like Chris?"

The church is to be a place where biblical justice is not only proclaimed, but also produced. Yet because God's people have failed to *be* the church as the church was designed to function, the society does not see a sufficient model of divine justice at work. Therefore, it loses an opportunity to learn how to operate properly which results in expanded civil government beyond its divinely ordained scope.

### *Biblical Justice and Reconciliation*

Not only does biblical justice focus on restitution, but it also comes tempered with the potential for mercy toward the offender. The cross of Jesus Christ is the greatest example of this appeal for mercy. While on the cross, Jesus asked His Father to forgive those who were killing Him (Luke 23:34). Through the parable of the two slaves who owed money, Jesus teaches that this principle of mercy should govern how we treat others as well (Matt. 18:21–35).

While mercy is not always granted in the execution of justice, the opportunity for it makes biblical justice distinct. This should cause each of us to be grateful, because without God's mercy, none of us would be here today. It should also cause each of us to be willing to extend mercy, when able, as an outgrowth of having received it ourselves.

When combining restitution with mercy, biblical justice then has the unique ability to lead toward reconciliation as well. A secular example of this combination happened in South Africa. Following apartheid, South Africa initiated what has come to be known as the model of Truth Commissions throughout the world. Then-newly elected president Nelson Mandela established the Truth and Reconciliation Commission (TRC) as a court-like restorative justice body tasked with discovering, revealing, and, inasmuch as possible, righting past wrongdoing by a government in the hope of fostering reconciliation through resolving conflict and its resultant consequences left over from the past.[2]

The key term in the Commission is "reconciliation." As Nelson Mandela said, "For to be free is not merely to cast off one's chains, but to live in a way that respects and enhances the freedom of others."[3] Justice was sought, in this case, toward the end goal of reconciliation leading South Africa to stand head and shoulders above other nations in its bid for cooperation and oneness within its governing institutions.

Our government has never enacted a Truth and Reconciliation Commission for the injustices committed by the founding members of our nation, as well as those who came after them, toward African Americans. These injustices lie largely in the past, but they do not lie dormant. Their tremors and repercussions remain as alive and active as ever, as evidenced in the schisms, racial unrest, and social upheavals still regularly bubbling to the surface in our country.

Yet we do not need to wait on a government run by men and women who may or may not know the God of the universe or operate by His standards to enact a Truth and Reconciliation Commission. After all, we know the One who is the Truth, and He came to us on a mission of reconciliation. As He is about His "Father's business," so we are to be about the same.

Biblical justice does not simply mean halting an evil that has been done to a group of people without being willing to also offer restitution and reconciliation to the victim in order to salve the psychological, sociological, and spiritual wounds it inflicted. Biblical justice contains more than an awareness of a past wrong.

Biblical justice can only bear its fruit with regard to the issue of race in America, in particular, when we acknowledge the sin of our division, repent of it, offer and receive forgiveness for it, address any appropriate restitution, and build a bridge of oneness with each other in place of it through mutual service toward the common goal of advancing God's kingdom. Then will we experience the freedom, power, and purpose that the functioning, healthy, holistic body of Christ was designed to know and transfer to a divided nation.

Biblical justice will have released African Americans from the bondage of the myth of inferiority, separatism, and the self-defeating view of victimization. Conversely, it will have released Anglo-Americans from the bondage of a belief of superiority, fear of other cultures, and an often-illegitimate guilt-induced relational style of condescension.

### *Biblical Justice and Responsibility*

Seldom in the discussion of the poor or biblical justice do we hear the word *empowerment*, a risky term simply because couched within it is another word: *power*. Human nature rarely lends itself to relinquishing power to another person whether it is done relationally, socially, spiritually, or politically.

In fact, the words often associated with the poor and social action in our contemporary language involve concepts such as relief, charity, and aid. The focus is on how to make life more palatable for the poor through temporal and often inadequate provisions of a meal, clothing, or housing. While well-intentioned and helpful in many ways, this often nurtures a paternalistic style of justice, causing us to forget that we are not our brother's keeper, but that we are our brother's brother. Rather, we need to seek to give the able-bodied poor the power that they need to ultimately rise above their situation into a position of personal responsibility and sustainability.

Injustice is not simply mistreating the poor or oppressing others. Injustice also involves a refusal to appropriately equip and empower the defenseless, poor, and oppressed in such a way so as to maximize their productive potential. Therefore, one of the primary purposes of biblical justice and social action should always be the creation of productivity that ultimately empowers people, calling and equipping them to take personal responsibility for their well-being.

In Scripture, charity was essentially an opportunity to work. This is illustrated by the process of gleaning, which we touched on earlier, whereby the needy could collect the overlooked, castoff, and leftover grain that God's people were expected to leave behind from their harvest for the benefit of the poor (Lev. 19:9–10; Deut. 24:17–22). Through taking responsibility for being productive, people could turn poverty into productivity in response to the charitable opportunities provided by others.

If a person can work, then biblically it is expected that the person should work (2 Thess. 3:10). Gleaning provided the opportunity for the poor to help themselves out of poverty while simultaneously upholding their dignity since they were participants in the system and not merely passive recipients of charity. The harder a person worked, even as a poor person, the more productive that individual became.

Since the biblical role of civil government is to maintain a safe, just, righteous, and compassionately responsible environment for freedom to flourish, then the free market is the freedom to buy and sell at will without hindrance or interference from the state, except when such enterprise is forbidden by Scripture.[4] *Biblical economics* is the best system, because it provides the incentive for the producers of wealth to maximize their abilities while concurrently encouraging responsibility through empowering opportunities, not exploitation, for those who have the ability to work and charity for those who can't.

Other economic systems that stifle, limit, and illegitimately control the ways and means of production not only hinder economic growth, but also limit the authentic responsible expression of biblical charity. These systems produce government-run welfare states that keep people trapped in the very poverty and oppression that they say they are seeking to eliminate. This results in the destruction of families, the loss of personal initiative, responsibility, and purpose while simultaneously undermining local community development. The illegitimate use of welfare is a contemporary form of systemic oppression, racism, and classism. Biblical economic justice is not obtained through a socialistic utopian vision of equity through government-controlled or ownership of the ways and means of production, as some social theorists argue. The economic responsibility of civil government is to remove fraud, coercion, and exploitation from the marketplace, thus keeping it free from tyranny. In this way it prioritizes, protects, and incentivizes personal and family responsibility rather than undermines it. It also allows for upward mobility of the lower classes. Capitalism isn't capitalism if it's not based on basic fair principles of ownership, competition, self-interest, and freedom of choice. It is also not to control the marketplace (statism). Centralized governmental control of trade is the economic system of the Antichrist (Rev. 13:17).

Another purpose of biblical justice and social action, along with empowerment, is the impartation of knowledge. Knowledge is one of the greatest tools that can be given to people to either lift themselves out of, or defend themselves within, a situation of injustice. The clearest biblical example of the benefits of knowledge in an unjust situation is demonstrated in the book of Esther. We often read the story of Esther focusing on the beauty of Esther as a heroine who rescued her people from certain death. However, Esther didn't rescue her people from certain death at all. She merely enabled her people to defend themselves from the threat of certain death through the knowledge of the upcoming battle, along with the right to bear arms (Est. 8:11).

The law of the land forbade the king from reversing the order he had made to exterminate all of the Jews in his nation. What the Jews gained through Esther's stand was the knowledge of the ensuing battle, which allowed them the time to amass and use arms to legally defend themselves from their oppressor. Esther didn't win the battle for her people; she simply gave her people the information that equipped and enabled them to fight for themselves.

Knowledge empowers. However, if the statistics from our schools are any indicator, a large number of our young people are failing to be empowered today. And yet our churches sit idly by, housing the largest, most-qualified volunteer force in the nation who can both infiltrate and impact the next generation for good.

Churches exist in every community. Therefore, the structure to address social problems is already in place. The church is ideally suited to serve as a unified force for change. It is only that we have misunderstood our calling. As we often do when reading the story of Esther, we have become enchanted by the beauty within the safety of our own four walls to such a degree that we have forgotten that there is a battle upon us. This issue of biblical justice—how we view it and how we address it as a church—will ultimately shape and define our impact over the next century. It has the potential to unite us or divide us. As Voddie Baucham states, "This is . . . the epicenter of the Big One that, when it finally shifts with all its force, threatens to split evangelicalism right down the middle. Our problem is a lack of clarity and charity in our debate over the place, priority, practice, and definition of justice."[5]

Whether we realize it or not, we are at war. Our enemy is well trained in lies, deception, and tactics to divide and destroy not only our nation but also the body of Christ. This war is ripping apart our families, our churches, our communities, and our land.

When you are in a war, you don't care about the color or class of the person next to you—as long as he is shooting in the same direction. When you are in a war, you don't debate about race or preference, nor do you hold seminars about how to get along. The only issue needing to be decided in a war is whether or not we are on the same side firing at the same enemy.

The church of Jesus Christ is on the same side. And we are firing at the same enemy. That truth alone should be enough to compel us to become one in our aim of applying the principles of biblical justice in order to take back our nation and our world for the kingdom.

**Notes**

1. John M. Perkins, *One Blood: Parting Words to the Church on Race and Love* (Chicago: Moody, 2020), 85.
2. See the summary given in "Truth and Reconciliation Commission (TRC)," South African History Online, March 21, 2011, www.sahistory.org.za/article/truth-and-reconciliation-commission-trc-0. Additionally, since Jesus is the fulfillment of the Jubilee in the Church Age, and since it is the responsibility of His body to reflect and extend what He has accomplished (Eph. 1:22–23), then it is the responsibility of the church to manifest Jubilee's liberating principle in history.
3. Nelson Mandela, *Long Walk to Freedom: The Autobiography of Nelson Mandela* (Boston: Little, Brown and Company, 1995), 624–25.
4. Statism is the infringement of God's limits on civil government where rulers progressively seek to illegitimately control the jurisdictions divinely given to His other covenantal institutions (family and church) while simultaneously restricting personal freedom and responsibility. Scripture rejects all forms of statism (socialism, communism, fascism, etc.); a constitutional republic best reflects God's ownership and rulership of His creation. Civil rulers are to serve as God's ministers who are authorized to administer His standards within civil government's important but limited sphere of authority (Deut. 17:18–20; Rom. 13:1–4).
5. Voddie Baucham, *Fault Lines: The Social Justice Movement and Evangelicalism's Looming Catastrophe* (Washington, DC: Salem Books, 2021), 5.

# Chapter 16

# KINGDOM RACE THEOLOGY

America, in particular, has continued to grapple with the unresolved, sinful, evil diseases of racism, culturalism, and classism. It is a sickness too deep for over-the-counter remedies. Any pandemic that lasts this long and runs this deep won't be solved by a trip to your local drugstore. Radical surgery is needed.

In chapter 10, we looked at contemporary social movements that called for racial justice, specifically Critical Race Theory, Black Lives Matter, and The 1619 Project. These movements give legitimate insights into some of the key areas that cannot be ignored if we are to address the problems of race and racism in our country. They fall short, however, in effectively addressing the spiritual cause and cure for this ongoing social malaise. This is because sociology that is not firmly rooted in proper theology will always fall short of fully evaluating and resolving the effects of sin in society that leads to injustice. Socialism in the name of equity, the redistribution of wealth, and compassion operate from a collectivistic worldview where civil government, to varying degrees, becomes the major means of either controlling, owning, or administrating the ways and means of production and the distribution of goods and services. Such a position illegitimately inverts God's limited purpose for civil government, *which is to maintain a safe, just, righteous, and compassionately responsible environment for freedom to flourish*. It is to free the marketplace from tyranny—starting with the individual. Scripture is clear that the centralized governmental control of trade is the economic system of the Antichrist (Rev. 13:16–17).

On the other hand, capitalism is an economic system based on the free market, limited government, personal productivity, and prosperity. But this system often opens the door to the sins of greed and exploitation in the name of profit. Slavery is an example of this, but the exploitation of the working class in a capitalist society is not limited to extremes such as slavery. These exploitations take place at a multiplicity of levels in our contemporary culture.

People are looking to a system to solve things today, but no system has truly solved the injustices in society because no system (capitalism, socialism, or any other) is free from the human imprint of sin. Without the sinful hearts of mankind being addressed, all political and economic systems will fall short of effectively addressing the injustices they wish to resolve. This is why righteous and just laws, enforced by civil government, are necessary to restrict the evil activity of sinful people (Rom. 13:1–7; 1 Tim. 1:8–10).

To address the chaotic racial confusion in our culture we need something much more effective, something that will not only address systemic issues but also the root of these systemic issues—sin. So as clearly as I know how, I would like this chapter to address as specifically as possible this issue of race, culture, and class that has been muddied by a million different voices. I'm offering a theological, kingdom-based approach to the issues of racism and injustices. As I've taught it, kingdomology is *the theological framework and belief system that asserts that God's purpose in history is the manifestation of His glory through the establishment and advancement of His eternal kingdom on earth*. Kingdomology views this purpose as the unifying theme of Scripture. This purpose is accomplished progressively in history through human instrumentality, over and against demonic and human opposition, as mankind functions in covenant with God.

Today we have voices making claims about *which* life matters. Or whose life matters *more*. Bear in mind, all human life is created in the image of God. Therefore, all lives matter.

However, underneath the banner that God has created all people in His image, there are inequities that must be addressed. For example, the life of the unborn matters. And thus there is an emphasis on justice for the life of the unborn. Few Bible-believing people question this emphasis. Many believe that injustice in the womb must be under the umbrella that the fetus is a human life, and since all life matters, that unborn life matters.

Now to emphasize that black lives matter is also a subset under the banner that all life matters. To say that black lives matter is not to say that other lives do not matter. It is to emphasize an injustice carried out over time toward a particular group of people. The problems of these various approaches arise once you extract any specific scenario and remove it from the umbrella of God's creation. You then create your own independent cause.

There is no discussion of sociology that from a Christian point of view should not be plugged into biblical theology. God's view on the matter should matter most. If people do not start with God in their viewpoints or discussions, they're not going to stay with you if you discuss these issues from a bibliocentric worldview. God does not want you to leave Him out just because others (sociologists, theorists, professional educators, media) don't bring Him in. Instead, followers of Jesus Christ must address these issues from a theocentric, Christocentric, and bibliocentric kingdom perspective: God, Christ, and Scripture.

There exists great legitimacy in looking at research and identifying problems from a sociological or sociopolitical standpoint in order to gain better awareness of the realities of life such as systemic racism, microaggressions, implicit biases, and the like. But for believers in Christ, the Bible must sit on top of all problems to serve as the defining reference point. If not, our methods, messages, and approaches to rectify racism and its schisms and stains in our land may be not only inept, but may even lead to greater division and furtherance of racism (from both sides).

Martin Luther King Jr. made such headway in a season where all odds stacked against him because his methods and messaging were rooted in truth. As he said, "Darkness cannot drive out darkness; only light can do that. Hate cannot drive out hate; only love can do that."[1] While we herald him and his accomplishments in our culture today, many have abandoned his framework through which he achieved so much in so little time, leaving us in a continual cycle of urban decay, defensiveness, and division.

As in His creation, God expresses Himself in a multiplicity of ways. Differences are intentional. Until we begin to realize and embrace this, we will fail to fully benefit from our differences.

You may have heard me say this before but it bears repeating. I don't drink black coffee. It's too bitter on its own. I put cream in my coffee, and sugar. When I mix the white cream with the black coffee, two very distinct colors come together to create something new. I now have brown coffee. Once combined, it is impossible to redivide because a merging has occurred to supplement each other.

In bringing us together across racial and ethnic lines, God is creating something new. He is producing the sweet-smelling savor of biblical reconciliation so that the broader society can see His handiwork. One hundred pianos tuned to the same tuning fork will intrinsically be tuned to one another. But it seems like today we've got too many people playing their own keys and their own rhythm with their own cadence, rather than operating under the reconciling rule of God.

This issue of illegitimate division is so critical that the Bible says in Romans 16:17, "Now I urge you, brethren, keep your eye on those who cause dissensions and hindrances contrary to the teaching which you learned, and turn away from them." Keep your eye on those who cause dissensions. Watch out for the dividers. Watch out for language politics that seeks to divide. Watch out for those who post hate-filled verbiage or condescending statements. Watch for the insulters. The belittlers. Those who judge. Watch out for those in the body who intentionally state or share divisive images or messages on their personal platforms, but then join together on Sunday morning singing about praising God. Division is straight from Satan's playbook. The enemy's number one approach is to stir up division, keeping the body of Christ from impacting the world for God and for good.

John 17:22–24 tells us why this is Satan's strategy where we read Jesus' own words:

> The glory which You have given Me I have given to them, that they may be one, just as We are one; I in them and You in Me, that they may be perfected in unity, so that the world may know

> that You sent Me, and loved them, even as You have loved Me. Father, I desire that they also, whom You have given Me, be with Me where I am, so that they may see My glory which You have given Me, for You loved Me before the foundation of the world.

The world is not seeing God's glory as it should see God's glory because we are illegitimately divided along racial, class, political, and ideological lines. Those who name the name of Christ still use culture, race, and preference as an excuse not to do the work of reconciliation among each other. Not to talk to each other. Not to listen to each other. Not to read each other's writings if we think they disagree with what we believe. Yet, if we are fighting, marginalizing, dismissing, and downright insulting each other in the global church, the same—and even worse—will be happening in the world.

In the midst of the social chaos swirling all around us, we have been positioned for impact as the church of Jesus Christ. Rather than allowing ourselves to be co-opted by the racial confusion of the culture, we should be operating with a kingdom agenda for race, racism, and reconciliation. Any use of the word *kingdom* that does not recognize and submit to the rule of God based on His self-revelation in Scripture is an abuse of the term. Therefore I am proposing a different, biblically framed paradigm for Christians to use when addressing contemporary racial issues and that is Kingdom Race Theology.

Again, I define Kingdom Race Theology as *the reconciled recognition, affirmation, and celebration of the divinely created ethnic differences through which God displays His multifaceted glory and advances His rule in history. God displays His glory through us as His people justly, righteously, and responsibly function personally and corporately in unity under the lordship of Jesus Christ.*

Kingdom Race Theology sees race, racism, and reconciliation as a kingdom issue and not merely a cultural or social one. As such, it must be first and foremost addressed biblically and theologically if true healing and reconciliation is to occur in the church for the benefit of the society. Biblical reconciliation is *the restoration of a previously broken relationship based on repentance and forgiveness.* It removes the hostility between parties and restores peace and harmony in the relationship. This reconciliation among people is based on the reconciliation God has provided to humanity when Jesus died on the cross for our sins (Rom. 5:10).

This biblical theology of race will examine, critique, analyze, and respond to all social movements against the backdrop of God's inerrant Word. Our theology must inform, affirm, or correct our sociology. Racism in any form must be seen as the humanistic evil expression of the sin of idolatry since it is an attack on the value of the image of God in which all humanity of every race is created. This means that the dignity of every human life must be maintained from the womb to the tomb (James 3:9). Kingdom Race Theology also argues that it is sinful not to recognize and appreciate, without apology, the legitimate distinctives and differences that God has intentionally endowed in the unique racial and cultural makeup of His creation. He is not colorblind as some would argue since He will even extend our racial distinctions into eternity (Rev. 5:9; 7:9). Our identity in Christ is designed to correct and enhance—not limit, cancel, or replace—our racial uniquenesses and their usefulness to the kingdom.

From a KRT perspective, Christians should be working together across racial lines to lead the way in repairing the damage done by the long history of racial injustice that affected generational, social, medical, educational, and economic progress. These opportunities were—and in many ways are—limited or denied to people of color, particularly in urban centers. White Christians, and churches in particular, must be willing to come out of the shadows to join with their minority brothers and sisters in identifying and correcting any remaining evils of racism, overt or covert. Biblical reconciliation is always measured by and achieved as we serve together to improve the lives of others. In KRT, unity is obtained through service, not just in seminars. It is a theology with solutions, not just a theory about our schisms.

Contemporary social movements should be able to look at the collective work of the church in our ability to be repairers of the breach as the most successful and impactful model of how the application of God's kingdom principles can restore the years the locust (of racism) has taken away (Joel 2:25). Rather than siding with, or spending all our time seeking to remove, the movements of the culture, we should be establishing a movement for the culture as Christ's kingdom representatives whose aim it is to influence the culture for God's glory and for humanity's collective good.

However, our illegitimate disunity has muted our voices and stripped our spiritual authority to set God's agenda on race within the context of our land. While biblically and spiritually sound discussions on racial history and issues are strategic, they are not sufficient in and of themselves. Biblical reconciliation is ultimately achieved as we do good works together to improve the lives of people, especially the lives of the poor, oppressed, and disenfranchised. Justice is something we are commanded to do, not merely to discuss (Mic. 6:8).

In KRT, much more time must be given to activating reconciliation strategies than reiterating the problems of racism. All discussions about the sin and evil of racism (which are necessary) and the need for genuine repentance must be quickly followed up with forgiveness and a plan to move forward as one. White guilt must never be utilized as a cudgel to promote a continuous mindset of black victimization or identity as "the oppressed." Forgiveness is key to overcoming a mindset that will keep a person locked in a helpless, inferior state.

Keep in mind, forgiveness never means ignoring the sin or denying your pain. As Latasha Morrison writes, "Bridge builders don't deny hurt. They experience it. Sit in it. Feel it. But they don't stay in that pain. They don't allow those who've wounded them to control them or constantly drive them back to anger and resentment. Instead, they allow that pain to continually push them into forgiveness."[2] Forgiveness is first and foremost a decision. It is *the decision to no longer credit an offense against an offender with a view to executing personal vengeance*. Unforgiveness is like an untreated injury of the soul. Left to fester, it can set in motion a cycle of events that only harm you more. Unforgiveness can keep you so focused on the pains of the past that you fail to recognize the goodness of God in the present. What's more, when you refuse to forgive, you and God are no longer on the same page.

Rather than siding with any of the conflicting and oft-confusing social and racial movements of the culture, KRT says we should clearly demonstrate on our own how God's approach to racial reconciliation dismantles the oppressor/oppressed distinction (rather than reinforcing it) in light of the supremacy of Jesus Christ (Eph. 6:5–9; Col. 3:22–4:1). In Christ we are now to know "no one according to the flesh" (2 Cor. 5:16). This means that divinely created racial and ethnic differences become secondary to and reflective of biblical principles and to spiritual and moral Christlike character.

As believers who ascribe to a Kingdom Race Theology, like God we are not colorblind but neither do we allow color to "blind us" from judging people based on who they are and the values they demonstrate through their choices. Character must always come before color. KRT always starts with a framework of personal responsibility, not group identity, since that is where God starts. After all, if racism is the primary cause of all contemporary challenges facing black America, then how do we explain the stability of the black family, the strength of the black church, and the progress and productivity of the black community during slavery and Jim Crow?

We experienced these things as a culture due to the emphasis on values, family, commitment, hard work, and God. As Wilfred Reilly points out, it is the de-emphasis and downright divorce from these values that have contributed to the demise of our culture, as well as the demise of other ethnic or class constructs. He writes, "Empirically, contemporary factor variables such as pay-per-child welfare, no-fault divorce and the normalization of illegitimacy, under-policing of black neighborhoods, and the outsourcing of blue-collar jobs seem primarily responsible for contemporary problems in black communities—and poor white ones. Just maybe, we should focus on and discuss these factors as much as we do the ethnic conflicts of two hundred years ago."[3]

A never-ending conversation of oppressed/oppressor categories in a nation will only exacerbate our divisions, escalating into mere emotional vituperation. It will also support the illegitimate expansion of civil government to resolve the conflict resulting in an increasing loss of personal freedom. We must be honest about what has caused the decline in our culture holistically. We must also approach social issues without yielding to a victim mindset of them being wholly determinative. There has to be an individual choice to view racism, or its repercussions, as no longer determinative in your life if you are black. You must look at it through a nondeterminative lens. You have personal power through the individual choices you make. Your choices shape your future, irrespective of challenges based on your race. If you don't choose to recognize your own power over your emotions, thoughts, and actions, you risk getting stuck in a hopeless cycle of self-sabotage negating any personal responsibility you have to rise up.

And if you are white, you need to no longer view separatism as saintly. The hope is that you will be motivated to make a difference for God's kingdom through the strategic connection with and working alongside others of a different race. The most effective spiritual movement in the Bible was the church in the book of Acts. One of the significant characteristics of this church was that it was culturally and racially diverse. God did wonders through the coming together of His people who merged strength with strength to impact their culture for Christ.

Kingdom Race Theology insists that our painful racial history should never be ignored, whitewashed, or marginalized since God is a God of truth. People need to know about the 4,500 lynchings that occurred, the destruction of Black Wall Street and an entire black-populated and successful town of Rosewood, Florida, by racists, the atrocity of slavery, the evil of peonage, and criminal leasing. Nor should we reject every aspect of racial social theories just because some of its connections, originations, or conclusions are overtly wrong. Nor should we allow those theories to cancel out necessary discourse on race, racism, and injustice. We must search for the kernels of truth and apply those to a biblical truth-based common ground. We must also celebrate the achievements of black people in spite of and through adversity. Much more time must be spent on our triumphs and hope for the future than simply rehearsing the pain of the past.

However, we must always reject racial conclusions that judge people by their racial identity, positioning them in a perpetual oppressor or oppressed status. This goes against God's Word (2 Cor. 5:16; Col. 3:11; Gal. 3:26–28). We must also reject anything that does not promote or prioritize God's goal of unity through reconciliation. In Kingdom Race Theology, the biblical principle of love must prevail. Biblical love is *the decision to seek the well-being of another person compassionately, righteously, and responsibly*. God makes it clear that this includes loving our enemies while simultaneously condemning or correcting falsehoods and evil actions, yet through a spirit of love, kindness, and dignity.

While we are arguing about ideologies as a culture, those of us who are bibliocentric and kingdom-minded ought to understand, espouse, and live under this unifying Kingdom Race Theology. There exists an alternative that overrules the divisions in our land for those who are kingdom people. When we live according to a Kingdom Race Theology, we will actively seek to overcome the reality of racism and its residual effects with the power of love through biblical reconciliation based on the truth that commands us to impact our culture for good.

## From Grace to Race

When writing to the church at Ephesus, Paul spends the first half of chapter 2 talking about the magnificent grace of God. He tells us we are saved by grace, through faith. He also tells us that God wants to manifest His grace in the ages to come (vv. 7–9). It is in this first half of chapter 2 that we read about our personal calling as "His workmanship, created in Christ Jesus for good works, which God prepared beforehand so that we would walk in them" (v. 10). But just as quickly as Paul finishes talking about grace, he moves to the subject of race. Paul goes from grace to race immediately following the verse on personal and corporate life purposes.

From this flow we can determine a few things, one of which is that a primary "good work" we are to walk in as saved people is the work of racial reconciliation. Experiencing the grace of God in our own lives should lead to seeking to address the injustices and inequities brought about in other people's lives, or our own lives, through issues of race. To put it another way, if a kingdom follower is not about the business of fixing the problems people face due to racism, it is because he or she does not fully understand the glory of God's grace. This grace motivation is at the heart of KRT.

Paul speaks to the racial calamity of his day by urging his readers to prioritize the removal of the plague, or spiritual pandemic, at hand. In Ephesians 2:11–18 he says,

> Therefore remember that formerly you, the Gentiles in the flesh, who are called "Uncircumcision" by the so-called "Circumcision," which is performed in the flesh by human hands—remember that you were at that time separate from Christ, excluded from the commonwealth of Israel, and strangers to the covenants of promise, having no hope and without God in the world. But now in Christ Jesus you who formerly were far off have been brought near by the blood of Christ. For He Himself is our peace, who made both groups into one and broke down the barrier of the dividing wall, by abolishing in His flesh the enmity, which is the Law of commandments contained in ordinances, so that in Himself He might make the two into one new man, thus establishing peace, and might reconcile them both in one body to God through the cross, by it having put to death the enmity. AND HE CAME AND PREACHED PEACE TO YOU WHO WERE FAR AWAY, AND PEACE TO THOSE WHO WERE NEAR; for through Him we both have our access in one Spirit to the Father.

Paul calls for an end to racial divisions. Any ideology (or vocal opposition to an ideology) that promotes division is of Satan. Now that they had named the name of Christ, they needed to solve the problem of an illegitimate racial division, in spite of how long it had existed or how deeply embedded in the culture its roots had become. Because even though they were on their way to heaven, they hadn't yet learned to get along on earth. It's like the old saying:

> *To live above with saints we love, oh, that would be glory;*
> *But to dwell below with saints we know, that's a whole different story!*

Paul was not willing for them to wait to get to heaven to fix this issue of the dividing walls on earth. Part of these dividing walls we erect between us based on race that leads to racism is bringing our histories with us into the present reality. The Gentiles only knew how to be Gentiles, and the Jews only knew how to be Jewish. And yet they both found themselves sharing the same faith and belonging to the same church. The issues arose when they both sought to bring their pasts with them.

It is important to retain cultural identity and cultural nuances, as well as the knowledge of our historical realities, such as Jesus did when interacting with the woman at the well (John 4:4–9), and Paul did in relating to his Jewish history and heritage (1 Cor. 9:20; Rom. 9:3–5; Phil. 3:5). But we need not impose our racial distinctives to everyone else around us (Rom. 14:1–16). When we seek to do that, we will remain stuck in the confines of our limited views and understandings, and become complicit in causing others to stumble (1 Cor. 8:13; Rom. 8:13–16). This attitude Paul proclaims is a kingdom issue (Rom. 8:17).

This reminds me of the story of the bear who was in a 12-foot-square cage at a zoo for the longest of time. That 12x12 space was all he had ever known. One day when the zoo expanded, he was transferred to a 36x36-foot living space. But whenever the bear would walk around, he remained in his self-imposed 12x12 space. That is where he felt comfortable. That is what he knew. He was so ingrained in yesterday that he refused to embrace the expansions of today. He had gotten so used to the confines of the past that he couldn't press on to the future.

And so it often is when a formerly confined minority cultural group seeks to expand more holistically into a majority culture. Established history often restricts each group (both the majority and the minority) to remain apart from the others. It just doesn't feel comfortable to stretch beyond how you were raised, what you were taught, what you expect to experience, and more. As a result, we have believers living in racially defined cages, or social media silos, unable to be released into a new environment of intentional integration. It was true back in Paul's day and unfortunately it remains true today.

One thing I find very interesting in all of this, though, is how easily individuals on sports teams can work together across color and racial lines. In fact, people seem to be able to do drugs together across racial lines as well. Activities somehow manage to pull people together when they are seeking a common goal and yet when it comes to the family of God, all we know to do, it seems, is to split up. I would assert that one reason we so easily split up is that we do not share a common goal—that of advancing God's holistic kingdom agenda on earth. Church, rather, is viewed as simply an extension of our various social lives. And since it is nothing more than an extension of our social lives, it winds up reflecting our social circles—which are far too often racially divided.

## But Now

Paul spends an inordinate amount of time in his letter to the church at Ephesus explaining how bad off we were apart from Christ and why we must become one under His rule. He does so in setting up his transition to how things have, or ought to have, changed. We read these transitionary statements where Paul moves from what God did in our lives to how that should affect us:

> "But God . . . " he says in Ephesians 2:4 as he sets the stage.
> "But now . . . " he continues in Ephesians 2:13, directing the readers to a better way.

Paul argues that because of what God has done in grace, we ought to be different now about race. Because of grace, we ought to view race and racism differently. In other words, this is a whole new situation. This is a whole new reality. This is a whole new circumstance. And if you do not understand this new thing that God has done through grace, you'll remain trapped in your own racial cage or socially segregated grid. Our problem today is that we have too many Christians trapped in their racial identity who miss the "but now" Christ came to initiate. It's worth reviewing what we saw earlier in Ephesians 2:13–16:

> But now in Christ Jesus you who formerly were far off have been brought near by the blood of Christ. For He Himself is our peace, who made both groups into one and broke down the barrier of the dividing wall, by abolishing in His flesh the enmity, which is the Law of commandments contained in ordinances, so that in Himself He might make the two into one new man, thus

establishing peace, and might reconcile them both in one body to God through the cross, by it having put to death the enmity.

If you'll recall from the entire passage we looked at earlier, Paul emphasizes one concept repeatedly: Peace. Four times he mentions the word *peace.* Racial unity evokes an atmosphere of peace. Racial division evokes chaos, hatred, and turmoil. You don't need me to tell you that. Just read any news article or watch any news program dealing with racial division. It doesn't matter which side of the debate you watch; you will witness divisive rhetoric on both these days. Rare is the person speaking a message of common ground, common goals, and shared solutions. It doesn't matter if the person speaking claims to be a Christian; division is always a tool of the enemy, Satan.

*Unity ushers in peace.*
*Disunity flames hearts of pride and hate.*

When you and I come to Christ and are born again as new creations in Christ, we are not tasked with the primary responsibility of trying to fix something old. Rather, we are made new. We are now called "one new man" (Eph. 2:15). This does not refer to losing your racial identity. What it means is that your racial identity is no longer your ultimate point of reference and identity (Col. 2:11; Gal. 2:20; Rom. 8:7–9).

Kingdom Race Theology argues that racial distinctions must always adjust to our new Christocentric identity when the two are in conflict. When this occurs, the uniqueness of our varied racial and ethnic identities, as bearers of the *imago Dei*, can be fully experienced, appreciated, and manifested for the benefit of others.

Let me say that again because it may sound simple, but the truth is profound to our souls. Paul is not saying that Jews are no longer Jews or Gentiles are no longer Gentiles. In fact, he goes on to talk about Jews and Gentiles throughout all of his letters. Paul did not become colorblind upon salvation. What he is saying is that this new relationship with Jesus Christ as a kingdom disciple is to be the starting point for everything else. It is the reference point for how we are to experience and interact with each other, and even how we are to view ourselves. If you choose not to allow this new identity in Christ to be the glasses through which you view life and make decisions, you will forever live in racial conflict, confusion, debate, and crisis. Why? Because you are starting at the wrong place. Paul says that Jesus, Himself, *is* our peace. He *is* our identity (Gal. 2:20).

Paul is emphatically reminding us here that we are Christian first. Christ is our point of reference. This new point of reference should enhance the uniqueness of our racial identity, not eradicate it. And, as we saw earlier when examining Galatians 2 more fully, Paul said Christ is our identity right in the middle of a racial conflict. He made this statement in the midst of a racial issue between Peter and the Gentiles. In fact, he went on to emphasize how damaging racism is by saying that Peter's racial "hypocrisy" maligned the good news of the gospel (Gal. 2:13–14). Contrary to what many Christians purport, race and racism *is* a gospel issue, according to the apostle Paul himself.

Jesus is the One who has established a whole new way of operating as believers so that people from different backgrounds can come together in one body, one purpose, and one spirit. When we recognize that our loyalty is to Christ first and not culture, we discover a new way of relating to one another across racial, class, and ethnic barriers. Jesus wants to reconcile us together through His sacrifice on the cross (Eph. 2:16). He wants to bring harmony, unity, togetherness, and like-mindedness to each of us. Kingdom Race Theology, then, while not ignoring racial history and identity, places its primary focus on "the one new man," which then allows us to visibly be the household of God and temple where His Spirit is free to express Himself (Eph. 2:17–22). When this happens, the reality and power of our Christian witness will become clearly manifested before a watching world (John 17:23–24).

When the orchestra is warming up, everything is in a state of discord. It's just noise. One instrument plays over on the right side. Another one plays scales behind it. Another plays something else entirely off to the left. It's noise. That is until the conductor comes out. When the conductor comes out, he taps the podium. Everyone gets silent. And what was at one point noise becomes a beautiful song.

Now, keep in mind, the instruments aren't the same. There's a violin being played. Or a tuba. Or a piano. All sorts of instruments are represented in the orchestra. And at one point, they all made a lot of noise. But when the conductor calls them together on one accord, they play his song.

What we have today in the church of Jesus Christ are black people playing one song, white people playing another song, Asians playing another, and so on. No one can hear each other because we're all making a lot of noise. But in the kingdom of God, we have a conductor. His name is Jesus Christ. Jesus has come, having died on the cross, so that we might play His song. And in this song called "one new man," racism is never to be tolerated.

The cross is not a two-thousand-year-old relic. The cross is a contemporary reality. The cross was established to deal with sin. And racism, in any form, is sin.

Racial reconciliation does not come about by simply stating we need to all get along. That's been our problem. This approach dismisses the reality of the sin that caused the division in the first place. Rather, we must identify the sin, apply the grace of the cross, address the sin through repentance and fruits of repentance so that the reconciling work of Jesus Christ can be ignited. Jesus has the final say-so because He is the foundation upon which all else rests. As Paul continues in his letter to the church of Ephesus, he makes this point clear:

> So then you are no longer strangers and aliens, but you are fellow citizens with the saints, and are of God's household, having been built on the foundation of the apostles and prophets, Christ Jesus Himself being the corner stone, in whom the whole building, being fitted together, is growing into a holy temple in the Lord, in whom you also are being built together into a dwelling of God in the Spirit. (Eph. 2:19–22)

The "cornerstone" was the alignment stone that was used to position all the other stones to it. Everything else depended on the location and strength of this cornerstone. Paul's point couldn't be more clear. If you and I align our thoughts, emotions, and will under Christ and His rule as revealed through the Word of God, everything else will fall into place.

If we are ever going to fix the racism problem in the church for the benefit of our nation, the Bible has to overrule our emotions, thoughts, words, actions, and histories. Our problem is that we have far too many people running to sociology books before searching the Scripture. We have far too many people quoting portions of content from Critical Race Theorists, or *White Fragility*, *Intellectuals and Race*, or *Shame* before going to the Bible. And while there are legitimate truths present in all of these things, and it is good to read and research various thoughts on the subjects as well as statistical analysis, they must be viewed through the grid of the gospel. They must be seen through the spectacles of Scripture and they must ultimately be made to surrender to the lordship of Jesus Christ.

And every Christian who names the name of Jesus Christ must be actively and purposefully involved in racial reconciliation, according to the Scripture. Not division. Not blame. Not divisive speech. Not dismissiveness. Why? Because unity is what glorifies God and allows His presence to be visibly seen in and through His people. Like a football team, we may come from different backgrounds and ethnicities, but we are to be one team, wearing one uniform. There are different cultures and different backgrounds, but there is only one uniform. We are to head toward the same goal line together, which is the exaltation of Jesus Christ through His reconciled body, advancing God's kingdom agenda on earth through the individual, family, church, and community. This is the goal of KRT.

Only when we get radical believers who take seriously the apostles and prophets as well as the teaching of Jesus Himself, will we offer a biblical solution to the racism problem in our society. As Colossians 1:21–22 puts it,

> And although you were formerly alienated and hostile in mind, engaged in evil deeds, yet He has now reconciled you in His fleshly body through death, in order to present you before Him holy and blameless and beyond reproach.

If you and I want to see God and His glory made manifest in our culture today, we had better start focusing more intentionally on reconciliation, which is best achieved through ministry together, rather than language and phrases that only further divide us. Christ came to reconcile us to each other and to God. If the church in America had operated according to a Kingdom Race Theology, the last 400+ years of our racial history wouldn't have happened as they have played out. Since Christians have helped to create the racial catastrophe, it is incumbent on us to lead the way in helping to fix it.

It is past time for racism to cease as a dominant force in our land and in the world, starting with the church. America is not unique to racial and ethnic oppression or inequities. White people are not the only race to have oppressed another race. This is a global sin manifested in racism, tribalism, and ethnic cleansings. It is a worldwide stain on humanity, steeped in historical genocides and racially motivated oppression and, at times, wars.

It is time we begin acknowledging the sin that causes the divide, both nationally and globally and ecclesiastically. This includes acknowledging the privilege (white privilege) that has benefited certain people over others in our own culture of America. We need to acknowledge the collective pain and trauma that resonates in the DNA of generational stigma through inequitable structures. We must confess and repent of the sin of racism. Black people must also confess and repent of the sin of unforgiveness and resentment and the failure to seek the improvement of the level of classism toward other black people who have not had our opportunities to advance.

I understand the cry for "no justice—no peace." But we also must cry out "no forgiveness—no peace." We need both. Both must simultaneously be true for those of us in Christ. Paul's letter to the church at Corinth gives us our mandate on how we are to be ambassadors for unity and spiritual warriors for peace:

> Therefore from now on we recognize no one according to the flesh; even though we have known Christ according to the flesh, yet now we know Him in this way no longer. Therefore if anyone is in Christ, he is a new creature; the old things passed away; behold, new things have come. Now all these things are from God, who reconciled us to Himself through Christ and gave us the ministry of reconciliation, namely, that God was in Christ reconciling the world to Himself, not counting their

> trespasses against them, and He has committed to us the word of reconciliation. (2 Cor. 5:16–19)

In short, we are to be "agents of reconciliation." We are not to judge others by their skin or physical humanity. That's the old life. That's old school. That's how Satan and his minions group and target people for destruction. Now that we are in Christ, we are ambassadors of heaven. We are carriers of Christ's views. We are to be about His purpose and ministry, which is reconciliation. Whether that is seeking to help people heal from past wounds or traumas, or even present ones, we are to be about a ministry of empathy, awareness, repentance, impact, change, forgiveness, respect, and grace.

Every Christian who names the name of Jesus Christ must be actively, intentionally involved in reconciliation. We are agents of reconciliation who demonstrate what it looks like when the Word of God has the last word. And when we get radical believers who take seriously the apostles and the prophets and the teachings of Jesus Christ the way we were called and created to do, we will reconcile people vertically to God as we reconcile people horizontally to each other in Christ's name.

As believers, we are headed toward the same goal line of exalting Jesus Christ through His reconciled Body. We are agents of reconciliation who are here to demonstrate what it looks like when the Word of God has the last word. And when we get radical believers who take seriously the apostles and the prophets and the teachings of Jesus Christ the way we were called and created to do, we will reconcile people vertically to God as we reconcile people horizontally to each other in Christ's name.

It's time for racism to end, especially in the church. It's time to live by 2 Corinthians 5:16 where we are told to no longer recognize anyone according to the flesh. We are not to judge, stereotype, dismiss, or reject someone because of their race. Rather, we are to live as ambassadors for Christ. An ambassador is someone who goes to another country on behalf of their country and represents their country on foreign soil. We are here on earth to be ambassadors of heaven. Earth is the foreign country. Our culture is the foreign country. We are here to show that in heaven, all humanity is reconciled.

There will be a myriad of races and ethnicities in heaven. God has set up eternity to operate this way. In the meantime, we are to be about reflecting the culture of heaven on earth. We are to reflect "thy kingdom come and thy will be done" on earth. We will be reconciled in heaven. Love will exist in heaven rather than hate and prejudice. But our role on earth is to reveal this kingdom now. We are to give the world a kingdom alternative that overrides racism, cancels classism, and countermands evil whether it is individual or structural. And we are to demonstrate what the kingdom of God looks like when people align themselves on earth underneath His overarching rule. Adopting a KRT worldview will help us accomplish this vision.

## Practical Steps You Can Take

Theology must never be limited to esoteric biblical conclusions void of practical strategies for bringing God's truth to life through our obedience and good works. Kingdom Race Theology seeks to encourage and challenge Christians and churches to lead the way in bringing unity to our land by visibly reflecting it in their lives and through our churches. Since this book has focused on the two dominant racial groups with a shared history of racism in America, I've chosen to include practical steps for both black and white Christians and their churches to take in addressing our disunity. But if you are not in either of these racial groups, you can apply the principles to your own personal life and church in ways you deem best.

## What Black Christians Should Do

1. Appreciate, celebrate, and affirm the uniqueness of our divinely created racial identity, while simultaneously guarding against an unbiblical pride that resists or detours us from biblical truth.
2. Highly value our special collective community dynamic and support righteous movements that seek to correct injustice and promote our corporate well-being. However, we must never allow our group racial identity to erase personal convictions, individual uniqueness, and responsibility. We must

never compromise biblical truth and personal integrity for group acceptance.

3. Make the restoration and preservation of the nuclear heterosexual family our highest priority since it is God's foundational institution for a stable, productive, and peaceful community. Fatherlessness and the demise of the nuclear black family is the greatest crisis we face as a people.
4. Reach back to use our gifts, talents, skills, influence, and opportunities to improve the lives of other black people who need the help and hope we have to offer for their spiritual, personal, and professional development. While charity is important, good, and necessary, empowerment is better, and the benefits last much longer. This will create sustainable and strong individuals, families, churches, and communities. Reject all worldviews and entertainment that belittle, dehumanize, sexualize, victimize, or otherwise demean us as image bearers of God.
5. Resist the temptation to automatically view every questionable action by those of another race as racism. Reject the tendency to stereotype people based on their racial identity, including all whites. Take the time to evaluate the motivation, knowledge, and intent of the person and the deed. Ask questions and seek clarification before making a final judgment. Also, accusations of racism should never be used as a tool to hold white people hostage to white guilt, and thus creating the need for them to prove their innocence as a means of exercising and legitimizing black power.
6. Reject a victim mentality. Victimology nurtures an unfocused strain of resentment rooted in a defeatist identity through which all realities are filtered. Instead, view us as God sees us and with the intrinsic value with which He created us. Even if we have been victimized, we are not victims. We must see ourselves as overcomers. This mindset empowers us with the appropriate mentality to properly address injustices. Where racism is real, it must be resisted and corrected. However, it must no longer be viewed as a substantive impediment to black progress. If our ancestors

persevered and made great progress during the worst of times, we have no excuse today for not maximizing the opportunities of freedom that are at our disposal. Victimhood must be replaced with a *victorhood* mentality.

7. Prioritize spiritual success as we pursue social, political, and economic equality. This will enable us to more quickly overcome the historical disparities that have limited or denied us equal access and opportunity, especially since we often have to work much harder to be viewed and treated as equals. Don't allow money, power, and position to take precedence over our pursuit of a growing intimate relationship with God. We must not automatically and uncritically make the secular cultural standards of success our own.
8. Become an active part of a solid, biblically centered disciple-making church where you use your time, talents, and treasures to advance God's kingdom agenda in the areas of both righteousness and justice.
9. Emphasize as great a focus on personal righteousness as we do on social justice since God holds them in equal balance. Additionally, black leaders and black people should be held accountable for more than their personal, professional, and political commitment and competence in the area of racial justice. They should also be held accountable for the quality of their character. We must not give black people a pass for bad character and destructive, irresponsible behavior just because we share the same complexion, culture, and social concerns.
10. Do not look to civil government to do for us what God holds us responsible for addressing ourselves, either personally, in our families, in our churches, or in our communities. We must accept, promote, and operate on God's definition regarding the responsibility and limitations of civil government.
11. Educate ourselves about the biblical role and responsibility of civil government and hold it locally and nationally accountable to fulfill that role. This includes civic involvement and voting without simultaneously and uncritically marrying ourselves to a political party.

12. Promote and support a whole-life agenda (womb-to-tomb) since abortion is not only an attack on the image of God in which all mankind has been created, but also contributes to the self-imposed genocide of our race's future.
13. Do not become guilty of the sin of racism or black privilege based on class that we condemn in others. We must pursue God's goal of reconciliation. Perpetual unaddressed anger about racism will drive us to sin and prohibit us from finding a godly solution to the problem.
14. Expand "the Talk" with our children beyond legitimate concerns about police brutality to include finishing school, developing strong character, hard work, skill development, entrepreneurship, the importance of family, and growing in their faith. We must never neglect the pain of our past, but we must prioritize the achievements in our history, opportunities in the present, and the potential of our future.

## What White Christians Should Do

1. Accept the fact that racism is a genuine historical and contemporary problem that needs to be addressed personally and corporately. Learn and grow in your understanding of the history of racism and the accompanying pain many African Americans and other racial groups have experienced at the hands of white people in general and evangelical Christians in particular. Many have created scars that still need healing. Such exposure will increase empathy while simultaneously decreasing microaggressive behavior.
2. Reject white guilt if you have not committed racial sins. White people should not apologize or seek to prove their innocence of racism, nor should they function with racial guilt for the legitimate blessings God has allowed them to experience, provided that these gifts are humbly, righteously, and responsibly used to bless and not disadvantage others. Conversely, if you find you are guilty of any form of

the sin of racism, you should repent, seek forgiveness, and correct the wrong.

3. Recognize how the Bible has been misused and even weaponized as a tool of oppression throughout history. Correct this errant use of Scripture. Bring people into a unified comprehensive kingdom understanding and application of God's revelation on the subjects of racism, injustice, and equality.
4. Support and partner with opportunities for responsible, non-paternalistic black progress, especially for the poor, oppressed, and underserved communities (allyship). This is needed since color alone has never been an impediment for white people in their personal, generational, social, medical, educational, and economic progress—though this had been the case with black people.
5. Understand that many of the generational benefits white people enjoy (i.e., white privilege) are built on the historical forced labor of black people.
6. Expose yourself, family, and friends to diverse racial environments and people who share God's kingdom values as outlined in His Word. Begin dismantling all forms of racism while simultaneously building authentic cross-racial bridges as God's agents and models of reconciliation.
7. Become an active part of a kingdom-minded discipling church that partners with minority churches to work together on social service and justice issues, especially those issues that can be connected to evangelism and discipleship. Consider becoming an active part of a kingdom-minded, minority-led church.
8. Clearly and publicly reject connecting and marrying your Christian faith to a political party, thus judging and rejecting other Christians who vote differently.
9. Challenge your spiritual leaders to spend as much time specifically addressing justice issues as they do righteousness issues since God holds them in equal balance. Hold spiritual leaders accountable for acts of unrepentant injustice, just as any other unrighteous activity.

10. Expose yourself to recommended black literature, black history, and accomplishments. Visit the National Museum of African American History and Culture in Washington, D.C. Discover the voices of black leadership, black theologians, and black ministries that can give you a larger and more comprehensive perspective on the history, experiences, and worldview of black people.
11. Promote and support a whole-life agenda, not just a pro-birth agenda, since humanity is created in the image of God imbued with inherent significance and dignity from the womb to the tomb. To be created in God's image is to value the dignity of life in all stages of life.
12. Recognize that it isn't enough to *not be racist*. In order to bring about positive changes in our country, you must also be verbally and visibly against all forms of racism (antiracist), whenever you encounter it on a personal and structural level.
13. Reject the tendency to stereotype people based on their racial identity. Such stereotyping serves to elevate white pride and privilege while simultaneously reducing the dignity and significance of others.
14. Be willing to dialogue with those you disagree with and read authors who do not share your viewpoints. Engage with documentaries, books, and articles that are outside your normative worldview. Understand that no true intellectual only reads authors with whom he or she agrees. Become truly informed, assess which parts are valuable, then draw your own conclusions. Always allow the Scripture to make the final decision.

After considering what individuals should do, we should also consider what we can do together. Since the church is the primary manifestation of the kingdom and is the primary means by which God is extending His kingdom rule in this world, local churches must be willing to work together across racial, denominational, and class lines. Churches should cooperate in a comprehensive program that connects both the spiritual and social. Churches must work together to extend their influence beyond their individual walls in order to impact the broader communities that they serve.

**Notes**

1. Martin Luther King Jr., *Strength to Love* (Boston: Beacon Press, 1963), 47.
2. Latasha Morrison, *Be the Bridge: Pursuing God's Heart for Racial Reconciliation* (Colorado Springs, CO: Waterbrook Publishing, 2019).
3. Wilfred Reilly, "Slavery Does Not Define the Black American Experience," in Robert L. Woodson Sr., ed., *Red, White, and Black: Rescuing American History from Revisionists and Race Hustlers* (New York: Emancipation Books, 2021), 41.

## Chapter 17

# KINGDOM STRATEGY FOR COMMUNITY TRANSFORMATION

The Christian church must accept the responsibility and challenge of leading the way in reversing our racial divide since we, to a large degree, are responsible for creating and maintaining it. I have frequently been asked to address communities and cities on the issue of disunity over the last four decades—at times in small congregations in local churches and at other times in football stadiums filled with twenty thousand people from the community. I've learned a lot through these experiences engaging with people from all walks of life and a variety of viewpoints.

Whatever the size, I am convinced that we share a vision across our racial divide. What we lack, however, is the implementation of an organized and cohesive strategy on how to bring about the fulfillment of that vision of biblical unity and community impact in our land. When less than 5 percent of the population can affect public policy and the cultural climate as we saw in the legalization of same-sex marriage, it makes me wonder why the church—comprising far greater numbers—is having such little impact in areas of social change and unity. One of the main reasons we are not having an impact is because we do not unite around a common goal or goals. Rarely do we go outside of our own church walls and join collective arms to bring about a lasting influence. Yet that is essential if we are going to change our culture for the good of others and the glory of God.

## The Salt of the Earth

One of the most concise yet comprehensive statements on this subject of how we are to impact society came from the lips of Jesus in His kingdom-based message recorded in Matthew 5:13–16. It's a story you have probably heard from Scripture before. Pastors preach on it. Authors write about it. But what I want to be careful not to do is to skip over it mentally just because you may be familiar with it. The principles within can literally—and should literally—change our world. In this Sermon on the Mount, Christ used two key metaphors to communicate the impact He wants us to make for Him in the world around us. The first one is salt.

### *Salt's Preserving Influence*

Jesus told us, "You are the salt of the earth." By declaring His kingdom ambassadors the salt of the earth, Jesus was making a clear statement about the decaying condition of this world and the role of Christians in delaying the decay. Of course, salt has been used as a preservative for thousands of years. Rubbing it into a piece of meat helps to preserve the meat from decay, because salt is an antibacterial agent.

Roman soldiers in biblical days were also said to receive some of their pay in salt. The value of salt in a world with no refrigeration was pretty obvious. Salt's value became part of the language, which we can see today in the word *salary*. The word *salary* is actually a derivative of the word *salt*. You're familiar with the expression that "so-and-so is not worth his salt." A person who didn't do his job right didn't receive his full allocation of salt.

Jesus put His church on earth to act as a preserving influence on a rotting world, to slow down the decay of sin. If Jesus had nothing on earth for His people to do, He would have taken us out of here the moment we trusted Him as Savior.

But, as someone has pointed out, salt can't do its job when it is sitting in the shaker. When followers of Jesus Christ are gathered in the house of God, that's salt in the shaker. When the doors open and we go out into the world, that's when the shaker should get turned over to spread the salt of God's kingdom where it is needed. If our communities are going to be better, and if our country is going to be stronger, then the salt must be at work.

### *When Salt Becomes Tasteless*

Jesus finished His illustration on salt by saying, "But if the salt has become tasteless, how can it be made salty again? It is no longer good for anything, except to be thrown out and trampled under foot by men" (Matt. 5:13b). In the culture of Jesus' day when salt was so crucial in preserving food, there was nothing worse than salt that had lost its usefulness.

A lot of people wonder about this statement because sodium chloride is a stable compound that cannot lose its saltiness or taste. What Jesus is referring to here is the fact that a lot of the salt in biblical days was distilled from marshes and other places where it was mixed with all manner of impurities. When the salt was used up, the impurities would remain and render the mixture useless. There was nothing to do but toss it out on the ground.

Tasteless salt was also "trampled under foot" because in biblical days people mixed gypsum with water to make a paste for patching holes in their roofs. The paste was solidified with salt, which was then good for nothing else because it was mixed with gypsum, which is bitter. The bitterness of the gypsum canceled out the saltiness of the salt.

This salt was trampled underfoot because in Jesus' days the homes in Israel had flat roofs that were the center of a lot of activity. People could fight from the rooftops, and they were the scene of many social occasions such as wedding receptions. Israelis used their roofs the way we use a veranda or porch.

All of that walking on the roofs would create holes, because the roofs were usually just earth. The gypsum and salt mixture was used to patch the holes, so the salt would literally be trampled underfoot by people. This is a graphic picture of God's people becoming so diluted by the world that we lose our impact and the world walks right over us without feeling any effect.

### *Salt's Thirst-Inducing Nature*

Besides its preserving qualities, salt also creates thirst. As believers gather together in the name of Jesus Christ, the church's impact should not only have a preserving influence against the decay of evil, but the quality of our lives should also make people so thirsty for what we have that they are drawn to Christ like a parched person to water.

I was at an airport one day with some time to spare before my flight boarded, so I went to a small lounge area and ordered a soft drink. The waitress brought me my drink, but she also brought something else I didn't order: a complimentary bowl of salty peanuts—"on the house."

Now you know she didn't do that because the establishment simply wanted to thank me for my business, or because they wanted to enhance my airport experience so I would come back. The only purpose for that salty snack was to dry out my mouth and make me so thirsty that I would open my wallet and say, "I'd like another drink, please."

The job of the kingdom-minded corporate church is to create a thirst in the culture that can only be satisfied by the living water of Jesus Christ. We don't have to worry about trying to make Christianity attractive, palatable, or relevant to the world. All we have to do is make people thirsty for Jesus.

A kingdom ambassador brings the pure salt of the kingdom to a world in desperate need of Christ.

## The Light of the World

Jesus used a second familiar metaphor in Matthew 5 when He said of His people, "You are the light of the world. A city set on a hill cannot be hidden; nor does anyone light a lamp and put it under a basket, but on the lampstand, and it gives light to all who are in the house" (vv. 14–15).

*Driving Back the Darkness*

The last time I checked, the role of light was to shine, and in so doing to drive back the darkness. The world needs light because it sits in spiritual darkness. We were saved out of that darkness, and now our job is to shine the light of Christ back on the world's darkness. Paul told the Ephesians, "You were formerly darkness, but now you are Light in the Lord; walk as children of Light" (Eph. 5:8).

When we are walking through this world as children of light, the world has a better chance to see things as they really are. "All things become visible when they are exposed by the light, for everything that becomes visible is light" (Eph. 5:13). You know how hard it is to sleep when someone comes in and turns the light on in your face. That's the effect we should have on unbelievers who are sleeping the sleep of eternal death.

If you're in a dark room where people are groping for light and you know where the light switch is, it's a waste of time to organize a panel discussion on the effects of darkness or shake your head over how terrible the darkness is. Your assignment is to turn on the light, and the darkness will automatically be overcome.

Jesus went on to say, "Let your light shine before men" (Matt. 5:16a). In other words, carry your light out where it's dark so that unsaved people can see it. It would be ridiculous to turn on a lamp and then put something over it to hide its glow.

Yet, all too often, that's what we do in the church. Our lights burn brightly inside the church, but we are the only ones benefiting from them. Meanwhile, the world outside goes on in its darkness. It's impossible to hide a light that's "set on a hill," and the farther the beam reaches, the more people who are affected by it. A local church that wants to measure its effectiveness only has to look into its community to see how far its light is penetrating the darkness. A community that has a church in its midst should be better off because of its presence (Jer. 29:7). More so than that, a country with hundreds of thousands of churches in its midst should be better off because of them.

## Reflecting God's Glory

Don't misunderstand this—we are not the light itself, but simply the reflector of Christ's light. It's interesting that before Satan fell into pride and rebelled against God, he was Lucifer, "the shining one" or "light-bearer." He is called "star of the morning" and "son of the dawn" in Scripture (Isa. 14:12). As the highest-ranking angel, Lucifer was to reflect God's glory by leading heaven's worship. But Lucifer decided he wanted to become the light instead of just reflecting it, and God cast him out of heaven into darkness (Isa. 12:14, Gen. 1:2). Satan has been the prince of darkness ever since, and he's still trying to put out the light of God's glory. But God has set the church in the world as a "city on a hill" to reflect His glory. Salt and light, then, refers to the collective influence God's people are to have in society.

## Kingdom Impact in the Culture

In order to understand the potential impact of the church in a community, we need to look more deeply at what the Bible says about the cause of social upheaval in the life of a community or nation.

In 2 Chronicles 15:3–6, we read that the nation of Judah found itself in the midst of widespread social chaos. Nation rose up against nation in international conflict. City rose up against city in urban conflict. "There was no peace to him who went out or to him who came in" (2 Chron. 15:5). High crime and safety concerns disturbed everyone. Upon initial reflection, one might think that Satan was behind this turmoil. However, God was shown to be responsible for the chaos in society (2 Chron. 15:6).

The thesis is simple. If God causes or allows the problems in society, only God is the solution. It matters not who is elected to office or what legislation is passed. It does not even matter what new economic initiatives or educational opportunities are put in place. If God is the one orchestrating the chaos—until one has dealt with Him, one has not dealt with the root cause of societal ills.

Much like the culture written about at the time of 2 Chronicles, we are experiencing chaos in our society today. We have international conflict (nation against nation), urban conflict (city against city), and individual and family conflict (no peace).

Second Chronicles 15:3 gives the insight to comprehend why God allowed such chaos in society: "Israel was without the true God." This does not mean there was no religion, worship, Bible reading, or programs at the temple. What it means is that the culture did not recognize the one true God because there were no teaching priests equipping the people to point them in that direction. Although Judah had many priests, they were not communicating truth about God. The temple had lost its impact. The result was that there was no law, so the people had no true representation of God's rule or governance over mankind. There was no accountability system to enforce or encourage correct and healthy behavior, and so social and political turmoil ensued.

If the visible, physical realm of social chaos and upheaval is to be corrected, the invisible, spiritual realm has to be addressed through the proclamation and application of God's Word. Otherwise, the spiritual causes of the chaos will be allowed to take place indefinitely.

Making an impact in our culture is not something that will come easily, though. As Martin Luther King Jr. once said, "Human progress is neither automatic nor inevitable. . . . Every step toward the goal of justice requires sacrifice, suffering, and struggle; the tireless exertions and passionate concern of dedicated individuals."[1]

Since the church is the primary manifestation of the kingdom and is the primary means by which God is extending His kingdom rule in this world, local churches must be willing to work across racial, denominational, and class lines in order to become intentional about having a comprehensive program that connects both the spiritual and social. Churches must work together to extend their influence beyond their individual walls in order to impact the broader communities that they serve.

I have proposed a three-point plan for invoking a national impact through the church. This plan involves the following three foundational components:

1. Assemble: Unified Sacred Gathering
2. Address: Unified Compassionate Voice
3. Act: Unified Social Impact

When we become intentional about assembling, addressing, and acting together on this issue of racial unity, we will make an impact. The problem in our society today is that too many people are looking for "salvation by government." They are looking to force God's hand, way, and will into the box of elected officials. They want a kingdom they can schedule, program, and understand, thus putting their hope in the political realm. But God warns us what happens when we put our confidence in kings (1 Sam. 8:9–18). There is no such thing as salvation by government (Judg. 8:22–23).

Even so, the Democrats are looking for a Democratic savior; the Republicans are looking for a Republican savior. However, God alone sits as the potentate of the universe, saying, as He did through the prophet in Ezekiel 43:6–9, "I am the only Savior in town." We shouldn't worship the elephant or the donkey. We should worship the Lamb.

What we need in our nation today is a radical comprehensive covenantal return to the God of the Bible—our true and only Savior—and this can be initiated through a collective approach in which we seek radical change and improvement in each of the four covenantal spheres: individual, family, church, and society. We need to integrate and influence our culture through all means possible. Almost everyone recognizes the fact that the task of national renewal in the areas of faith and freedom is too big for any one group or church to accomplish effectively. It will require the collective cooperation of the masses to leave a lasting impact for good.

One way of getting a jump-start on this collective impact, which I'll go over briefly before outlining in more detail the Three-Point Plan, is by identifying the Christian agencies and individuals who already have intellectual affinity and integration within the spheres of typical American society: education, health care, entertainment, news media, literary, government, business, research, family issues, law, national security, economics, community organizations, and social activism. The primary goal of such identification is to take advantage of opportunities of cross-pollinating efforts while also sharing research on cultural trends and indicators. In doing so, we provide a more synergistic approach to shaping the moral framework of our land.

Some of the goals of this partner platform might include:

- To awaken and initiate the desire for national revival, personal responsibility, spiritual integration, and progressive reformation.
- Developing a national strategy of social impact, scalable and implementable across cultural, geographical, and class lines.
- To increase the efficiency and effectiveness of the mobilization and management of American Christian resources for national kingdom impact.
- Developing a national ongoing prayer movement to support the initiatives.
- Building and promoting collaboration among churches, nonprofits, training institutions, and agencies.
- Facilitate research and discussion on national trends within the various mediums in order to stimulate strategic influence.
- To reduce wasteful duplication of efforts.
- To create a forum for the sharing of strategies and techniques while providing responsible forecasting.
- Producing artistically excellent, compelling means of storytelling to encourage kingdom thinking and personal responsibility through mainstream distribution channels.
- Leveraging social and digital media to transform thinking toward national renewal and kingdom values.
- To devise a corporate approach to deal with collective felt needs.
- To encourage thinking about community and national impact as also a local church strategy rather than solely a parachurch strategy.
- And the promotion and production of a National Solemn Assembly drawing together spiritual leaders and laity to seek God's face and invoke His hand in our land.

## The Elements of the Three-Point Plan

The Three-Point Plan for Community Transformation involves the steps of Assembling, Addressing, and Acting in unison on this subject. We begin through assembling.

### *Assemble*

Over the years and even in the last decade, we have had localized gatherings of believers seeking God's face in order to invoke His hand of involvement in our nation. People have met in cities, churches, and in their homes to call on God and access heaven's intervention in our nation. Many, if not most, of these gatherings lasted one night, one Sunday, or perhaps two Sundays back-to-back. Yet in the busyness of the American lifestyle, it is easy for these experiences to be lumped into another long list of good things to do, and—as a result—lose the collective impact they were intended to have. Likewise, because many, if not most, of these gatherings occurred segmented by denomination, church, or location, we did not experience renewal on the greater level that is so desperately needed.

I have also noticed that while there has been much emphasis on 2 Chronicles 7:14 reminding believers that if "My people who are called by My name humble themselves and pray," there has been less ardent proclamation and awareness of the variety of elements that historically comprised collective solemn assemblies. As I mentioned in an earlier chapter, the "fast" God chooses goes deeper than a prayer said without a meal (Isa. 58). It even goes deeper than confessing sins. Rather, it involves the intentional application of His two greatest commandments of loving Him and loving others.

Have we gathered as groups to seek God's face in our land? Yes. Have we met in churches every so often and scattered across our nation to seek revival? Yes. But have we ever done this collectively and comprehensively with unity from our nation's spiritual leaders? No. Have we ever done it coupled with the intentional applicational realities of carrying out God's command of love? Not that I'm aware of. Lastly, have we truly experienced God's hand of national revival in the last century? I would also argue—no.

If we, as His people, are going to seek His face, we will need to set aside personal agendas, organizations, denominations, structures, and the like, and come together once and for all as the body of disciples whom Christ died to procure, and call on the name of our great God and King.

Have you ever noticed how special-interest groups in our country carry far more weight in influencing our land (policies, opinions, etc.) even though their numbers are but a small fraction of the number of believers in America? The reason they carry so much weight and influence is because they unite. We may have the numbers in our favor as an overall body of believers, but we have rarely, if ever, truly united over anything at all.

It is time to set our preferences and egos aside and go before the Lord as one body. It is also time for more than an evening event or Sunday morning assembly. It is time for a comprehensive season of seeking our Lord's hand and face in our great land. One of the ways to do this is to focus an entire segment of time—whether that be a week or several days—on each of the four covenantal areas of God's involvement with humanity: individual, family, church, and society.

Every year in January for the last several decades, I have led our congregation in a weeklong solemn assembly starting on Sunday morning and culminating with a "Break the Fast" breakfast on Saturday morning. This solemn assembly involves giving up some personal physical need or desire every day to call on God for His presence throughout the year. It also involves meeting together as a church body six times in the week, and as individual families one night.

I'm not proposing this as a standard process for carrying out a national solemn assembly, but I am proposing that we enter into something that is more comprehensive and more collective nationwide than a gathering on a Sunday or two.

If every serious Bible-believing church would do their own solemn assembly simultaneously with the others—whether that be for a solid week or spread out over four weeks, allowing time for personal reflection during the weekdays, we would seek God as a nation together. If church and organizational leadership would come together in humility and unity, we could actually see the hand of God move in our midst in a way we may have never imagined.

The problem is not merely our waiting on God to involve Himself in our country's demise, but it is also that God is waiting on us to call on Him collectively, and according to His prescribed manner. I have compiled the following action items (aimed at spiritual leaders) to help us achieve this first point of the Three-Point Plan:

- Start or join a racially and denominationally diverse fellowship of kingdom-minded pastors in your local area.
- Meet regularly with kingdom-minded pastors to strengthen relationships, provide mutual encouragement, and to meet the needs of one another.
- Worship together and seek God in prayer.
- Use social and digital media to facilitate communication with your fellow spiritual leaders.
- Train and develop lay leaders who can provide practical assistance and support for meeting your goals.
- Plan and host a local solemn assembly at least once a year, gathering congregations together to seek God on behalf of their community and the nation.
- Share your pulpit on occasion with like-minded pastors across racial, class, and denominational divides.

Whenever a solemn assembly or sacred gathering was called in Scripture, it was often called by those in leadership—whether that be a priest, prophet, or king.[1] Often it would first be called for a specific smaller leadership sphere before spreading to the entire nation. Even in America, our historical records verify that prior to every national awakening, the spiritual leadership of the day placed a heavy emphasis on fasting and gathering for times of solemn assemblies, typically in smaller groups that then led to larger gatherings.

During its inception, God will often speak to people in separate locations giving them the similar vision of the need for this type of gathering. When leaders and people meet who may not see each other often or even know each other, they find that conversations turn to God's movement within their hearts. As a result, synergy arises between denominations and leadership that might not have been there before. And people who may have never worked together across church, denominational, or organizational lines now have their paths cross in this one overarching purpose.

A solemn assembly for the purpose of restoration is a sacred gathering where God's people, during a specific time of fasting and prayer, seek the renewal of their relationship with Him through the repentance of sin and the passionate pursuit of the return of His presence in their midst. It can also be defined as *a specific move of God, by His Holy Spirit, through His leadership where He gathers the saints to Himself.*

Biblical history is replete with this similar theme of the assembling of the saints and God's subsequent restoration. After all, God has a heart for reconciliation. From the garden in Genesis to the heavens in Revelation, God issues a call time and again for reconciliation prior to issuing judgment. He is swift to spare if we will but ask Him for the new heart and the new spirit as His prescribed pathway to seeing hope restored and lives transformed (Ezek. 18:30–31).

### *Address*

The second point in the Three-Point Plan is to address the issues at hand through a unified compassionate voice. I touched on the Tower of Babel in an earlier chapter but I want to return to it here simply because it is the best illustration in Scripture of the power of unity and oneness. As you recall, when the evil citizens of Babel got together to work in unity toward a specific goal, God said, "Nothing which they purpose to do will be impossible for them" (Gen. 11:6b). Because of this, God intentionally disrupted their unity through the alteration of the languages they spoke—introducing multiple languages into a people group who had previously spoken the same thing and in the same way. He disrupts their ability to communicate.

Far too often in the Christian church today, we come across to the outside culture and world as if we are not even speaking the same language. We don't even look like we are on the same page when it comes to various issues facing our land. Part of the cause of this is because we have neglected to work across denominational and racial boundaries in order to create and pursue a synergistic strategy toward cultural impact. When national times of crisis erupt, the church should have a greater collective voice in addressing responses to the chaos. Protests take place, which can be very good, but often anger becomes displaced and results are not accomplished. Thus, we need more than a protest—we need a plan.

We need an approach to add to the protests which will bring about a lasting level of change for good. The best way to position ourselves to create and carry out a national plan of restoration that can be implemented community by community involves this kingdom strategy I'm offering in this chapter, and a crucial step is on how we collectively speak on the issues we face. I watch a lot of news and read a lot of books and articles, and I have yet to hear a cohesive voice on the issue of race from the body of Christ. We have become so focused on arguing certain semantics and originations of Critical Race Theory or systemic racism that we have neglected to address the glaring issues we can all agree on.

The Christian fundamentalist or evangelical seminaries and their students often get accused of neglecting real issues in the real world while getting bogged down in arguing the minutiae of the details in dispensationalism, pretribulation, and eschatological nuances while the world goes to hell in a handbasket. And rightly so. Similarly, I have seen the current racial climate produce myriads of meetings, lectures, papers, statements, even referendums for pages on end discussing whether or not Critical Race Theory should be accepted or rejected, or whether or not systemic racism exists, all the while racial inequities grow larger and cross-racial relationships collapse beneath the mountains of suspicion, blame, and critiques. And while these terms, definitions, and intentions are important to discuss, it appears that we have allowed them to dominate and even snuff out any real effort toward discussing and voicing a solution toward the existing racial and class problems at large, whatever a person wants to "label" them.

If we could agree to speak in unison on the ideologies and theologies of agreement rather than spend all our time arguing the portions in disagreement, we would do better at calming the anger and hostilities in our churches and land. In so doing, we could offer several productive yet impactful options for restoration and biblically based equity. A number of special-interest groups have been successful in influencing culture because they have managed to unify their collective voice both in the media and entertainment, even though they are small in number. It is time to set our platforms and personal agendas aside when it comes to the matters of national importance so that we can effectively speak into and address the concerns of our day.

Steps our spiritual leaders can take in order to do this include:

- Seek common ground and shared goals which foster biblical solutions to contemporary issues needing to be addressed, rather than get hung up on the areas of disagreement. Show grace.
- Hold discussion groups and prayer sessions to explore the biblical answers to cultural issues.
- Read and discuss relevant books and videos together to form a basis for common understanding.
- Commit to serving together to work for cultural transformation and biblical values.
- Host community forums to address relevant social issues.
- Collectively meet with civic leaders for relationship building to address issues related to justice and righteousness, and in an effort to influence needed policy reforms.
- Reestablish the biblical importance, permanence, and centrality of marriage and the family as the foundation for a stable and productive society.
- Equip and deploy church members to be kingdom disciples who have transformed lives that visibly transfer the values of the kingdom of God into the societal spheres of politics, education, law, medicine, business, entertainment, etc.
- Utilize the pulpit, platforms, and other ministry opportunities to give an equal emphasis to the issue of justice as is done with righteousness.

### *Act*

The third point in the Three-Point Plan is to act together to bring about unified social impact. We will make a bigger impact when we intentionally align our actions with each other in order to produce greater momentum. As an example, one of the ways we can collectively impact our communities and our nation is done through what we have established in Dallas of a local model of church-school partnerships. Churches partnering with schools seek to rebuild communities by comprehensively influencing the lives of urban youth and their families in addressing the education, health, economic, and social needs of hurting people based on spiritual principles.

A significant advantage that churches have in being agents of impact for a community is that they are located everywhere. There is an average of three to five churches for every public school in America. Churches are also closer to the needs of the people since they are located in the heart of the community. They also offer the largest volunteer force in the nation. Further, churches already have buildings to use for community-based programs. By providing a moral frame of reference for making wise choices, churches can equip the community members for social transformation.

One avenue of broadening the churches' impact on their communities is to recognize that churches and schools represent the social, educational, familial, and potentially spiritual nucleus of the community. As people and businesses come and go, churches and schools remain and are ready to accommodate newcomers to their neighborhoods. If these two institutions share common ground as well as longevity, a strategic alliance between the two can precipitate, to a greater degree, positive outcomes for children, youth, and families living in the community.

A few additional action items that can assist ministry and lay leaders in bringing this about include:

- Start or join a racially and denominationally diverse fellowship of kingdom-minded pastors in your local area.
- Meet regularly with kingdom-minded pastors to strengthen relationships, provide mutual encouragement, and to meet the needs of one another.
- Worship together and seek God in prayer.
- Use social and digital media to facilitate communication with your fellow spiritual leaders.
- Train and develop lay leaders who can provide practical assistance and support for meeting your goals.
- Plan and host a local solemn assembly at least once a year, gathering congregations together to seek God on behalf of their community and the nation.

- Share your pulpit on occasion with like-minded pastors across racial, class, and denominational divides.

When we come together to Assemble, Address and Act on behalf of God's kingdom principles in society at large, we will bring about a greater impact as a whole. Remember, it is the scope of our unity that will determine the scope of God's presence and the level of our impact (John 17:23–24).

## Collective Community Impact History

As we end this book and specifically this chapter on making an impact, I want to share some history on how the concept of this impact was given to me by God. It came about when I was a young pastor in a predominantly urban community. A nearby high school was experiencing increased difficulties at the time, including delinquencies and low academic achievement. The principal of the school decided to reach out to me for help. Gang activity had broken out affecting all areas of performance within the school. After I got the call, I decided to go over to the school with around twenty-five men from our church. The principal stopped all the classes and brought all of the male students into the gymnasium, and we shared what it was like to be a real man.

What's more, we did it in the name of God. In fact, I even used the name of Jesus Christ, and the school was fine with it because when things have broken down so much that you can't even conduct classes for your students, you don't get so picky about what you will allow or not allow in an effort to help. After our time together, and after some of the men from the church began hanging out in the hallways—offering help and hope to those in need, plus accountability for those who wanted to cause trouble—the gang activity shut down. Student grades went up, delinquency was lowered, and the school acknowledged that the church connection was good for producing a more productive learning environment.

In fact, the principal later became the superintendent of the district of eighteen schools and requested our church's involvement in all eighteen schools. We then organized ourselves and adopted all of the schools, expanding our support services to each through mentoring, tutoring, counseling, offering skills training and wraparound family support services. When the word got out to neighboring school districts, the eighteen schools soon became thirty-six, and eventually increased upwards of over forty schools at this time.

In addition to that, I initiated a meeting with the principals once a month for Bible study, discussion, and prayer—typically seeing an average of thirty to forty in attendance each month for more than two decades.

One interesting discovery we made in this process was that in helping the students in the schools, we also gained access to the parents. Many of the problems students had in school were an extension of brokenness in the homes. When we adopted the school, we also connected with the families, which in turn allowed us to connect at a deeper level with the entire community.

As our church positioned itself to be the major social service delivery system to the schools, the church provided an avenue to community transformation. We provide comprehensive family services. We help people get an education and acquire job skills through our Technology Institute, then help them find jobs and get homes. We have a thrift store to help sustain and expand the economic growth in the community, as well as a credit union. We develop businesses and provide medical assistance on a regular basis free of charge to the community.

Well-known pastor Bryan Loritts describes our church's approach in his book *Insider Outsider* when he writes,

> One particular Sunday during my time with Dr. Evans remains tattooed across my mind. Wrapping up his sermon, he invited everyone in the church who was on welfare to come down front. I remember thinking, This ought to be interesting, and then, I think I'd rather walk down the aisle to confess shacking up with another woman than admit to this. But sure enough, the altar was flooded with people. Then Dr. Evans pronounced that he was going to provide a tangible fix to their situation. In the weeks to come, a computer lab was set up for all who had come to the altar, and a partnership was formed with an

> affluent church on the other side of town, where several of their members owned businesses and had promised jobs to those who were trained in computer literacy at the church Dr. Evans pastored. Months later, scores of people waved goodbye to welfare and had been given the dignity of work.[2]

Why did I do that? Why do we do this as a church? Because the church has been uniquely called to impact our society for good. Churches around the country are to set the agenda for effecting positive values, beliefs, and real-life impact.

The rebuilding and development of urban America can be achieved by churches replicating the model of Nehemiah. The scriptural book bearing his name clearly demonstrates that when kingdom visionary leadership implements biblical principles of justice, righteousness, and compassion in a context of responsible freedom, urban decay can be reversed in a surprisingly short period of time. Through the reestablishment of the nuclear family, economic and educational development, and reducing and controlling crime, things can change. Such leadership achieves one overarching goal that is at the root of urban disintegration: replacing hopelessness with hopefulness (Neh. 2:17–20).

The mission of revitalizing and transforming communities begins with the individual along with this foundational truth: What a man thinks, so he is (Prov. 23:7). To put it another way, one's behavior is controlled by one's thoughts. If one's thought life is changed, the person is changed. Changed individuals transform families, and transformed families restore communities. While there are many, one way this can be done is by partnering with public schools and reaching into their communities to bring about a higher quality of life in their areas. When churches can set the agenda for the communities, positive returns are compounded.

The church and school partnership initiative strengthens communities and our nation through seeking to correct improper responses to God's Word, which is at the root cause for the dilemmas in society. This successful model has become a national effort through our National Church Adopt-a-School Initiative where we seek to train church and lay leaders across the country on how to implement the scalable model in their community. The church and school partnership model exists as a blueprint on how to apply the principles of the kingdom of God while meeting the needs of hurting people through caring interventions underlined with the message of hope.

One of the most exciting aspects of this community outreach strategy is that it is scalable. The program works whether you have a church of forty members or forty thousand. Our church serves more than forty public schools because we have enough members to sustain that level of impact. However, smaller churches can still make a significant impact in their communities by adopting just one public school (elementary, middle, or high school) and a collection of churches can assure that every school in their community is adopted.

Additionally, the program is cost-effective because the basics of what you need are already in place at both the church and the public school. The actual program cost is contingent on the scope of services your church wants to offer and your capacity to deliver those services.

Whenever I go into a community to speak, I seek to rally the pastors and community leaders around a shared vision for a unified community-wide impact through the adoption of schools. My vision is to have ministerial associations, church denominations, or a group of churches in a local area band together to adopt all of the public schools in their community. I also encourage them to plan an annual time of celebration where they can get together to share what God has done through the various outreach ministries as well as to strategize for the upcoming year.

This strategy enables us to be the salt and the light in our communities that Christ has called us to be. The interesting thing to note about light is that it is not as it appears. It is not one color. A prism reveals the true nature of light when it refracts it into a spectrum of colors. Likewise, the light we shine for God through good works is not a removal of our color, culture, or uniqueness, but an embracing of ourselves personally as well as each other in such a way as to create something we could have never created on our own. This allows us to carry out strategies for lasting impact and transformation in the lives of those around us. As we combine strength with strength across racial lines, we form something stronger than what would have been formed alone.

When churches operate properly under the kingdom agenda, progress and transformation naturally occur as the spiritual and social aspects of life work in a coordinated way, positively affecting individuals, families, schools, and communities.

For far too long, believers have looked to political, economic, social, and education-based agendas to address the decay now engulfing us. But spiritual success in spiritual war depends entirely upon spiritual solutions. God has given us this three-pronged strategy for kingdom-minded pastors, churches, and individuals to adopt and implement across racial lines in every community. It is my hope that the more people implementing these principles and points in the plan will enable us to collectively develop more kingdom disciples who will lead the way in impact, unity, and societal transformation by equipping them to build families and infiltrate the culture in order to reflect and transfer kingdom values, all the while taking advantage of opportunities to share the gospel of Jesus Christ so that those who see our good works are given the opportunity to trust Christ for the forgiveness of sins and the free gift of eternal life.

The decay of our culture is, at its core, a spiritual issue. That is why I believe when the church decides to operate in unity on a kingdom-based agenda that we will usher in true and lasting hope for our land. Believers must come together across class and cultural lines and work toward reconciliation. We must heed the clarion call—from heaven into history and from eternity into time—for Christians to live fully as kingdom disciples reflecting one body of Christ.

Unless kingdom-minded influencers significantly enter the discussion and assume the leadership for promoting justice and righteousness in society in order to resolve the division crisis, we will be hopelessly deadlocked in a sea of relativity regarding this issue, resulting in restating more questions than providing permanent answers. God is not going to bless a country or a culture that comes up with its own rules and asks Him to bless it. God expects kingdom-minded churches and Christ followers to lead the way.

This is a defining moment for us as churches and kingdom citizens to decide whether we want to be one nation under or a divided nation apart from God. If we don't answer that question correctly and if we don't answer it quickly, we won't be much of a nation at all.

**Notes**

1. Quoted in Julianna Monjeau, "Martin Luther King, Jr. at NYU: A Catalyst for Change," NYU *Alumni & Friends Connect*, January 15, 2021, from a speech King gave on the NYU campus, February 11, 1961.
2. 2 Chron. 12:1–8, Rehoboam; 2 Chron. 15:1–19, Asa; 2 Chron. 20:1–29, Jehoshaphat; 2 Chron. 29–32, Hezekiah; 2 Chron. 34, Josiah; Ezra 10:7–9, Ezra; Neh. 8–9, Nehemiah; Joel 1–2.
3. Bryan Loritts, *Insider Outsider: My Journey as a Stranger in White Evangelicalism and My Hope for Us All* (Grand Rapids, MI: Zondervan, 2018), 58.

# Appendix:

# THE URBAN ALTERNATIVE

The Urban Alternative equips, empowers, and unites Christians to impact *individuals, families, churches,* and *communities* through a thoroughly kingdom agenda worldview. In teaching truth, we seek to transform lives.

The core cause of the problems we face in our personal lives, homes, churches, and societies is a spiritual one; therefore, the only way to address it is spiritually. We've tried a political, social, economic, and even a religious agenda.

It's time for a **kingdom agenda.**

> The kingdom agenda can be defined as *the visible manifestation of the comprehensive rule of God over every area of life.*

The unifying central theme throughout the Bible is the glory of God and the advancement of His kingdom. The conjoining thread from Genesis to Revelation—from beginning to end—is focused on one thing: God's glory through advancing God's kingdom.

When you do not recognize that theme, the Bible becomes disconnected stories that are great for inspiration but seem to be unrelated in purpose and direction. Understanding the role of the kingdom in Scripture increases the relevancy of this several-thousand-year-old text to your day-to-day living, because the kingdom is not only then; it is now.

The absence of the kingdom's influence in our personal lives, family lives, churches, and communities has led to a deterioration in our world of immense proportions:

- People live segmented, compartmentalized lives because they lack God's kingdom worldview.
- Families disintegrate because they exist for their own satisfaction rather than for the kingdom.
- Churches are limited in the scope of their impact because they fail to comprehend that the goal of the church is not the church itself, but the kingdom.
- Communities have nowhere to turn to find real solutions for real people who have real problems because the church has become divided, ingrown, and unable to transform the cultural and political landscape in any relevant way.

The kingdom agenda offers us a way to see and live life with a solid hope by optimizing the solutions of heaven. When God is no longer the final and authoritative standard under which all else falls, order and hope leaves with Him. But the reverse of that is true as well: as long as you have God, you have hope. If God is still in the picture, and as long as His agenda is still on the table, it's not over.

Even if relationships collapse, God will sustain you. Even if finances dwindle, God will keep you. Even if dreams die, God will revive you. As long as God and His rule are still the overarching standard in your life, family, church, and community, there is always hope.

Our world needs the King's agenda. Our churches need the King's agenda. Our families need the King's agenda.

We've put together a three-part plan to direct us to heal the divisions and strive for unity as we move toward the goal of truly being one nation under God. This three-part plan calls us to assemble with others in unity, address the issues that divide us, and to act together for social impact. Following this plan, we will see individuals, families, churches, and communities transformed as we follow God's kingdom agenda in every area of our lives. You can request this plan by emailing info@tonyevans.org or by going online to tonyevans.org.

In many major cities, there is a loop that drivers can take when they want to get somewhere on the other side of the city but don't necessarily want to head straight through downtown. This loop will take you close enough to the city so that you can see its towering buildings and skyline, but not close enough to actually experience it.

This is precisely what we, as a culture, have done with God. We have put Him on the "loop" of our personal, family, church, and community lives. He's close enough to be at hand should we need Him in an emergency, but far enough away that He can't be the center of who we are.

We want God on the loop, not the King of the Bible who comes downtown into the very heart of our ways. Leaving God on the loop brings about dire consequences as we have seen in our own lives and with others. But when we make God and His rule the centerpiece of all we think, do, or say, it is then that we will experience Him in the way He longs for us to experience Him.

He wants us to be kingdom people with kingdom minds set on fulfilling His kingdom's purposes. He wants us to pray, as Jesus did, "Not my will, but Thy will be done," because His is the kingdom, the power, and the glory.

There is only one God, and we are not Him. As King and Creator, God calls the shots. It is only when we align ourselves underneath His comprehensive hand that we will access His full power and authority in all spheres of life: personal, familial, ecclesiastical, and government.

As we learn how to govern ourselves under God, we then transform the institutions of family, church, and society using a biblically based kingdom worldview.

*Under Him, we touch heaven and change earth.*

To achieve our goal, we use a variety of strategies, approaches, and resources for reaching and equipping as many people as possible.

## Broadcast Media

Millions of individuals experience *The Alternative with Dr. Tony Evans* through the daily radio broadcast playing on nearly **1,400 radio outlets** and in over **130 countries**. The broadcast can also be seen on several television networks and is available online at tonyevans.org. You can also listen or view the daily broadcast by downloading the Tony Evans app for free in the app store. Over 30 million message downloads and streams occur each year.

## Leadership Training

*The Tony Evans Training Center* facilitates a comprehensive discipleship platform which provides an educational program that embodies the ministry philosophy of Dr. Tony Evans as expressed through the kingdom agenda. The training courses focus on leadership development and discipleship in the following five tracks:

- Bible and Theology
- Personal Growth
- Family and Relationships
- Church Health and Leadership Development
- Society and Community Impact Strategies

The TETC program includes courses for both local and online students. Furthermore, TETC programming includes course work for nonstudent attendees. Pastors, Christian leaders, and Christian laity, both local and at a distance, can seek out The Kingdom Agenda Certificate for personal, spiritual, and professional development. For more information, visit TonyEvansTraining.org.

*The Kingdom Agenda Pastors* provides a *viable network* for *like-minded pastors* who embrace the kingdom agenda philosophy. Pastors have the opportunity to go deeper with Dr. Tony Evans as they are given greater biblical knowledge, practical applications, and resources to impact individuals, families, churches, and communities. KAP welcomes *senior and associate pastors* of all churches. KAP also offers an annual Summit held each year in Dallas with intensive seminars, workshops, and resources. For more information, visit KAFellowshiporg.

*Pastors' Wives Ministry*, founded by Dr. Lois Evans, provides *counsel, encouragement*, and *spiritual resources* for pastors' wives as they serve with their husbands in the ministry. A primary focus of the ministry is the KAP Summit that offers senior pastors' wives a safe place to *reflect, renew*, and *relax* along with training in personal development, spiritual growth, and care for their emotional and physical well-being. For more information, visit: LoisEvans.org.

## Kingdom Community Impact

The outreach programs of The Urban Alternative seek to provide positive impact to individuals, churches, families, and communities through a variety of ministries. We see these efforts as necessary to our calling as a ministry and essential to the communities we serve. With training on how to initiate and maintain programs to adopt schools, or provide homeless services, or partner toward unity and justice with local police precincts which creates a connection between the police and our community, we, as a ministry, live out God's kingdom agenda according to our *Kingdom Strategy for Community Transformation*.

*The Kingdom Strategy for Community Transformation* is a three-part plan that equips churches to have a positive impact on their communities for the kingdom of God. It also provides numerous practical suggestions for how this three-part plan can be implemented in your community, and it serves as a blueprint for unifying churches around the common goal of creating a better world for all of us. For more information, visit tonyevans.org and click on the link to access the three-point plan.

*National Church Adopt-a-School Initiative* (*NCAASI*) prepares churches across the country to impact communities by using *public schools as the primary vehicle for effecting positive social change* in urban youth and families. Leaders of churches, school districts, faith-based organizations, and other nonprofit organizations are equipped with the knowledge and tools to *forge partnerships* and build *strong social service delivery systems*. This training is based on the comprehensive church-based community impact strategy conducted by Oak Cliff Bible Fellowship. It addresses such areas as economic development, education, housing, health revitalization, family renewal, and racial reconciliation. We assist churches in tailoring the model to meet specific needs of their communities while simultaneously addressing the spiritual and moral frame of reference. Training events are held annually in the Dallas area at Oak Cliff Bible Fellowship. For more information, visit: ChurchAdoptaSchool.org.

*Athlete's Impact* (*AI*) exists as an outreach both into and through the sports arena. Coaches can be the most influential factor in young people's lives, even ahead of their parents. With the growing rise of fatherlessness in our culture, more young people are looking to their coaches for guidance, character development, practical needs, and hope. After coaches on the influencer scale fall athletes. Athletes (whether professional or amateur) influence younger athletes and kids within their spheres of impact. Knowing this, we have made it our aim to equip and train coaches and athletes on how to live out and utilize their God-given roles for the benefit of the kingdom. We aim to do this through our iCoach App as well as resources such as *The Playbook: A Life Strategy Guide for Athletes*. For more information, visit: ICoachApp.org.

*Tony Evans Films* ushers in positive life change through compelling video-shorts, animation, and feature-length films. We seek to build kingdom disciples through the power of story. We use a variety of platforms for viewer consumption and have over 100,000,000+ digital views. We also merge video-shorts and film with relevant Bible study materials to bring people to the saving knowledge of Jesus Christ and to strengthen the body of Christ worldwide. *Tony Evans Films* released the first feature-length film, *Kingdom Men Rising*, in April 2019 in over 800 theaters nationwide, in partnership with Lifeway Films. The second release, *Journey With Jesus*, is in partnership with RightNow Media.

## Resource Development

We are fostering lifelong learning partnerships with the people we serve by providing a variety of published materials. Dr. Evans has published more than 125 unique titles based on over 50 years of preaching, whether that is in booklet, book, or Bible study format. He also holds the honor of writing and publishing the first full-Bible commentary and study Bible by an African American, released in 2019. This Bible sits in permanent display as a historic release in the Museum of the Bible in Washington, DC.

See tonyevans.org/oneness for video resources including "Tony's Message to Christian Whites," "Tony's Message to Christian Blacks," "What is Systemic Racism?," and "Three-Point Plan."

For more information and a complimentary copy of Dr. Evans's devotional newsletter, call (800) 800–3222 or write TUA at PO Box 4000, Dallas, TX 75208, or visit us online:

www.tonyevans.org

# SUBJECT INDEX

**B**

# SCRIPTURE INDEX